W9-BCD-207

THE BASEBALL
HALL OF FAME
50ᵀᴴ ANNIVERSARY
B · O · O · K

THE BASEBALL HALL OF FAME 50TH ANNIVERSARY

BOOK

The National Baseball Hall of Fame and Museum, Inc.,
the National Baseball Library, and Gerald Astor
with essays by
ROY BLOUNT, JR. ◇ THOMAS BOSWELL
ROBERT CREAMER ◇ RON FIMRITE ◇ ROGER KAHN
ED LINN ◇ ROBERT LIPSYTE ◇ SHIRLEY POVICH
GEORGE VECSEY

PRENTICE HALL PRESS

NEW YORK LONDON TORONTO SYDNEY TOKYO

Where there is disagreement on statistics among the available sources, the text uses the figures in The Baseball Encyclopedia, *6th ed., Joseph Reichler, ed., Macmillan Publishing Company, 1985.*

The Glory of Their Times by Lawrence Ritter, new enlarged edition, William Morrow & Co., 1984. Copyright © 1984 by Lawrence Ritter. Reprinted by permission of the author.

Baseball as I Have Known It. Reprinted by permission of The Putnam Publishing Group from *Baseball as I Have Known It* by Frederick G. Lieb. Copyright © 1977 by Frederick G. Lieb.

From *Nobody Asked Me, but . . . The World of Jimmy Cannon* edited by Jack Cannon and Tom Cannon. Copyright © 1978 by The Estate of Jimmy Cannon. Reprinted by permission of Henry Holt and Company, Inc.

From *The Red Smith Reader* by Red Smith, edited by Dave Anderson. Copyright © 1982 Random House, Inc. Reprinted by permission of Random House, Inc.

From *Sport Magazine's All Time All-Star's,* edited by Tom Murray. Copyright © 1977 by MVP Sports, Inc. Reprinted by arrangement with the New American Library Penguin, New York, New York.

Baseball for the Love of It. Reprinted by permission of Macmillan Publishing Company from *Baseball for the Love of It* by Anthony J. Connor. Copyright © 1982 by Anthony J. Connor.

Babe: The Legend Comes To Life by Robert W. Creamer. Copyright © 1974. Reprinted by permission of Simon & Schuster, Inc.

Branch Rickey by Murray Polner, New York: Atheneum Publishers, 1982. Copyright © 1982. Reprinted by permission of The Julian Bach Literary Agency.

Late Innings by Roger Angell. Copyright © 1982. Reprinted by permission of Simon & Schuster, Inc.

Prentice Hall Press
Gulf+Western Building
One Gulf+Western Plaza
New York, New York   10023

Copyright © 1988 by The National Baseball Hall of Fame and Museum, Inc., the National Baseball Library, and Gerald Astor

All rights reserved
including the right of reproduction
in whole or in part in any form.

PRENTICE HALL PRESS and colophon are registered
trademarks of Simon & Schuster, Inc.

Library of Congress Cataloging-in-Publication Data
Astor, Gerald, 1926–
    Baseball Hall of Fame book: celebrating 50 years of the hall and
150 years of the game / by Gerald Astor and the National Baseball
Hall of Fame and Museum.—1st Prentice Hall Press ed.
        p.   cm.
    Includes index.
    1. Baseball—United States—History.   2. National Baseball Hall of
Fame and Museum—History.   I. National Baseball Hall of Fame and Museum.   II. Title.
GV863.A1A87   1988   796.357′0973—dc19   87-33401
ISBN 0-13-056573-3

Designed by J. C. Suarès and Michael J. Freeland

Manufactured in the United States of America

10 9 8 7 6 5 4 3 2 1

First Edition

A C K N O W L E D G M E N T S

Pat Kelly of the National Baseball Hall of Fame Library cheerfully gathered many of the photographs for the book. Thanks to the professional skills of Tom Heitz, librarian for the Hall of Fame; Bill Deane, senior researcher; and the rest of the staff, research was comparatively painless and obscure questions were authoritatively answered. Ted Spencer, curator of the Hall of Fame Museum treasures, identified the objects of significance and Peter Clark, registrar, was enormously helpful in gathering items for photography.

The interviews with Hall of Famers, done by Rod Roberts, provided valuable material. Larry Berger gave his time and expertise to the composition of some of the photographs at the museum.

Howard C. Talbot, Jr., director of the Hall, was not only a source of information about the life of the institution but with Ed Stack, president, gave me free rein along with unflagging encouragement. And Bill Guilfoile, associate director, in whose imagination the project originated, never flagged in his hospitality and support, while guarding me from factual errors. Although the Hall of Fame has a proprietary interest in the book, the words, opinions, and conclusions expressed are solely those of the writers, myself, and the sources listed.

Agents Gerard McCauley and Toni Mendez, who represented the Hall and me, guided the project through the sometimes difficult shoals of literary–commercial enterprise. Prentice Hall Press editor Paul Aron exercised much-appreciated tolerance for the occasional crankiness of his author and contributed substantially to the work.

C O N T E N T S

vii

On June 12, 1939, a modest brick building billed as the National Baseball Hall of Fame and Museum officially opened its door on Main Street in the bucolic village of Cooperstown, New York. Thus, we now approach the 50th anniversary of the Baseball Hall of Fame, while not-so-incidentally closing in on the 150th anniversary of what is generally acknowledged to be the first baseball game with rules resembling the modern ones.

We live by the decimal system—base 10 if you're a product of modern mathematics—and we set landmark anniversaries accordingly. Logically, there is nothing sacred about the number 50; it's one more than 49 and one less than 51. But round numbers confer moments to focus larger thoughts about a subject. (Thus our shorthand for the ".300 hitter" who hits somewhat above that figure or the "20-game winner" who has notched one or two more.) So this golden anniversary of baseball's special place at Cooperstown—the town itself is irrevocably tied to the Hall and fans speak of the site as a synonym for the shrine—affords an opportunity to ask: Why a Baseball Hall of Fame?

Institutions honoring the great have been with Americans for more than fifty years. In 1900, the Hall of Fame for Great Americans was founded at New York University to celebrate statesmen, authors, inventors, painters, explorers, and generals, but no baseball players. Nor were athletes the only ones who seemed excluded. In a nation of specialists, redress came in the form of halls of fame devoted to more narrow fields of endeavor. So now we have the Hall of Immortals and the Hall of Murals in the International College of Surgeons, the National Cowboy Hall of Fame, the National Hall of Fame for American Indians, the Merchandise Mart Hall of Fame (in praise of those who come to sell), the Candy Makers Hall of Fame, the Alabama Turkey Hunters Hall of Fame, the National Humor Hall of Fame (address, Box HoHo, Le Claire, Iowa), the Big Band Hall of Fame, the Dog Mushers Hall of Fame (Kuik, Alaska), and even halls proclaiming the renowned from the fields of accounting, insurance, and drainage (all three in Colum-

bus, Ohio). Hitting closer to home are the sports-centered halls: those created for professional and college football, hockey, basketball, soccer, tennis, and horse racing.

A penchant for halls of fame may seem an odd tangent for American inspiration. Yet, a noble foundation for hall building can be found in a quote by the nineteenth-century essayist and student of the French Revolution, Thomas Carlyle, who said: "History is the biography of great men."* And if we look at the lives of the fellows in the Baseball Hall of Fame we indeed see the history of the game. The major isms of the world that govern political and economic systems, particularly those associated with Georg Wilhelm Friedrich Hegel, Adam Smith, and Karl Marx, stress vast forces beyond the influence of a single man or even a small united band. But in baseball one or two or a few have transformed affairs. By their skills and their imaginations they have changed the rules, shifted the emphasis, restructured the geography, and above all stirred the passions of tens of millions of their fellow Americans. Their deeds are justly commemorated at Cooperstown, a worthy successor to Valhalla, the hall into which the Scandinavian god Odin took his heroes. (The name Valhalla, however, comes from the combination of the Icelandic words *val* and *hal,* meaning "slaughter" and "hall"; Odin accepted only dead heroes. Happily, the Baseball Hall of Fame frequently extols the living as well as the deceased.)

Alexander Cartwright, the most ancient member of the Hall, made his mark in 1845. The nearly 150 years that have passed since then have of course been chockful of events, natural as well as humanmade astonishments, mighty upheavals, times of individual and mass tears, terror, trial, jubilation, victory, defeat—a thesaurus of human experiences. For all of their unique individual efforts, the people named to the Hall have played against and within this backdrop. This book, on the occasion of the 50th anniversary of the Baseball Hall of Fame, is an attempt to capture the story of the game in terms of its great men and the times in which they have lived.

*Carlyle came from that long-since-discredited school that believed women should bend to the authority of their male betters. There were no women admitted to the New York University Hall of Fame in its first election, although several were honored the second time around. One can still speak in masculine terminology when it comes to the Baseball Hall of Fame. However, we now have women owners and executives, women baseball writers, minor league women umpires, and perhaps some day we will have major league female players.

The ball was described as "made out of parchment covered with catgut" and measured roughly three times the size of a modern one. The bat was a flat-faced club and no one wore a glove. A game consisted of twenty-one counts or aces—runs in modern parlance. The pitcher threw underhand from a distance of 45 feet and the batter could call his preference for a high or low pitch. Still, the bases for the first time were set 90 feet apart and there were flat markers on the ground rather than stakes, poles, or even rocks. The shape of the field, instead of a square or rectangle, amounted to a diamond.

This was the game begat in 1845 by bank teller and volunteer fireman, Alexander Joy Cartwright, ★ * as one of a group of New York City men who for several years engaged in ball games in a Manhattan park area at 27th Street and Fourth Avenue, a plot soon appropriated for the Harlem River Railroad Depot. On hand was a friend of Cartwright, Duncan F. Curry. Thirty-two years later Curry recalled the scene:

Well do I remember the afternoon when Alex Cartwright came up to the ball field with a new scheme for playing ball. The sun shone beautifully, never do I remember noting its beams fall with a more sweet and mellow radiance than on that particular Spring day. [The heavens appeared to bless the moment.] For several years it had been our habit to casually assemble. . . . We would take our bats and balls with us and play any sort of a game. We had no name in particular for it. Sometimes we batted the ball to one another or sometimes played one o'cat.

On this afternoon . . . Cartwright came to the field—the march of improvement had driven us further north and we located on a piece of property on the slope of Murray Hill between the railroad cut and Third Avenue—with his plans drawn up on a paper. He had arranged for two nines, the ins and outs. . ... He had laid out a diamond-shaped field, with canvas bags filled with sand or sawdust for bases at three of the points and an iron plate for the home base. He had arranged for a catcher, a pitcher, three basemen, a short fielder and three outfielders. His plan met with much good natured derision, but he was so persistent in having us try his new game that

we finally consented more to humor him than with any thought of it becoming a reality.

Cartwright's prescription had changed the outfield from a stage for all otherwise unassigned hands to the current three. He had removed one of the customary "short fielders," retaining only the position now known as shortstop. The pitcher covered the middle of the infield, leaving the second baseman to balance the right side of the diamond.

The bank cashier also pruned away one of the two catchers usually stationed behind the batter. Like all other fielders, the now solitary catcher wore no glove. Furthermore, he lacked the most elementary tools of ignorance, bearing neither mask, nor chest protector, nor shin guards, but as a sop he was allowed to snag balls on one bounce. Thus, an early account of a game lauded one backstop, "Smith caught a remarkable game, having but five passed balls against."

Equally important to Cartwright's structuring of the game were his codified rules. Fielders were now required to throw to the bases rather than at the runners or hitters to gain an out. He decreed, "Three balls being struck at and missed and the last one caught is a hand out, if not caught is considered fair, and the striker bound to run." The dropped third strike, of course, remains part of today's game. Three hands out and the side was out with all players required to take their chances hitting. A ball hit outside "the range of first or third base is foul." Until Cartwright's innovation, nothing was foul; all balls were in play as is the case in cricket.

It was still a game with some significant differences from the modern version—batters were out if the ball was caught on the fly or on the first bounce, and it took a few years before Cartwright changed from 21 aces a game to the standard 9 innings. However, the first incarnation captured the local fancy. According to Duncan Curry:

At that time, none of us had any experience in that style of play and as there were no rules for playing the game, we had to do the best we could under [the] circumstances, aided by Cartwright's judgment. . . . When we saw what a great game Cartwright had given us, and as

Alexander Cartwright, a New York City bank cashier, surveyor, and draftsman, set down the basic rules of modern baseball in 1845, including the ninety-foot distance between bases, the nines of innings and players, the three outs per inning. He carried his game as far west as Hawaii where he prospered in business, and in his dotage was photographed with the helmet and "hailer" (to bawl orders) while serving as chief of the Honolulu fire fighters.

Courtesy National Baseball Library (NBL)

---

*Wherever a member of the Hall of Fame is first introduced, a star (★) will follow his name.

his suggestion for forming a club to play it met with our approval, we set about to organize a club.

Curry was elected president of the group named the Knickerbockers. On June 19, 1846, the twenty-six-year-old, full-bearded, husky Cartwright and his fellow Knickerbockers boarded a ferry to demonstrate their brand of baseball in a contest against "a party of gentlemen who styled themselves the New York Club" on a cricket pitch at the Elysian Fields in Hoboken, New Jersey. (Already real estate values in New York City were driving teams across the Hudson River.) "Well do I remember that game," said Curry, "the first regular game of baseball ever played hereabouts and the New Yorks won it by a score of 23 to 1."

Curry blamed the defeat on the failure of the Knickerbockers to take their opponents seriously—an excuse still bandied about by managers. He also noted that the New York club was well stocked with expert cricketers who batted very skillfully. Furthermore, the enemy hurler "could pitch an awfully speedy ball." Some baseball historians point out that neither Cartwright nor Curry played in this first match game. They appeared to use their "muffins" rather than their first stringers and the box score indicates the Knickerbockers racked up more than the single "ace" mentioned by Curry. Cartwright made one major on-field contribution; he served as umpire and recorded another first—he levied a fine upon player James Whyte Davis for swearing.

"Success," noted President John F. Kennedy, "has many fathers" and the honor of starting the game has been attributed to General Abner Doubleday, club owner and sporting goods magnate Albert Goodwill Spalding, ★ player-manager Harry Wright, ★ and sportswriter Henry Chadwick. ★ But baseball historians agree that the Elysian Fields game truly marks the first public introduction of something close to modern baseball and, as the fellow who formulated the rules published by his Knickerbocker club, Cartwright deserves the credit for paternity above all others.

Of course the roots of baseball are buried so deep in human experience that no one can identify its origins. People enjoyed whacking projectiles with clubs and chasing one another long before Cartwright proposed his brand of ball. Robert Henderson in *Ball, Bat, and Bishop* and Harold Peterson in *The Man Who Invented Baseball* cite a Puritan bluenose of the 1700s who railed against "Morris-dancing, cudgel playing, baseball, and cricketts." There are eighteenth-century references to scholars amusing themselves with balls and stick in a "low and unbecoming" manner. Jane Austen in *Northanger Abbey* mentions a tomboy who prefers "cricket, base-ball . . . ," naming the two separately.

An 1834 tome, *The Book of Sports*, described a number of entertainments, including Puss in the Corner, Blowing Bubbles, Dick, Duck, and Drake, along with "Base or Goal Ball . . . sometimes known as 'round ball' . . ." and the accompanying diagram showed a diamond shape for the play. The Colonies saw much of what was known as "rounders," "town ball," "the Massachusetts game," and the various "old or o'cats—one, two, three, four." To all of this Cartwright added his own ingenious notions.

The Knickerbockers, who decked themselves out in uniforms of blue pantaloons, white flannel shirts, and straw hats, expanded to a large membership devoted to intramural baseball and postgame imbibing. Within less than ten years, according to Peterson, "baseball became no less than a mania." Clubs sprang up all over the city and employers inquired not only about applicants' business and industrial skills but also about how well they could hit and field. Those who could not play watched and the most devoted of them were known as "kranks" (sometimes spelled with a *c*; female devotees were "kranklets"), perhaps because when disappointed, they noisily vented their unhappiness. Somewhat later, spectators were "bugs" until "fans" (believed to be derived from "fanatics") became the accepted term. The labels all express the ambivalence of players and writers.

The father of baseball, however, was not around to see the swift growth of his child. In 1849, Cartwright, who came from a tradition of seafaring adventurers, trekked westward, lured by the highly publicized gold strike at the California mill owned by August Sutter. Cartwright kept a log of his journey.

". . . they crossed the Barclay Street fer[ry] a body, like unto the Pilgrims of yore, [and] marched up the country road on the J[ersey] side, prospecting here and there for sui[table] grounds, until they reached the Ely[sian] Fields, where they settled. Then they [per]fected their organization, calling it [']Knickerbockers,' which was the nucle[us of] the great American game of baseball [wrote] Seymour R. Church, early twentieth-cen[tury] baseball historian. A Currier & Ives l[itho]graph memorialized the Grand Matc[h for] the Championship at the Elysian Fiel[ds.]

Courtesy NBL

The Knickerbockers of New York, 185[?], a] social organization as much as an ath[letic] one, after one encounter the Knickerbo[ckers] entertained their rivals, the Excelsiors, [at] a splendid party for two hundred gents [at the] Hoboken Odd Fellows Club. Cartwrigh[t had] begun his trek westward almost ten [years] earlier.

Courtesy NBL

Based on its contents (the actual diary has since disappeared), his grandson, Bruce Cartwright, Jr., claimed the inventor of baseball spent 156 days getting from Newark to San Francisco, introducing his game of baseball whenever the caravan paused. Eventually Alex wound up in the Hawaiian Islands where he continued preaching the gospel of his game.

Back in the continental United States baseball continued to boom. British-born Henry Chadwick, who witnessed his first game—a contest between the Knickerbockers and the Gothams—in 1856, was an enthusiastic convert. Acknowledged as the creator of the box score, the one-time music teacher quickly sought to promote the game. In Chadwick's "Base Ball Manual," "Beadle's Dime Base Ball Player," and "De Witt's Base Ball Guide," he explained the game and described techniques. His reporting in the *New York Clipper*, a journal of show business and sports, popularized the game and its players. From Chadwick one learned that loudmouths supplied "chin music" and was taught the meanings of a "balk," "daisy cutter," "fungo," "white wash," and "assist." He was elected to the first organization for the sport, the National Association of Base Ball Players, founded in 1858. In one of his accounts of the evolution of baseball, Chadwick noted that the National Association required a ball 6¼ ounces in weight, and a robust 10¼ inches in circumference. Compare that heavyweight sphere with the modern version, which is 5 to 5¼ ounces and a tight 9 to 9¼ inches around. The 1858 ball contained 2 or 3 ounces of rubber, making it in Chadwick's memory "too elastic for the uses of scientific play alike at the bat and in fielding it."

In this almost prehistoric era of baseball, pitchers made an underhand delivery and could run forward to the 12-foot-long line 45 feet from home plate before releasing the ball. However, the striker, as the batter was known, was armed with a bat of unlimited length and size and was under no obligation to swing even at fat pitches. Only if he persisted in passing up "good balls repeatedly" could the umpire call a strike.

For the first few years of the National Association, baseball was almost exclusively an eastern pastime. New York City was a hotbed of baseball, with the Knickerbockers meeting the likes of the Empires, Atlantics, Eagles, Putnams, Washingtons, Gothams, Eckfords, Phantoms, and Pocahontases, whose rosters included cops, dairy workers, saloon-keepers, bank employees, lawyers, and respectable citizens from all vocations. In the Northeast, cricket warred with baseball for club favor with many outfits fielding teams in both sports. The Elysian Fields continued to play host to the games; a cricket match with a touring British squad and some top Americans drew 24,000 spectators.

Gradually, however, the Johnny Appleseed peregrination of Cartwright wrought a bumper baseball crop across the map. The Minerva, Winona, United, and Benedict clubs sprouted in Philadelphia in 1857 and two years later the Athletics took the field. Indeed, according to some baseball chroniclers, the seed sown by Cartwright in his passage through Illinois had so infected local citizens that when a delegation interrupted a game in 1860 to inform Abraham Lincoln of his nomination for president, he allegedly admonished, "Tell them to wait until I make another hit." Lincoln experts indicated this is pure fable but the Great Emancipator was enough of a fan to watch a game with son Tad while president.

The Civil War of 1861–1865 spread baseball fever as troops in the North and South whiled away time between engagements with baseball. Diaries and letters from enlisted men carry frequent references to the sport. Baseball also owes to the War between the States its controversial connection with Abner Doubleday. A major in command of the federal troops at Fort Sumter, it was Doubleday who gave the order to heave the first cannonball at the Secessionists after they fired upon his forces. The Union's first hero went on to become a general, undistinguished by either failure or achievement. As the possessor of such an impeccable record he could subsequently become the center of the argument about who invented baseball.

Peace brought rapid development of baseball. A. G. Spalding, in a handwritten manuscript prepared around 1905, reported more than a thousand "regular organized clubs" from all over the nation belonged to the Association in 1866. Some were organized along ethnic lines like the Fenian Baseball

"Henry Chadwick has been called the [fa]ther of Base Ball for many years, no[t be]cause he invented the game, thoug[h he] assisted materially in its gradual evolu[tion] in the first half of the last century, fro[m the] simple old game of town ball, the 'one[-old-] cat' and 'three-old-cat' of the early boy[hood] of men now aged. Mr. Chadwick fos[tered,] encouraged, and helped to develop [Base] Ball through more than half a century[, and] for more than half that time had bee[n the] editor of the Official Guide. *He believ[ed in] the efficacy and good moral influen[ce of] hearty outdoor sports, and for the full[mea-] sure of his active life had devoted hi[mself] zealously as a newspaper writer to in[creas-] ing the public interest in them."—[New] York Times*

"It may be truly said that the ye[ar] 1856 was the birth year of the evoluti[on of] baseball; for it was in that year that a [move-] ment was made to improve the crude co[de of] playing rules which had previously [gov-] erned the clubs of the period.

"It was in that year that we first s[aw a] regular match game of base ball, the [occa-] sion being a contest between the old Kn[icker-] bocker and Gotham clubs—the two stro[ng] clubs of the city that year. It was there [that] we took note of the possibilities of the [game] and saw in it a lever which could be a[dvan-] tageously used to lift up athletic sport[s to] a desired popularity."—Henry Chad[wick]

Courtesy NBL

Club and the Landwehrs; others represented volunteer fire companies, political clubs, businesses, including saloons, and even cities. By the 1880s, one could find the *Chicago Tribune* reporting the score of a game between the Paregorics of Morrison, Plumber and Co. and the Castor Oils of Lord, Stoutenburg and Co. Even more exotic was a series of games between the Snorkeys and the Hoppers in Philadelphia. Prerequisites for membership in the former was the absence of an arm, for the latter the lack of a leg.

Amateur teams comprised of gentlemen like the original Knickerbockers were increasingly supplanted by rough-and-tumble semiprofessional or entirely professional clubs seeking to supplement or earn their livelihood by playing ball. As early as 1864, the Philadelphia Athletics hired the star second baseman of the New York Eckfords, Albert Reach, for $1,000 per season. A year later the highly skilled Athletics campaigned around the state, rolling up scores of 101–8 and 162–14. Forty thousand cranks, paying anywhere from $5 for a privileged elevated seat to 25 cents for simple admission, showed up for a "Grand Match" featuring the Athletics against the Brooklyn Atlantics in October 1866. Fans clung to trees, scaled roofs, and perched on fences. All went for naught as the overflowing crowd poured onto the field in the very first inning to halt the game.

The Cincinnati Red Stockings became an all-professional team after the 1868 season and shortstop George Wright ★ was recruited from New Jersey for the lofty sum of $1,400. The boys of Cincy barnstormed across the country in 1869 under the management of George's brother, Harry Wright, by trade a jeweler's apprentice. He exhorted his troops with the cry, "You need a little ginger" as they met the likes of the New York Mutuals in Brooklyn. Harry was British born, George, a native of Yonkers, New York. The Wrights were the sons of a professional cricketer; their first sport in the United States had involved wickets and bowlers. The Red Stocking team, garbed in flannel knickers with a below-the-knee clasp, brilliant scarlet stockings, square-cut locomotive engineer caps, shirts laced at the throat with a cross drawstring, and collars that flared about the neck, strutted their stuff before President Ulysses S. Grant. They finished the 1869 season with 65 victories, 1 tie, and no losses. The club traveled almost 12,000 miles, using trains, stagecoaches, and boats, and 200,000 people saw them play. However, the tour supposedly netted only $1.39 profit.

By 1871, recognition of the dominance of paid hands led to a split away from the National Association of Base Ball* Players (NABBP) of 1858 and formation of a more ambitious organization, the National Association of Professional Base Ball Players. The league's constitution carried specifications on player contracts, franchise requirements, admission prices, and attempted to establish a schedule. A charter member of the new outfit, the Philadelphia Athletics, won the 1871 championship with a record of 22–7.

The NABBP suffered a series of reverses. Players jumped from club to club, sometimes in midseason. Teams often failed to honor the schedules, particularly when required to travel some distance late in the season. The silk-hatted umpires, generally unpaid and unprofessional, staggered under abuse; they frequently lost control of the games. And gambling by both the men on the field and the spectators threatened the integrity of play. Newspapers described ball players as "worthless," "dissipated," and not far above the most reprehensible of nineteenth-century athletes, "the professional pugilist." Teams like the Troy Haymakers and the New York Mutuals, owned by the notorious William Marcy "Boss" Tweed, earned a justifiable reputation for "hippodroming," or dumping games.

Professional baseball in the spirit of today began with an 1876 meeting at the Grand Central Hotel in New York City. The leading public figure was William Hulbert, owner of the Chicago White Stockings. The National League of Professional Base Ball Clubs, as the new enterprise dubbed itself, is noteworthy first for its exclusion of players from any proprietary role and for strict limitations placed on their ability to move to greener pastures. The actual reserve clause that bound a player to a team for life came in 1882. The National League set admission prices, paid umpires, and, in a bid for re-

*Not until the 1930s did everyone make "baseball" one word.

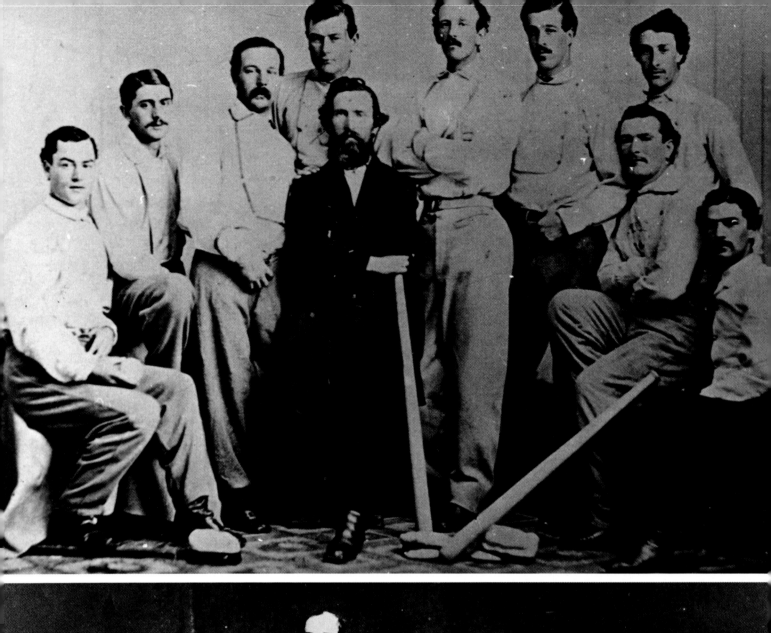

spectability, banned Sunday games and gambling. Only cities with populations of at least 75,000 were deemed eligible for franchises—the initial teams came from Boston, Cincinnati, St. Louis, Hartford, New York, Philadelphia, Louisville, and Chicago.

The delegates chose Morgan G. Bulkeley, ★ president of the Hartford club and a banker who also presided over the Aetna Life Insurance Company, to be the first president of the National League. Bulkeley, a compromise candidate satisfactory to the eastern and western teams, served for only a year and went on to become governor of Connecticut. The second head of the National League, Hulbert, in office until his death in 1882, governed with a strong hand and his rigorous enforcement of what was known as "the National Agreement"—the constitution of the league—kept organized baseball going.

The first years of the League were not without their troubles. In 1876, it was discovered that four Louisville players had conspired to throw the pennant to Boston. Hulbert set a precedent, barring them for life. Subsequently the Louisville franchise folded along with those in Hartford and St. Louis. But other cities replaced them. Providence, Indianapolis, and Milwaukee all fielded clubs in 1878.

Just as professionalism assumed command in the organization of the game, so did it now appear on the field. A hitter could still call for location of a pitch. If he wished a high ball, the umpire informed the pitcher to throw between the waist and shoulder, and a prescribed low ball was to arrive between the waist and one foot above the ground. But nine balls not meeting desires meant a walk. Pitchers still could not throw overhand, but instead of being limited to a full submarine delivery, could raise the arm to a 90-degree angle for a sidearm release. (Not until 1884 did men on the mound gain full freedom of delivery.)

Already the bane of batters, the curve had been introduced. William Arthur "Candy" Cummings, ★ a slight 5'9", 120 pounder, is regarded as the pitch's progenitor. He subsequently recalled:

In the summer of 1863 a number of boys and myself were amusing ourselves by throwing clam shells . . . and watching them sail along through the air, turning now to the right and now to the left. We became interested in the mechanics of it. . . .

. . . it came to me that it would be a good joke on the boys if I could make a baseball curve the same way. We had been playing "three-old-cat" and town-ball, and I had been doing the pitching.

Cummings sought the secret of ball movement, practicing "every spare moment" out of school. He experimented with his posture, "doubling up in all manner of positions," thinking that controlled the trajectory. Then he tried "holding the ball in different shapes." Occasionally he was rewarded with success but for the most part his comrades regarded the joke as on him.

In 1867, Cummings was playing with the New York Excelsior Club and traveled to Boston for a series of games. Finally, against a Harvard team he said his wrinkle proved effective:

I became fully convinced that I had succeeded . . . the batters were missing a lot of balls; I began to watch the flight of the ball through the air, and distinctly saw it curve.

A surge of joy flooded over me that I shall never forget. I felt like shouting out that I had made a ball curve; I wanted to tell everybody; it was too good to keep to myself.

Cummings restrained his exultation. He was above all a competitor: "I said not a word, and saw many a batter at that game throw down his stick in disgust. Every time I was successful I could scarcely keep from dancing for pure joy. The secret was mine." But not for long, of course, as others quickly learned the skill. The reality of the curve was not immediately accepted. In 1877, baseball men like Colonel J. B. Joyce of the original Cincinnati Red Stockings as well as academicians argued that a change in the path of a thrown ball by any other means than wind deflection was an absurdity. To prove movement, proponents arranged for three posts to be set in a row in Cincinnati with a low board fence running in a straight line between the posts. The first major leaguer to wear spectacles on the field, Will White—"one of the most expert twirlers of the day," in the words of A. G. Spalding—stood to the left of the fence at one end. He threw a ball that

Among the Brooklyn Atlantics, Dickey Pearce (third from left) *supposedly perfected the bunt. Flat-sided bats, preferred for bunting, were legal until 1893.*

Courtesy NBL

Challenging the Atlantics were the Brooklyn Excelsiors with their natty long trousers, emblematic belts, and high collars.

Courtesy NBL

passed to the right of the middle post and then sailed a good 6 inches to the left of the third marker.

Colonel Joyce, however, remained unconvinced. Indeed, learned professors from Ohio Agricultural College, Worcester University, and the University of Rochester all debated for and against. It is an argument that survived even into the 1950s when *Life* and *Look* took to photographs to prove the curve an illusion *(Life)* and a fact *(Look)*.

As early as 1864, a man was no longer out if a fielder caught a ball on a single bounce. Ross Barnes, a clever fellow with the bat, specialized in slicing balls that struck the turf in fair ground and caromed across the baseline before reaching the base. Within one year of the National League's creation, it ruled a ball must remain in fair territory until it passes beyond the base or is fielded.

In 1875, the glove came to the game. Spalding wrote:

> The first glove I ever saw on the hand of a ball player in a game was worn by Charles C. Waite in Boston in 1875. He had come from New Haven and was playing at first base. The glove worn by him was of flesh color, with a large, round opening in the back. Now, I had for a good while felt the need of some sort of hand protection for myself. In those days clubs did not carry an extra carload of pitchers, as now. For several years I had pitched in every game . . . and had developed severe bruises on the inside of my left hand. For every ball pitched it had to be returned, every swift one coming my way from infielders, outfielders or hot from the bat must be caught or stopped, some idea may be gained of the punishment received.

Waite apparently was "a bit ashamed to wear it" so to keep the glove inconspicuous he chose a flesh-colored one. The open back provided ventilation. By 1877, in a mild show of defiance, Spalding adopted a black glove to join what he called "the kid-glove aristocracy." Skin tight with the finger tips cut off, much like some golf gloves of today, these early mitts did soften the impact of the ball, however slightly. Sore and swollen hands remained an occupational hazard; errors abounded and high scores marked games.

In 1883, Arthur Irwin, shortstop for Providence, broke the third and fourth fingers of his left hand. With only ten- or eleven-man rosters, more serious injuries were required to gain a day off. Irwin visited a glover who took a buckskin driving glove several sizes too large, padded it, made a large opening at the back for ventilation, and sewed the third and fourth fingers together to allow for Irwin's bandaged digits. Irwin said some years later the fans forgave the use of the mitt because they were aware of his mangled bones. More important, he immediately noticed an unexpected benefit; he could "meet" a ball solidly instead of easing off to avoid trauma. He thus threw quicker. After New York's John Montgomery Ward ★ observed the added efficiency of Irwin's contraption he ordered a similar one. When fans failed to jeer at him for cowardice, Ward went a step further. He and Irwin showed their gloves to other players and a sporting goods firm picked up hundreds of orders. Within a year almost every major leaguer wore them.

Players like first basemen Joe Start and Charles Comiskey, ★ who would eventually own the Chicago White Sox, introduced such innovations as playing off the bag. Infielders backed one another up; there was a new tactic called the bunt, probably invented by a shortstop named Dickey Pearce. Some thought the technique effeminate but others used bats with one side flattened for more effective bunts. Runners now took leads to enable them to steal bases, although sliding on the hard, hewn surfaces exacted a toll of broken bones and skinned torsos. The advent of gloves also ended the practice in which fielders were allowed to catch balls in their caps for an out. (Al Spalding's proficiency with his hat also led to outlawing the technique.)

If any figure dominated the nineteenth-century pro game, at least in management and front-office circles, it was Albert Goodwill Spalding. In his autobiography, Spalding said his first memory of the game dated to 1863 when as a twelve-year-old in Rockford, Illinois, he was invited to play on a club organized by "a young man from the East, who had brought with him a *Beadle's Base Ball Guide.*" Spalding described watching baseball on the commons as "the only bright skies for me in those dark days of utter loneliness. . . . no mother, parted from her young, ever had a stronger yearning to see her beloved offspring than I had to break into those crude games of baseball."

The game already had enough of a hold for a cartoonist to use baseball as a metaphor for the 1860 elections.

Courtesy NBL

Baseball fever, caught during the Civil War, raged through the land after the peace of Appomattox. The New York Daily Graphic, *like many newspapers, boosted circulation with extensive coverage.*

Courtesy NBL

In an incident foreshadowing 1930s movies, Spalding alleged that while mooning about somewhere beyond center field a ball suddenly flew in his direction: "Impulsively I sprang to my feet, reached out for it with my right hand, held it for a moment and then threw it home on an air line to the catcher."

Supposedly, the feat brought congratulations and the invitation to join a team. Within a few years, the adolescent Spalding had been enlisted as a pitcher for the local Forest City Club. Like many such aggregations, the Forest City team's chief purpose was to foster the reputation of Rockford rather than to make a profit. Although ostensibly composed of amateurs, Forest City included a number of paid, skilled hands. They were good enough to whip the touring Washington Nationals, a squad of government employees reportedly tops in the country, by an ugly 29–23. (George Wright was a member of the Washington squad, listed as a clerk, but probably hired only for his baseball prowess.) In spite of the score, Henry Chadwick, writing for "Beadle's Dime Base Ball Player" as well as New York newspapers, observed that Spalding was "undoubtedly the best pitcher in the West."

His talent attracted notice from would-be baseball magnates in Chicago. In the fashion of the day, the Chicago Excelsiors recruited Spalding with the promise of a job with a wholesale grocer for $40 a week. The young pitcher was assured that his mercantile duties would not interfere with his baseball. Unfortunately, the employer went bankrupt after Spalding had played only a single game. He returned to Rockford to star again for the Forest City team.

Meanwhile, with professionalism now established through the National Association of Base Ball Players, Harry Wright (some insist he is "The Father of Professional Baseball") left the first play-for-pay outfit in Cincinnati to set up shop in Boston. He hired Spalding after losing an exhibition game to the Rockford youth. The salary was set at $1,500 per year and eventually reached $2,000 per year. The sum was handsome enough but the occupation lacked respectability. Remarked Spalding:

> I had determined to enter Base Ball as a profession. I was neither ashamed of the game nor of my attachment to it. . . . The assumption of non-professionalism would not deceive anybody. It was not possible that any could be found so simple as to believe that . . . Harry Wright . . . and the rest were in the game merely for health or philanthropic reasons.

Spalding handsomely justified Wright's investment by winning 20, 37, 41, 52, and finally a staggering 57 games as the Boston Red Stockings carried off the pennant every year from 1872 through 1875. To triumph 57 times he pitched in a total of 66 games and went 24 consecutive contests without a defeat.

His contribution to the Boston club struck Chicago coal merchant William Hulbert as a necessary ingredient in making the Chicago White Stockings a winner. Hulbert saw baseball prowess as a means to rebuild the pride and reputation of his home city after its disastrous fire. To seduce Spalding, Hulbert offered him the dual roles of field captain and management of the White Stockings business affairs with a salary of $2,000 annually plus 25 percent of the gate. Furthermore, he wooed Spalding with appeals to his duty as a "western boy." Hulbert and Spalding sealed a deal in the middle of the 1875 season, and it included other members of the team as well. The *Worcester Spy*, noting the defection of Spalding and three others, said: "Boston is in mourning. Like Rachel weeping for her children, she refuses to be comforted because the famous baseball nine, the perennial champion, the city's most cherished possession, has been captured by Chicago."

Spalding had Hulbert's ear during the crucial meeting that established the National League and the structure of the teams. Some of the rules undoubtedly sprang from his genius. Hulbert, with the advice of Spalding, also recruited a redoubtable Philadelphia Athletics first baseman, Adrian "Cap" Anson. ★ All of the newly acquired White Stockings reported to Chicago for the following season. Hulbert had bought a winner; with Spalding winning 46 of the 53 games in which he played, the White Stockings captured the championship. And Spalding was just as busy off the field, arranging exhibition games; handling correspondence concerned with standards for the ball, umpires, and other league matters; and establishing

Harry Wright, British-born son of a [profes]sional cricket player, known as "The [Father] of Professional Baseball," introduced [numb]ers to the uniform. "Every magnate [in the] country is indebted to this man [Harry Wright] for the establishment of base b[all as] a business, and every patron for furni[shing] him with a systematic recreation. [Every] player is indebted to him for inaugur[ating] an occupation by which he gains a [liveli]hood, and the country at large for a[dding] one more industry (for industry it is i[n that] respect) to furnish employment."—Spo[rting] Life

Courtesy NBL

George Wright

Courtesy NBL

his own business. With $800 borrowed from his mother, Spalding and his brother opened a sporting goods store in Chicago.

In time, through Spalding's position, the store would obtain the exclusive right to supply baseballs to the organized professional game, publish the *Official League Book* that carried league rules, and sell tens of thousands of *Spalding's Official Baseball Guide*, an unsanctioned compendium of team and individual records and articles, many of which pushed Spalding's viewpoint on issues. Over the years, the *Guide*s not only preserved stats but also sold carloads of equipment manufactured by Spalding and even earned added revenue through ads from nonbaseball businesses. Spalding and his brother sought to take over the budding market in uniforms. His imagination bested him with his notion that every player in the league wear the same white pants, white belts, and white ties; only the color of the stockings would distinguish one club from the other. The *pièce de résistance* of the scheme called for shirts and caps to be color coded by position. Thus, while those in the field all sported white pants, belts, and ties, they displayed a gaudy riot of shirt and cap hues that appalled everyone. This blast of color was described by the *Chicago Tribune* as looking like "a Dutch bed of tulips" and faded from sight after a single season. Perhaps that rainbow outburst so shocked the baseball world that it caused only the most modest color to be permitted for the next ninety years, until the advent of Charles O. Finley in Kansas City.

A sore arm severely curtailed Spalding's effectiveness in 1877 and the team fell to fifth place. Peter Levine says Spalding took to heart the chiding of Henry Chadwick, who said it was not possible to play, manage on and off the field, and run a sporting goods business. Spalding gave up pitching and yielded the post of field manager to Cap Anson. From 1878 on, he devoted himself to the life of an entrepreneur, taking on the presidency and ownership of the team after Hulbert died in 1882.

With Anson running the show on the field, the White Stockings flew the pennant for five out of seven seasons between 1880 and 1886. The Sox also boasted pitcher John Clarkson ★ whose repertoire included the curve and a "drop" good enough to win 53

games for Chicago in the 1885 championship season.

A utility man for the Sox outfield during this era was a slim Iowa youth, William Ashley Sunday, whom Anson rated as the fastest fellow in the game. According to Sunday, he was in center field in 1886 when, with the pennant on the line, Detroit put two men on base in the ninth inning. Catcher Charlie Bennett drove the ball deep. Sunday said he chased the ball with glove extended, his open mouth full of prayer. "As though wings were carrying [him]," Sunday claimed to have leaped over benches crowded with fans (it was common practice for them to sit or stand in the outfield and along the foul lines then) and caught the ball. "I am sure the Lord helped me catch that ball and it was my first experience in prayer." The latter-day evangelist asserted that this was the initial revelation of the power of Christ as revealed to him. He went on to a journeyman baseball career with other teams; his lifetime batting average of .248 indicates either that he failed to invoke prayer frequently or the Higher Power was busy elsewhere when Sunday came to the plate.

Michael J. "King" Kelly ★ was a genuine star. Probably the first player to catch the public's fancy as much for his personality as for his skill on the diamond, the 5'10", 180-pound, extravagantly mustachioed Kelly began his baseball career as a sixteen-year-old right fielder with the Troy, New York, Haymakers. His openly professional debut came with the Paterson, New Jersey, Olympics and subsequently he starred as a catcher for Ohio clubs, including the Cincinnati Red Stockings, before Al Spalding brought him to the White Stockings in 1880 to serve as catcher and outfielder.

Kelly, whose lifetime batting average was .307, twice led the league in hitting and three times in runs scored, aided no doubt by his penchant for dashing from first to third by way of the shortstop, even going directly home from there whenever the solitary umpire was engaged in observing other activities. Fred Pfeffer, who was a second baseman with Kelly on the Chicago club, said:

He was a creator. . . . His strongest playing point was that he was always ready. He could take advantage of a misplay which others wouldn't see until afterward. . . . He played the

(Previous page) *William Arthur (Car Cummings* (left) *pitched for the Broo**Excelsiors, New York Mutuals, the **Baltimores, Philadelphias, and Hartfo**He perfected the curveball in 1867 a**four years of experimentation.*

Courtesy NBL

". . . it was his [Charles Comiskey's] *w**on the bases and in fielding which bec**distinctive. He was fast on his feet bu**could hardly be regarded as a 'ten sec**man.' Yet there were few who had the a**base-stealing down to a finer science. **ting on, he was a runner not to be tr**with. If the chances were even he was cer**to advance a base or two. If they were **he was smart enough to wait for the ine**ble break.*

*"It was risky to slide in the early day**the game on any except the best kept **monds. Feet first and it might mean a bro**leg or a twisted ankle. Head first and it **'raw meat' from the shoulders to the h**With Comiskey it was the latter and n**give him the credit for originating **trick."—G. W. Axelson, "Commy"*

Courtesy NBL (Ted Astor)

umpire as intelligently as he did the opposing nine. He would make a friend of him, engage his confidence, and in various ways get the best of close decisions.

He achieved notoriety as a base stealer during an era when no one kept complete stats on the tactic. In an 1890 game he swiped six bases. He was so skilled at the feat that he received due homage with a popular song, "Slide, Kelly, Slide."

Joe Quinn, who played with and against Kelly, recalled Kelly as the first perfecter of the hit and run:

. . . the Chicago Whites would have their man on first and feint the opposing infield into showing its hand by having the baserunner make a bluff to steal on the first ball pitched.

The batsman would take a strike in order to help the play along. The trick was to see who was going to cover the bag. If it was the second baseman's duty to take the throw, Kelly would try to place a hit through right field. On the other hand, if the shortstop covered the bag, Kelly would aim to hit through second and third.

At least part of Kelly's ability to place the ball lay in his rather unique stance. According to Quinn, he stood with his back square to the catcher to "look the pitcher straight in the eye." He held his bat down, raising it only when the pitcher delivered the ball, thereby concealing where he hoped to hit until he actually started to swing.

Behind the plate, Kelly fooled runners with a fake, wild pickoff throw. As the runner saw the ball sail over the head of the first baseman, he would take off for second, only to find that Kelly had signaled his right fielder to sneak in, catch the ball, and relay it to the second baseman. He himself possessed a prodigious arm; Quinn insisted Kelly was the first to trap a ball on first bounce in right field and fire it to first to nab a hitter. Other accounts note that, along with catcher Buck Ewing, ★ Kelly could throw to second without shifting from his receiver posture. He popularized the hook slide. Quinn said, "He would jump into the air 10 feet from the sack, dive directly for it, dig one of his spiked shoes into the bag and then swerve clear over on his side. Few second basemen . . . had the nerve to block his hurricane dives."

John J. McGraw, ★ whose Baltimore Orioles and then New York Giants fed regularly on the hit and run, said:

The greatest play from the standpoint of quick thinking that I have ever seen was one made by King Kelly. . . . Kelly was catching in a close game. In the ninth inning his team led by a run when the other side stepped to bat. Two men were retired easily. Then a base on balls and an error put the tying run on second and the winning run on first.

The next batter shot a hot single to right, and the man on second tore for the plate. The outfielder's throw came in true enough but to Kelly's left, on his gloved hand. As the ball was in the air Mike saw that he had to take it with his left hand. If he used two hands he would miss the runner. Yet taking the ball with the glove and swinging into the sliding man, he ran the chance of dropping the throw.

Kelly figured this out quicker than it takes me to tell it. He flung off his glove, caught the bounding ball with his bared left hand and touched the runner out.

I've seen many great plays in my twenty-seven years in baseball. This one has always stood out as the headiest play of them all.

Runners racing toward home against Kelly sometimes were unnerved by his trick of dropping his mask on the plate just as they prepared to slide. This and other deeds by King Kel constantly frazzled the brains of rules writers. In a moment of carelessness before one season the guardians of the game had decided managers could substitute during play. In a game between Chicago and Detroit, the White Stockings were in the field but Kelly was on the bench with Flint catching. Detroit loaded the bases and the situation was perilous. A high foul rose near the dugout, just beyond the reach of Flint and first baseman Cap Anson. Kelly leaped off the bench and yelled, "Flint, you're out of the game" and he proceeded to catch the ball. Then he took Flint's mask, put on his glove, and nonchalantly attempted to continue as the new catcher. Umpire John Gaffney, aghast at the sudden turn of events, denied him and remained obdurate even though Kelly pulled out a rule book to prove his point. The rule was amended immediately to avoid any further refinements by Kelly.

King Kel endeared himself to Chicagoans by openly pursuing the pleasures they ef-

Albert Goodwill Spalding began as a pitcher for the club in Rockford, Illinois. "On receiving the ball he [Spalding] raises it in both hands until it is on a level with his left eye. Striking an attitude he gazes at it, two or three minutes in a contemplative way, and then turns it around once or twice to be sure that it is not an orange or coconut. Assured that he has the genuine article . . . and after a scowl at the shortstop, and a glance at homeplate, [he] finally delivers the ball with a precision and rapidity of a cannon shot."—New York Star

Courtesy NBL

"The nine [Cincinnati Red Stockings] had plenty of exercise and practice, a so well regulated that it should avail of its capabilities of defeating every with which it contests."—Henry M Cincinnati Commercial Appeal

The Cincinnati Red Stockings, the all-pro club of 1869, won 79 games, ti before the first loss in 1870. Harry W (seated, center) put the team together his star associate was his brother G (back row, second from left).

Courtesy NBL

Harry Wright (center) decamped from cinnati to create a Boston powerhous 1875 squad included brother George left) and Al Spalding (holding ball d behind George Wright).

Courtesy NBL

fected. He bet on the horses, bellied up to the bar in saloons nightly, and was a devotee of the stage. Indeed, like a number of his contemporaries and his successors—Ty Cobb, ★ Christy Mathewson, ★ Rube Marquard, ★ among others—he trod the boards of vaudeville and the legitimate stage, starring in a skit entitled "He Would Be an Actor, or The Ball Player's Revenge."

His consumption of whiskey was public knowledge. Joe Quinn remembered an incident in Indianapolis: "An old Irishman in the bleachers yelled to Kelly, 'You're a fine-lookin' tin-thousand dollar beauty, ain't you now?' 'Well, I got the best of you, old man,' replied Mike. 'I'm eating strawberries and ice cream off the salary I earn performing for suckers like you.' 'Yes, and the bartenders get yours, all of it,' snapped the fan."

The liquor guzzling exasperated White Stocking boss Spalding, a near-fanatical dry. Spalding assigned Pinkerton detectives to trail Kelly and report on his activities. One of them filed a detailed report that accused Kelly of hanging out in a dive until 3 A.M., swigging lemonade. Confronted with the accusation, Kelly protested: "It was straight whiskey. I never drank a lemonade at that hour in my life."

Unamused, Spalding engineered the sale of the high-salaried ($2,500 per year) Kelly after the 1886 season (in which he hit a blistering .388) to the Boston club for the huge sum of $10,000. Kelly agreed to terms with Boston that guaranteed him $4,000 per year.

"Mugwump," the pen name of the local correspondent for *Sporting Life,* wrote:

> The effect Kelly's presence will have on the Boston nine is very pleasant to contemplate. We have long needed such a man. There are not a great many of them in the business but one man like Kelly on a team is of inestimable value. His style of playing ball is catching. Put him on a team and the other men cannot help trying to play as he does. His good nature and even temper helps him in trying times, and the fact that he never gets rattled will hold the boys together.

In his conversation with Mugwump, Kelly demonstrated that the gap between players and sportswriters existed even one hundred years ago. Kelly complained that "interviews which have been going all over the country are big fakes. . . . Now that's a nice business,

ain't it, writing interviews with me when I haven't said a word?"

On another occasion, a newspaper described a furious Kelly, armed with a horsewhip, prowling the Fifth Avenue Hotel in search of a *Boston Herald* reporter who wrote that Kelly was aggrieved over a dispute with other players about a bill for expenses on a benefit show. Mugwump at least sought to capture Kelly's speech down to his "ain't." Other journalists, possibly persuaded by owners like Spalding to glorify the athletes, described Kelly as "educated for the priesthood at Georgetown College." This was highly improbable indeed. Until he was securely launched as a professional ball player, Kelly labored for $3 a week in a paper mill.

In Boston, Kelly performed credibly, stealing 84 bases during his first season as a club member and adding another 124 the following two years. He averaged over .300 during the three seasons, and played outfield and catcher as well as pitching occasionally and filling in at second base, third, and shortstop. His good efforts, however, were not enough to bring a championship to Boston but neither did his former club, Chicago, prosper without him.

Kelly jumped to the short-lived Players League Boston entry in 1890 as a player-manager and his team captured the league title. His defection along with other stars from the National League brought attempts to woo him back. His former boss, Spalding, met with Kelly in Boston and offered him the huge sum of $10,000 for the next three years if he would bolt the Players League. Spalding said Kelly responded, "Aw, I want the ten thousand bad enough . . . but I've thought the matter all over, and I can't go back on the boys. And neither would you." Spalding said he was so taken with Kelly's loyalty to the comrades who had followed him out of the National League that he felt compelled to praise his virtue and lend Kelly $500 on the spot.

With the collapse of the Players League after a single season Kelly finished his career with Boston and finally New York in 1893. He died penniless, a few weeks short of his thirty-seventh birthday. Allegedly, as a stretcher bore him to the hospital the day of his death, Kelly slipped off the litter and whispered his final words, "This is my last slide."

"Mike Kelly was the trickiest player who ever handled a baseball. There was nothing he would not attempt. . . . Baseball rules were never made for Kel. He had his own way of interpreting them and it was in his own characteristic way that he made them conform to his ideas."—Sam Crane, New York Evening Journal

Courtesy NBL

Sold off to Boston for $10,000 by Al Spalding because of his carousing, Kelly continued his free-booting ways, then in 1890 led the short-lived Boston Players League entry to an easy championship.

Courtesy NBL

Some years ago a group of baseball writers would occasionally play a wordgame they called "L. Peter B." One person would give the first initial, middle name, and last initial of a prominent ball player, and the others would try to guess who the player was. Experts would toss in toughies like C. Gardner R. (for Charles Gardner "Old Hoss" Radbourne) and the eponymous L. Peter B. (for Lawrence Peter "Yogi" Berra); less expert practitioners might try W. Perry J. (Walter Johnson) or W. Howard M. (Willie Mays), or even something as obvious as G. Herman R. or T. Raymond C. But no one tried to fool anyone with A. Constantine A.

Adrian Constantine Anson not only had one of the most distinctive names in baseball history but he was the most dominant player in the premodern era of the game, the years before 1900. He played twenty-seven consecutive seasons as a regular in the National League and its predecessor, the old National Association, in which Anson was a star for five years before the National League was established. He batted over .300 in twenty-four of those twenty-seven years. He hit .352 as a nineteen-year-old rookie in 1871 and .395 as a forty-two-year-old veteran in 1894. He was also a major league manager for twenty years, from 1879 to 1898, so far back in baseball antiquity that his long and successful managerial career (he won five pennants) was over and done with before John McGraw's began.

Anson was a large, imperious man, standing more than six feet tall and weighing more than 200 pounds. Precise details vary: His height is given as anywhere from six-feet even to 6'3½", and his weight from 200 to 230 pounds. Whatever the actual figures, Anson was big—a huge man really—in an era when the average big leaguer was about 5'9" and weighed 165 pounds. His famous Chicago White Stockings of the 1880s at that time were noted for their size. Anson's greatest player, the colorful outfielder-infielder-catcher Mike "King" Kelly, said in later years, "Where can you get a team with so many big men on its payroll? . . . We had most of 'em [other teams] whipped before we threw a ball. They were scared to death." Yet on this team of big men Anson was taller and (with the exception of a fat pitcher named Jim McCormick) heavier than every other man on the club—taller and heavier than most other men in baseball.

He had blond hair and blue eyes (he was called "Swede" in his early years in the game, although his ancestry on both sides was English), fair skin, and a truculent temper. For a long time he wore a waxed, pointed moustache that made him look something like a Prussian army officer. He

" . . . in the third game of the last B Chicago series when Madden and Ta ing two men on bases for the B deliberately sent Anson to first on five balls. . . . The captain of the Boston preferred to see three Chicago men or with two men out than to take the ce of Anson's hitting the ball as an alter This leads the Chicago Journal to re 'If there is such a thing as scientific b Anson has mastered the points th . . . With a quick, sharp stroke he wi a ball on a dead line between sho second, second and first, along the ba just inside the bag or on a bounding just over the heads of the infielders t or left centre. . . . And when Anson h ball it travels. It does not linger point along its line of route but cuts on its way to the goal the big fellow in it to reach, with a warning screech th infielders have the highest possible for." —Sporting Life, 1886

Courtesy NBL

16

was a persistent baiter of umpires and a stern manager who demanded a great deal from his players. One of his stars, outfielder Jimmy Ryan, declared angrily at one point that he would never play for Anson again. Ryan did, but he didn't like it, and when Anson was finally let go as manager he claimed that Ryan was a ringleader in the move to have him dismissed.

Aside from his temperament, Anson was much like his father, another big, forceful (but more amiable) man. Henry Anson was born in New York State, where his family had lived for five generations in Dutchess County. As a young man, scarcely more than a boy, Henry went out on his own, left New York, and settled in southern Michigan. By the time he was nineteen, he had married a large, strapping girl named Jeannette Rice (A. C. Anson remembered his mother as being 5'10½" and over 200 pounds) and had fathered a son, named Sturgis Ransome Anson.

Henry Anson liked Michigan but there was more opportunity farther west, so in 1851, with his wife and infant son and other pioneer families, he pushed on to Iowa, which recently had become a state. With the help of friends he built a log cabin on high ground near the Iowa River and founded a town (really a hamlet then) that he named Marshall after a town he had liked in Michigan. Later, when it was learned that there was already a post office called Marshall in Iowa, it was renamed Marshalltown.

There, in his father's log cabin, Adrian Constantine Anson was born on April 17, 1852. He liked to boast that he was "the first white child" born in Marshalltown. His odd name came from his parents' lingering affection for the state they had left: Adrian is a southern Michigan town, and so is Constantine. (For that matter, so are Sturgis and Ransome.) When he was seven years old his mother died, but his father, who was both a successful farmer and a businessman (he later ran a hotel called The Anson House in rapidly growing Marshalltown), seems to have been a caring, if indulgent, parent. That was fortunate because Adrian, reared as much by relatives as by his father, was by his own account a hell-raiser. "I was a natural-born kicker," he wrote in his autobiography, "bent upon making trouble for others." He said he had "an instinctive dislike both to study and work, and I shirked them whenever the opportunity offered." When his father was away on business, Adrian would play hookey from school and get into trouble. The elder Anson would administer some punishment on his return, but not too severely, and life would go on, with his unruly son learning as little as possible in school and playing as much as he could out of it.

The favorite games were variants of baseball: one o' cat, two o' cat, something called "bull pen," and, most frequently, "soakball," in which base runners were put out by hitting or "soaking" them with the ball. The more formal game of baseball, which had been codified by Alexander Cartwright only a few years earlier, in 1845, reached Marshalltown when Anson was still a boy. He took to it eagerly, as did his older brother and his father. Henry Anson was only in his thirties when the Marshalltown Baseball Club was organized in 1866, and he played on it along with both his teenage sons. Baseball fever was rampant in those post–Civil War days, and the Marshalltown nine played in games and tournaments all over Iowa and even as far away as Omaha, Nebraska.

At the same time, the elder Anson was trying to get a proper education into his son, and he sent him off to the University of Iowa. Adrian failed his first entrance examination, passed the second, and then behaved just as badly as he had back in Marshalltown. "The scrapes I managed to get into were too numerous to mention," Anson admitted, and he was sent home. His father then dispatched him to Notre Dame, which at the time, Anson said, was "noted as being one of the strictest schools in the country." It was also in northern Indiana, only a few miles from friends and relatives the Ansons had left behind in southern Michigan. At Notre Dame, Adrian was an early version of the total jock. He studied little, but he played a lot of football in the fall and did a lot of ice skating in the winter ("As a fancy skater, I excelled," Anson claimed). He also played second base for the Juniatas, the baseball team that represented Notre Dame (college sports were informal then), before once again leaving the groves of academe, this time for good.

Back in Marshalltown, still in his teens, Adrian took on all comers at billiards in the family hotel (he loved to bet) and really blossomed as a baseball player, to his father's evident satisfaction. "From my early years," Anson wrote, "he allowed me to participate in any sort of game that took my fancy." But, he added, "He had no idea at that time of my ever becoming a professional. Neither had I."

Then, in 1870, a crack professional team from Rockford, Illinois, called the Forest City club, came to Marshalltown to play the local nine. The Rockford pitcher was a tall, slim youngster only a year or two older than Anson named Al Spalding, who would have a profound influence on his life. Spalding and the Forest Cities won both the games they played against Marshalltown, but they were impressed by the quality of the local team. When the season was over they asked Anson and his brother Sturgis to play for Rockford in 1871. Henry Anson said that Rockford

The Chicago White Stockings of 1885 was basically the same club that also won the championships of 1881 and 1882. Anson stands third from left in the back row. Other notables include the irrepressible Mike "King" Kelly (back row, second from right), pitcher John Clarkson, winner of 326 games (front row, second from right), and the clean-shaven right fielder Billy Sunday (at Clarkson's right), who made his reputation as a preacher.

Courtesy NBL

The White Stockings of 1895 with the portly Anson seated at center no longer dominated the league. The mustache was then out of fashion; fewer than half of the team wore one. Cap's bat work seemed slipping in the early 1890s, but the lengthening of the pitching distance from fifty-five feet to sixty revived him, and he hit .332 in 1893, .394 in 1894, .338 in 1895, .335 in 1896, and .302 for his final major league season in 1897.

Courtesy NBL

"tried to seduce the whole Anson family, and Adrian, who was only a boy, was allowed to sign with them, I retaining his older brother at home to aid me in my business."

The elder Anson apparently assumed that his son would play one summer with Rockford and then return to Marshalltown, but before the 1871 season began professional baseball changed suddenly. Until that time, teams like the Forest Cities and the Red Stockings of Boston and the Atlantics of Brooklyn played haphazardly, scheduling games when and where they liked. But in March 1871, players from Rockford, the Red Stockings, the Atlantics, and seven other clubs formed a loose-knit league called the National Association of Professional Base Ball Players. The teams continued to play here and there as games could be arranged, but they also agreed to play one another a specific number of times, with the club achieving the best record in those games winning the Association championship. Young Anson, playing third base for Rockford, traveled to the biggest cities in the country—Chicago, Philadelphia, New York, Boston. His father may have expected him home again after Rockford's season ended, but Adrian's life had changed forever. Earlier, Al Spalding had jumped from the Forest Cities to the Boston Red Stockings. Now the Philadelphia Athletics, who had won the Association championship in 1871, offered Anson $1,250 to play with them in 1872, a vast increase over the $65 a month he had been earning with Rockford.

His business-oriented father had impressed upon young Anson the sanctity of contracts, and while he did not discuss Philadelphia's invitation with either his father or his older brother (possibly anticipating disapproval of his intention to continue playing professional baseball), he did inform the Rockford club of the Athletics' offer and said he would stay if his salary were increased to $100 a month. The Forest Cities, in over their heads financially in the competition with teams from the big cities, were unable to meet his figure. Twenty-year-old Anson left for Philadelphia and didn't return home to Marshalltown for five years.

Although Spalding and the Red Stockings dominated the Association, winning the championship in 1872, 1873, 1874, and 1875, Anson had a great time in Philadelphia, playing every position except pitcher at one time or another and quickly establishing himself as one of the two or three best hitters in the league. Off the field he played billiards, hung around saloons, got drunk, fought with policemen, punched a man he got into an argument with on a streetcar, and, ultimately, fell in love with a girl named Virginia Fiegal (and at her request gave up drinking). In the summer of 1874, he traveled overseas to England with the Athletics and

"Player, manager, business man, a actor, politician, billiard player, b baseball critic, reporter, and vaudevil ist were many of the lines in Anson's life, but his greatest success was as player and he will go down in baseba tory as one of the best and the gr characters the sport ever knew."— Crane, New York Evening Journal

Courtesy NBL

the Red Stockings on a baseball/cricket tour arranged right in the middle of the Association season by the enterprising young Spalding; the two American teams played each other in a series of baseball exhibitions and combined to play British sides in cricket. Anson, swinging the wide cricket bat with un-British abandon, proved just as able a batsman in the English game.

After the 1875 season, William Hulbert, owner of the Chicago White Stockings, disturbed by the increasing informality of the Association structure, forced the establishment of the stronger, more cohesive National League. He lured Spalding and three other Boston stars to Chicago, with Spalding at age twenty-five taking over as manager of the club. Spalding, in turn, got Hulbert to sign Anson and another Philadelphia standout, third baseman Ezra Sutton. The Athletics made counteroffers, and Sutton changed his mind and decided to stay in Philadelphia. Anson wanted to change his mind, too, particularly since Virginia Fiegal, whom he wanted to marry, declared that she didn't want to move to Chicago. But he had signed a contract. Even though players routinely jumped back and forth in those days, Anson traveled to Chicago twice to ask Hulbert to let him out of the deal, the second time just before the 1876 season was to begin, when he offered to pay $1,000 for his release.

Hulbert was inclined to let the player go, but Spalding, convinced that Anson would not break the contract, persuaded Hulbert to hold on to him. The story then goes that Anson, in street clothes, stopped by the White Stockings' field to watch them practice and after standing around for a while said to Spalding, "Toss me one, Al." Eventually, he took off his hat and coat and joined in the practice, after which Spalding said, "Now, Anse, come tomorrow in uniform." Anson did and stayed with Chicago for the next twenty-two seasons.

The White Stockings won the National League pennant in 1876 but they did badly the next two years. Spalding, more interested in the business end of baseball (and in his own sporting goods company), gave up pitching and managing to run the Chicago front office. Anson, consistently among the top hitters in the league, was obviously the best player the White Stockings had, and in 1879 Spalding and Hulbert made him captain and manager of the team. In his eight previous seasons as a professional, Anson had been used as a catcher, a third baseman, a first baseman, and an outfielder (along with brief stints at shortstop and second base). Now he put himself at first base, where with rare exceptions he remained for the next nineteen years.

In his first season as manager he missed more than a third of his team's

As an actor after he quit baseball, the former manager and first baseman of the White Stockings toured for five years in "Cap Anson and His Daughters," a vehicle created by Ring Lardner and George M. Cohan.

Courtesy NBL

games because of a badly inflamed finger, but the team improved under his direction. A year later, in 1880, bolstered by the addition of the flamboyant Kelly and a splendid pitcher named Larry Corcoran, Anson and his White Stockings ran away with the National League pennant, winning it by 15 games. They won again the next year, when Anson had a tremendous season, batting .399 to lead all other hitters in the league by more than 60 points, and again in 1882, when Anson was a close second in the batting race. Runs-batted-in totals weren't paid as much attention to in those days, but modern research shows that Anson was the best RBI man in the league, consistently coming through for Chicago with men on base. Teams played fewer games then (Anson was in his fourteenth season before any of his teams played as many as 100 games a year), but from 1884 to 1891 he drove in 100 runs or more six times when the league was playing an average of 128 games a season.

The White Stockings fell to second place in 1883 as Corcoran's arm gave out, but with a new pitching star named John Clarkson ("the best that Chicago ever had," according to Anson) they came back to win two more pennants in 1885 and 1886. After the 1886 season, in an astonishing move, Spalding sold the glamorous Kelly, the best all-around player in the game that year (he beat out Anson for the batting title), to Boston for $10,000. A year later he sold Clarkson to the same club. Despite the loss of his two finest players (both are in the Hall of Fame) Anson managed to keep the White Stockings in contention, finishing second or third for five straight years.

By now he was a folk hero, not just in Chicago but all over the country. He married showmanship to sport. During the 1888 Republican Convention in Chicago, Anson paraded his men onto the field dressed in black swallow-tailed coats. Everybody had heard of "Captain Anson of the Chicagos" or, as he was more familiarly known, Cap Anson. "His name became a household word," wrote baseball historian Harold Seymour, "better known, it was said, than that of any statesman or soldier of his time."

People kept photographs and drawings of him. Boys bought "Anson bats." Indeed, years later when Chicago-born poet Vachel Lindsay sought to describe his childhood in verse he wrote: "Pop Anson was our darling, pet and pride. . . ."

Young players imitated his style at the plate and according to Sam Crane, a big leaguer then who later became a baseball writer, "To hit like the big Chicago giant, or at least to imagine so was glory enough for all time."

He was a phenomenon, a major force at bat even after twenty years as a professional (in 1891, nearing forty, he drove in 120 runs, 35 more than anyone else in the league). Anson batted right-handed, in an open stance almost facing the pitcher. He didn't take a full swing, going for the fences, but snapped at the ball, sending line drives between the fielders. He finished with 3,041 hits, the first player ever to reach such an acclaimed level, even though during his twenty-two years with Chicago he played an average of only 103 games a season. Project Anson's hit figures to today's 162-game schedule, and he would have had close to 4,500 hits for his National League career. Add his five seasons in the National Association, projected the same way, and he would have had over 5,000.

As he turned forty he put on weight, getting bulky through the middle and looking his age. Scorned as elderly when he played at that age, he mocked his critics in an 1892 game by taking the field wearing fake whiskers. His last Chicago teams finished well down in the standings, and people began to poke fun at him (despite his temper, or perhaps because of it, he was frequently the butt of jokes). They called him Uncle Anse and Old Anse and, finally and lastingly, Pop Anson.

Although everyone had high regard for his extraordinary skills, he was never overwhelmingly popular with other players. He could hardly have endeared himself to his lessers after Hugh Fullerton, the baseball correspondent for *Chicago Inter-Ocean*, carried the item: "Captain A. C. Anson desires me to announce in black type, at the head of this column, that the Chicago baseball club is composed of a bunch of drunkards and loafers who ARE THROWING HIM DOWN" [sic].

As a young man Anson admittedly liked his brew when the "beer was in and the wit was out," resulting in saloon brawls and a brief stay in jail for insobriety. But as manager he enforced stern discipline, fining beer drinkers as much as $100 and holding bed checks.

Anson became particularly unpopular during the abortive players' revolt of 1890, when rebellious stars broke away to start their own independent league. A majority of National Leaguers jumped to the Players League, including all but two of Anson's 1889 Chicago team, but Old Anse, who had a ten-year contract with Spalding and the White Stockings as well as some stock in the club, refused to follow. Some held that Anson's presence in the old league was instrumental in holding it together until the rebel league faltered and died.

Earlier, in 1884, he had etched his name in baseball infamy when before an exhibition game in Toledo he threatened to take his team off the field unless Fleet Walker, Toledo's black catcher, was removed from the lineup. The Toledo manager refused, and Anson reluctantly played the game. But three years later, in July 1887, when Chicago played an exhibition game in Newark, New Jersey, and a big crowd showed up to see how Anson and the White Stockings would fare against Newark's superb black pitcher, George Stovey, the Newark management announced just before the game that Stovey was "ill" and substituted a white pitcher and catcher (Fleet Walker, Anson's *bête noire* in Toledo, was slated to catch Stovey). A contemporary newspaper account said flatly that Stovey was not ill and that the substitution had been made because "Anson objected to him playing on account of his color." A year after that in an exhibition game in Syracuse, New York, Walker again was not allowed to play against Anson and the White Stockings.

Anson employed black mascots for his team, but his attitude toward blacks was stupidly racist. In telling a long story in his autobiography about a mascot he hired named Clarence Duval, he used such derogatory terms as "darkey," "coon," and "no-account nigger." Such blatant bigotry was common in (and out of) professional baseball then, and before the 1889 season, the game's leaders instituted the infamous color bar that lasted until Jackie Robinson's debut almost sixty years later. Anson was not involved in the owners' decision to exclude blacks, but having the most important player in the game display such a racist attitude must have hastened the process. Oddly, a decade after his major league career ended, when he was running a semiprofessional team called Anson's Colts in Chicago, he played games frequently against the Leland Giants and other all-black teams without incident.

Anson was a marvelous athlete and in his own way an honest, steadfast man, happily married (to Virginia, after the 1876 season) and devoted to his four daughters (he also had three sons, all of whom died in early infancy), but there is little evidence to show that he was very intelligent. Spalding, shrewd and manipulative, had affection for Anson (he took him on another baseball tour abroad, this one around the world, after the 1888 season) but he conned his gullible manager time and again, finally helping to ease him out as the White Stockings' leader after the 1897 season, when the naive Anson was under the impression that Spalding was going to help him buy control of the club. When Spalding later proposed that a testimonial purse be gathered for presentation to the old hero, Anson stiffly refused to let the money be raised, saying, "I am not a pauper, the public owes me nothing, and I believe I am still capable of making my own living."

Anson was bitter in his autobiography (published in 1900, the first

24

Generally regarded as the foremost opponent of nonwhites in organized baseball during the nineteenth century, in later years Anson conferred with Andrew "Rube" Foster, the Chicagoan who is regarded as the patriarch of the Negro Leagues.

Courtesy NBL

such ghostwritten autobiography of a ball player), saying, "I trusted implicitly in Mr. Spalding. . . . I made a mistake in trusting him." His life after he left the White Stockings was never as rewarding as he felt it should have been. He managed the New York Giants for one brief month in the middle of the 1898 season, sold ginger beer, operated a billiard parlor, managed his semipro team, went on a vaudeville tour with two of his daughters (Ring Lardner wrote a sketch for the act and George M. Cohan prepared a monologue for Anson to deliver), gave interviews in which he said the old-time ball players of his day were superior to the "modern" breed (those of 1915 and 1920, like Ty Cobb and Babe Ruth), went to World Series games, and on April 14, 1922, three days before his seventieth birthday, Anson died in Chicago.

He was an oddly anachronistic figure at his death, like a rugged fragment of an ancient mountain jutting from the plain—not forgotten but not really part of the world around him anymore. His time was too far back in baseball's past. But in baseball's early years Cap Anson was a mountain, a towering mountain.

The early dominance of the Spalding–Anson operation yielded to stiffening competition from a number of teams. For a few brief years the Providence Grays battled Chicago for the championship. Four future Hall of Famers graced their lineup. George Wright guided the Grays and played shortstop. Of Wright, one contemporary writer said:

> Whenever he would pull off one of those grand, unexpected plays that were so dazzlingly surprising as to dumbfound his opponents, his prominent teeth would gleam and glisten in an array of white molars that would put our own Teddy Roosevelt and his famed dentistry . . . far in the shadow.

Along with the flashy smiles, Wright added dimension to the shortstop position through the innovation of playing deep, behind the baseline. George Wright had far more impact on the sport than just a new wrinkle at shortstop. After finishing third in the six-team competition of 1878, the Grays lured Wright and Jim O'Rourke, ★ a hard-hitting outfielder from Boston, with generous salary offers. The coup, which led to Providence's first championship, alarmed the baseball tycoons. They foresaw ruinous bidding wars at the end of every season. Supposedly, the first championship season of the Grays had produced only a $2,000 profit and much of that was spent on ballpark improvements. To forestall any consequent payroll rise, the 1879 National League meeting in Buffalo produced an agreement whereby each team could "reserve" five players for the succeeding season. Eventually, baseball extended the reservations to cover for life all players under contract to a major league team.

The Grays pitching ace for several years was Charles (Old Hoss) Radbourne, ★ a twenty-five-year-old rookie for Buffalo in 1880 before shuffling off to Providence. He won 31 in 1882, 49 the next year, and an incredible 60 for the 1884 season, including 26 wins in the final 27 games. During that season, Radbourne started and completed 73 of the Grays' 112 games. He led the league with his 441 strikeouts, an earned run average of 1.38, and he worked 678⅔ innings. Because of Old Hoss's contentious nature, his catcher was described by one writer as an unsung martyr for putting up with the "erratic, ill tempered and capricious Lord Radbourne . . . without a murmur." The pitcher went to Boston for the 1886 season and won 20 games or more for four seasons before his overworked right arm quit.

The third stellar performer was John Montgomery Ward who began at Providence as a pitcher and right fielder. On the mound he collected 47 wins in 1879 and 40 the following year. An injury reduced his effectiveness and he served in the outfield while spelling Radbourne on the hill enough to add another 37 wins in two seasons. (In those days of twelve-man rosters nobody spent much time on the bench and Radbourne also filled an outfield slot when not pitching.)

In spite of two pennants and three second-place finishes, the Grays could not muster sufficient attendance to support the club. (The annual payroll for the entire team in 1881 was a lusty $13,175, slightly less than what Dave Winfield earned in 1988 every game.) Providence bellied up after the 1885 season; the franchise along with player contracts was sold to the Boston club whose chief gain was the tireless arm of Old Hoss Radbourne.

The eight-year life of the Grays in the National League was hardly singular. Between 1877 and 1890, twenty-three cities—among them Indianapolis, Worcester, Buffalo, Troy, and Syracuse, along with more familiar places—fielded National League teams. During that period only Chicago and Boston survived without missing a single season.

The National League was not the sole wheel in town. The American Association, established in 1882, placed clubs in St. Louis, Cincinnati, Baltimore, Columbus, Pittsburgh, and New York, among others. For a brief period the two leagues were at odds. By cutting the usual 50-cents admission in half, scheduling games on Sundays, and selling alcoholic drinks in their parks, the American Association prospered enough to win a peace treaty in 1883. The terms of the agreement included respect for territorial rights, an extension of the reserve clause to fourteen men, and granting clubs the right to do business as they saw fit. That opened the way for Sunday games where permitted by

From Providence, Radbourne moved to [Bos]ton, but his only championship club was the 1890 Players League entry.

Courtesy NBL

"[John] Ward is one of the younges[t] most promising players in the country although less than 20 years of age, second to none in his position."—[H.] Chadwick (1879)

"Probably no player has ever la[bored] under the mental strain that John M. [Ward] has done in the past few weeks. Whatev[er the] Brotherhood has accomplished it l[argely] owes to this energetic player. War[d has] worked night and day, and the strai[n] naturally told upon him. He is round[ing] in great shape, however, and will und[oubt]edly 'play the game of his life' this su[mmer] now that his interests are more closely [tied] up with base ball than ever before."—S[port]ing Life (1890)

Ward joined the Giants in 1883 aft[er] years with the Providence Grays.

Courtesy NBL

local law* and opened sales of whiskey and beer, bitter medicine for the straitlaced Spalding. But the game was thriving. Philadelphia boasted a pair of clubs while the New York area housed the Metropolitans, New Yorks, and Brooklyns.

The two leagues played a kind of World Series starting in 1884. The Spalding–Anson team met the St. Louis Browns led by twenty-four-year-old Charlie Comiskey. The opening game ended in a tie when darkness prevented further play. In the second contest, a disputed call by an umpire unleashed a riot by hometown St. Louis kranks. The official fled the premises to the safety of his hotel and awarded the game to Chicago as a forfeit. That decision was still in dispute when the Browns won the next 3 out of 5. Comiskey claimed the championship. A year later the same teams fought again under more structured circumstances; the series was the best of 7 games with home and away competition. All income was consigned to the winner. To goad his employees, Spalding telegraphed Anson, offering "as a token of my appreciation . . . each man a suit of clothes . . . and the team collectively one-half of the receipts in the coming series with the Browns." The promised reward failed to inspire the club, and the Browns took the series 4–2.

Even before the Grays vanished, J. M. "Monte" Ward had already left Providence, switching to the New York National League entry in 1883, and two years later his manager was Jim Mutrie, formerly with the American Association's New Yorkers. In the late 1890s, the club deployed five other Hall of Famers, leading the ecstatic Mutrie to wheeze, "My Giants" and thus permanently endow the team with its name. (As a more dubious honor, after raiding other teams' rosters to sign Louis Bierbauer of the Athletics and catcher Connie Mack, ★ Pittsburgh became known as the Pirates.)

William (Buck) Ewing, adept at all positions, starred behind the plate for the Giants, achieving notoriety for his ability to peg the ball to second without rising from his squat receivership. In seventeen years he compiled a lifetime batting average of .303. Later he

would manage at Cincinnati. Francis Richter wrote in the *1919 Reach Guide:*

> . . . we have always been inclined to consider Catcher–Manager William ("Buck") Ewing in his prime from 1884–1890 as the greatest player of the game from the standpoint of supreme excellence in all departments—batting, catching, fielding, base running, throwing and base ball brains—a player without a weakness of any kind, physical, mental or temperamental.

Richter made this judgment after having seen both Ty Cobb and Honus Wagner ★ in their primes and he concluded: "As a thrower to the bases Ewing never had a superior. . . . Ewing was the man of whom it was said, 'He handed the ball to the second baseman from the batter's box.' "

Jim O'Rourke, who had accompanied George Wright from Boston to Providence, was equally versatile, playing outfield, first base, or catcher for New York. Dubbed "The Orator" because of his Yale Law School studies, O'Rourke already had thirteen major league years of service when he joined the Giants for eight more. He retired after a year with Washington as player-manager, hitting .287 in 1893. He returned to the Giants eleven years later at age fifty-two to catch 1 game, and his career batting average stands at .310.

Tim Keefe, ★ like Buck Ewing, started out with the Troy (N.Y.) Haymakers before joining the New York Metropolitans, the club name until Mutrie's nomenclating sigh. "Sir Timothy" to some and "Smiling Tim" to others, Keefe possessed both fastball and curve to which he added a new pitch, the change of pace. Twice he won more than 40 games. To Jacob Morse, a sportswriter for Boston newspapers and the founder of *Baseball* magazine, Tim Keefe revealed a strategy of tight pitches to hitters who crowded the plate and outside ones for those who stood back.

Alternating with Keefe was Michael (Mickey) Welch. ★ Welch on occasion pitched doubleheaders, winning both games against the Cleveland Spiders, for example.

"[Buck] Ewing's gilt-edged team lowered its colors twice to the Clevelands at Cleveland yesterday. In both games the local club led at the bat and won by their opportune work with the ash."—New York Times, *1890*

Ewing caught and managed the ill-fated New York team of the Players League but returned to the Giants in 1891.

Courtesy NBL

Mickey Welch went the distance in his first 105 starts and won 17 in a row in 1885.

Courtesy NBL

---

*At an 1891 Sunday game in Cincinnati, two thousand customers were on hand and advised to save their tickets for a refund if the cops halted the game. During the first inning the police appeared and arrested the players. They were released on $300 bond each. Until Ohio allowed Sunday ball, the club played in Covington, Kentucky, just across the river from town. Sunday baseball came to places like New York in 1918, Boston in 1929, and, the last holdouts, Pittsburgh and Philadelphia, in 1934.

Opening Day at the Polo Grounds in 1
featured a crowd of derby-hatted men; a
York team starring home-run hitter R
O'Connor; Monte Ward at shortstop w
he committed a ghastly 86 errors; the
catcher of the nineteenth century, B
Ewing; pitcher Tim Keefe, who won 35
an ERA of 1.74; and hurler Mickey W
with 26 victories and an ERA of 1.93

Courtesy NBL

Manager Jim Mutrie endowed the New
National League entry with its perma
name when he boasted, "My Giants."
club in the early 1890s included pitc
Mickey Welch and Amos Rusie, and
fielder Jimmy O'Rourke, all elected t
Hall of Fame.

Courtesy NBL

He completed his first 105 starts in the League and was only the third man to win more than 300 games.

Giant first baseman Roger Connor ★ was celebrated for the long ball; his 136 homers stood as the record until Babe Ruth swept past him in 1921 while on the way to another 576. The left-handed Connor was 6'3", weighed 220 pounds, and also graduated from the Troy Haymakers. In ten years with the Giants he smote .320.

The Giants beat Chicago out by 9 games in 1888 and Boston by a single contest in 1889. But the team fell to sixth in 1890 as a direct result of the upstart Players League. Monte Ward was the man most responsible for this challenge to organized baseball.

In 1885, the bright, articulate Ward, dismayed by the owners' extension of their proprietary rights and the loss of player bargaining power, created the National Brotherhood of Professional Baseball Players. He described the reserve clause as a "fugitive slave law" and the Brotherhood quickly won the allegiance of many players. Initially, management viewed the quasi-union with tolerance, even recognizing its existence.

However, the desire to control expenditures led to an ever-widening gap. Spalding proposed an overall agreement to cover even minor leaguers. Furthermore, the league officials envisioned a pay schedule divided into five categories ranging from $1,500 to $2,500 annually. Among the determinants of compensation were "habits," "earnestness," and "special qualifications," that presumably covered base hits, strikeouts, steals, wins, and the like. "Habits" and "earnestness" reflected Spalding's Carrie Nation–like crusade against boozing. He offered bonuses for total abstinence and announced: "We don't intend to . . . insult ladies and gentlemen in this city or any other by allowing men who are full of beer and whiskey to go upon the diamond in the uniform of the Chicago club."

Spalding's proposal provoked open rebellion by the Brotherhood. Ward denounced the proprietors as a combination "stronger than the strongest trust." It was a well-calculated tocsin as many thinking people had discerned the menace in the trusts being organized by the industrialists and financiers of the era. Ward flung down his gauntlet, a

Players League, an operation that put teams in five National League cities and two that housed American Association clubs. The Brotherhood itself was in no position to finance clubs. Instead it solicited well-heeled businessmen eager to become sportsmen.

The investors hoped to turn profits but dispensed with the reserve clause, guaranteed salaries for three-year contracts, and agreed to share the profits with the workers. The proposals had obvious appeal and many major leaguers enthusiastically jumped ship.

The old establishment fought back with a "war committee." It fired salvos of propaganda, portraying the National League as "responsible for making professional baseball a dignified, honest business that guaranteed ballplayers the dignity of profession and . . . munificent salary."

The efforts of the Brotherhood and its offspring, the Players League, were doused with fire and brimstone. Spalding's *Guide* declared that if the insurgency were successful "dishonor and disintegration" would "smear the most glorious and honorable sport on the green earth." Spalding decried the new entrepreneurs as that nineteenth-century anathema, "speculators from Wall Street." He called them ignorant of baseball enterprise: "They take all the risks; they pay their employees fabulously high salaries and in addition to all that they divide with them the profits of the business half and half. . . . A shrewd businessman would laugh in their faces at their temerity."

There is no sign, however, that shrewd businessman Spalding ever giggled over his rivals' efforts. The players received an even more severe drubbing from Henry Chadwick whom Spalding had hired to edit his *Guides*. In a section of the 1890 edition, Chadwick blasted the Brotherhood leadership as a cabal that hatched its plans in "secret council." He declared the sinister nature of the plot was made obvious by the Brotherhood's timing for its announcement of revolt: Guy Fawkes Day. British-born Chadwick may have been stirred by his schoolboy lessons on the 1604 plot of dissident Roman Catholics to blow up the House of Lords. It is most unlikely that the largely uneducated, predominantly Irish Catholic American players knew anything of Guy Fawkes. Chadwick seems to have tried to exploit fears of union

Roger Connor wielded the heavy bat of the nineteenth century; his career total of 138 homers stood as the record until surpassed by Babe Ruth in 1921.

Courtesy NBL

Dan Brouthers was the other slugger of the era. His .343 lifetime average ranks ninth and his 206 triples give him eighth among all-time records.

Courtesy NBL

James Francis "Pud" Galvin posed with a bat but his turf was the mound, where he was the first to compile 300 wins.

Courtesy NBL

(Left) The Providence Grays won their pennant with this 1884 squad whose notable member was Old Hoss—nee Ch. Gardner—Radbourne (standing, extr. left). Other notables: Jerry Denny, amb. trous third sacker and reputedly the last to play without a glove (standing, fo. from left); Joe Start, first baseman ar fielding innovator (standing, sixth left); Arthur Irwin, shortstop and se. baseman and an early adherent of the (standing, second from right).

Courtesy NBL

and worker violence and the festering animosity toward Roman Catholics in America. Fresh enough in memory lay the 1886 Haymarket Square riot in Chicago that touched off a bomb and pistol barrage leaving eight cops dead, and New York City among other municipalities regularly witnessed pitched battles between Irish Catholics and Protestants.

Initially, the Players League outdrew its elder by as much as 50 percent. Soon, however, both circuits, struggling to persuade customers of their staying power, started to paper the houses and wildly inflate figures.

Top names jumped to the Players League. Beefy first baseman Dan Brouthers, ★ perhaps the outstanding slugger of the nineteenth century and a man who hit better than .300 for sixteen dead-ball seasons including a high-water mark of .419 in 1887 (a feat only slightly tarnished by walks that then counted as hits), moved from the Boston National League club to the Beantown Players League team.

James Francis (Pud) Galvin, ★ the Pittsburgh veteran who was the first 300-game winner, took his stocky 5'8", 190 pounds to the Pittsburgh Players League version. Sometimes known as the "Little Steam Engine," Galvin was near the end of his career in which he threw more innings (5,941) and complete games (639) than anyone except the incredible Cy Young, ★ who happened to make his debut the starting year of the Players League.

A refugee particularly galling to Spalding was outfielder Hugh Duffy, ★ who broke away from the Chicago White Stockings to toil for the crosstown Players League outfit. The diminutive Duffy was just beginning his legerdemain with the bat; in 1894, he was to hit .438 as part of a string of ten consecutive .300-or-better years.

Ed Delahanty, ★ the oldest of the five Delahanty brothers who made it to the major leagues (setting an all-time sibling record), quit the Philadelphia Athletics for his hometown of Cleveland at the invitation of the local Players League aggregation. His sixteen-year career as an outfielder and longball dealer—521 doubles, 183 triples, 100 homers including the first four in a single game—came to a mysterious end when he disappeared from a train crossing Niagara Falls in 1903.

Nowhere was the fight for players and fans fiercer than in New York. The Players League fielded a Brooklyn team under Monte Ward and a Manhattan one skippered by Buck Ewing that featured three other former Giants: O'Rourke, Connor, and Keefe. Actually, the season began with three clubs in Brooklyn: the National League entry, the newcomer from the Players League, and the American Association squad that decamped in midseason to Baltimore. The Giants came perilously close to folding. Having lost all but three members of the championship 1889 team, attendance fell to an average of two hundred per day. A hasty trip by Spalding raised $80,000 to rescue owner John B. Day.

In the end, the tyro sportsmen lacked the staying power of the established owners. The Players League collapsed as Boston ran away with the pennant race under King Kelly. Although the National League retained a policy of blacklisting anyone who defied its regulations, it extended a general amnesty to the defectors who were returned to their former clubs. Ringleader Ward even became manager for Brooklyn. The National League, in an effort to avoid further conflict, set up a three-man board to control all contracts and resolve all questions on franchises. The reserve clause remained stronger than ever.

Outfielder Ed Delahanty, one of five b. ers who reached the major leagues t went 6 for 6 and was the first to str. homers in a single game.

"Del was a whole-souled fellow, soc. inclined, and even when under the fat. management and watchful core of the eran Harry Wright he never grasped the that the game afforded a field for imp. ment and betterment of habits and char. that could have firmly established hi. life as a prosperous and successful man. Sam Crane, New York Evening Jour.

Courtesy NBL

With the surrender of the players, management focused on an alarming aspect of the game itself. Ever since 1884, when pitchers were granted the power to throw overhand—with the attendant improvement in velocity and ball movement; great strides in control of curves; techniques to persuade balls to drop; the appearance of the screwball, a sort of reverse curve around 1880; and the discovery of ways to doctor the ball for added deflection—offense had suffered. Batting averages declined steadily, particularly after 1890. The number of .300 hitters fell into the single digits.

To spike the punch from the batter's box, the poobahs in 1893 set the pitcher's mound at 60 feet 6 inches from home plate, 10 feet farther than specified a dozen years earlier. Results were immediate—runs per game rose by more than 25 percent while strikeouts were nearly halved. While only nine men achieved .300 in 1892, twenty-six did so in 1893 (based on a minimum of 400 at-bats). No one held a slugging average better than .495 in 1892; the five leaders for the next year were above .523. The stage was set for Hugh Duffy's historic 1894 average of .438 with his 18 homers and 145 runs batted in. That same season Sam Thompson, ★ a Phillie outfielder, pushed his average to .404, but that was good enough for only third place among league leaders. Lifetime, Thompson achieved .331. In contrast, there were players like Jake Beckley, ★ who kept his average largely above .300 from 1888 through 1892 while with Pittsburgh clubs, and continued to show a sharp eye for a lifetime .308 over a twenty-year period.

The introduction of batting practice before the game sharpened offenses. A professor from Princeton University modified a cannon to fire baseballs. Curved prongs at the muzzle caused balls to curve, drop, or even rise for the edification of troubled hitters. Adjustments in the amount of gunpowder controlled the velocity of the balls. Wily managers platooned players,* partly for extra efficiency, but also sought versatility to protect teams in cases of injuries. The first

pinch hitter allegedly came to bat in 1889 in the form of Mickey Welch, who swung for Hank O'Day.

Most hitters continued to wield great, heavy clubs, choking up to ensure contact. Naturally, the defenders countered with their own tactics. Catchers signaled pitchers what to throw and where. In the mid-1890s, Brooklyn demonstrated the cutoff, wherein an infielder intercepted a throw to home from an outfielder and trapped an unwary player trying for an extra base. As a catcher, Connie Mack perfected a technique of tipping the hitter's bat with his mitt, leading to the rule that awarded a man first base in such cases. With two strikes on a batter, Mack also would remove his mask as if to adjust it. When the hitter relaxed, the pitcher would suddenly fire a strike. That stunt forced some limitations of quick pitches.

A few men had begun to swing for the fences, engendering controversy. Writer Sam Crane plumped for the long ball: "Who wants to see big Roger Connor—who . . . can hit the ball a mile . . . make a puny little feminine bunt."

However, Henry Chadwick scoffed at would-be sluggers trying to knock it out of the park. He bemoaned unsophisticated fans who delighted in the "splurgy long hit ball which yields a home run" and failed to appreciate the nuances of scientific hitting.

A crude sort of sports medicine appeared. Jacob Morse in his book *Sphere and Ash* quoted a Philadelphia physician and fan:

> Do not pitch when you have an off day; when you do not feel able to do yourself justice, don't try to pitch hard. Let your average be considered less than your arm; but, to be in good form, a pitcher must practise about an hour morning and afternoon, holidays included [the need to throw on off days is still deemed essential for modern conditioning]. If the thermometer is below 60, vigorous pitching is risky, and the danger increases as the temperature falls. Never use linaments. They are not good. Rubbing too is bad [articles of faith now discarded]. Hot water is good, as is also mild galvanism [electrical stimulation of the arm].

Hugh Duffy, a 5′7″ outfielder for the Boston Beaneaters, set the all-time high of .438 in his 1894 season.

Courtesy NBL

---

*Bill James in his *Historical Abstract* reported Bob "Death to Flying Things" Ferguson, who played from 1871 to 1884, switch-hit, indicating an early recognition of the circumstances favorable to actual platooning. George Stallings, manager of the Miracle Braves of 1914, alternated outfielders to exploit the advantages of righties swinging against lefties and vice versa. Tris Speaker, as manager at Cleveland, experimented with platooning in 1921 at four positions. The technique waned until Casey Stengel revived it with great effect during his tenure with the Yankees in the late 1940s and 1950s.

The infatuation of the public with baseball caught the attention of publishers. Francis C. Richter, according to historian David Quentin Voigt in his book *American Baseball,* founded *Sporting Life* in 1883, increased the coverage of baseball, and was rewarded with circulation gains of tens of thousands. Daily newspapers also recognized the market and made sports into separate departments on a par with the financial pages.

Like the players, the writers failed to profit immediately. Voigt quotes the studies on American journalism that show top baseball reporters earned $15 a week less than their counterparts on the police beat and $25 less than general-assignment men. While sports reporting bore a glamorous connotation, the journalists also suffered the general opprobrium accorded professional athletes; President Charles William Eliot of Harvard, who despised the game, labeled them "drunkards, deadbeats, and bummers."*

Many of those recruited to write, like Sam Crane, Tim Murname, and even Harry Wright, were former ball players. As much as the players who constantly attacked the officiating, some reporters seemed intent on building their reputations through abuse of umpires. Despite their affinity with those on the field, the naturally adversarial relationship developed with the players. At the same time, the journalists frequently stooped to the most blatant bias when the home nine faced an alien club.

Competition for reader interest led to rhetorical excesses. Among the more inventive was Ithuriel Ellery Sanborn, correspondent for the *Chicago Tribune,* who within a single week offered: "The Cardinals were outbatted by many parasangs [a Persian distance measure]"; "Big Jeff Overall cut the cardiac region of the plate"; "The turnout from Bugville was surprisingly large"; "One on a pass, the other on a puncture"; "Arbiter Klem showed him a slewfoot print on the edge of the rubber."

Empurpled prose was not exclusive to the Midwest. In New York one might have relished the voice of William F. Kirk of the *New York American:* "To come down to cases, the Giants played like a lot of suffragettes. When the stern voice of duty called, with eager base runners on the bags, the local swatsmiths had their ears stuffed with cotton." Or suffered along with Sam Crane: "In the sixth yesterday things got tangled up dangerously and I could feel the carmine perspiration oozing from every pore." In Pittsburgh, C. B. Power of the *Dispatch* offered: "There was a noise like the fall of a truck horse on a board sidewalk. The ball and bat kissed and parted forever. 'I am going on a long journey' shrieked the blistered bulb and the bat chuckled, 'On your way, and I don't care if you never come back.' "

Instead of a dialogue between ball and bat, W. W. Aulick of the *New York Times* created on-field chatter:

When Matty had puzzled him [Johnny Evers] three times, Umpire Klem made the customary decision. Mr. Evers then spoke. He spoke eloquently, pointedly, and for a long time.

"Is that all?" asked Mr. Klem.

"It is all I can think of now," admitted Mr. Evers.

"Perhaps if you had a little leisure you could think of something more," said the umpire kindly. "Suppose you go over to that nice, quiet clubhouse for the rest of the afternoon and think up some more things. You may tell them to me Monday."

As the flavor of the game subtly changed, the Boston Beaneaters, guided by Frank Selee, now enjoyed hegemony in the National League. King Kelly had rejoined the club and Duffy, the erstwhile Chicago White Stocking, had come east to bolster the outfield. Duffy was one-half of what local writers labeled the "Heavenly Twins." The other member of the tandem was Tommy McCarthy, ★ a swift runner and strong hitter. At least of equal importance was Charles Augustus (Kid) Nichols, ★ a twenty-year-old rookie in 1890 when he won 27 games and embarked on a streak of seven straight years of better than 30 victories a season, slipping to a mere 29 in the eighth year. His career totals added up to 360 wins and the Beaneaters flew the pennant five times during his

"Sliding" Billy Hamilton's 937 c[a]reer steals, including 115 during 1891, wa[s] most until Lou Brock exceeded the figu[re on] a single base in 1979.

Courtesy NBL

---

*When Harvard students enthusiastically took up the game, in 1884 the dismayed Eliot recommended the sport be banned from the athletic program: "I think it is a wretched game. . . . There are only nine men who can play a game . . . and out of the nine there are only two desirable positions—pitcher and catcher."

first nine years with the team. "Sliding" Billy Hamilton ★ arrived in Boston from the Philadelphia Athletics in 1896. Hamilton's lifetime .344 is eighth on the list of all-time leaders. He earned his nickname with 937 total stolen bases, a mark that stood until Lou Brock ★ swiped 938 overall.

While the Beaneaters performed their shining deeds on the diamond, business problems and skulduggery in the backroom offices continued to plague baseball. The battle with the Players League and the limitations of the market squeezed the holders of franchises in both the National League and American Association. To preserve solvency, the American Association disappeared into the maw of the older organization and 1892 witnessed a single twelve-team National League. Gone were the competing outfits in Boston, Philadelphia, and Cincinnati as well as the weak show in Columbus, Ohio.

That solved some troubles, but the restructuring increased situations where some stockholders held investments in more than a single club. That in turn led to some peculiar shifts of players. The lairds of Baltimore shipped their best merchandise to their Brooklyn Superbas store, eliminating the Orioles as a competitive team, while Brooklyn won the 1899 pennant. St. Louis profited at the expense of the Cleveland Spiders as the proprietor of both outfits dispatched to St. Louis Jess Burkett, ★ the outfielder who had already hit .400 twice, and pitcher Denton Cy Young, with more than 200 of his eventual 511 wins registered. The affair squashed the Spiders; they finished last in 1899 and a boycott of fans ended Cleveland's existence in the National League.

Ownership of the New York Giants had passed into the grasping hands of a Tammany politician, Andrew Freedman, a pal of the nefarious Richard Croker, the boss of New York City. Freedman went through twelve managers during his eight years of ownership, perhaps setting a precedent for some of his modern counterparts. After Amos Rusie ★ won 22 games for the ninth-place Giants in 1895, Freedman docked him $200 for breaking training and a slovenly effort in his final appearance. Rusie, who said his baseball career began on Indianapolis corner lots with a team called the Never Sweats, believed it was nothing more than an attempt to trim his salary. He balked at playing in 1896 unless the money was returned.

Freedman refused and Rusie became one of the first to sit out an entire season because of a salary dispute. The public and press sided with the ball player. Said the *Sporting News,* "Every independent fair thinking man is with Rusie in his stand. . . . Every ball player of standing is with him." New Yorkers fulminated against Freedman; some in the financial district displayed a banner urging a boycott of the Giants.

John Montgomery Ward, who had earned his law degree from Columbia only a year earlier, acted as Rusie's advocate when the pitcher put his case to League officials. He was, however, up against those whose interests matched Freedman's no matter how much they loathed the New Yorker. Rejected by the League Board, Rusie remained adamant as the 1897 season neared. He went so far as to apply for relief through the courts. That step frightened the owners; monopolies and trusts were beginning to come under heavy fire from legislators and the judiciary.

The other proprietors met with Freedman and pushed him to settle but he was as stubborn as his opponent. In a compromise that brought victory to both parties, Freedman's colleagues passed the hat and paid Rusie his $3,000 for 1896. He put on his uniform to win 29 for the Giants in 1897 and 20 more a year later in a ten-year career of 243 victories.

Unabashed, Freedman and some cronies of similarly dubious character now sought to transform organized baseball into a trust like those that governed oil, coal, and steel enterprises. In 1901, he proposed that the National Baseball Trust issue stock that would buy up the eight franchises of the National League (the twelve-team setup had survived until the 1900 season when Cleveland, Washington, Baltimore, and Louisville all lost their charters). Under the Trust the distinct identities of the teams and their cities would be lost. Players, as employees of the central corporation, could be transferred at whim, and towns eager for major league baseball held in thrall by the Trust. Freedman and his supporters argued that they could thus ensure maximum rivalry among the eight entries and thereby retain fan interest. They pointed out that elimination of the four teams opened the Na-

Cantankerous Amos Rusie lasted only ten years but in eight years with the Giants he won 230 games. The first celebrated salary holdout, Rusie missed the 1896 season. "The Giants without Rusie would be like Hamlet without the Melancholy Dane." —O. P. Caylor, New York Herald

Courtesy NBL

tional League to competition from a new source, the Western Association, revitalized by a near-300-pound, former Cincinnati sportswriter, Byron Bancroft Johnson, ★ who had renamed the group the American League. Johnson had begun to raid the National League for players and his organization moved into cities where the older circuit formerly held a monopoly.

Al Spalding vigorously opposed the trust scheme. He inveighed with almost radical pietism: "Think of a trust in baseball. Is it all commercialism? Is there no more of the glorious sentiment attached to our national sport?"

While these were the words of a fellow who always strove mightily to make the game pay, and in fact once had proposed a restructuring that smacked of a trust, Spalding typified that rare nineteenth-century capitalist who streaked his infatuation for profit with a strain of idealism. No man ever preached the gospel of virtue through baseball more passionately than Spalding.

Spalding, noting that he had combated gambling, pool selling, and collusion between ball players and the gaming fraternity, said he had struggled to free the sport from "irresponsible, unreliable drunkards" and other abuses. He later recalled: "Now for the first time I was face to face with a situation full of graver menace than any of the others had been, because those who were seeking its ruin now were men of real power, men of ability, men of acute business instincts—an enemy that knew how to fight."

In his memoirs, Spalding described Freedman as "obnoxious" and a fellow who spoke of other members of the baseball fraternity in terms "so coarse and offensive as to be unprintable." Spalding's brother, J. Walter, had been a stockholder in the Giants and a director of the club but Freedman dismissed him. That undoubtedly accounted for some of Spalding's hatred for Freedman, whose Jewish background also made him an outsider. Joe Vila of the *New York Sun* inserted derogatory remarks aimed at Jews on several occasions and no one protested. Such was the tenor of the times.

The Chicago magnate expressed particular umbrage over an incident during a game in which Freedman exchanged words with a former Giant, James "Ducky" Holmes, then an outfielder for Baltimore. Enraged supposedly by Ducky Holmes's anti-Semitic jibes (allegedly, "I'm glad I don't have to work for a Sheeny any more"), Freedman ran from his box in the stands onto the field and insisted the umpire banish Holmes because of his insults. When umpire Lynch refused, Freedman summoned a detective and a uniformed cop to oust Holmes. Lynch cried "Play ball!" But Freedman declared the game could not continue with Holmes. Lynch announced a forfeit in favor of Baltimore and Spalding recounted how the hometown New Yorkers not only approved the decision but demanded their money back from Freedman. Spalding reported, "One man yelled, 'You ought to be expelled from the League. You're killing Base Ball in New York deader than a herring.' "

For that matter, *Sporting Life* saw no justification for Freedman's outburst, dismissing Holmes's bigotry of "insulting the Hebrew race . . . as a 'trifling offense.' " The League suspended Holmes for the remainder of the season, "a perversion of justice" in the eyes of the publication.

Spalding drew vigorous support from Barney Dreyfuss, who had profited by an agreement that allowed him to buy the Pittsburgh franchise after the League dumped his Louisville club. When Dreyfuss went from Kentucky to Pittsburgh he brought with him Honus Wagner and Fred Clarke, ★ the nucleus of a strong entry. Push came to shove at a stormy series of meetings to elect a new head of the National League. Freedman and his cohorts backed the incumbent Nick Young; Spalding ran as the opposition. Each candidate drew four votes. When the Freedman faction withdrew from the process, Spalding was elected although clearly the balloting lacked the constitutionally mandated quorum. In a compromise, most agreeable to Spalding, he abdicated his office and Freedman sold his ownership in the Giants to John T. Brush. The threat of syndication through a trust vanished.

This internecine warfare enabled Ban Johnson's upstart organization to establish a beachhead. The new American League had discarded its former identity as a western operation by invading Boston, Baltimore, Washington, and Philadelphia, the last of these under part-owner and manager Corne-

Elmer Flick thrilled Phillies fans in [with a .378 average but along with an[local favorite, Nap Lajoie, he took his s to Cleveland until a stomach ailment e[his career in 1908.

Courtesy NBL

lius McGillicuddy, or Connie Mack as he became better known. The Mack men were the Athletics, transported from Milwaukee, the earlier Philadelphia establishment having taken the label of Phillies.

Most galling to the crosstown rivals was the seduction of second baseman Napoleon Lajoie. ★ The Phillies obtained a court injunction against Lajoie playing for the Athletics. The new Cleveland club promptly seized the opportunity to sign him. During the turbulent year of 1902, with a judicial order banning him throughout Pennsylvania, Lajoie starred for Cleveland in seven cities; when scheduled for action in Philadelphia, however, Lajoie idled away his time in Atlantic City, safely over the state line. Travel for Lajoie was a railroad nightmare; to get from Washington back to Cleveland required a detour via Virginia and West Virginia. Going from Boston to Washington involved a route through New Jersey that allowed him to cross into Maryland by way of Wilmington, Delaware. Whenever the Cleveland club entered Pennsylvania, sheriffs' deputies boarded the trains in search of Lajoie.

One year after Lajoie emigrated from the National League the Phillies lost a second star, Elmer Flick, ★ a .300-hitting outfielder whose high-water mark was .378 in 1900. Flick, like Lajoie, moved across town to the Athletics and then to the Cleveland Naps, so dubbed in honor of Lajoie.

Philadelphia was one of four markets where Ban Johnson directly confronted the National League. Charles Comiskey operated a Chicago entry run by pitcher-manager Clark Griffith ★ to compete with Spalding's show. There were teams in St. Louis and Boston. In addition to Lajoie, other National League players who chafed under the $2,400 salary limit scarpered to the new circuit. Émigrés to the Boston Pilgrims included Cy Young and Jimmy Collins, ★ a third baseman renowned for a fielding stance off the sack, for his wizardry at grabbing bunts, and for his consistent power at the plate. Joe McGinnity ★ the Iron Man pitcher, John McGraw the youthful third baseman, and soon-to-be manager, and catcher Wilbert Robinson, ★ all hired on at Baltimore. Ban Johnson particularly coveted McGraw as a symbol of major league presence in his league. They would, however, fall out almost immediately because of McGraw's habitual umpire baiting.

The anarchy and potentially ruinous bidding for players forced the National League to accept Ban Johnson's offspring as legitimate. A new national agreement early in 1903 proclaimed the two leagues separate but equal. All player contracts, which of course included the reserve clauses, were to be respected. Rules of the game were standardized and schedules set cooperatively. Furthermore, it was agreed that at the end of the season, the winners of the two leagues would meet for a championship series.

The first such classic followed the conclusion of two-league play in 1903 and featured the Pittsburgh Pirates and Boston Americans. The home of the Pirates, Exposition Park in Allegheny, sat only eight thousand. Boston's Huntington Avenue grounds accommodated several thousand more, but overflow crowds at both sites stood behind outfield ropes. Ground rules for the series awarded 3 bases for a ball into the packed standees; in the 8 games (it was scheduled as a best of nine) 25 triples were recorded.

Against that handicap, Boston overwhelmed the National Leaguers, with pitchers Bill Dinneen and Cy Young on the mound for 69 of the 71 innings played. Dinneen won 3, lost 1 (earned run average 2.06) and Young accounted for 2 victories while dropping 1 (earned run average 1.59 with 3 complete games plus 7 innings of relief). Admissions were pegged at $1.50 for lesser seats, and the players received two weeks' pay plus a share of the gate.

Following his resignation as the illegally elected head of the National League, A. G. Spalding contented himself with publication of his guides and sales of his sporting goods. Ownership of the White Stockings had been relinquished. But he took center stage one more time to wage a splendid paper war to prove baseball wholly American.

In an essay on baseball's origins, Henry Chadwick, as editor of the 1903 *Spalding Guide*, declared the game an offshoot of the British pastime of rounders. To Spalding, who believed baseball exemplified all the virtues of his native land (he called the game "a man maker," and "a soul builder"), Chad-

"As the players came from the clubhouse for practice an uncouth figure that brought a titter from the stands, shambled along behind them. It was Denton T. Young, the new 'phenom.'

"Darius Green, the Pied Piper and other noted characters of fact and fiction had nothing on Young for weirdness of appearance. The baseball knickerbockers he wore had been made for a man many inches shorter, and served the recruit little better than a bluff. His jersey shirt stretched across his massive body like a drumhead, and his arms dangled through its sleeves almost to the shoulder. He dragged himself across the field bashfully, every angle of his great frame exaggerated and emphasized, and the stands tittered again.

"The great Anson saw Young. 'Is that the phenom?' he asked with a sneer. . . . The gaunt figure lost its uncouthness as he warmed to his work, and the ball shot to the catcher's thin glove with a crack that betokened even greater speed than the flash of the sphere in the sunlight. . . . The game began and the Chicago batters strode to the plate arrogant and confident. One after the other they threw down their bats and returned to the bench puzzled and baffled. . . . Young grew even more effective as the innings passed and Chicago left the field beaten and blind with rage. Then the crowd which had laughed at the unique figure of the new pitcher arose in a mass and gave him an ovation."—Sporting Life

Courtesy NBL

wick had committed an obscene blasphemy. Spalding biographer Peter Levine has noted: "As A. G. saw it, if baseball truly had a special contribution to make to the shaping of American character, its pedigree had to be impeccably American."

Spalding's attitude sprang from fertile soil. Rank chauvinism infused the nation; publishers Pulitzer and Hearst and their lessers celebrated in florid print their versions of the unique American character. In the White House Theodore Roosevelt was hell-bent on making the world aware of U.S. power. In spite of, or perhaps because of, the flood tide of immigrants, the antiforeign spirit of the country remained virulent.

Baseball jingoism also flourished. Walt Whitman sang its praises: "I see great things in baseball. It's our game—the American game. It will take our people out-of-doors, fill them with oxygen, give them a larger physical stoicism. Tend to relieve us from being a nervous dyspeptic set. Repair these losses, and be a blessing to us."

Mark Twain in a rather uncharacteristic gush at a testimonial dinner for the returning heroes of a Spalding international tour declared: "Baseball is the very symbol, the outward and visible expression of the drive and push and rush and struggle of the raging, tearing, booming nineteenth century."

And the *Chicago American* of 1906 reasoned:

> We owe a great deal to Base Ball. . . . It is one of the reasons why American soldiers are the best in the world—quick witted, swift to act, ready of judgment, capable of going into action without officers. . . . It is one of the reasons why as a nation we impress visitors as quick, alert, confident and trained for independent action.

Great Britain defeated Napoleon thanks to the playing fields at Eton; the United States had whipped the Spanish as a consequence of strife on the diamond.

The 1905 annual from the Spalding presses trumpeted his defiance of his subordinate's scholarship.

> I hereby challenge the Grand Old Man of Base Ball to produce his proofs and demonstrate in some tangible way, if he can, that our national game derived its origin from Rounders.

Mr Chadwick, who by the way, is of English birth, and was probably rocked in a "Rounders" cradle, says, in support of his theory that "there is but one field game now in vogue on this continent which is strictly American in its origin and that one is the old Indian game of Lacrosse, now known as the Canadian national game. Base Ball originated from the old English schoolboy game of Rounders, as plainly shown by the fact that the basic principle of both games is the field use of a bat, a ball and bases."

I have been fed on this kind of "Rounder pap" for upward of forty years, and I refuse to swallow any more of it without some substantial proof sauce with it.

Spalding continued his argument with a rousing denigration of rounders as sissified and akin to "Drop the handkerchief" and "Ring Around the Rosy." He flatly declared baseball had American antecedents and noted that a prominent baseball writer (actually it was Chadwick himself) "can prove that one of the founders of the old Knickerbocker club came onto the field one day in the early forties with the original game of Base Ball worked out described on a sheet of paper," which was indeed credit where due to Alexander Cartwright.

Carried away by his zeal, Spalding returned to the debate a year later with further explication. And he subsequently created a committee of seven to establish the facts. The hand-chosen bunch was headed by the former National League President Andrew Mills and it also numbered in its ranks James Sullivan, an employee of Spalding who went on to become a benefactor of U.S. amateurism. (The Amateur Athletic Union's Sullivan Award to the outstanding nonpro each year is named in his honor.) Also on the board were U.S. Senators Arthur Gorman and Morgan Bulkeley, the first National League President; Al Reach, the former ball player and a competitor in sporting goods and baseball guides; Nick Young, who had been head of the National League at the time Freedman sought to create a trust; and George Wright.

None possessed the requisites for scholarly research and no genuine research was done. Sullivan collected a pile of unsubstantiated statements on baseball's origin but it was Spalding who produced the commission's chief "evidence." He submitted a let-

So when a stalwart steps out from throng
On with the tribute, let garlands flung—
Here's to the sturdy and here's the strong—
Here's to the king of them all, Denton Young
—Grantland Rice

Courtesy NBL

Byron Bancroft Johnson, a former Cincinnati sportswriter, an irascible 300-pound zealot in the cause of baseball expansion headed the Western Association which became the American League following disputes with the National League.

Courtesy NBL

ter written in 1907 by an octogenarian Colorado mining engineer named Abner Graves. Digging sixty-eight years into his memory, Graves reported that in 1839 a schoolmate named Abner Doubleday halted a game of marbles behind the tailor shop in Cooperstown, New York, to show a diagram of a game created out of one old cat. The field was diamond shaped and Doubleday even named it "base ball."

The Graves document satisfied Spalding and his group. A. G. wrote to the commission: "It certainly appeals to Americans' pride to have had the great national game of Baseball created and named by a Major–General in the United States Army."

Mills, who had served with Doubleday in the military, made a perfunctory and futile effort to prove that one of the original Knick-

erbockers had grown up in Cooperstown, which would account for the role of Cartwright. The committee ignored Graves's recollection that Doubleday's plan called for eleven men on a side, a characteristic of Town Ball and not the game devised by Alexander Cartwright.

Actually, only Spalding and company took the issue seriously. Chadwick considered the matter unimportant; the current game was to him a thoroughly American institution. Rival publishers like the *Sporting News* dismissed the findings as absurd; historians subsequently demonstrated that in the summer of 1839, Doubleday was a cadet at West Point and could not possibly have been in Cooperstown as Graves claimed, because the military academy did not grant leave to cadets until the end of their second year.

"His face is that of a Greek hero, his manner that of a Church of England Bishop. When I first talked with him he was a candidate for United States Senator from California and he is the father of the greatest sport the world has ever known.

"You don't know him? You are unfortunate. There are in the United States at least a million men who do and who will yell at the sight of him. I am writing now of A. G. Spalding."—Edward Marshall, New York Times

Courtesy NBL

HUNTINGTON
AND AVENUE
BASE BALL
GROUNDS

The first World Series pitted the Boston Americans against the Pittsburgh Pirates. The Boston games were played at a site on Huntington Avenue, now the home of Northeastern University. Games were interrupted by surges of fans onto the field, particularly those sold standing room behind the outfielders.

Courtesy AP/Wide World

37

(Left) *Baseball first went internation
1874 with a visit to Europe by G
Wright, Al Spalding, and some of the
horts. A much more ambitious tour too
White Stockings plus players from
teams around the world on a six-month
that started in October 1888. Afte
games in the U.S. West, the entou
which included wives and one newsp
man, sailed first to Hawaii and then
tralia. Spalding and company pause
Ceylon before passing through the
Canal. During a sojourn in Egypt, the
ers mounted camels, put on an exhibiti
the shadow of the Pyramids, and cau
about the Sphinx. Spalding, however,
off the Egyptians as potential converts
game: ". . . in a country where they
stick for a plow, and hitch a donkey c
camel together to draw it and do many
things as they did twenty centuries age
hardly reasonable to expect that the m
game of base-ball will become one
sports."*

Courtesy NBL

(Opposite) *From Egypt the baseball
ets journeyed across the Mediterr
where the Italian government huffily re
an improbable request to demonstra
game in the Coliseum. However, the
hese Gardens served as a diamond (to
though Spalding noted: "We found
little interest in athletic sports in Ita
France (bottom); in fact it was wi
greatest difficulty that we could find a
to play a game of baseball in either o
countries, and not in a single place
find an enclosed ground."*

Courtesy NBL

38

"Once upon a time, three descenda
Irishmen took two ball clubs aroun
world. The purpose of the trip was t
—to prove to the foreign element tha
ball is a better game than cricket, ro
hopscotch, baccarat, parchesi or any
other sports in vogue abroad, and t
vince Herman Schaefer and the rest
heathen included in the roster of th
clubs that Ireland, one of the ste
points, is the second best country
atlas. The dual purpose was practical
filled although it is asserted that Au
and England still prefer cricket. . . . F
the Australians and Britishers, 'base
nothing more than rounders,' an
statement, although we are willing to
that there are plenty of rounders in
ball."—Ring Lardner.

The occasion was the winter of
1914 when John J. McGraw (seated
enth from left) and Charles Comiskey
of McGraw) carted a melange of New
Giants and Chicago White Stockings,
with pressmen like Lardner, about the
A British writer scoffed, ". . . rounde
a bigger stick."

Courtesy NBL

The Giants returned to the British s
1924, enabling King George V to
Casey Stengel, recent hero in a losing
Series cause.

Courtesy NBL

Plus fours, argyle stockings, brown and white shoes were shipboard attire for a 1931 tour of Japan starring Mickey Cochrane (seated, far right), Frank Frisch *(Cochrane's right), and Lou Gehrig (standing, far right).*

Courtesy NBL

On the edge of retirement, Babe Ruth came to baseball-mad Japan. Half a million people jammed Tokyo's Ginza to see a motorcade led by Beibu Rusu *and Gehrig, Jimmie Foxx, and Lefty Gomez.*

Courtesy UPI/Bettmann News photos

At the close of a visit by the Baltimor[e] [Ori]oles to Japan in 1971, Brooks Ro[binson] said goodbye to a local Hall of [Famer] Shigeo Nagashima. Among those w[ho vi]sited the troops in Vietnam during t[he war] were Joe DiMaggio and Pete Rose.

Courtesy Baltimore Orioles

(Opposite, bottom) Some historians [claim] that after a soda pop bottle thrown b[y a St.] Louis fan in 1907 fractured the sk[ull of] umpire Billy Evans, ★ public animos[ity to]ward his trade began to slacken. Kno[wn for] his fastidious, refined manner, Evans [began] his career in 1906 and officiated t[hrough] 1927 before accepting a post as a fron[t office] executive and farm director.

Courtesy NBL

(Top) *"Give the Umpire a Chance"* pleaded an 1886 cartoon in Puck. *In his quest to perfect the product, A. G. Spalding recognized the need for officials whose decisions could not be doubted. He wrote: "To secure the presence of intelligent, honest, unprejudiced, quick witted, courageous umpires at all contests in scheduled games has been one of the most vexatious problems confronting those in control of our national sport."*

Baseball began with only a single individual responsible for all calls. Inevitably, the hapless official missed plays. Also, the first arbiters hired often lacked either the proper temperament or skills, further lowering the general esteem. Aside from contentious players and managers like John J. McGraw, the early umpires were lashed by owners who disputed them on the field, sportswriters who denounced them for verdicts against the home club, and, of course, fans who followed the great nineteenth century tradition of disrespect for authority.

Early umps worked exclusively from behind the pitcher but in 1888 John Gaffney moved behind the catcher for a better look at balls and strikes until a runner reached base. Gaffney then took up the stance at the rear of the mound. Addition of a second official enabled one man to station himself permanently behind the plate but calling shots hit down the line and hustling to the three bases for close plays was more than a single roving fellow could handle. Still, until the umpire corps was expanded to place additional men in the field, the efforts of Spalding and other executives gradually enhanced the prestige of officials. A. G. could boast: "There was a time when the umpire was simply tolerated as a necessary evil. He was known to be essential to the playing of the game; . . . but he was feared and hated alike by members of both teams engaged, and was the special object of derision and abuse on the part of occupants of both grandstand and bleachers. . . . The slugging of umpires by players is no longer an essential part of the programme [sic], and their mobbing by spectators, though occasionally indulged in, is not encouraged by public opinion."—Albert Spalding, America's National Game

Courtesy NBL

(Top, left) *Tom Connolly,* ★ *an E.
émigré, started with the National Leag
1899 but switched to the employ of
Johnson who saw Connolly as a mec
demonstrate the high caliber of his le
Connolly's magisterial service lasted a
of thirty-four years. Soft-spoken, a ma.
the rules, he was a firm disciplinaria.
managed nevertheless to go ten conse
years of rambunctious games and argu
without ejecting a single player.*

Courtesy NBL

(Top, right) *"The foundation stone
national pastime is its umpires. Ar
foundation stone on which that foun
stone rests is William J. Klem. He b.
a dignity to the job that it never had.
He brought it respect and authorit
brought it a certain element of infalli
'I never missed one in my life,' he r
And meant it."—Arthur Daley, New
Times.*

    Bill Klem ★ *joined the National L
in 1905. He spent his first sixteen
behind the plate because of his
vaunted skill at determining ball.
strikes. Klem originated the arm sign
announce judgments.*

Courtesy NBL

(Bottom, left) *Burly former pro fo
player Cal Hubbard* ★ *could not be
by protests from such huskies as Lou
and Bill Dickey of the New York Ya
Hubbard trained for eight years in t
nors and put in fifteen major league se
He holds the distinction of election
College and Professional Football H
Fame as well as the Cooperstown sh.*

Courtesy NBL

(Bottom, right) *Jocko (nee John) Cor.
was a mediocre White Sox outfielder in
when umpire Red Ormsby collapsed fr
summer heat. Conlan was nominated
place Ormsby. The following season
a new career to which he brought a po
bow tie, a willingness to jaw with th.
cantankerous of players, and a keen
to judge the plays of the game.*

Courtesy NBL

44

The settlement for 1903 brought a peace that would last twelve years and allow for maximum focus on the game and the players. And there was no shortage of oversize figures for fandom. Among these was the aforementioned Lajoie. A strapping 6′1″, 195 pounder, the Rhode Island native of French descent stands as one of the biggest second basemen of the game. Although he lacked speed, he possessed a sure grace that established him as a premier fielder. His prowess with the bat marked him for the Hall of Fame.

Lajoie, born in Woonsocket, Rhode Island, in 1875, was a twenty-year-old hack driver playing ball with the local youths between fares, when the manager at Fall River in the New England League signed him up on the back of an envelope. Less than a full season later, Lajoie entered the majors via Philadelphia.

An instant success, he hit .328 that first partial year and a robust .363 the second. Somewhat unsure of his future, however, Lajoie spent his first few off-seasons back in Woonsocket, chauffeuring a cab about town. But he continued to pound the ball season after season with a peak of .422 in 1901, after which he deserted the Phillies for Cleveland. For many years he was credited with a mere .405 as the result of a careless statistician of the day who recorded 220 hits instead of the correct figure of 229.

In the 1910 race for the American League batting title, which carried with it the gift of a new Chalmers automobile, Lajoie and Ty Cobb battled for the honors. On the final day of the season—a doubleheader for Lajoie and his Cleveland teammates against the St. Louis Browns—Cobb, comfortably ahead, chose to sit out the last game. While fans and other players regarded Larry Lajoie fondly, Cobb already had earned the enmity of most of the men in the League as well as his fellow Tigers. According to some, St. Louis manager Jack O'Connor instructed his rookie third sacker, Johnny Corriden, to play deep for Lajoie. Lajoie opened the day with a triple, but then took advantage of the alignment, bunting safely three times. In the second game the burly Lajoie continued to dump the ball toward third. On his second at bat, with a runner on first, Corriden fumbled the bunt and threw too late to catch Lajoie

at first. Official scorer E. V. Parish refused to allow it as a base hit; he credited Lajoie only with a sacrifice. Lajoie put down 2 more successful bunts and with a line single finished the doubleheader with 8 hits in 8 official trips to the plate. His final average, however, fell just shy of Cobb's: .3841 to .385.

The Chalmers firm generously awarded cars to both men but the tactics of the Browns drew an investigation by Ban Johnson. He quickly absolved Corriden who said his only instructions were to back off when Lajoie hit—the Cleveland star was known for driving fierce liners injurious to bold third basemen. Umpire Billy Evans ★ supplied Johnson with a four-page report in which he saw nothing untoward in the way the Browns defended against Lajoie (although the slow-footed Lajoie ordinarily eschewed the bunt). However, official scorer Parish stated that while at his press-box job he was offered a bribe of a $40 suit to give Lajoie a hit instead of a sacrifice on the fumbled bunt. Furthermore, Browns player-coach Harry Howell made frequent trips to the press box to learn whether Parish scored hits for Lajoie. Johnson apparently forced the St. Louis owner to sack both O'Connor and Howell and neither ever returned to major league ball in any capacity.

Cobb never regarded Lajoie favorably and he left him off his all-time list thirty-five years later. "Lajoie could not go out, nor come in, and did not cover too much ground to his right or left." Having given up the diamond for the pulpit, Spalding's former outfielder the Rev. Billy Sunday, generously praised Lajoie: "He works as noiselessly as a Corliss engine, makes hard plays easy, is great in a pinch, and never gets cold feet." The 1911 *Reach Guide* noted: ". . . he was a superb fielder at first base, second base and in the outfield. He was . . . the personification of a peculiar grace, in the expression of which he made the hardest plays look easy." Statistics show Lajoie among the all-time top ten in putouts, putouts per game, assists, chances, and thirteenth in double plays.

Lajoie spent from 1903 to 1914 with Cleveland, even managing the club from 1905 to 1909, but never serving on a pennant winner. He wound up his career back with the Philadelphia Athletics for his final

"Those who are cognizant of my great age ask me sometimes what Larry Lajoie would do in this 'game.' Well, he wouldn't do anything after one day. Larry wasn't a fly-ball hitter. When he got a hold of one, it usually hit the fence on the first bounce, traveling about five feet three inches above the ground most of the way and removing the ears of all infielders who didn't throw themselves flat on their stomachs the instant they saw him swing. They wouldn't have time to duck this ball, and after the battle there would be a meeting of earless infielders, threatening a general walkout if that big French gunman were allowed in the park again, even with a toothpick in his hand."—Ring Lardner, New Yorker

Courtesy NBL

two years, finishing with a lifetime .339. He was a near fanatic about his eyes, refusing to read while on trains or to see movies, a regimen endorsed by one of his great successors as a second-base batting terror, Rogers Hornsby. ★

Some years after he retired, Lajoie spoke of the tricks of the game during his prime.

> . . . all pitchers and infielders sewed emery paper on their gloves and you were a sissy if you didn't keep a man sized chew of tobacco in your mouth . . . when a new ball was put into the play the pitcher let the catcher's toss roll out to the second baseman or shortstop. Emery paper and tobacco juice had done a good job on the ball before it was tossed back to the pitcher who then worked on the seams.
>
> Nor was it unusual for a pitcher to scrape the cover with his spikes to give it grooves and cause it to wobble through the air. We often played five or six innings with one ball. And after two or three innings you thought you were hitting a rotten tomato.

The tiny, barely larger than hand-size gloves with infinitesimal pockets and perfunctory padding reduced infielder capacity well below the levels of the 1980s. The top five lifetime fielding percentages for infielders are all drawn from men who played after World War II when significant modifications in size and construction of gloves began.* Indeed, even during the 1930s, the equipment restricted abilities. Charlie Gehringer, ★ the expert second sacker of the Detroit Tigers from 1924 to 1942, has said:

> In our day you didn't see the plays you do today. I can't remember anybody catching one like jumping over the fence and it would stick in the big glove, 'cause it wouldn't. Maybe I dove for a ball once or twice, but you'd only hurt yourself probably and still wouldn't do more than knock it down. Today they [balls] stick and you can get up and throw them out if they're hit hard. Nobody seemed to think fielding was that important . . . hitting made all the difference.

Nevertheless, aside from Lajoie, others achieved fame for their fielding talents. Jimmy Collins, ★ a turn-of-the-century third baseman in Boston, excelled when confronted by bunts. John B. Foster of the *Spalding Guide* declared:

> Few bunts were made so skillfully that Collins could not make a play on the ball. . . . With a swoop like that of a chicken hawk, Collins would gather up the ball and throw it accurately to whoever should receive it. . . . The beauty about Collins was that he could throw from any angle, any position on the ground or in the air . . . the unstudied grace of the professional dancer characterized Collins' every movement while in pursuit of the ball. He could not bend ungracefully if he made an effort to do so.

Still, Collins probably would not have remained a big leaguer had he not performed such feats as 15 homers in 1898, 132 RBIs in 1897, and five seasons well over .300.

Bobby Wallace ★ commenced his twenty-four-year career in 1894, and gave the fans of the St. Louis Browns something to cheer for with his graceful glove. But the most celebrated field reps owed as much to the literary arts as to those of the glove. The famous Chicago Cub trio of shortstop Joe Tinker, ★ second sacker Johnny Evers, ★ and first baseman Frank Chance ★ first took the field in 1903.

Earliest of that triumvirate on the Chicago scene was the California-bred Chance. Word of "Husk" Chance, who could hit like Anson, run like Billy Hamilton, and throw like Bill Bergen (a receiver who must indeed have had an incredible arm in order to last eleven years while batting .170), reached Chicago. The twenty-one-year-old Chance debuted as a catcher and outfielder, continuing his dual role until his alarming tendency to stop balls behind the plate with his fingertips, knees, and head rendered him a too-frequent case for first aid and even hospitalization. For his protection, in 1903 manager Frank Selee assigned Chance to first base. That reduced damage partially; he still managed to spike himself several times and had an unfortunate habit of being hit in the head by pitchers. The battering took a toll, resulting later in a loss of hearing, neurological problems, and probably shortened his

After Lajoie arrived in Cleveland a[nd] came manager in 1905, the club was named the "Naps."

Courtesy NBL

Beaky Bobby Wallace began as a p[itcher,] switched to shortstop during his St. [Louis] Browns days, led all American Leagu[e at] the position in assists and fielding p[ercent-] age three times. His 17 chances in a [single] game remains the record.

Courtesy NBL

---

*Following the addition of fingertips and modest padding in the nineteenth century, the next great advance was a mitt devised by "Spittin' Bill" Doak, a skinny pitcher who spent most of his sixteen years with the Cardinals. Doak created a glove with a preformed pocket and reinforced webbing that Rawlings agreed to manufacture in 1920.

life. But by 1905, he was a fixture at first base and also managed the outfit.

Twice during his career the rangy Chance led the league in stolen bases, with a high of 67, and he hit for a lifetime .297. Four times his Cubs won the pennant and twice the World Series. After his stellar performance in 1906, hitting .319 and swiping 57 bases, although his club fell to the local rivals in the Series, Chance was dubbed "the peerless leader."

Fiercely combative, Chance forbade his players from shaking hands with opponents while in uniform. "You're a ballplayer and not a society dancer at a pink tea" raged the peerless leader. "I want to see some fight in you and not this social stuff." He made good on his threat, fining players $10, a considerable sum then, for violating the rule. No less an authority than the one-time heavyweight champion of the world Jim Corbett, dubbed Chance, "the greatest amateur brawler in the world."

The first of his celebrated accomplices to arrive in Chicago was Joseph Bert Tinker, a graduate of the Kansas City League. According to Tinker, at the tender age of fourteen he was sold by the John Taylors club to Hagen's Tailors for the grand sum of $3. The story had a happy ending: The new team won the championship that carried with it a prize of $50, and Tinker's share was $2.50. Determined to make his living on the diamond, Tinker abandoned his job as an apprentice paperhanger and caught on with the first of four minor league clubs that would hire him, then dish him off.

Tinker divided his minor-league time between third and second base, preferring the former, botching the latter, which was the only job open. He joined ten other candidates for the three infield posts with the Cubs in 1902 and was resigned to a trip back to Portland when the shrewd Selee transformed him into a shortstop. Selee may have been attracted by Tinker's obvious determination; a feisty, aggressive style marked his play.

Last of the trio to take the stage was the matchstick thin Evers, 5'9" and between 115 and 125 pounds. A former $4-a-week laborer in a collar factory, Evers had a brief introduction to pro ball at Troy in 1902. He was summoned by the Cubs in the fall of that year, raising his pay from $60 a month to

$100. His Troy background earned him the nickname "The Trojan." He had the open, innocent look of a choirboy with his hair neatly parted in the middle; the only hint of combativeness was a thrusting, long lower jaw. Evers was also known as "The Crab," in recognition of his distinctive gait as he sidled left and right to field balls and perhaps because of his low flash point. Joe Tinker once remarked: "How he could ride you! Chance use to say he wished Evers was an outfielder so he couldn't hear him."

Neither Evers nor Tinker posted such impressive offensive marks as Chance but they were dependable hitters for their positions; they hit .260 to .270 and stole 30 to 40 bases per season apiece; Evers was particularly good at begging walks, with 108 in 1910. It was in the field where they shone, consistently finishing at or near the top for their positions.

Working together game after game for eleven seasons, they developed an almost musical harmony of play, with hardly ever a discordant note afield. Their fine synchronization was all the more remarkable in that for much of their active careers they mutually detested one another. Tinker said they stopped speaking after an exhibition game in 1908 or 1909:

We dressed in the hotel and went to the ball park in hacks. Evers got in a hack all by himself and drove off, leaving me and several others to wait until the hack returned. I was mad. As soon as I got to the ball park I went up to him and said, "Who the hell are you that you've got to have a hack all to yourself?"

One word led to another and presently we were at it, rolling around among the bats on the ball field. After we were pulled apart, and it was all over, I said to Evers, "Now listen: if you and I talk to each other we're only going to be fighting all the time. So don't talk to me and I won't talk to you. You play your position and I'll play mine and let it go at that."

"That suits me," Evers said. We went along two or three years without speaking.

Evers remembers a different confrontation. He insisted: ". . . early in 1907—he threw me a hard ball [indicating a distance of perhaps ten feet]. It was a real hard ball. Like a catcher throwing to second. And the ball broke my finger. I yelled at him. He

"The Peerless Leader," Frank Chance, first sacker and manager of the Chicago Cubs, also was known as "Husk" because of his physique and willingness to punch when doubted. He knocked only 20 homers in seventeen years, since Chance, playing in the dead-ball era, like most of his contemporaries, preferred to choke up on the heavy clubs in vogue.

Courtesy NBL

Chance and his wife showed off their newest runabout; note the right-hand drive.

Courtesy NBL

laughed. That's the last word we had for—well, I just don't know how long."

Silent they may have been, but still they communicated, to the rage of Ty Cobb. During the 1907 World Series, Cobb occupied second base. Tinker remarked to the Tiger star, "Don't get too far from the bag or the Jew will nip you," referring to catcher Johnny Kling. The shortstop discreetly signaled to Evers as Cobb swiveled his head to jeer at Tinker. Kling fired the ball and Evers, who had snuck up on the bag, slapped a tag on the apoplectic Cobb.

In 1908,* with a furious pennant battle between the Cubs, Giants, and Pirates, fame came to Evers and infamy to a young New York Giant, Fred Merkle. It was Evers's habit to dissipate nightly with a copy of his hometown *Troy Times,* one of the New York City papers, the *Sporting News,* the *Spalding Guide,* and a candy bar. In the course of his studies, he was struck by the rule that implied a runner must advance to the next base on a game-winning hit before the lead run can be scored. But the custom of the day was for anyone on base to scamper to the clubhouse as soon as the lead runner crossed home. On September 4, during a game with Pittsburgh, Evers saw Pirate Warren Gill wheel in the base paths before he reached second and sprint for the showers the moment his teammate scored for a 1–0 win.

Evers immediately accosted Umpire Hank O'Day, cited the rules, demanded Gill be declared out and the run negated. O'Day denied the appeal, even laughing at The Crab as a sore loser. I. E. Sanborn in his account for the *Chicago Tribune* remarked that if O'Day had seen what actually occurred he could not have ruled otherwise than in Chicago's favor, leaving the score 0–0. And Cub owner Charles W. Murphy telegraphed National League President Harry C. Pulliam to protest. Pulliam rejected the Cub claim: "I think the public prefers to see games settled on the field and not in this office." The *Pittsburgh Post,* reporting on the incident, warned: "The final play of Friday's game between the Cubs and Pirates is one that does not come often, but next time it happens it is safe to predict that none who took part in the game will overlook the im-

portance of touching the next base."

O'Day was regarded as one of the better umpires and later even spent several years managing clubs. He apparently had second thoughts. It was logical that just as the man who scored must actually reach the plate, so must every runner who is obligated, move up a base. However, in spite of the newspaper stories, few people paid attention to the affair. But Harry Pulliam, whose decision rested only on the fact of a protest of an umpire's ruling after the game, cautioned his umpires about a possible reoccurrence.

On September 23, the Cubs met the Giants in New York's Polo Grounds. Both cities were caught in the frenzy of the pennant race. The *Chicago Tribune* and the *New York Times* built makeshift scoreboards outside their headquarters. The progress of runners was marked with light bulbs as thousands clogged the streets to watch. The score was 1–1 in the bottom of the ninth with two men out. Pinch hitter Moose McCormick led off third base while nineteen-year-old Fred Merkle edged off first. At bat was Al Bridwell who lined a sharp single to center. The umpire in chief behind the plate was none other than Hank O'Day.

Later Evers recalled the events:

After Merkle singled . . . I tipped Tinker to watch out for the play. I knew that Merkle had only recently come up from the bushes and might make a bonehead at a critical moment.

. . . instead of watching the ball I kept my eyes glued on Merkle. He ran a few yards down the baseline and then [to] the clubhouse, thinking the game was over as the runner on third had scored. I yelled to our man to throw the ball to me. He was ready for the play and knew what was up. We caught the Giants off their guard except old Joe McGinnity, coaching third. Hofman [the outfielder] made a poor throw in as the players and spectators were all over the field by this time. [Tinker claimed the throw struck him in the back of the neck.] There was a scramble for the ball and McGinnity got it and threw it over into the crowd behind third base. Tinker and Steinfeldt [the third baseman] dived after it. [Steinfeldt, said Tinker, actually punched a fan who picked up the ball.] Tinker got it and threw it to me and I touched second base.

"The defensive work of Chicago was [?] the stops of Evers [right] and Tinker [le[ft] the crowd mad with applause. B[ut] Chance was reserved the major honors, the eighth by one of the most astou[nding] plays ever made, he stopped the Pira[tes]

"Leach hit a fierce line drive straig[ht] first, and it looked like a sure double. Chance, with a running jump, shove[d] one hand, turned backwards and clu[tched] the ball. Against that kind of defensive [play] Pittsburgh had no chance."—Hugh S[ul-]lerton, New York American

Courtesy NBL

*G. H. Fleming in *The Unforgettable Season* records what was one of the most extraordinary years in baseball history.

◆ 48 ◆

Indeed, because of the confusion, it was necessary for Evers to stand on his toes, hands high in the air, waving the ball, to catch Hank O'Day's attention. Then Evers ran to home plate to confront the umpire. Having made his point, there was nothing more for Evers to do but hurry off the field, now a mob scene of Giant celebrators.

Only later that evening was it announced that O'Day had canceled the apparent winning run and declared the game a 1–1 tie, necessitating a replay. Actually, McGinnity always swore that he had heaved the ball far into the stands and Evers used a substitute. Merkle long insisted he did touch second but that defies the tradition of the period. In the Giant clubhouse they were soon aware of the contretemps on the field. McCormick assumed that Bridwell might be at fault for failing to touch first. To get Bridwell's attention, he booted him in the butt, then the pair pushed their way through the crowd so Bridwell might put his foot to the bag, an absurd gesture in that the runner had departed from the baseline beyond redemption.

The reversal of the outcome proved critical in the pennant race. The Cubs and Giants finished the season deadlocked, and in a one-game playoff, Chicago won the pennant.

Two years later, a columnist for the *New York Evening Mail* dashed off a quick tribute to the trio that ensured their remembrance. Franklin P. Adams was not a regular baseball writer but he was, according to a letter he subsequently wrote, in July 1910, about to leave for the Polo Grounds when the foreman of the *Evening Mail* composing room said he needed eight more lines to fill his column. And so Adams put together his doggerel:

These are the saddest of possible words,
    Tinker to Evers to Chance
Trio of bear cubs and fleeter than birds,
    Tinker to Evers to Chance
Thoughtlessly pricking our gonfalon bubble,
    Making a Giant hit into a double.
Words that are weighty with nothing but
    trouble
Tinker to Evers to Chance.

Because of its dirgelike tone and use of "our," latter-day students describe Adams as a frustrated Giant fan. In fact, in his memoir about the creation of the piece, Adams noted he was "the only Cub rooter in the Polo Grounds press box." Nor did he think highly of his effort, saying the lines "weren't much good." But they ensured his presence in quotation tomes and enshrined Tinker, Evers, and Chance as a super combine.

Illnesses cut short Chance's career and he died at age forty-seven. Both Tinker and Evers had brief flings at managing and did some scouting toward the ends of their lives.

Undoubtedly, the greatest infielder of the day was the barrel-chested, bowlegged, superficially awkward John Peter Wagner whose Germanic Christian name of Johannes was corrupted into Honus. Said John McGraw in 1912: "You can have your Cobbs, your Lajoies, your Chases [Hal], your Bakers [Frank "Home Run"] ★ but I'll take Wagner as my pick of the greatest. He is not only a marvelous mechanical player, but he has the quickest base ball brain I have ever observed."

Born in Pennsylvania in 1874, by age twelve Wagner had gone to work like his father in the local coal mines where he earned 70 cents for every ton he loaded. His income came to about $3.50 a week, which made the seemingly paltry ball player salaries of $1,000 to $2,500 much more attractive.

He had begun to study the barber trade when his brother Al recommended him to George Moreland who managed Steubenville in the Inter State League. Moreland offered Honus Wagner $35 a month with the proviso that Wagner lay out the money for his uniform and shoes. Of course he had to supply his own glove. The rookie rode an overnight freight to join the club. When he paid off his obligations he had $3 left from his first month's pay.

Actually, during this season, Wagner claimed he played for no less than six teams. The Steubenville franchise shifted first to Akron, then Kent, and finally Mansfield in the Tri-State League. The Mansfield owner asked him to help out a brother who operated a team in Adrian, Michigan.

According to A. D. Suesdorf in a piece for the *National Pastime*, the Adrian Demons or Reformers were part of a six-club circuit that also included the Battle Creek Adventists, the Kalamazoo Kazoos, Zooloos, or Celery Eaters, among others. The Adrian roster car-

Fred Merkle set off baseball's memorable 1908 argument.

Courtesy NBL

ried an outstanding black battery, pitcher George H. Wilson and catcher Vasco Graham. They were recruited from a black semi-pro outfit, the Page Fence Giants. The unwritten color bar against nonwhites had been in place about ten years.

After 20 games at Adrian, the homesick Wagner secured his release and finished the year with the Warren, Pennsylvania, club in the Iron and Coal League.

On the prowl for talent to stock his Paterson, New Jersey, club, bush-browed Ed Barrow, ★ whose acumen in finding and developing players made him the most famous general manager for the first half of the twentieth century, traveled to Wagner's hometown of Mansfield, Pennsylvania, to size up the candidate. Supposedly, Barrow stepped from the train and inquired the whereabouts of Wagner. Told he might find him with other youths idling up the railroad tracks, Barrow struck off on foot. He heard a series of loud booms and, his curiosity aroused, quickened his pace. Barrow came upon a bunch of young men diverting themselves by firing lumps of coal at an empty hopper. Barrow watched, fascinated by the scene and in particular by one strong fellow whose cannon shots with coal indicated he was Wagner. Barrow of course proceeded on more than just Wagner's skills with pieces of anthracite. He was well aware of his quarry's accomplishments during his initial professional season. Wagner's first impression of his discoverer was less enthusiastic. "We sized him up as a railroad cop and ran like the dickens." Barrow, however, obtained Wagner's services for 1896 at Paterson.

He hit .349 that year and was ripping along at .379 the following season when Barrow sold his contract to Louisville, then a National League team. Tommy Leach was a twenty-year-old rookie in Louisville, hoping to catch on at third base. He recalled being mightily discouraged after he saw his rival for the post, Wagner, whom Leach insisted used a first baseman's glove, knocked down a line drive to his right with his bare hand, then fired to first to nip a runner. Said Leach to Lawrence Ritter:

It also turned out that while Honus was the best third baseman in the league, he was also the best first baseman, the best second base-

man, the best shortstop, and the best outfielder. That was in fielding. And since he led the league in batting eight times between 1900 and 1911 you know that he was the best hitter, too. As well as the best base runner. [As a major leaguer, Wagner stole 722 bases, good enough to make him fifth on the all-time list, even though he hung up his spikes back in 1917.]

After the franchise collapsed in 1900, Wagner moved to Pittsburgh, along with twelve others including Leach, where he spent his entire playing career hardly more than a long fly ball from his birthplace.

As a Pirate Wagner spent most of his first few years in the outfield with short stints at first, second, and third, even pitching three innings of a game. Not until 1903 did he settle into his niche as a shortstop. Thick-legged and oversize as he seemed for the position, Wagner exploited his upper-body attributes. Contemporaries swore his arms were so long that he could tie his shoes without bending over. The hands were huge, like shovels on an earth-excavating machine. First basemen spoke of throws from Wagner in which the ball arrived accompanied by a shower of dirt clods and tiny pebbles all scooped up and included in the package.

His speed was more than adequate but his base-stealing success lay in a marvelous ability to anticipate a pitcher's moves and his excellent technique with hook or head-first slides. He rated a triple "sprint and slide" feat as his greatest thrill and with 252 of these heart quickeners, he stands third on the lifetime list. For more than forty years after he quit he led the National League in total games played and at bats, and for seventeen years he bettered the .300 mark.

Slumps obviously bothered Wagner infrequently, although in the 1903 World Series against the Boston Red Sox, he committed 6 errors and hit a dismal .222. However, he redeemed himself in the 1909 championship against Detroit and Ty Cobb. Wagner hit .333 and stole 6 bases while his arch rival for honors received credit for only two thefts. Cobb did steal home to break open a game but Wagner uncharacteristically hotly disputed the call of Cobb's other theft, claiming he'd made the tag. From that Series came a persistent legend that placed Cobb on first base from where he yelled to Wagner, "Out

Pittsburgh ruled the National League 1901 to 1903. Fred Clarke (middle third from left) starred in left field av ing .331 for the trio of seasons and m ing the club. Jack Chesbro (middle row left), an early exponent of the spitter, aged 25 wins per season from 1901 to 1 laboring for the American League New Highlanders starting in 1903. At Cla right sits owner Barney Dreyfuss, and right, the inimitable Honus Wagner. to be hoped that Louisville didn't t away very much money on the Wagner as times are hard, and Wagner won't se world afire as a third baseman. He is a t outfielder than infielder."—Sporting 1897 (on Wagner's entry into the r leagues)

Courtesy NBL

"If a man with a voice loud enough to himself heard all over the United S should stand on top of Pike's Peak and 'Who is the greatest ball player?' 27, 009 persons would shout 'Wagner!' are great baseball players, but only Wagner. . . . He looked like a prospe contented German worker. One would thought to watch the massive shoulder the powerful bowed legs that probab had been a brewery wagon driver or a man. . . . For a dozen years every playe every pitcher has searched for Wag weakness and found none. He has p every position in baseball, is as great i outfield, perhaps greater than in the in He is the best batter, possibly exce Cobb, in the land, he is the greatest bas ner. . . .—Hugh S. Fullerton, Ame Magazine

Courtesy NBL

of my way Krauthead, I'm coming down on the next pitch," or suitably dramatic words to that effect. When the throw from the catcher arrived, Wagner supposedly slapped it down on Cobb's mouth, splitting his lip for three stitches worth. In one of his as-told-to autobiographies, even Wagner repeated this tale but baseball historians declare the incident never occurred.

Wagner ordinarily never lent himself to such fictions. He refused to capitalize on his fame when invited on a vaudeville trip at $1,000 a week with Cobb and Lajoie. He rejected an offer to put his byline on syndicated newspaper coverage of baseball. He turned down a local clothing store's offer to front for their wares. Tobacco companies had started using baseball stars on cards with cigarettes and a local reporter was offered a fee if he could secure Wagner's permission. Wagner killed the proposal on the grounds that he opposed smoking (he did chew) but in his letter to the journalist enclosed his personal check to cover the amount promised the reporter by the tobacco concern. Actually, the company had already begun producing the cards. Although they recalled them, some continued to circulate,

making the item, known as the "1909–1910 T-206 tobacco card," one of the most valuable of baseball collectibles.

When Ban Johnson opened his campaign to raid the National League, Clark Griffith approached Wagner, whose salary was about $2,500 per season. According to some, Griffith flashed twenty $1,000 bills as an inducement to the Pittsburgh star. While the sum may be exaggerated, certainly the offer easily surpassed Wagner's pay. Nevertheless, Wagner refused to desert his club. By 1909, he achieved his highest salary level, $10,000 a year. He remained at that plateau, without complaint, until he retired.

Gentle, bashful, fond of the corniest jokes, Wagner showed a fine solicitude for rookies and an openness to those denied access to organized ball. Of Andrew "Rube" Foster, ★ the black player who was a major force in establishing the Negro Leagues, Wagner said: "He was the smartest pitcher I have ever seen in all my years of baseball." And when someone called John "Pop" Lloyd, ★ arguably the finest shortstop of the Negro Leagues, "the black Honus Wagner," the white man responded that it was he who had been honored.

"Good batsman, fast base-runner, fir[e] fielder, grand thrower and a hustler Wagner is all over the field. Let a lo[n] go to the outfield, even to right and will chase out to be in position to re[ceive] and many a runner has stopped sud[den] when warned that Wagner had the rather than take the risk on drawing [of] the German's hard throws. . . . "—Spo[rting] Life

Courtesy NBL

(Bottom) Wagner stole home and five bases against Detroit in the 1909 [World] Series. "No one ever saw anything gr[aceful] or picturesque about Wagner on the [dia]mond. His movements have been liken[ed to] the gambols of a caracoling elephant. ungainly and so bowlegged that wh[en he] runs his limbs seem to be moving in a after the fashion of a propellor. But h[e can] run like the wind. When he starts a[fter a] grounder every outlying portion of his [anat]omy apparently has ideas of its own [as to] the proper line of direction to be taken position at the bat is less awkward an[d the] muscular swing of his great arms and s[houl]ders is strong enough to drive the ball f[urther] than most batters who hit from the spikes up. . . . There is no question Wagner is the greatest all around player of this or probably any othe[r sea]son."—New York American

Courtesy NBL

(Opposite) Following Pittsburgh's tr[iumph] over Detroit, the Sporting News featur[ed the] two great rivals in a preview of the c[oming] season.

Courtesy NBL

The semipro who earned his living as a phone linesman was known as "The W[Idaho] Wonder."

Courtesy NBL

Let there be no more understanding, no more delusion, that Walter Perry Johnson is, or was, a baseball legend. Not only inaccurate is that description; it demeans him. This, on the authority of that great arbiter, Noah Webster. Legend: Any story coming out of the past, popularly known as historical . . . unverifiable.

Walter Johnson's deeds with a baseball in his pitching fist, unverifiable? Gadzooks! Put the question to the 3,508 batsmen he dismissed with his strikeout pitch, a record unbettered for more than half a century. Ask it of that mortified 1910 Yankee team, the one he shut out in consecutive starts on Friday, Saturday, and Monday. Call up, among other witnesses, the four Red Sox he made a reluctant footnote to history, the four he fanned in the same inning. I speak here only of the iceberg's tip. Beneath lies a great mass of other truths about the swiftness that came out of Johnson's delivery. They're in baseball's official *Red Book,* in fifty-two categories.

Let others be legends if the word fulfills their admirers and biographers. For Johnson there is need for something more fitting as tribute to all those heroics in his twenty-one years of indentured service with the mostly ragtag Washington Senators, those inadequate companions he had need to rise above while creating more records than any ball player of his time, or before, or since.

Only by sometimes overdrawing the tales of Johnson's speed, only by embroidery, could the man and his fastball be limned in proper perspective. Of all the stories that come down to us in baseball lore, how best to convey the image of Walter Johnson and his speed pitch than to recite the episode of Ray Chapman's truncated appearance against him in the batter's box on a day in 1915.

Chapman took one, then a second futile swing against Johnson pitches, with Umpire Billy Evans intoning "Strike two!" Whereupon Chapman suddenly flung his bat away and headed for the Cleveland bench. Evans yelled he had another strike coming. Without breaking stride, Chapman told Evans over his shoulder, "I know, and you can have the next one. It won't do me any good."

And the story goes that Bing Bodie, another Johnson strikeout victim, returned to the Yankee bench muttering, "You can't hit what you can't see." Did he really say it? Did Bodie give that aphorism to the language? No matter. It served to dramatize Johnson's fastball. When the speed of his pitch was the topic, one could never be certain where truth ended and fancy began.

Ring Lardner found it useful to haul Johnson into his script when he wrote "Horseshoes," quoting his fictional rookie like this:

They can't tell me he throws them balls with his arm. He's got a gun concealed on his person and he shoots 'em up there. I was leading off in Murphy's place and I just tried to meet the first one and stuck my bat out. When I did, Henry [a John Henry once caught for the Senators] was throwing the pill back to Johnson. Then I thought maybe if I start swinging at the second one, I'll hit the third one.

Such is the stuff that stemmed from the fastball Johnson brought to the big leagues in 1907 when, described by one writer as "the big galoot from Weiser, Idaho," he walked onto the Washington Senators as a nineteen-year-old rookie right-hander and began to make pitching history. No pitcher spawned as many tales of the unhittable speed. Velocity was a word unused in Johnson's era. Otherwise, it would have been overworked in compliment to him.

Johnson's fame became so progressively wide—local idol, best pitcher in the American League, national hero—that it became a mark of distinction in Washington to boast, "I saw Walter Johnson pitch his first game." Those who said it, said it proudly, as if they were there at the beginning of time.

Honest folks who otherwise wouldn't bandy the truth found an urge to hop on the "I was there" bandwagon. In the 1930s, the Washington club invited all those who had witnessed Johnson's debut on August 2, 1907, to sit in a special section with appropriate badges. Out of the original 2,841 fans in the park that day in 1907, a delegation of 8,000 showed up. For the phonies, a wonderful lack of conclusive guilt.

Johnson pitched under the worst working conditions of any long-career man in baseball. It was the ne'er-do-well Senators of his early years who spawned the repeated joke that might have killed vaudeville—"Washington, first in war, first in peace, and last in the American League." Not until Johnson's sixth year with the club did the Senators rise above seventh place.

Joe Cantillon, the Senators manager in those dismal times, best understood the difficulty of winning games for the inept Washington club. In the fall of 1910, Cantillon, in Chicago, read in a news dispatch that an off-season fire had destroyed a large hunk of the wooden stands behind third base in Washington's American League Park. When he also learned that the District of Columbia fire chief had remarked, "A plumber's

He arrived in Washington, D.C., the ultimate rube, black patent-leather shoes, a high riding derby, and a horseshoe ring on his finger. "I was the greenest rookie that ever was . . . the evening after the first game I ever pitched in Washington, . . . a man approached and said, 'You're famous already, kid. See? They've named a hotel for you.' I looked across the street and, sure enough, there was a big illuminated sign that said, 'Johnson Hotel.' . . . you know I was so green I actually belived the man."—Walter Johnson

Courtesy NBL

blowtorch probably started the blaze," Cantillon said, "The chief is probably right, and the plumber was probably playing third base."

In 1983, a day before Nolan Ryan topped Johnson's lifetime strikeout record, I asked him by telephone to Houston if he was familiar with Johnson's career.

"Not really," Ryan said. "All I know about Johnson is that he's supposed to be a legend. Really, I don't know much about him."

Well . . . Mr. Ryan, meet Mr. Johnson. You're justifiably proud, I am sure, of leading the league seven times in strikeouts. How does twelve times by Johnson strike you? And about those two 20-victory seasons of yours (21–16 and 22–16), please know Johnson had ten of those in a row, including a couple that read 32–12 and 36–7.

And, Nolan, about that 8-game winning streak you had in 1983; exactly seventy years before, Johnson reeled off 16 in a row and the next season he had ministreaks of 14, 11, and 10. Your career 3.10 earned run average is excellent; Johnson had an ERA of 2.00 in ten different years.

Not to disparage Ryan, who will present very impressive crendentials as a Hall of Fame candidate once he retires, but strikeouts come easier today. Since 1963, pitchers have worked with ten more inches of vertical strike zone because Commissioner Ford Frick convinced the majors to expand the zone from "the space between the armpits and the top of the knees" to include "the area from the top of the shoulders to the bottom of the knees." (In 1988, the area was reduced to again boost hitting.)

Batters in Johnson's time were less likely to strike out. They weren't down on the end of the bat taking big swings aimed at home runs and the big money. In Johnson's time, hitters poked at the pitches, aiming to make contact and diminishing strikeouts. Those were the types Johnson fanned.

Significantly, Home Run Baker led the league with homer totals of 11, 12, and 9 in 1911, 1913, and 1914. In 1915, Bob Roth's mere 7 homers for Cleveland gave him the league title. In 1913, there were only 160 homers for the entire American League. In 1983, the Orioles hit 158 homers and the American League total was 1,903.

The records Johnson set almost defy comparison. He would lead the American League in career games won (416); in games won annually (6 times); in shutouts (7 times), in strikeouts (12 times, 8 in a row), in earned runs with 1.14 the first year that statistic was kept; and in one season 36 of his 37 starts were complete games.

Ask how many pitchers could win 25 games for a seventh-place team,

"On August 2, 1907, I encountered the most threatening sight I ever saw on a ball field. He was only a rookie, and we licked our lips as we warmed up for the first game of a doubleheader in Washington. Evidently manager Pongo Joe Cantillon of the Nats had picked a rube out of the cornfields of the deepest bushes to pitch against us. . . . He was a tall, shambling galoot of about twenty, with arms so long they hung far out of his sleeves and with a side-arm delivery that looked unimpressive at first glance. . . . One of the Tigers imitated a cow mooing and we hollered at Cantillon: 'Get the pitchfork ready, Joe—your hayseed's on his way back to the barn.' . . . The first time I faced him, I watched him take that easy windup—and then something went past me that made me flinch. The thing just hissed with danger. We couldn't touch him. . . . every one of us knew we'd met the most powerful arm ever turned loose in a ball park."—Ty Cobb

Courtesy NBL

as Johnson did for the Senators in 1910. He slumped to 23 victories for the Senators who again finished seventh the following year.

On the subject of slumps, Johnson posted a notable one in 1914, or so the Senators insisted. He was denied a pay raise by the club for winning "only" 28 games, a comedown from his 36–7 record of the season before.

To appreciate Walter, it may help to recall that Dizzy Dean was voted into the Hall of Fame for winning 150 games in his career. No disrespect to Dean, but no big deal. Was Dean aware that Johnson licked the Detroit Tigers 66 times?

Always bothersome to Walter Johnson fans were the claims that the Giants' Christy Mathewson outranked him in the pitching arts. These were put forth mainly by New York baseball writers of an earlier generation, who godded Mathewson up for those four 30-victory seasons (Johnson had two) and the three shutouts he pitched in the 1905 World Series. When Johnson came along to surpass Mathewson by almost every measure, they had neither the will nor the honesty to retreat.

Give Mathewson his deserved fame, but to confuse him as a pitcher with Johnson's skills shows a poverty of understanding of their comparative records. Transpose Matty and Johnson in terms of the caliber of teams they pitched for and you get a telling fix on Johnson's greater capacity for winning.

Place Matty with the futile Senators of Johnson's years, those teams that played .438 ball, and an algebraic projection says Mathewson would have won 96 fewer than his 372 victories. Give Johnson a team that played .591 ball like Matty's Giants and that extrapolates to an additional 145 games won for a career total of 567, sending into smithereens Cy Young's 507, the only total that topped him.

In addition to his pitching feats, and for all his fame, a case could be made that Walter Johnson also led the major leagues in humility. For example, his teammate of fifteen years, Joe Judge, described one incident in St. Louis when they were leaving the hotel bound for a movie. A fan in the lobby asked Johnson for his autograph. Recounted Judge: "He began a long conversation with Walter and I wondered if we would make the start of the movie. Finally, when Johnson broke away I asked what took him so long. He said, 'The man said he knew my sister in Kansas.' I told Johnson I didn't know he had a sister. Walter said, 'I don't.' "

For years, baseball writers referred to Johnson as "The Big Swede" without eliciting from him the slightest murmur that he was not Swedish. Why so long a silence on that point? "The Swedes are nice people,"

Johnson explained. "I didn't want to offend them." He said his ancestry was Scotch–German.

His gentle nature and sensitivity toward others was also affirmed that day when he lost a game in the sixteenth inning on a dropped fly ball by Outfielder Clyde Milan. There was no display of righteous anger. Johnson's only comment: "Clyde doesn't do that very often."

It was a personal shock when this writer, as a teenage arrival in Washington in 1922, for the first time beheld the figure of Walter Johnson working from the pitching mound in Griffith Stadium. Not at all did he fit my concept of Johnson as the big right-hander coming in overhand with the world's fastest pitch—the one I had envisioned from reading accounts of his speed in the *Sporting News,* in my baseball books, and in the newspapers deposited every evening in Bar Harbor, Maine, by the six o'clock boat from Boston.

Why, this fellow wasn't even throwing overhand, like big right-handers should. Elmer Cleaves always threw overhand; he was the fastest pitcher in eastern Maine, and he struck out all those guys for our Bar Harbor team. He could hum it, and he always threw overhand. But this fellow they claimed was Walter Johnson threw sidearm with a sweeping motion, and he was even throwing a bit underhand, too, if you could believe that. I couldn't.

There was a time in his retirement years when Johnson talked of his sidearm delivery. It came up in 1938 when Bob Feller was the American League's new, exciting strikeout king, whose speed was being equated with Johnson's. At my invitation, Johnson made the excursion from his Germantown, Maryland, farm to Griffith Stadium to watch Feller pitch for the first time.

From a seat behind the Senators' dugout, Johnson watched and approved. "My he's fast . . . he does throw that ball hard," was Johnson's first comment. And later, "He's got a good one, very fast."

In the third inning that day, after Feller was properly warmed up, the burning question was put to Johnson: "Does he throw as fast as you did?" From the most humble and modest man to play the game came the surprising answer, "No." His modesty had collided with his integrity, and honesty won.

Later, in the same guileless manner that in no way sought to disparage Feller, Johnson also offered, "I don't think he throws as fast as [Lefty] Grove." This was Johnson speaking out, but only after he was asked.

Of Feller, Johnson also noted, "Look and you can see he's got that advantage, with him throwing overhand and following through like he

The musculature held up for 416 wins, ond only to Cy Young's 511.

Courtesy NBL

Among his other virtues Johnson swun effective bat and the Senators frequ called him to pinch hit. He hit 21 ho and on a few occasions played out Early in his career they called him ' ney," referring to the speedy race-car a Barney Oldfield. "The Big Train" wa other nickname hung on Johnson.

Courtesy NBL

does with the ball coming out of his shirt the way it does. . . . That's good for him and bad for the hitters who can't pick it up so quick. . . . I used to give the hitters a good look at my pitch," and he simulated the motion he used to deliver the ball with his sweep from far outside.

In 1907, big league baseball was a hard game, seemingly unsuited to the mannerly rookie from Weiser, Idaho, when he reported to the Washington team. Ty Cobb typified the high success of the ball player of that period with his tough-guy tactics and his jabbering contempt for umpires. When it came to fisticuffs, Cobb did not lack willing opponents.

The ball players of that era were not regarded by everybody as socially acceptable. The stuffier hotels scorned their patronage. Baseball athletes rated only one cut above the plug-uglies of the professional prize ring; the chaw of tobacco was their badge and the corner saloon the hangout of so many.

Into that brawling business walked Walter Johnson, the gangling farm boy from Idaho with arms that dangled to his knees in near-gorilla length, and with a gait that smacked of the plowfield. To the other players on the Washington team in 1907, he was a rube sure enough, with his high-button shoes and celluloid collar. They played poker. He played checkers and casino and went to church.

Walter Johnson, gentleman ball player, hadn't changed when refinement came to baseball later and the game became a more honorable profession, attracting the college bred and dropping pugnacity as a requisite. Johnson had simply been ahead of his time.

In all the romance of baseball, the story of Walter Johnson's discovery and acquisition by the Senators rates recalling. The club stumbled across him by a stroke of luck, prodded by an anonymous and self-appointed scout, a traveling salesman whose territory took him as far west as Idaho–California, and who bombarded Manager Cantillon with tall tales of a local, young semipro pitcher.

Cantillon paid little heed to the letters until he read: "This boy throws so fast you can't see 'em . . . and he knows where he is throwing, because if he didn't there would be dead bodies all over Idaho." Cantillon dispatched an injured catcher, Cliff Blankenship, to have a look at young Walter Johnson.

It was not Blankenship's primary mission, though. En route to Idaho he was instructed to sign a talented young outfielder in Wichita named Clyde Milan. Milan, who signed for $1,250, later related: "Blankenship said 'I'm on my way to Idaho to look over some palooka they say is striking out everybody. Probably isn't worth a dime and I'm on a wild goose chase.' " Little did Milan guess that Blankenship would be scouting the man who would be Milan's roommate for the next sixteen years and the most famous pitcher in American League history.

Blankenship's first look in Weiser at the nineteen-year-old Johnson in a game was a 12-inning eye-filler. He saw the big country boy throwing a fastball that smoked, but he would lose 1–0, done in by two booted ground balls in the twelfth.

When he sought out Johnson after the game to talk business, he flashed a $100 bill to impress the lad, and guaranteed him $350 a month to join the Senators. Johnson was eager, but cautious, asking if there would be traveling expenses to Washington. Satisfied on that point, Johnson took the proposition to his dad who asked for one more stipulation, a return train ticket to Idaho if Johnson failed to make good. Blankenship had Johnson's agreement that day, on a piece of rough brown wrapping paper.

After his one-game look at Johnson, Blankenship was ecstatic, wiring Cantillon in New York with the Senators: "Signed Johnson today. Fastest pitcher since Amos Rusie."

The next day the *Washington Star* carried the story with exclamation points. "New York, June 29—Manager Joe Cantillon has added a great baseball phenom to his pitching staff. The young man's name is Walter Johnson, premier pitcher of the Idaho State League. Cantillon received word today telling of the capture!"

The newspaper's story continued: "Johnson pitched 75 innings in the Idaho State League without allowing a run, and had a wonderful strikeout record of 166 in 11 games, or more than 15 strikeouts a game. Blankenship is very enthusiastic but fails to state whether this great phenomenon is right-handed or left-handed."

When the Senators unveiled him for the first time, on August 2, 1907, Washington fans confirmed that Johnson was, indeed, a right-hander. Also he was a husky lad of 200 pounds and 6'1", broad of back and with arms of uncommon length. What they saw spelled leverage. Perhaps his fastball was indeed as good as publicized.

The Senators had picked no soft spot for Johnson, sending him against the Detroit Tigers, leading the league in hitting and on their way to the 1907 pennant. They had to resort to 3 bunts to get 6 hits off the white comets that came out of Johnson's sweeping right arm. Ty Cobb broke a 1–1 tie by beating out a bunt and scrambling to third on another bunt that followed, later scoring. Johnson was trailing 2–1 when removed in the eighth for a pinch hitter, and the Senators eventually lost, 3–2.

Cantillon unwittingly subjected himself to the supreme second guess

"In the most dramatic moment of baseball's sixty years of history, the wall-eyed goddess known as Fate, after waiting eighteen years, led Walter Johnson to the pot of shining gold that waits at the rainbow's end."—Grantland Rice, New York Herald Tribune

"When the Senators took the field it was behind the broad shoulders of Walter Johnson and this time their hero did not fail them. In danger every one of the four innings that he worked, he rose superbly to every emergency. In each succeeding crisis he became a little more the master, a little more the terrible blond Swede of baseball fable. Twice he struck out Long George Kelly when the game hung by a thread so fine that thousands in the tense silent throng turned their heads away with every pitch. Somewhere, perhaps in that little patch of sunlight that was filtering through the shadowy stands and down in front of the pitcher's mound the once mightiest arm of all was finding the strength to do the thing that twice before had balked it."—Bill Corum, New York Times, 1924

Courtesy NBL

in later years by taking Johnson out for a pinch hitter. Johnson eventually became the best-hitting pitcher in the league. Often he served as the Senators' prime pinch hitter. In 1925 he hit .433, the highest average ever attained by any pitcher. On August 1 of that season he was hitting .546.

And it was not long before other teams learned it was not wise to bunt against Johnson. By 1913, he was the best fielding pitcher in the league, with an average of 1.00 that season on 103 chances accepted—another record.

It is not generally known that Detroit manager Hughie Jennings told Cantillon after Johnson's first game, "If I were you, Joe, I'd tell that big green kid of yours to quit fooling around with that spitball he was throwing against us. He doesn't need anything but the speed he's got. All spitballers except Ed Walsh are in-and-outers who throw their arms away." This is the only known reference to Johnson as a spitballer.

Johnson achieved victory in his second start—a four-hitter against Cleveland. It produced a newspaper comment that hinted how Johnson intimidated hitters: "Johnson's speed was so terrific several Cleveland players acted as though they took no particular delight in being at the plate."

Perhaps more than any other pitcher, it was necessary for Johnson to pitch shutouts to guarantee himself a win. He could never rely on the Senators to get him a run. He pitched 54 1–0 games, losing 26 of those for lack of Senator bats. He couldn't even win on a day when he retired twenty-eight Yankees in a row, getting no better than a 0–0 tie in 12 innings. The Senators got 10 hits off Jack Quinn but squandered them. How many hits did Johnson allow in those 12 innings? Two.

In Chicago, he had to go 18 innings to win a 1–0 game. He lost 3 1–0 games to a Red Sox pitcher named George Herman Ruth. Even George Sisler, who had a brief 5-game pitching career, beat Johnson in a 1–0 game.

But Johnson proved at the age of thirty-eight that he could still win, 1–0, although it took him 15 innings to beat Ed Rommel in a season opener in Washington. He pitched 14 season openers, winning 7 of them by shutouts. Among his shutouts was, of course, his no-hitter against the Red Sox in 1920, the one he pitched with a sore arm that dogged him all year in the worst season he knew as a Senators regular.

Johnson often expressed his dread of hitting batters. "I know I throw hard and I don't want to hurt anybody." Ballpark crowds gasped whenever Johnson did hit a batter, fearing death at worst or a fracture if the victim was fortunate.

I remember the scene in Griffith Stadium when Eddie Collins was felled by a Johnson pitch he took in his ribs. It produced a hush over the crowd. Johnson, racing from the mound, was the first to reach Collins writhing in the batter's box and was the most solicitous of the group that gathered there.

For five minutes Collins lay prone while taking first aid. There was a cheer when he rose unsteadily and indicated he would stay in the game. He received a pat from Johnson and hobbled to first base with a gimpy stride. On Johnson's next pitch the wily Collins stole second. It was Johnson's loss of innocence.

Ty Cobb exploited Johnson's fear of hitting a batter. In his retirement years, Cobb said:

> It was useless to try for more than a single off Johnson. You had to poke and try to meet the ball. If you swung you were dead. . . . After he told me he was afraid he might kill a hitter, I used to cheat. I'd crowd the plate 'til I was actually sticking my toes on it, knowing he'd be so timid he'd pitch me wide. Then with two balls and no strikes he'd ease up to get one over. That's the Johnson pitch I hit.

The belief that Johnson would not throw at hitters did not mean one could belly up to the plate without risk. In fact, faith in his benign attitude probably contributed to Johnson's dubious record of having hit more men than anyone in baseball with the exception of a wild thrower named Chick Fraser (1896–1909). Undoubtedly, many of the 206 battered by a Johnson delivery became vulnerable by crowding the plate, unable to avoid an otherwise innocent inside fastball.

Johnson was in the league barely a year when he vaulted into wide public notice. In what possibly became the most remembered Walter Johnson feat, he shut out the Yankees (then called the Highlanders) 3–0 on a Friday. On Saturday he shut them out again 6–0. On Sunday, blue laws banned baseball in New York. On Monday he took the mound again, shut them out again 4–0. By that time was Johnson tiring? Humph. The first shutout was a four-hitter, the second a three-hitter, and the third a two-hitter. And the next time he saw the Yankees a month later, he shut them out again.

All of this by a pitcher who, his teammates said, "wasn't even trying for shutouts, or strikeouts, either, if he had a big lead." The Senators trainer, Mike Martin, called Johnson "an artistic loafer satisfied to win by any score." Martin remembered a 1909 game against the Browns when Johnson, after striking out eight men in the first 3 innings, was content with his big lead and fanned nobody thereafter.

Washington fans were jolted when their hero who had never asked for a raise suddenly showed an interest in money, and declared himself a holdout after winning 25 games in 1910. "I want $9,000 a year, just as much as Ty Cobb," he said. Thomas Noyes, the Senators' president, was furious, snarling, "No other pitcher in the league is earning as much as the $6,500 we're offering Johnson." He might have added no other pitcher could have won 25 games with a seventh-place club. The holdout lasted thirty hours with Johnson accepting a $7,000 offer.

Johnson gave the Senators back-to-back seasons of 32–12 and 36–7 in 1912 and 1913, lifting the seventh-place team to two second-place finishes. One of his contributions in 1912 was a record-tying 16-game winning streak ended through a scoring miscarriage. As a relief pitcher, Johnson faced the Browns and was charged with the defeat when two runners left on base by the previous pitcher scored on a hit off Johnson.

His 1913 season included winning streaks of 10, 11, and 14 games. He struck out 243, pitched 12 shutouts, had a 56-inning scoreless streak, 5 one-hitters, and an earned run average of 1.14.

But in the winter of 1914 to 1915, the entire nation was startled. Good, honest, dependable Walter Johnson "jumped" to the new Federal League, signing with its Chicago team for a $16,000 salary and $10,000 bonus. His decision was brought on by the Senators' refusal to increase his $12,000 salary, the owner calling him ungrateful and saying, "You had a poor year in 1914 and we did not give you a salary cut." In 1914, Johnson won "only" 28 games.

Clark Griffith, the Senators' manager, maneuvered successfully to bring Johnson back. He could match the Feds' $16,000 salary offer but not the $10,000 bonus. The canny Griffith persuaded White Sox owner Charles Comiskey that Johnson playing for the Feds on the North Side of town would be an attraction ruinous to the South-Side White Sox. Comiskey anted up, Johnson returned the $10,000 to the Feds, and was forgiven instantly by Washington fans.

In latter-day jargon, Johnson would have been called "The Franchise," so important was he to the Senators' gate receipts. In those simple days before public relations departments, Manager Griffith used to telephone Washington sports editors with the plea, "Gimme a headline tomorrow, Johnson's pitching."

President Calvin Coolidge greeted Jo on opening day in 1926. Between th the fading American League chief Johnson.

Courtesy NBL

Suddenly, when it appeared in 1924 that the Senators had a shot at winning the pennant, Johnson's long-deferred dream of pitching in a World Series became a national cause. Other ball players were famous; none became an American symbol in the mold of Johnson—gentleman ball player and great pitcher shackled so long in the service of the inept Senators. As in the case of the latter-day futile New York Mets, affection increased with each passing year.

And they won that pennant. Johnson, almost thirty-seven years old, did his part by the simple act of leading the league in pitching for the sixth time in his career (23–7). When the race became nip-and-tuck with the Yankees, the Big Train won 13 in a row. It was certain Johnson would pitch the World Series opener against the Giants. And when he did his locker held $360 worth of unclaimed tickets he had bought for purported friends who didn't show.

Bittersweet though was his long-deferred World Series debut. Ironically, on a day when he set a series record with 12 strikeouts, the Giants licked him, 4–3, in 12 innings. They beat him again in the fifth game, leaving all but the New York fans saddened by the fate of the aging hero.

But there was a seventh game, and this time the country would rejoice. Johnson won it—not right away; he didn't start. But with the score tied at 3–3 in the eighth, Manager Bucky Harris eyed Johnson, who nodded he could get ready in a hurry.

After a short warm-up he faced the Giants in the ninth, tenth, eleven, and twelfth. They didn't get a run. Twice when he was in trouble with men in scoring position he walked Ross Youngs to pitch to George Kelly and set Kelly down both times on wickedly pitched strikes. The Senators won in the twelfth on Earl McNeely's famous or infamous "pebble" hit that bounced over Freddie Lindstrom's head and brought Muddy Ruel home with the winning run.

Johnson rode in the lead car of the victory parade up Pennsylvania Avenue to the White House to be greeted by President Coolidge. The exuberance of Washington fans who crowded the parade line by the thousands was best spelled out by the banner on the decorated float of the Cherrydale, Virginia, Fire Department: "Let Cherrydale burn."

To the Senators in 1925, Johnson contributed a 20–7 record and they captured a second pennant. This time he got his World Series victory early, in the opener against Pittsburgh, and he also beat the Pirates in his second start. But he couldn't wrap it up for the Senators in game seven, losing a 4–0 lead when rain turned the pitching mound to mud and slime. For their own pitchers, the Pirates rushed sawdust to the mound

66

to provide a better footing, but Johnson received no such help. With the aid of Roger Peckinpaugh's eighth error of the Series, a new record, the Pirates rallied and Johnson lost on Kiki Cuyler's bases-loaded double, 9–7.

American League president Ban Johnson grew wroth at Manager Bucky Harris for allowing Johnson to stay in the seventh game for so long, blaming it in a telegram to "maudlin sentiment." The ebullient Harris wired back, "I'd do it again and again with my best pitcher."

At the start of his twenty-first season, Johnson pitched batting practice in the Tampa training camp. A line drive off Joe Judge's bat struck his leg. Ball players, with their rough sense of humor, always laugh when a teammate gets pinked. As Johnson went down, Coach Al Schacht galloped to the mound and, clowning, counted him out.

Schacht and Johnson's other teammates were unaware that Johnson's leg was broken. He would never pitch again except with a brace on it. He won 5 games that season, lost 6, and called it a career on a note of widespread sadness.

There would be managerial flings with the Senators and Cleveland Indians, not notably successful. In 1930 came his greatest sorrow—the death of Hazel Roberts Johnson, his wife and mother of their five children. Periodically, he would come out of retirement from his Germantown, Maryland, farm, lending his presence to benefit causes. In 1936, he agreed to participate in the celebration of George Washington's 204th birthday by attempting to duplicate the Founding Father's storied feat of throwing a silver dollar across the Rappahannock River, in Fredericksburg, Virginia.

On his second try, Johnson hurled the coin 372 feet, far beyond the opposite shore. Characteristically reverting to his aw-shucks mode he said, "I guess the River was wider in Washington's time." Dozens of reporters covered the event, watched by thousands. Edward T. Folliard of the *Washington Post,* a Pulitzer Prize winner who had covered presidents, kings, queens, wars, and popes, confided in later years, "That was my proudest day. When Walter Johnson took off his coat to try the throw, I was the one who held his coat."

Johnson was persuaded to run for Congress on a Republican ticket from his district in Maryland in 1940, and he agreed reluctantly, saying he would neither campaign nor make speeches. In a Democratic landslide year he was beaten in a close race. He filed an expense report totaling 50 cents.

Reporters proposed to Johnson in 1942 that he don a Washington

After retiring from baseball Johnson [tested] politics as a Republican. In 19[.] duplicated a feat allegedly perform[ed by] George Washington, throwing a silver [dollar] across the Rappahannock River at F[reder-]icksburg, Virginia.

Courtesy UPI/Bettmann News photos

uniform and pitch again, to Babe Ruth in a war bond benefit in Yankee Stadium. They publicized it as a classic Babe Ruth versus Walter Johnson confrontation, the greatest slugger versus the greatest pitcher. Yankee Stadium was packed for the show.

With Johnson taking his warm-ups and Ruth taking practice swings in the batter's circle, the excitement was heightened. Actually, they were long-time friends with high respect for each other. Johnson had known Ruth as a pitcher and played him often, not always with success. Ruth had known what it was to go down swinging at a Johnson fastball.

Now as he faced Ruth from the mound once more, on Johnson's face was a friendly smile. It was not Chaucer's "smile with a dagger under its cloak." Johnson wasn't planning any discomfiture for the Babe by burning a fastball past him, if he could.

Ruth hit Johnson's third pitch into the seats. There were other home runs by Ruth and the huge crowd was joyed. When the show was over, Johnson and the Babe shook hands.

Later when I suggested to Johnson, "You were laying them up for the Babe to hit, weren't you?" Johnson didn't answer the question directly. Instead he said, "They came to see the Babe hit, not to see me pitch." Johnson had voiced esteem for Ruth before. There was the time when he was asked to compare the home runs of the game's long hitters, Ruth, Gehrig, Foxx, and Greenberg. As usual, Johnson was not about to hurt anybody's feelings. What he said was, "I only know one thing. Those balls Ruth hit got smaller quicker than anybody else's." That was another nice touch.

As a boy, John Joseph McGraw supposedly knocked a baseball through a window and his crusty father, who considered the game purely frivolous, punished him with a severe hiding. Writes baseball historian Donald Honig, "The very thought of *anyone* putting bruises on John J. McGraw is barely thinkable, like goosing William Howard Taft or slipping a whoopee cushion under Woodrow Wilson." That awe-inspiring persona plus a positive genius for tactics and handling men explains why McGraw dominated baseball for the first two decades of the twentieth century.

Like so many of his period, McGraw sprang out of the Northeast with Irish antecedents. "I was born in Truxton, New York [an upstate rural area]," said McGraw. "After grammar school, during which I devoted more time to the problems of baseball than those of history, geography and English, I decided it was time to embark on my career as a ball player and got a job on a professional team."

He glosses over the horrifying circumstances that may have driven him to overachievement; at the age of twelve he lost his mother, two sisters, and two brothers to a diphtheria epidemic and when he could not please his cantankerous surviving parent, he boarded with a neighbor. Only 5'7" and 150 pounds at maturity, the slightly built sixteen-year-old McGraw began his pro life picking up $2 a contest for a team in East Homer, five miles from his home.

Just short of his seventeenth birthday he tried out as a third baseman for Olean, part of the New York–Pennsylvania League in 1890. "I thought I could play," reminisced McGraw, "but after a few days the manager decided I couldn't so I went to Wellsville, in western New York, and finished the season." (The sagas of McGraw and others of the era bespeak the incredible plethora of teams to whom hopefuls could apply for paid positions. McGraw's experience is also a cautionary tale of the fragility of franchises.)

Knocking around with a pickup squad known as the Ocala (Florida) Giants, McGraw caught the eyes of higher league bird dogs and he accepted an offer from Cedar Rapids in the Illinois and Iowa League. But what started out as an eight-club organization dropped first to seven, then six, and finally to a meager four. Fortunately for McGraw, Baltimore in the American Association had taken him on as a shortstop.

When the National League swallowed the American Association in 1892, the Orioles and McGraw became bona fide major leaguers. He found his playing niche at third for the 1894 season and sparked Baltimore to the first of its three consecutive championships. A bout with typhoid fever limited him to 23 games in 1896, but he bounced back to hit .325 the following year.

During those incandescent Baltimore seasons, a style of play exemplified by McGraw swept over the game. In addition to McGraw, the Orioles boasted the "Hit 'em where they ain't" expert Willie Keeler ★ in right field (lifetime batting average .345), Hughie Jennings ★ at short (lifetime BA .312), and Joe Kelley ★ in left (lifetime BA .319). Wilbert Robinson, who caught for Baltimore and was McGraw's closest pal until they quarreled, said:

> Take the bunt. It may have been seen occasionally somewhere before, but if so it made no lasting impression. The first men to realize its practical value were Keeler and McGraw. Both were fast runners. Dumping the ball was an astonishing thing to players of those days. Unprepared as the third and first basemen were for a thing like that, before they could handle the ball, fleet Keeler or McGraw were across the bag, kidding the other fellows . . . there were great old days and great old teams, but I'll always swear to the end that Baltimore had all the others skinned.

Playing and managing mostly in the "dead-ball" era, McGraw teams pursued a run at a time. The Orioles and then the Giants typically relied on an offense that began with a base on balls, followed by a stolen base (in 1911 and 1912 four of the National League leaders in stolen bases were Giants), sacrifice bunt, and finally a run on a fly to the outfield or a grounder, adding up to a run without a hit. It was McGraw, according to sportswriter H. C. Salsinger of Detroit, who made the cutoff throw from the outfield an integral part of the game, demonstrating its worth to advantage five times against the New York Yankees in the 1922 World Series.

McGraw skinned his baseball cats with other tricks, some of which earned him vituperation if not retaliatory fists. As a third

(Following page) As a slim sixteen-year-old, John J. McGraw wore the uniform of Olean in the New York–Pennsylvania League in 1890.

Courtesy NBL

baseman, McGraw had few peers in the arts of grabbing a base runner's belt or shirt out of umpire sight as he rounded the sack. The Orioles were known for their roughhouse style of play; nothing was sacred when they rode the enemy, and critics scorned them as "hoodlums." Always contentious with umpires, McGraw's battles with the arbiters became his trademark once he became a manager.

With the New York Giants in 1905, he became embroiled in a shouting match with Pittsburgh Pirate owner Barney Dreyfuss who demanded that the league censure the Giant manager. National League President Harry Pulliam and the league's directors held a hearing on the charges of misconduct and violations of the rules (McGraw's alleged denunciation of Dreyfuss came from the clubhouse balcony after he had been thumbed from a game for offenses against an umpire). Pulliam already had slammed McGraw with a $150 fine and a fifteen-day suspension for his "abusive language." The National League Board of Directors listened to testimony for better than five hours and McGraw's defense included himself, newspapermen, club officials, a New York City detective, and a petition on his behalf signed by twelve thousand fans. He was exonerated.

One year later, when a pair of umpires arrived at the gates of the Polo Grounds before a New York Giants–Chicago Cubs game, one of them named James Johnstone was denied admission. He promptly forfeited the game to the Cubs by the official score of 9–0, which of course caused a deafening hullabaloo. The Giants pleaded McGraw's innocence, insisting that Police Inspector Sweeney decided not to permit Johnstone to umpire for fear of a riot if he put in an appearance. In a previous game, Johnstone had called Giant third baseman Art Devlin out on a close play at the plate. Devlin and McGraw had protested angrily and the New York fans supported their opinion with a fusillade of seat cushions and beer glasses aimed at Johnstone. Only the intervention of cops suppressed the riot. McGraw-haters such as a correspondent for the *Sporting News* dismissed the defense that the Inspector did it on his own. Indeed, Sweeney cried: "That is a contemptible lie. I never advised such a thing, as it was not my province. I

stood ready to protect the umpire if I had to call every policeman in the city to the grounds."

McGraw boldly argued that the Giants should be awarded a forfeit, saying that he and his troops had waited the prescribed five minutes for the umpires to show, then proposed to supply their own officials. When the Cubs balked at the suggestion and then decamped, McGraw claimed the win. The Giants had summoned Joe Humphreys, a manager of prize fighters, to address the crowd: "Ladies and Gents! This here game has been forfeited to New York by Umpire Strang [a fellow picked by McGraw to fill in at the post] because the Chicagos will not play. The police barred Johnstone from the grounds!"

Pulliam upheld the decision of Johnstone and the game went into the record books as a 9–0 victory for Chicago. When Johnstone showed up for work at the Polo Grounds the day after his exclusion he was admitted with no fuss.

But the following spring, McGraw barred an umpire nominated to work a spring training game, forfeited a pair of contests, and even got the Giants declared persona non grata at a New Orleans ballpark.

Then there was an encounter with an umpire named Bill "Lord" Byron after a Giant loss to Cincinnati. The arbiter's calls had gone against the New Yorkers and after the Reds pushed across the winning run, the umpire, according to writer Sam Crane, accosted McGraw.

"I hear you were run out of Baltimore," offered Byron with ill intent.

"What's that?" demanded McGraw.

"I hear you were run out of Baltimore," repeated Byron.

"Well, do you say that yourself?" asked McGraw.

"Yes, I say it myself," said the uncautious Byron.

Crane reported that McGraw then smacked his tormentor with a hard blow to the mouth. "The umpire went down, his mouth bleeding profusely. He made no attempt to regain his feet."

McGraw fared more poorly several years later when Patrick Newnam, manager of the minor league Houston Buffalos, sucker-punched McGraw unconscious in response to

At age twenty-one, McGraw was an established star with the Baltimore Orioles, hitting .340, stealing 78 bases, and well known for his truculence. "The game was replete with incidents. The wild shouts of the onlookers, the strains of the Catholic Protectory Band, . . . and the general outbreak that follows the gathering of thousands of cranks caused a stampede in the horseshed.

"One of the side rails of the free seats gave way, and a dozen persons fell to the ground below, but luckily none was injured. Umpire Emslie and third baseman McGraw had a tilt, and for a time a fight was imminent. Catcher Farrell prevented them from spoiling each other's appearance.

"Throughout the contest the spectators kept jeering at McGraw. . . . But McGraw was apparently undisturbed and appeared rather to like the distinction given him. Umpire Hurst was knocked unconscious by a foul tip. After he recovered he rubbed a lump as big as a walnut on his forehead, and, . . . resumed his duties. . . . As the Baltimores left the field with measured tread, the picture of gloom and despair, a mighty shout went up from the assemblage, cheer after cheer was given to the victors, and the band played 'Carry the News to Mary' "— New York Times *account of Temple Cup competition, 1894.*

"[McGraw] was a master tactician in a time when runs were scratched out singly, out of luck and speed and connivance. He was too impatient to qualify as a great developer of talent, but he was a marvelous coach and a cold and deadly trader."—Roger Angell

Courtesy NBL

an earlier sneer by McGraw that he employed "bush league language." Art Fletcher, sitting nearby, then decked Newnam.

Both the *Sporting News* and *Sporting Life*, reflecting the extreme feelings McGraw aroused, used words like "ruffian," "obstreperous," "rowdy," and "hoodlum" when speaking of him. Articles accused him of vilifying opponents and of obnoxious language, and spoke of the "filthy lips of his subordinates."

Detractors called him "Muggsy," a name derived not from his puggish physiognomy but from the label for criminals. Admirers dubbed him "Little Napoleon."

He was only twenty-six in 1899, when by an astonishing maneuver, Oriole manager Ned Hanlon signed on with Brooklyn, taking with him most of the top Baltimore hands. More or less by default, the young third sacker became a playing manager of Baltimore. Consigned by the experts to a dismal season, the Orioles under McGraw, relying mostly on scrubs, surprised everyone with a fourth-place finish in a twelve-team circuit. Two big assets were his pal Wilbert Robinson behind the plate and a strong-armed rookie, Iron Man Joe McGinnity, who won 28 games with a 2.58 earned run average. McGraw himself hit better than ever at .391 (third best in the National League), stole 73 bases (second best), and topped everyone with 124 walks and 140 runs scored.

But such heroics could not save the Baltimore National League franchise. McGraw spent 1900 in St. Louis before Ban Johnson, determined to give his fledgling American League credibility, engineered a franchise for Baltimore with McGraw as manager. Inevitably, two such hard-headed, cantankerous individuals as Johnson and McGraw clashed, particularly over McGraw's noisome efforts to intimidate umpires. In a plot allegedly directed by McGraw, that even Machiavelli might have admired, a spectacular series of midseason 1902 coups repositioned some major performers. The owner of the National League Cincinnati Reds, John T. Brush, bought an interest in the American League Orioles. He brazenly issued unconditional releases to first baseman Dan McGann, catcher Roger Bresnahan, ★ outfielders Cy Seymour and Joe Kelley, pitcher Joe McGinnity, and manager-third baseman

McGraw. McGann, Bresnahan, and McGinnity quickly signed on with the New York Giants with McGraw as field boss. As part of the machinations, Brush disposed of his shares in Cincinnati and bought control of the Giants for $125,000. The notorious Andrew Freedman continued to hold some shares, bar reporters from the park, and bawl threats of libel suits.

Ban Johnson struck back. He stocked the depleted Baltimore club with players from other clubs and a pair of notables lured from the National League, outfielder Willie Keeler and pitcher Jack Chesbro. ★ Johnson then sacrificed Baltimore, advancing the club to New York City as a direct challenge to the Giants. The American League entry set up shop around 168th Street on the West Side of Manhattan on a hilly section, earning the team its original name of Highlanders. The ownership consisted of Frank Farrell, a Tammany hustler and gambler, and William Devery, a former police chief who is regarded as the all-time king of law enforcement corruption. It was Devery who lectured his troops, "If there's any graftin' to be done I'm goin' to be the one that does it." Not surprisingly, some referred to the new team as the "Burglars."

In 1903, his first full year of command, McGraw brought the Giants in second and the following year captured the pennant. Still furious at Ban Johnson, he refused to allow his team to meet the winner of the American League and there was no 1904 World Series.

Even the imperious McGraw could not resist the public clamor for a World Series the following year. The absence of World Series loot had cost each player about $1,000—as much as half a season's salary. Giant owner John T. Brush proposed the standards to govern the postseason championship, a four out of seven match with 60 percent of the receipts of the first 4 games for the player pool, which would be divided into 75 percent for the winners, the remainder to the losers.

To McGraw's enormous satisfaction the Giants demolished Connie Mack's Athletics four to one, with Christy Mathewson shutting out the foes three times; Joe McGinnity did the trick once. McGraw sneered at the Mackmen as "white elephants" (pachyderms became part of the club logo for many years).

"McGraw the umpire baiter, the dictato king of the diamond! Who shall say th word must not be law this year?"—Joe New York Sun

Courtesy AP/Wide World

"McGraw's very walk across the field hostile town is a challenge to the tude."—Grantland Rice

Courtesy UPI/Bettmann News photos

(Top) *Owner John T. Brush (in cap) orchestrated the bizarre shifts that brought McGraw to New York. Next to Brush sits his wife, and the fellow in the derby is Harry M. Stevens whose ballpark catering service became a near monopoly.*

Courtesy NBL

(Bottom, left) *Upstart rivals of the Giants were the American League New York Highlanders. Awaiting transportation to their quarters in Gray, Georgia, for spring training in 1909, a trio played pinochle by the tracks. The most notable Highlander was Wee Willie Keeler (second from right), a former teammate of McGraw in Baltimore.*

   K is for Keeler
   As fresh as green paint
   The fastest and mostest
   To hit where they ain't
—*Ogden Nash*

Courtesy NBL

"In a hot game when things begin to go wrong he [Roger Bresnahan] is a composite of ginger and bad language. In his clumsy shinguards and wind-pad, his head in a wire cage, through which at intervals comes a stream of reproof and comment as he fusses around the plate, he suggests a grotesque overgrown hen trying to get the family in out of the rain. . . . Bresnahan does not have a delightful personality. He once made a speech to Art Devlin which brought in return a punch on the nose. But Bresnahan isn't there to be loved."—J. W. McConaughy, New York Evening Journal

Courtesy NBL

The first game of the Series in wooden Shibe Park drew 17,955, six thousand more than the seating capacity, and the second encounter brought 24,992 to the Polo Grounds in New York. The victorious players were rewarded with $1,142 apiece while the losers, entitled to only $370, carried off $823 per man after the club, following a brief tradition begun by Pittsburgh in 1903, tossed its share into the player pot.

The anchor for McGraw's pitching staff during the Series as he had been during the Oriole days was a pugnacious immigrant from Ireland, Roger Bresnahan. The squatty Bresnahan originally tried pitching; he had major league speed but sandlot control. With the Orioles in 1901, he pitched, played outfield, second and third base, but most of all, catcher. When McGraw permanently installed him as a receiver in 1905, Bresnahan set new standards for the position.

Bresnahan's contributions included the introduction of shin guards and face-mask padding to the catcher position in 1907, completing the basic armor for receivers. Thus shielded, Bresnahan caught an unprecedented 139 games in 1908.

Bresnahan was ahead of his time with another form of protection, too. Andy Coakley, pitching for Cincinnati, beaned Bresnahan in 1907, rendering him unconscious. At high risk when he returned some days later, Bresnahan entered the batter's box wearing a crude helmet. In 1905, the A. J. Reach Co. patented its "Reach Pneumatic Head Protector for Batters." An ad for the $5 device declared:

> So many batters have been put out of the game by being struck in the head by pitched balls that the demand for some protection for the batter caused us to design this Pneumatic Protector. . . . It is not only the loss of the player's services that is involved, but his usefulness to the team is impaired, even after he recovers he is timid when approaching the plate, which necessarily affects his batting.

It was another fifty years and countless beanings later, including one major league fatality and several career enders, before baseball took its cue from Bresnahan and A. J. Reach.

Bresnahan fitted the McGraw player profile neatly. He ran well enough to lead off, a singular role for a catcher. He sought to con umpires. He habitually pulled his shirtfront out when at bat and would groan in pain as a ball nicked the wool. Umpires then awarded him first base for being struck by the pitch. When pickoffs caught him off first base, Bresnahan would stroll toward second as if it were obvious that the pitcher had balked. Apart from his skills with bat, ball, and glove, he baited and battled umpires, field foes, and fans. In Philadelphia only the arrival of the cops saved him after he attacked a heckling mob outside the ballpark.

When traded to St. Louis, Bresnahan sought to lift his club from its habitual cellar status through sheer aggressiveness. A 1910 league directive to curb "vile and unbecoming behavior" named Bresnahan and only him as the perpetrator of the offense. That same year the *Reach Guide* noted:

> Bresnahan's numerous disputes with and ejections by the umpires, in their cumulative effect, caused his team much loss in prestige and possible victories. In all other respects, Bresnahan . . . scored a decided success, as he infused aggressiveness and ambition and kept the team keyed up to its best efforts nearly all season.

However, the report pointed out Cardinal catching declined sharply "when Bresnahan was off duty and he was off a great deal due to frequent suspension for umpire baiting."

McGraw might have been excused for thinking that the trade of Bresnahan opened the way for a series of Giant disasters. The Merkle blunder or the Evers trick, depending on whether one rooted for or against the Giants, cost McGraw the 1908 pennant, if one disregards the club's loss of 3 straight to the Phillies before the playoff with the Cubs. But McGraw put together pennant winners for 1911–1913 with Mathewson and Rube Marquard ★ winning 147 games over the three seasons.

Mathewson, in his seventeen seasons with the Giants, notched 372 wins for McGraw. (He was 1–0 for Cincinnati at the end of his career.) The Bucknell grad frustrated hitters with a good fastball, a sweeping curve, and above all his fabulous fadeaway, the progenitor of the modern screwball. Contemporary accounts indicate others could throw what was called a "reverse curve" or an "in-drop"

"There's a flock o' pitchers that kno batter's weakness and works accordin' they ain't nobody else in the world tha stick a ball as near where they want to it as he [Christy Mathewson] can. I b could shave you if he wanted to and had a razor blade to throw instead of a If you can't hit a fast one a inch a quarter inside and he knows it, you' three fast ones a inch and a quarter ir and then, if you've swung at 'em you c and get a drink o' water. . . . I ain't to make you believe that he don't neve to pitch where he's aimin' at. If he don he wouldn't be here; he'd be working the angels in St. Peter's league. But he 10 to 1 better control than any guy seen and I've seen the best of them."—Lardner

Courtesy NBL

but Matty alone delivered it from the same overhand motion as his other pitches. Under one of his not-infrequent bylines he offered the arcana of his powers:

> Of various balls used by latter-day pitchers the fast ball, which may end with an inward shoot, outward shoot or upward shoot, comes first. All pitchers must be able to use this ball with more or less success. Then comes the slow ball, which does not curve or revolve; the drop curve, one of the most popular curves, the out-curve, which is seldom used in the big leagues, the rise ball, an underhand curve used with very little success by anyone except McGinnity; the fall-away [sic] which I have used, if I may be pardoned for saying so, with greater effectiveness than any other pitcher (it is my favorite); and the spit ball, a style of delivery the science of which cannot be explained, and one very difficult to control.*

To a reporter he confided:

> It is an exceptionally slow ball and relieves the strain on the pitcher as well as puzzling batsmen. A simple definition for the fall-away is a ball that curves out from a left-handed batter when pitched by a right-handed pitcher.
>
> The ball sails through the air at a deceptive gait until it is about six feet from the batsman, where it begins to curve outward and downward. The rotary motion of hand just before the ball is let go imparts the outward curve to the ball. . . .
>
> Such a ball is calculated to deceive the greatest batter. He is deceived at the start as to the speed of the ball. As it rushes toward him it looks like a fast high ball; six feet from him, when it begins to drop, it has the appearance of a slow drop ball, and then as he swings it is traveling in two directions at once.

His erstwhile colleague McGinnity, who called his submarine riser "Old Sal," argued vehemently that Mathewson was mistaken: "It is not possible for a right-hand pitcher to so twist his hand as to curve the ball in. It would require a man without any bones in his fingers to do it."

With John Meyers behind the plate, Merkle at first, and Larry Doyle at second, the Giants led the league in hitting for those pennant-winning seasons. But the club dropped all of the World Series. In 1911, the

Philadelphians revenged themselves for 1905 with 4 wins to the Giants' 2. The mighty Mathewson lost 2 of his 3 starts while the Athletic ace, Charles Albert "Chief" Bender, ★ beat him twice after dropping the first game to Matty. In 1912, the Giants and Boston met in a festival of farce combined with a monumental tragedy of errors. Smoky Joe Wood struck out eleven Giants to take game one. Five Giant errors with 4 unearned runs betrayed Mathewson in game two and, after 11 innings, darkness stopped play at 6–6. The Giants finally won the third meeting but Wood returned to put the Sox ahead two games to one. The lead increased the following day when Mathewson, again victim of an error, lost 2–1. However, Rube Marquard pitched the Giants to a victory in game six.

Boston politics literally took the field in the seventh game. Ordinarily, the Boston Royal Rooters (an odd name for a citadel of the American revolution), a contingent of bugs whose adoration of the locals dated back to 1897, occupied prime pavilion seats. The 6–6 game, however, had confused the ticket sellers and when the Rooters arrived at the park they were aghast to find paying plebians usurping their royal prerogatives.

Led by Mayor John "Honey" Fitzgerald (whose grandson was to be the thirty-fifth U.S. President), the aggrieved mob with its own brass band at the forefront marched onto the field, delaying the game. Mounted cops sought to shove them from the diamond. After thirty minutes order had been restored but all the while Joe Wood had been patiently throwing. Having left his game in the ruck of the Royal Rooters demonstration, Wood was pounded early and hard. The Series was tied at three apiece.

The assault on the Royal Rooters momentarily disaffected Boston from its beloved Sox. Newspapers compared the police action to that of Russian Cossacks. The city turned its back on the eighth and deciding game; only 17,034 fans showed. The finale went into the tenth at 1–1. In the Giant half, the New Yorkers scored a run but that only added to the agony incurred when the home team batted. First up was Clyde Engle, a pinch hitter for relief pitcher Smoky Joe Wood (winner of 34 games during the season plus three more in the Series). Mathewson

"Just after Steve Yerkes had crossed the plate with the run that gave Boston's Red Sox the world's championship in the deciding game of the greatest series ever played for the big title [1912], while the thousands, made temporarily crazy by a triumph entirely unexpected, yelled, screamed, stamped their feet, smashed hats and hugged one another, there was seen one of the saddest sights in the history of a sport that is a strange and wonderful mixture of joy and gloom. It was the spectacle of a man, old as baseball players are reckoned, walking from the middle of the field to the New York players' bench with bowed head and drooping shoulders, with tears streaming from his eyes, a man on whom his team's fortune had been staked and lost and a man who would have conquered if he had been given the support deserved by his wonderful pitching. Matty tonight is greater in the eyes of New York's public than ever before. Even the joy-mad population of Boston confesses that his should have been the victory and his the praise."—Ring Lardner, Chicago Examiner

Courtesy NBL

---

*Mathewson does not mention the knuckle ball, which as early as 1908 one reporter labeled a "new-fangled" pitch.

coaxed a routine fly ball out of Engle. But Fred Snodgrass in center field muffed it. Harry Hooper ★ fouled off a bunt effort, then lined a ball to deep left center. Remembered Hooper: "Ninety-nine times out of a hundred no outfielder could possibly have come close to that ball. But in some way, I don't know how, Snodgrass ran like the wind, and dang if he didn't catch it. I think he *outran* the ball. Robbed me of a sure triple."

Unfortunately, in light of what followed, poor Snodgrass is recalled only for his previous boot, rather than his spectacular grab. The catch was only a delay in the fall of the Giants. Steve Yerkes mooched a walk. Then Tris Speaker, ★ a .344 lifetime hitter who stroked the ball for .383 in 1912, managed to lift a puny foul near first base. For some inexplicable reason, Mathewson shouted for catcher Chief Meyers to take it when either the pitcher or first baseman Merkle had a much better shot at it. Meyers lumbered down the baseline in slow pursuit; his glove hit the ball but he couldn't hold it. Speaker yelled at Mathewson: "You just called for the wrong man. It's gonna cost you this ball game." Speaker made good, singling to score Engle and put Yerkes on third with only one away. Larry Gardner drove a sacrifice fly to bring in the winning run.

The McGraw legions fared even worse the following year as the Athletics crushed them 4–1. Four years later the Giants again dropped a World Series, this time to the Chicago White Sox, a strong club that featured seven of the players who would blacken baseball history in 1919.

Closer to home, McGraw and his Giants dominated the New York scene; the names that lit up Broadway, drove the engines of finance, and battled in the political arena all graced the Polo Grounds. Douglas Fairbanks, soon to become Hollywood's hero; De Wolf Hopper who made a fair living from recitations of *Casey at the Bat;* Lillian Russell, the sex symbol of the age; Mayor James Gaynor, who survived a bullet to his head from a fired city employee; former Governor Charles Evans Hughes, then a Supreme Court justice; Big Tim Sullivan, the former saloonkeeper and then Tammany sachem; Colonel E. H. Green, son of Hetty Green, the richest woman in the country; Harry Payne Whitney, "hunter, explorer, and pet of society"; and stockbroker "Bet A Million" Gates—all were devoted fans. McGraw returned the compliment; he frequented the theater, hobbed with the nobs, and eyed the racetrack horses with the local sportsmen.

The manager brought to his role much more than an ability to mesh with the flash of the city. He understood baseball tactics as perhaps no other. He was a peerless shepherd of men and a master of psychology. He explained his credo:

> You've got to know your men before you can get this [crazy to win] spirit into them. You've got to study your men individually to learn his weak as well as his strong points. When you know him then you have to handle him accordingly. Treat one man in a friendly manner and he'll go out on the field and fight his head off for you. Take another man and you have to ride him hard sometimes. In handling the latter type I never for one instant let him forget that I am the boss. Because of that they once called me "the czar." Well, the real czar has lost his job lately, but I'm still holding down mine.

On another occasion, McGraw declared, "With my team I am an absolute czar. My men know it. I order plays and they obey. If they don't, I fine them."

Al Bridwell, whose single to right center triggered the famous Fred Marke faux pas, spent almost four seasons as a shortstop for McGraw (1908–1911). He told Lawrence Ritter in *The Glory of Their Times:*

> The reason McGraw was a great manager— and he was the greatest—was because he knew how to handle men. Some players he rode, and others he didn't. He got the most out of each man. It wasn't so much knowing baseball. All of them know that. One manager knows about as much about the fundamentals of baseball as another. What makes the difference is knowing each player and how to handle him. And at that sort of thing nobody came anywhere close to McGraw.

For all of his passion for his own authority, McGraw favored intelligence and initiative. Outfielder Fred Snodgrass, the second of McGraw's pair of unlucky Freds (Merkle was the other), told Ritter:

Mathewson (left) and Iron Man Joe M[.] *nity (right, flanking McGraw) acc[.]* *for 230 Giant wins in four years (I[.]* *1906). "McGraw is a born leader o[.]* *players and there is not a Giant or any[.]* *player who has ever played under hi[.]* *did not appreciate the value of his l[.]* *ship and the results he obtained by his[.]* *ough knowledge of the game."—[.]* *Crane, New York Evening Journal*

". . . it was an important pa[.] *McGraw's great capacity for leadershi[.]* *he could take kids out of coal mine[.]* *wheat fields and make them walk an[.]* *and chatter and play with the look [.]* *gles."—Heywood Broun*

Courtesy NBL

. . . it was an education to play under John J. McGraw. He was a great man, really a wonderful fellow, and a great manager to play for.

Naturally, McGraw and I didn't always see things alike. I was a headstrong, quick-tempered, twenty-year-old kid when I joined the Giants in 1908. And sometimes Mr. McGraw would bawl the dickens out of me as he did everybody else. Any mental error, any failure to think and McGraw would be all over you. And I do believe he had the most vicious tongue of any man who ever lived. Absolutely! . . .

However, he'd never get on you for a mechanical mistake, a fielding error or a failure to get a hit. He was a very fair man, and it was only when you really had it coming to you that you got it . . . and in public he would always stand up for his players.

Snodgrass asserted that on their own, the Giants "stole when we thought we had the jump. . . . We played hit and run when we felt that was what was called for. We bunted when we thought it was appropriate," and "every player on the team was expected to know how to play baseball."

John (Chief) Meyers—the racism of the period burdened anyone of Indian blood with the nickname of Chief—caught for McGraw during the times of Bridwell, Merkle, and Snodgrass:

What a great man he was! Oh, we held him in high esteem. We respected him in every way. According to Mr. McGraw his team never lost a game; he lost it, not his players. He fought for his ballplayers and protected them. You couldn't come around and second-guess McGraw's players in his presence without having a fight on your hands right there. He stood up for us at all times.

We always called him *Mr. McGraw.* Never John, or Mac. Always Mr. McGraw.

Of all his players, Mathewson, who combined intelligence, education, competitive zeal, and balanced temper, attracted McGraw most. Matty alone socialized with McGraw who, many felt, regarded the pitcher as the son he never had.

Even in his front-office capacities, McGraw was known for his generosity to his field hands. He was the first manager to insist on top accommodations in hotels. When he learned the Giants paid only $2.50 a day for food and lodgings per man he immedi-

ately doubled the expense. Charles Ebbets, the owner of the Brooklyn Dodgers, whose father had been Alexander Cartwright's boss, was outraged by the Giants' extravagance.

"This man McGraw will break us all. He is giving the players high-toned notions. Ball players are not accustomed to live in first class hotels, and this league must stop that foolishness." (Ebbets lost control of his club because of his extravagance in spending $750,000 to build in 1912 the Brooklyn ballpark that bore his name.)

Waite Hoyt, ★ a child prodigy when McGraw signed him, recalled McGraw with affection: "He was one of the kindliest martinets that you could possibly know. A rough and tumble roisterer . . . a very tough individual. But one of the kindliest, considerate fellows that you could meet. Especially with old timers, very sarcastic, very profane, very rough."

Hoyt remembered how McGraw, irate over umpire decisions, would arm both fists with gobs of black dirt when the Giants were behind with 2 out in the ninth. As soon as the game ended McGraw would follow the officials toward the dressing room. As he excoriated them for their failings, McGraw hurled the dirt in their faces.

On one occasion, McGraw ordered Hoyt to station himself in a hidden cubicle at the end of the dugout and heckle Umpire Bill Klem. McGraw instructed Hoyt to chirp, "Hey, Catfish," a name so detested by Klem that use of it meant immediate expulsion. Klem could neither detect where the voice came from nor its owner. McGraw added prime insult to festering injury by having Hoyt yell, "Hey, Catfish, where did you take your wife in Paris?" (It seems that the innocent Klem, while touring with the Giants and White Sox in Europe, sought to avoid the company of players and stayed with his wife in a secluded hotel. Only the place he chose proved to be a house of ill repute.) Klem never discovered the source of the barbs and spent the game at a parboil.

McGraw kept his distance from his subordinates, with the exception of Mathewson. When Matty's arm gave out in 1916, McGraw arranged a trade that gave his pal new life as manager for Cincinnati. It was a typical gesture. According to Waite Hoyt,

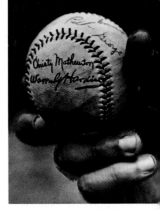

Christy Mathewson, in retirement, graphed a ball over the signature of dent Warren G. Harding and demonst his grip for his fadeaway.

Courtesy NBL

The McGraws (standing) socialized wi Mathewsons; the manager seemed to r the younger man as his surrogate son

Courtesy NBL

"The Little Round Man has gone out and thus the curtain goes down on the leader, the last and greatest of the old Giants. It was some ten or more years ago, when the fiery, peppery, trim McGraw of other days had changed to the portly genius of the high chair on the left end of the Giant bench. . . . All through his 'Thirty Years War' as commander of the Giants he was an absolute monarch. In the forepart of his reign he was also guide, philosopher and friend to his players. But there came a change some ten years ago . . . the increasing age of the Little Napoleon, the introduction of the lively ball into the game . . . the lively ball came in and any hillbilly, hay shaker or plow jockey might walk up there with a blundering bludgeon to ruin a whole afternoon of fine strategy by slapping the jackrabbit ball over a distance fence. It made a new game, a slambang affair in which stolen bases didn't count, inside stuff ran for Sweeney and the hit-and-run gave way to the hit-and-walk style of play; hit one into the bleachers and walk around the bases. That wasn't McGraw's type of game. He was smart enough to meet it, but he had no enthusiasm for it. He didn't sit up nights figuring it out as he sat up nights with Hughie Jennings in his old Oriole days, doping out trick plays for a coming series.

". . . Connie Mack says that John McGraw was the greatest leader the diamond ever knew. John McGraw was also one of the great players of the game. But going beyond the cold figures that placed him at the top of his profession, it was his fiery spirit, his fertile brain, his driving force and his amazing energy that carried him, his team and the whole game of baseball to a high peak."—John Kieran, New York Times

Courtesy NBL

many old ball players would be given some kind of job at the Polo Grounds, almost as if they had earned pensions. Among these was the nineteenth-century slugger, Dan Brouthers, who served as a pressroom attendant and night watchman from 1912 until his death in 1932.

For all his crustiness and authoritarianism, McGraw could work with very young ball players. Snodgrass was a twenty-year-old when he joined the Giants; Hoyt was a teenager and Mel Ott ★ was a sixteen-year-old with an odd way of lifting his right leg, almost like a pitcher as he swung. Others might have changed Ott's style, but McGraw perceived that however singular the boy's moves, they made him a powerful hitter. And when an excellent graduate of Fordham Uni-

versity with a degree in chemistry and a national reputation as a collegiate football and baseball star signed with the Giants, McGraw recognized that although he and Frank Frisch ★ had the sort of temperaments that inevitably clashed, the Fordham Flash could make an important contribution to Giant hopes.

McGraw won ten pennants and three World Series. But after 1924, he seemed to have lost his touch. No matter how he shifted players, no matter what he paid, he could not put together a winner. Babe Ruth had demonstrated that one no longer need strive for a single run through a combined effort. McGraw quit as manager in 1932, remaining with the team as club vice-president until his death in 1934.

One man rivaled John J. McGraw for managerial honors during the period, and for the most part he stands in vivid contrast to the man known as "Little Napoleon," a fitting description for the diminutive Giant despot. The best they could come up with for his opposite number in the American League, Connie Mack, was "The Tall Tactician," a bland label that probably owes more to an alliteration-happy sportswriter than to anything else. Yeasty anecdotes about McGraw abound; there is a paucity of tales about Mack. He eschewed controversy and preferred to spend his nights home with the family rather than carousing with the writers, coaches, and convivial souls of the sports world.

Where McGraw brought to bear a coruscating profanity, Mack spoke rather gently to his athletes, addressing them as "Mr. Groves" (the actual name was Grove), "Mr. Plank," or occasionally by their baptismal names as a father might do. When he disagreed with an interpretation by an umpire, Mack would ask the official to step over to the dugout. "The man looked safe to me, Mr. McGowan," Mack once mildly protested to an umpire.

"No, Mr. Mack," replied McGowan, respecting the courtesy shown him. "He was out. I wouldn't lie to you, Mr. Mack."

"No, you wouldn't, Mr. McGowan," responded Mack, thereby completing a dialogue that certainly never ensued between McGraw and an official. While McGraw wore a uniform that enabled him to charge onto the field for verbal combat with umpires, once Connie Mack assumed his managerial role full-time he dressed in a suit, usually black or gray with a starched shirt and stiff collar and necktie. In the spring and fall he wore a derby hat; a straw boater garnished his head in summer and as a concession to heat he might shuck his coat and sit in his vest or, if really oppressed by the temperature, in his gartered shirt sleeves. Photo relics show the youthful Mack as thin, intense, jug-eared, his elongated neck surrounded by a high, thin collar. Most fans today remember a tall, ascetically slim, white-haired Mack in tie and shirt, the steward of a series of futile teams, the image of a benevolent grandfather whom time made obsolete.

Make no mistake—Mack fiercely wanted to win. The Mack whose catching tricks of tipping the hitter's bat, chattering to distract him, slapping his glove as if the ball had smacked into the pocket to mislead an umpire, and who was known to store the baseballs in a refrigerator to deaden them did not always strictly hew to the sportsmanship line. And like McGraw he was a profound student of the sport. He was celebrated for wagging his scorecard from the dugout to shift players; Wilfrid Sheed said he waved it as if the document were "a papal bull and lesser men were running." Sheed compared him to an Irish city boss operating from the dugout shadows, but Mack was more than just the power behind the scenes. He possessed an excellent understanding of who was likely to hit the ball where and he endowed his less strategically minded outfielders with that awareness.

Together the rowdy McGraw and the more genteel Mack helped make baseball a more respectable occupation. To be sure, McGraw perpetuated the image of the quarrelsome, profane athlete that contributed to the low esteem of ball players in the eyes of many respectable citizens. But McGraw insisted that his men go first class; he would not accept the old shabby rooming houses or seedy hotels. He argued that their calling deserved the same accommodations as those accorded professionals in any endeavor. As general manager and a small share owner, McGraw never skimped on salaries. He operated on the raw principles of businessmen during the era—win at all costs—but like some of his counterparts in other enterprises, he was soft-spoken, polite, a gentleman in the presence of women.

Mack's demeanor oozed respectability; a teetotaler and a nonsmoker who never swore, it was difficult to believe that such a gentleman could resort to low trickery. There was never a breath of scandal around him and he tended to rid the team of those who might consciously or otherwise sully the game. However, Mack was parsimonious to an extreme, selling off dynasties of stars twice during his long regime, ostensibly because Philadelphians became bored by winners (a condition that never seemed to afflict supposedly blasé New Yorkers).

While McGraw's minions for the most part feared or even hated him, Mack's gradu-

(Opposite) ". . . it would require at le years to tell about this glorious ol [Connie Mack] who has been baseball priest and patriarch, one of its f minds, its priceless ambassador, one sharpest businessmen. . . . The man ballplayer in the days when baseball roughneck's game and he did all right game. He was not a roughneck and n fane by habit, but on occasion he cou like any honest mule-skinner.

"He could be as tough as rawhide gentle as a mother, reasonable and ob. beyond reason, and courtly and bene and fierce. He was kindhearted and fisted, drove a close bargain, and wa ered in a hundred deals. He was ge and thoughtful and autocratic and sh independent and altogether complete able."—Red Smith, New York F Tribune

Courtesy NBL

The Mack trademarks: stiff collar a even in the heat of summer, and the gling scorecard to indicate fielder pos

Courtesy NBL

D. MURPHY. R.F.

COLLINS, CAPT. & 2. b

Mc INNIS. 1ST B

COOMBS, P

SHAWKEY, P

SCHA

CONNIE MACK, MGR
PHOTO COPYRIGHTED BY UNDERWOOD & UNDERWOOD

P. C.

SH. C.F.

OLDRING. L

BENDER. P

PLANK. P

E. MURPHY. R.F.

BAKER. 3RD. B.

THOMAS, C

PHOTOGRAPHS BY

UNDERWOOD & UNDERWOOD, N.Y.

Philadelphia Athletics

CHAMPIONS
of the
AMERICAN LEAGUE

ates almost invariably sang his praises even as they bemoaned his tight purse strings. Rube Bressler, a true utility man—he pitched, played first base, and outfielded during a nineteen-year career in which he hit .301—emerged with the Athletics in 1914 as a fill-in on the mound. He was gone after three years but his brief encounter with Mack left an indelible impression that he gave to Lawrence Ritter for *The Glory of Their Times.*

> Connie Mack. There was a wonderful person. A truly religious man. I mean *really* religious. Not a hypocrite, like some are. He really respected his fellow man. If you made a mistake, Connie never bawled you out on the bench, or in front of anybody else. He'd get you alone a few days later, and then he'd say something like, "Don't you think it would have been better if you'd made the play this way?"
>
> And you knew damn well it would have been better. . . . He knew what he was talking about. Never raised his voice. Never used profanity of any sort. Oh, he might say, "Good grief, look at that!"
>
> In my opinion, Connie Mack did more for baseball than any other living human being—by the example he set, his attitude, the way he handled himself and his players.

The Civil War was only in its second year and the Emancipation Proclamation that freed the slaves lay a year in the future when Cornelius McGillicuddy squalled to life in East Brookfield, Massachusetts. It was probably the last time in his life that Connie Mack ever raised an unseemly racket.

In his later years Mack remembered his introduction to his vocation:

> It wasn't exactly baseball, but a sort of rounders or town ball. With our bare toes, we drew two rings thirty feet apart with a batter in each ring. The pitcher stood outside the ring and tossed the ball to the batter. When the batter hit it, he ran for the opposite ring. He had to hit the ball out of the ring to be safe and keep his time at bat, and I can still recall the thrill of knocking the ball over the heads of the boys . . . not until I was older and bigger . . . we had a big bat and a leather-covered ball, three bases and a home plate.

As a twenty-two-year-old, the sapling-skinny Mack broke into the majors as a catcher for Washington. After he spent a

year with Buffalo in the Players League he returned to the good graces of the National League at Pittsburgh, serving as a player-manager, starting in 1894. He guided teams for the next fifty-three years.

Ban Johnson brought him to the American League, giving him a piece of the ownership in Milwaukee. When the club shifted to the City of Brotherly Love, Mack came as a minority stockholder. Ben Shibe, a businessman who also owned a chunk of the A. J. Reach Sporting Goods Company, was the principal investor.

Despite the loss of Lajoie, Mack still led his team to first place in 1902. The victory rested on a pair of pitchers, two men who seemed to have in common only their uniforms and their left-handed deliveries. Eddie Plank ★ represented the ideal ball player in Mack's eyes, an intelligent, well-educated, disciplined athlete. Plank went straight from graduation at Gettysburg College to the Athletics in 1901, proving himself immediately with 17 wins. And in seventeen seasons, all but the last three toiling for Mack, Plank totaled 327 triumphs. Only Warren Spahn ★ recorded more career wins by a southpaw.

The other chief contributor to the success of the White Elephants was of a violently different hue. George Edward Waddell, ★ already the despair of three teams and exiled to play on the Pacific Coast, was taken on by Mack against the advice of most experts. It wasn't that Waddell couldn't throw hard. The talent was obvious. But his behavior, variously ascribed to alcoholism, emotional immaturity, or retardation, exceeded the tolerable limits for most employers.

A farm boy from Butler, Pennsylvania, left-hander Waddell displayed an open, bumptious ignorance of the ways people were expected to behave. Naturally, he was nicknamed "Rube." He seemed equally passionate about baseball, fishing, fire engines, and matrimony. The last three interests occasionally seriously interfered with the first.

Rube Waddell pitched his first major league game for Louisville in 1897, losing 5–1 to a Baltimore squad that included four men who eventually entered the Hall of Fame. Despite that inauspicious debut a local reporter commented, "It looks like the club has made a good haul in the hayseed."

The bat-thin Mack of 1887 caught Washington Nationals.

Courtesy NBL

The following year, however, Waddell found himself in the minors, throwing for Detroit in the Western League. Sam Crawford, ★ the superb outfielder who went on to play center for the major league Tigers, remembered Waddell as a good-humored flake. He recalled Waddell becoming fearful that he might burn up the catcher's glove with his blazing fastball. Allegedly, to avoid the conflagration he would pour ice water over his left arm to cool down the deliveries. Said Crawford: "He was always laughing out there on the mound. That's because the other side tried to keep him in good humor, even when he was striking them all out. They figured he was tough enough to hit against when he was happy; get him mad and there was no telling."

When he was fined $50 for playing in a sandlot game with kids during his day off, Waddell deserted Detroit. He surfaced in Canada briefly before hiring on with Western League clubs, first in Columbus, Ohio, and then Grand Rapids, Michigan, for a total of 26 wins. In Grand Rapids, posters advertised Waddell's appearances to guarantee packed houses. He showed an early appreciation for the dramatic, arriving at the park just before game time, strolling through the grandstand to generate a commotion. Remembered Crawford: "He'd jump down onto the field, cut across the infield to the clubhouse, taking off his shirt as he went. In about three minutes—he never wore any underwear—he'd run back out in uniform and yell 'All right, let's get 'em.' "

The Louisville club was in Pittsburgh for the 1900 season and Waddell rejoined teammates like Honus Wagner and manager Fred Clarke there. Records indicate he was 8–13 and led the league with a 2.37 earned run average. But Rube stayed with Pittsburgh only part of the season; he had a losing record in the early months. Manager Clarke suspended him, upset with Waddell's undisciplined ways, his penchant for toting firearms on the road, and perhaps his lack of consistency. Waddell allegedly threatened, "Next time I see you I will shoot you full of holes." On that note he left for Punxsutawney, Pennsylvania, to play for an independent team.

Connie Mack was in Milwaukee with his American League entry and he obtained permission from Pittsburgh to use Waddell, who quickly won 9 and lost 3. In mid-August, Mack called on Rube for an extraordinary series of performances. On August 16, the lefty went 12 innings in a 3–3 tie. Three days later he pitched the opener of a doubleheader against front-runner Chicago. It was a 17-inning marathon but this time Waddell won 3–2. When he struck out the last hitter, Waddell exuberantly performed cartwheels on the mound. Mack, encouraged by his pitcher's zest, offered a proposition. If Waddell would pitch the second game he could have a three-day vacation for fishing. Waddell could not resist the invitation to indulge in two of his passions. Darkness trimmed the second game to only 5 innings but Waddell put away the enemy with one hit for a 1–0 win.

Newspapers widely covered his 22-inning stint. Among the readers was Barney Dreyfuss, owner of Pittsburgh, then fighting for the National League pennant. He insisted Fred Clarke repossess Waddell. Mack surrendered and Waddell chipped in 5 wins during the stretch drive. It was not enough; Brooklyn beat out the Pirates and Connie Mack also wound up second best after losing his most effective pitcher.

Waddell began anew at Pittsburgh in 1901 but Clarke could not deal with him; after he dropped his first two decisions, Pittsburgh dealt him to Chicago. He found the atmosphere there less than congenial and quit, announcing to sportswriters that he would rather play the piano in the streets of Chicago because "the piano can be made to play as you want it to." Thus he was in his self-imposed California exile when Mack, desperate for pitching, sought him out again. He joined the team, bearing a $1 paper suitcase and $40 worth of fishing gear.

He quickly established himself as a hero in Philadelphia, winning 24 games, losing only 7, and striking out 210 in a season that for him began at the end of June. Between August 22 and September 22, he won 12 out of 14 games he started, a feat unlikely to ever be matched. Actually, combining his time in Los Angeles and his efforts in Philadelphia, he won a total of 35 and whiffed 344. He followed up that year with seasons of 21, 25, and 26 wins, including 349 strikeouts for 1904.

George "Rube" Waddell won 130 games for Mack but not even the wily Mack could control him.

Courtesy NBL

Because McGraw and the National League huffily refused to grant their counterpart equality, Waddell lost his opportunity to pitch in a 1904 World Series. He squandered his other chance when the White Elephants took the 1905 pennant because he dislocated a shoulder in September during a wrestling match with teammate Andy Coakley.

In his naive way, Waddell once bragged that he would give thirty-seven-year-old Cy Young the same treatment he had administered to another Red Sox pitcher whom he bested with a one-hitter. Said Young later: "I'd been watching him. He was a damned fine pitcher, but he ran his mouth quite a bit. I figured he was calling me out and I had better do something about it." What Young did was toss a perfect game with only 6 balls leaving the infield, and Waddell wound up a loser.

Neither failure nor success changed Waddell's character. Philadelphians delighted in a star who would show up at saloons, don a white apron, and work the bar. On other occasions he would appear at playgrounds to play ball with worshipful kids or he might be found at local firehouses, chatting with the fire fighters.

Showmen capitalized on his popularity. One autumn, he starred in a stage play, *The Stain of Guilt.* A critic remarked:

> Mr. Waddell is one of the finest examples of the strenuous actor now appearing before the public gaze. He is in fact so strenuous that the management has to curb him. He is "let out" for only two minutes in each scene—and the ensuing damage is awesome to behold.
>
> Mr. Waddell's capabilities are numerous. He is taller than James K. Hackett, has larger feet than Richard Mansfield and can throw a villain twice as far as Kyle Bellew.

He was forced to abandon his stage career when the second Mrs. Waddell sought to attack his wages for nonsupport.

During his short life Waddell frequently alternated between the roles of buffoon and hero. Within the space of three days one February, Waddell was cited for preventing a serious fire in a crowded department store after he picked up a blazing oil stove and carried it from the building, but then he was forced to flee town because the police wanted to charge him with having assaulted and badly injured his father-in-law. And then he was arrested for bigamy and locked up. When a teammate named Danny Hoffman was struck in the head by a pitch, everyone stood there uncertain of what to do. Waddell picked up the unconscious player, carried him out an exit, hailed a cab that took them to a hospital. Waddell stayed at the bedside, in uniform, ministering cold compresses until Hoffman began to recover.

His fielding was the despair of teammates and manager. One researcher of his career claims he lost close to 50 games because of bobbled bunts and wild throws to first. And there were suspicions that his sprees and sulks limited his effectiveness. A 1907 headline disparaged him as a "Disgrace to Game." The account claimed:

> . . . [he] disgusts patrons and players, booting games to unworthy opponents. Manager Mack could easily find cause to suspend him indefinitely and it would not be a difficult matter for the powers that be to set a trap for him to expel him from baseball. One of these days there will be an awful baseball scandal and Waddell will be the chief actor.

There were hints he could be bought by gamblers and that the injury allegedly incurred while horsing about with Coakley was actually a cover-up for a scheme by heavy bettors to ensure a win by the Giants. No evidence supported the accusation. But even Mack eventually despaired of the man he subsequently rated faster than even Robert Moses Grove, ★ who brought pennants to Philadelphia during Mack's second reign of power some twenty years later. He dished Waddell off to St. Louis and the hard living showed its toll; Waddell dropped to 33 wins in a little more than two seasons with the Browns. In 1912, he was visiting in Kentucky when floods swept the area. Waddell spent hours in icy water up to his armpits stacking sandbags to fortify levees. The exposure brought a severe infection that later developed into tuberculosis, which ended his life at age thirty-seven.

Waddell departed from the Athletics just before Mack put together the first of his two great teams. The Macksters, who won the pennant in 1910, 1911, 1913, and 1914,

"*Rube Waddell, the gigantic south* the Philadelphia Athletics, is a wo pitcher and has recently furnished pre he is now capable of pitching the mo liant baseball of his entire career. . . claimed for him that the striking ou teen men is a new record for a 9-innin . . . 8 of the strike outs were in succe . . . Waddell is a wonderful pitcher, is more wonderful when he does not pitch."—New York Globe

Courtesy NBL

"*Eddie Collins is the best ball player* seen during my career on the dian —John McGraw

Courtesy NBL

taking the Series in three of these campaigns, relied on pitching from Chief Bender, Plank, Jack Combs, and Joe Bush, and what was known as the $100,000 infield.

Mack had carefully nurtured the infield quartet; they grew into their positions, developing confidence with bat and glove. One team member, shortstop Joe Barry, never quite flowered as expected, and first baseman Stuffy McInnis, although a lifetime .308 hitter after nineteen seasons in the majors, was outshone by the others.

Second baseman Eddie Collins ★ and third sacker Frank Baker ★ bloomed magnificently; they were prized specimens grown by Mack and he was rewarded well for his husbandry. A Columbia College student, the chunky Collins starred there in football as well as baseball. In the fall of 1906, Collins, using the alias "Eddie Sullivan," appeared for the Athletics in 6 games on the road. College authorities heard of the new Athletic phenom and confronted Collins with photos of him playing major league ball. That ended his college ball but upon graduation he joined the Athletics team in earnest. Mack converted him from a shortstop into the regular second sacker for Philadelphia in 1908. From 1909 through 1914, Collins hit from .322 to .365, although never enough in that era for a batting title. He preferred to edge close to the plate; pitchers could not readily coax him to swing at a questionable pitch and he had that ability to hit balls where they were pitched, spraying base hits to all areas of the park. For a man who stood 5'9" and weighed a hefty 175, he flashed surprising speed, ranking third in total stolen bases until supplanted by Rickey Henderson in the late 1980s. His quickness in the field puts him at the top in career number of lifetime assists, putouts, and chances. (Admittedly very few others in the game lasted twenty-five seasons.)

The one-time prelaw student, according to a contemporary observer, was generous with his opinions: "His face is always open, and some of these days he will inhale a grounder if he isn't careful." Collins vocally encouraged and judged his associates' play. His self-assurance brought him the nickname "Cocky."

Frank Baker, a greener specimen whom

Mack plucked from the peach and cantaloupe fields of Maryland after a strong season with Reading (Pennsylvania) in the Tri-State League in 1909, finally curbed his tendency to overthrow first, and took over third. Barry also became the shortstop that year, with McInnis taking the field for the bulk of the season in 1911, and the triumphant Athletics opened a 13½-game gap over Detroit, making it two pennants in succession.

The World Series that year gave the Athletics an opportunity to avenge the sneers of McGraw after the 1905 meeting. Jack Combs, who'd won three for Philadelphia the previous year against the Cubs, pitched one victory, Chief Bender took a pair, and Plank the fourth. But the standout was Baker, whose homer in the second contest broke up a 1–1 tie, and whose second shot into the seats in the ninth inning of game three off Mathewson tied the score and allowed Philadelphia to win in the eleventh. Reporters hung the nickname "Home Run" on Baker, who led the American League that year with 11. Baker took his reputation seriously enough to repeat as home-run king for 1913 and 1914, with the grand totals of 12 and 9.

Mack's club finished second in 1912 but was back on top for the next two seasons. In the 1913 Series, the Athletics again cut the Giants down with Baker good for only a sole homer but a .450 average. Collins was only slightly less effective, hitting .421 while stealing three bases. But even the $100,000 infield, plus pitchers Bender, Plank, and a twenty-year-old boy wonder named Herb Pennock, ★ could not overcome the Miracle Boston Braves of the 1914 season who had resurrected themselves from the cellar in mid-July on the wings of a 34-wins-in-44-games flight.

After being swept 4 in a row by the Braves, Mack dismembered his team. He explained in *Sporting Life:*

> The claim has been made that I broke up my team for the sake of economy. In fact you cannot convince some people that I did not. . . . Before last season the boys thought only of victories, but when the Federal League [a third major league organized in 1913] agents started offering salaries all out of proportion, they forgot there was something else besides

"Never did a young slugger live up to his reputation more than Baker in the World's Series of 1910. The Mackmen surely did punish the sphere most barbarously in that event and Baker was one of the stalwarts hitting the Cub boxmen for an average of .409. . . . Baker is a solid sort of an athlete, hates publicity, and was rather bashful when he first came to Penn's town on the Delaware, and though he has not much to say on the diamond, he plays with his heart and soul in his work. He is always in the game, in the thick of every play, and does not know the word 'quit.' Many a time with the Mackmen far behind, a long-distance swat from 'Bake's' war club has put the White Jumbos back in the game."—Fred Lieb, The Baseball Magazine

Courtesy NBL

Left-hander Eddie Plank, a graduate of Gettysburg College, won 285 games for the Athletics, another 42 as a deserter to the Federal League in 1915 and with the St. Louis Browns from 1916 to 1917.

Courtesy NBL

Frank "Home Run" Baker strides
ball while Roger Bresnahan rises f
catcher's squat.

Courtesy NBL

money in the world. . . . Money had nothing to do with the breaking up of my team, except that I saw the time had come when some of the players thought of nothing but money, and sooner or later the team must go to pieces . . . there was no chance for me to hold any of the players I let go. They were responsible for the breaking up of the famous machine, and not the club or its policies.

In fact, Mack sold Collins to the White Sox for $50,000, top dollar for baseball flesh until the Yankees bought Babe Ruth ★ in 1920. Mack exchanged Jack Barry and Herb Pennock for about $10,000 from the Red Sox; Bender and Plank both succumbed to the fiscal charms of the Federal League; Frank Baker sat out the entire 1915 season because he and Mack could not come to terms and he joined the Yankees in 1916. Only McInnis remained an Athletic for several more years. Fifteen desolate, second-division years elapsed before Mack once more dominated the baseball scene.

86

Above all others, with the possible exception of Wagner, the benchmark for excellence on the field during the first two decades of the twentieth century was Tyrus Raymond Cobb. To baseball he brought a vaulting desire unmatched then and probably impossible to sustain today. Donald Honig wrote: "He was tough, aggressive, unforgiving, contentious, mean-spirited, bigoted. And that, according to the evidence of some, was his sunny side." A teammate said every time Cobb batted "was like a crusade."

Ossie Bluege was a rookie third sacker for the Washington Senators when Cobb at age thirty-six came racing toward the bag. The ball reached Bluege while Cobb was still several yards away. Bluege moved up the line, crouching for the tag. Recalled Bluege:

He didn't slide. He just took off and came at me in midair, spikes first, about four or five feet off the ground, so help me just like a rocket. He hit me in the upper part of my arm, just grazing the flesh but tearing open the sleeve. I made the play. I tagged him out, but I was so mad I was going to konk him with the ball while he was lying on the ground. But Billy Evans, the umpire, pulled me away. Then he threw Cobb out of the game for making such a vicious slide.

A day later, Cobb approached Bluege and apologized, adding he hoped the infielder was unhurt. However, his face darkened, the pale blue eyes glittered, and he warned, "Never come up the line for me."

They may have hated Cobb but all recognized his incredible talent. Jimmy McAleer, manager of the St. Louis Browns and Washington Senators, called him "the wonder of baseball, the greatest piece of baseball machinery that ever stepped on a diamond."

Comiskey rated him "the greatest player of all time . . . plays ball with his whole anatomy, his head, his arms, his hands, his legs, his feet." Casey Stengel, ★ who began as an outfielder in 1912, labeled Cobb as "the most sensational player I ever saw."

Sam Crawford, a teammate, detested him, but defended his style to Ritter: "They always talk about Cobb playing dirty, trying to spike guys and all. Cobb never tried to spike anybody. The base line belongs to the runner. If the infielders get in the way, that's

their lookout." Crawford contended that Cobb added a dimension to the sport: "There were others who were faster . . . Cobb was so fast in his *thinking*. He didn't outrun them. He outthought them!"

The pair had a play where with Cobb on third and ball four thrown to Crawford, the latter would trot partway toward first and suddenly on signal from Cobb break into a sprint, round the bag, and head for second. Nonplussed, opponents might hurriedly try to cut Crawford down. If the peg went toward second, Cobb, creeping off third, broke for home. If the foe held the ball to keep Ty from scoring, Crawford wound up at second.

Cobb described baseball as "not unlike a war. If we cannot only beat them but run wild on them in addition, treat them like a bunch of bush leaguers, it is liable to put them up in the air for a week." On another occasion he growled: "Baseball is a red-blooded sport for red-blooded men. It's no pink tea, and mollycoddles had better stay out. It's a struggle for supremacy, a survival of the fittest."

A child of the Reconstruction South, Cobb coupled the violent streak of the Georgia redneck with a yearning for the niceties of antebellum days where menials knew their place and nonwhites had none. His father, William H. Cobb, a North Carolinian from a respectable family fallen on hard times, bootstrapped himself from a humble start as a small-town teacher, to educator, newspaper publisher, and businessman.

W. H. Cobb preferred the title of "professor" and thought baseball an unworthy pursuit, but when his headstrong son insisted on seeking a career in the game, he installed the first of the furies that drove Ty. "Don't come home a failure," admonished the parent.

The son's response: "My overwhelming need was to prove myself as a man." Perhaps aware of his boy's volatile temper, the father also counseled: "Be good and dutiful, conquer your anger and wild passions . . . be guided by the better angel of your nature . . . not the demon that works in all human blood . . . ready and anxious and restless to arise and to reign."

Cobb was an eighteen-year-old minor leaguer in 1905 when his mother Amanda fatally blasted W. H. Cobb with a shotgun. The husband had secretly returned to his home

(Following page) *"Baseball was changed by Babe Ruth. The sport belonged to Ty Cobb . . . until Ruth took it away from him. There is small doubt that Cobb was the greatest of all players, though some of his contemporaries held out for either Ruth or Honus Wagner. Their opinions may have been formed by hate.*

"The game, as practised by Cobb, was a ceremony of deceit and brutal recklessness. He slashed other people with his spikes and fought them with his hands. But his precise skills were neglected when Ruth permanently altered baseball with the home run. It was as if a violin virtuoso attempted to compete with a brass band on the same stage. . . . The cruelty of Cobb's style fascinated the multitudes . . . but it also alienated them. He played in a climate of hostility, friendless by choice in a violent world he populated with enemies. Other players resented his calculated meanness. Their respect was reluctant but they were forced to present him with the trophy of their crabbed admiration. . . . He was the strangest of all our national sports idols. But not even his disagreeable character could destroy the image of his greatness as a ballplayer. Ty Cobb was the best. That seemed to be all he wanted. I wonder."—Jimmy Cannon, New York Post

Courtesy NBL

Jimmy Austin of the New York Highlanders in 1909 swipes a too-late tag at third. "[Ty Cobb] would climb a mountain to take a punch at an echo."—Arthur "Bugs" Baer

Courtesy NBL

After Ty allegedly slashed Home Run Baker in 1909, even Connie Mack called him a dirty player. Years later, Cobb wrote a letter about the photograph of the event: "I have resented this charge since 1909. He is clearly on the offensive, blocking me away from third base. I am on the inside trying to get to the bag. My foot has passed by his arm and yet his arm was not knocked aside. I am trying only to reach the bag with my toe. He had a slight cut on his forearm, never lost an inning of play. Cobb was a dirty spiker— look how far I am inside the bag."

Courtesy NBL

89

one night from a purported business trip. The shooter claimed she mistook her husband for an intruder. Some surmise his intent was to trap his wife in an affair. Less than three weeks after the slaying, the Detroit Tigers brought up the youngster, and on August 27, he appeared in the first of his 3,034 games.

Still agonizing over his idolized father's mysterious death, Cobb suffered the slings, arrows, and subtle japes of his teammates. They sawed his bats in half, ripped up his hat, locked him in a hotel bathroom, and the northerners, aware of Cobb's emotional attachments, ragged him unmercifully about his origins. He assumed the mantle of Johnny Reb, resisted the clique, fought his fellow Tigers with his fists (as well as other players, fans, and anyone else).

On the field he also absorbed punishment. Norman Arthur "Tabasco Kid" Elberfeld, shortstop for the New York Highlanders, jammed his knee into Cobb's neck and shoved his face in the dirt during an unsuccessful try to steal second. Cobb insisted unconvincingly: "I was just a mild-mannered Sunday School boy. But those old-timers turned me into a snarling wildcat."

In his autobiography, *My Life in Baseball*, Cobb asserted that only twice in his career did he deliberately seek to slash a man. One intended victim was a Cleveland catcher who "roughed me up when I slid into home." Cobb said he missed the target but the catcher took the lesson to heart. The other case involved Boston Red Sox pitcher Hub Leonard:

> [He would] aim bullets at your head, left handed to boot. . . . I dragged a bunt . . . which the first baseman was forced to field. Leonard sprinted for first to take the throw and saw that I was after him. He didn't stop at the bag, kept right on going, into the coaching box, which looked like safe territory to him. He wouldn't have been safe that day if he'd scrambled into the top bleachers. I ignored the bag—since I was already out—and drove feet first right through the coaching box. He managed to duck, but . . . the escape was close enough medicine for him. He never threw another beanball at me.

After Cobb mauled Home Run Baker at third in a game in Philadelphia, even mild-spoken Connie Mack called him "the dirtiest player the game has known." The natives from the City of Brotherly Love became so restless that 250 cops stationed themselves in front of the fans who ringed the field in right. On fly balls curving to the foul line, Cobb found himself grazing among policemen.

His reputation for ferocity increased when he started packing a pistol except while in uniform. When three Detroit toughs tried to stick him up he assaulted them. In a difference of opinion with a hotel watchman who swung his club, Cobb rebutted by stabbing him. No one could doubt his competitive toughness after he had his tonsils removed one morning in a Toledo hotel room (by a doctor who shortly took up residence in an insane asylum) and that afternoon played in an exhibition game, although his throat bled for three weeks.

The young Cobb quickly caught the fancy of press and public. His aggressive style produced heroic plays and foolhardy gambles that dismayed his early managers. That first partial season in Detroit he batted only .240, but he rose to .320 in 1906 and .350 the following year, his first as a full-time regular. The *New York American* spoke of his "superbly insolent confidence in himself." *Sporting Life* praised him as an "infant prodigy," "a sensational fielder and thrower," although in truth his arm was never special. Joe Jackson of the *Detroit Free Press* in 1906 first cast him as "The Georgia Peach."

As his touch with bat and glove markedly improved, Cobb substituted brains for sheer energy. He noticed shortstops habitually failed to cover for a third baseman fielding a sacrifice bunt; Cobb shook them up by going from first to third on such plays. He artfully interposed his body in the way of outfield throws, shutting off an infielder's sight of the ball or guilefully allowing it to bounce off him. He sought to score from second on groundouts and gambled heavily on steals. Being thrown out never fazed Cobb; he believed his free-running attitude forced errors and wild throws. What some perceived as reckless abandon were actually calculated pieces of strategy. He was perhaps the first to perceive that if he charged a ball he added velocity to his throw. He caught runners on first trying to reach third on a

Cobb with the bat; a split-handed gr everything from the bunts to power—his strength, late in his career he clo homers in 2 consecutive games.

Courtesy NBL

single to him in right. He even threw out a hitter who seemingly singled but loafed down the baseline.

Using a split grip with the bat, Cobb seldom missed contact; he struck out only 357 times in 11,429 times at bat, an average of fewer than 15 times a year. To pull to right he brought the top hand down; to slice to left he split his grip more. Until Pete Rose passed him, Cobb held the record for hits in a career with 4,191. His .367 remains the top lifetime batting average; his 892 stolen bases, with 35 swipes of home, is second only to Lou Brock. No one has scored more runs, and he is fourth and second, respectively, in doubles and triples. His .367 lifetime average is 9 points ahead of his nearest competitor. He led his league twelve times in hitting; three times he rose over the .400 mark. Detractors fault Cobb as a singles hitter but late in his career, in 1925, he resolved to demonstrate power; the result was 5 homers in 2 games.

Cobb against Walter Johnson was a classic duel. Cobb crowded the plate against the Senator star whose fearsome sidearm fastball he said "looked about the size of a watermelon seed and it *hissed* at you as it passed."

For his part, Johnson said of his foe: "If you put the ball on the outside where he likes it, he will drop it into left field. Keep it inside and he is liable to kill your first baseman. About the best way to fool him is to get the ball up there faster than he can get his bat around."

Unlike the less sophisticated Wagner, Cobb exploited his success at the bargaining table and off the field. He quickly ascended to the highest salary of the day, topping out at $50,000 as a player-manager in 1920. He took to the stage in a vehicle entitled *The College Widow*. Cobb became the first ball player to star in a movie, a drama by Grantland Rice, *Somewhere in Georgia*. The script concerned a baseball-playing bank clerk kidnapped on the eve of a big game; Rice may have originated the hoariest of sports melodramas. Cobb endorsed a chewing gum, a brand of suspenders, and underwear. He associated with financiers and industrialists, golfed with President William Howard Taft, visited President Woodrow Wilson in the White House, invested wisely in real estate

and securities, and owned an auto dealership. His best investment was in an Atlanta-based soft drink, Coca-Cola.

Age did not soften Cobb's furies nor wither his prejudice. In a 1917 exhibition against the Giants he spiked Buck Herzog during a steal of second. Later he beat up Herzog in a hotel room brawl. After a shouting confrontation with McGraw in the lobby, he refused to take the field against the Giants, huffing: "McGraw is a mucker and always has been and I don't intend to stand for his dirty work." When the Tigers faced the Yankees in 1924, Cobb baited them so roughly that even a mild-mannered new recruit, Lou Gehrig, ★ tried to fight him.

His on-field brawls irked baseball governors and they could not ignore his most infamous skirmish. In 1912, Cobb entered the stands in New York to assault a particularly abusive heckler. Horrified at the attack on a paying customer, who also happened to be physically handicapped, a hack politician, and a newspaper employee, officials promptly suspended Cobb. Fellow Tigers, for once, rallied to their teammate and refused to play while Cobb was under suspension. Manager Hughie Jennings scurried about and signed up a collection of collegians and sandlotters to avoid a forfeit. A seminarian bent on the priesthood pitched and his fellows received $10 per man for the game. The lambs in Tiger skins lost to the Athletics 24–2. The travesty sat poorly with Ban Johnson. He canceled a game scheduled for the next day and threatened to permanently bar every Tiger on strike. Cobb urged his teammates to get back in uniform and the drama petered out. But he continued to brawl, beating up a black groundskeeper and the man's wife, and felling a black member of a street-paving crew who complained when Cobb walked over freshly poured asphalt.

In 1928, at age forty-two, Cobb hit .323 in 95 games with Mack's Athletics and then retired. It was his second year in Philadelphia after having served as a player-manager with the Tigers from 1921 to 1926. The best he could do for Detroit was to bring them in second in 1923; he lacked the temperament for a field boss.

Charlie Gehringer first came across Cobb in spring training and for a time the older man smiled at him:

A newspaper hired Cobb to lend his name for 1911 World Series coverage and he posed with his temperamental opposite, Mathewson.

Courtesy NBL

Hugh Jennings was the shortstop for the Orioles in the days of McGraw. As the Tiger manager he gave Cobb free rein and was famous for his cry of "E-yah," a tight condensation of his original cheer, "That's the way." Jennings explained he first tacked on an exultant "ah" at the end, then cut away all but the drawn-out addition.

Courtesy NBL

He treated me like he was my father, sat with me on the trains and he told me all of the ways of hitting and the secrets of base running. He made me use his own bat which was a very thin handled job. I preferred something a little bigger, but he insisted that Heinie Manush and I use his bat. They were good bats, the best wood.

In spring training he was hollerin' at us infielders to "live it up out there" and in spring training you don't have much life; it's so hot and you're just putting in your time. I came back to the bench and I says, "I'm makin' as much noise as anybody else out there" and whether that was the thing that started me off or him off, from then on it was downhill.

One of the first things he ever said to me was if so and so or some guy you thought liked you but couldn't do anything for you, there's no use having him as a friend.

Gehringer added, "He put in 100 percent. If anybody got in his way, why you're in trouble. And maybe that's what got him where he is." Gehringer believed the zeal "took a lot out of him as far as being a human being. . . . You can't turn that kind of competitive drive on and off. He was the same off the field as he was on; he was always fighting with somebody. He was a holy terror."

Others brought to the game the religion of winning baseball but none combined the skills and fanaticism of Ty Cobb. Jimmy Cannon offered a fitting epitaph on the occasion of Cobb's death: "He was the strangest of all our national sports idols. But not even his disagreeable character could destroy the image of his greatness as a ballplayer. Ty Cobb was the best. That seemed to be all he wanted."

Few approached his level of play during or after his era. On his own club, Sam Crawford, from Wahoo, Nebraska, who deserted the barber trade, achieved one record unlikely ever to be broken: 312 triples in his nineteen major league years. The 3-base hit is the one offensive blow that has suffered a severe decline over the years. Stan Musial, ★ with 177 triples, is the only ball player since 1950 to break into the top twenty for career totals. The first nine names all quit playing before 1930.

Crawford is regarded as a preeminent bomber of the dead-ball period. Twice he was out front in home runs, including a sensational (for those days) 16 in 1901 with Cincinnati. During his nineteen seasons he smashed a total of 97 compared with 96 credited to Home Run Baker. (Unsung is Gavvy Cravath, who amassed 119 homers in fewer than eleven full seasons with a high mark of 24 for the Phillies in their pennant-winning 1915 year.)

Most notable as a rival to Cobb was Texan Tris Speaker, who broke in with the Boston Red Sox in 1907, two years after Cobb's debut, and laid down his bat with Cobb in 1928. His major league batting average was .344, 23 points below Cobb, but as a center fielder he had no peer. With a career that began in the dead-ball period, Speaker played extraordinarily shallow, so close that some referred to him as the fifth infielder. Only Willie Mays ★ caught more fly balls. In the 1912 World Series against the Giants, Speaker turned an unassisted double play at second; in April 1918, he performed that feat twice.

Oddly enough, Speaker credited a pitcher with helping him learn his trade. Cy Young, in the twilight of his baseball life, schooled the raw Speaker:

> He'd take me out on the practice field and hit fungos to me by the hour. I got to watching, and studying his fungo swing, and by doing that I could start after the ball before he actually hit it. It later served a good purpose when I started playing regularly center field. By closely observing the batsman at the plate after he had reached a certain arc in his batting swing, I knew whether the ball would go to the right or left, and I could also gauge the power of the swing. In that way I got the jump on the ball.

Because he stationed himself so close to the bag, Speaker sometimes covered second in an obvious bunt situation, thereby freeing up the shortstop or second baseman for the infield play. His strategic defense initiatives made him the all-time leader in assists from the outfield.

With his hair silvered prematurely and since he so swiftly glided in pursuit of fly balls, Speaker earned the nickname "The Gray Eagle." His strong left-handed throws were all the more remarkable since "Spoke" was not a natural southpaw. Only after he

A natural righty, Tris Speaker switc[hed to] the other side of the plate as a child [when a] bronco threw him, breaking his coll[arbone] and right arm.

Courtesy NBL

"To say that Tris Speaker revolut[ionized] outfield play wouldn't be quite right [because] the suggestion would be that the fame[d Gray] Eagle of Boston and Cleveland set a p[attern.] The fact is, he didn't. He broke the [mold.] Neither before nor since has an ou[tfielder] played so shallowly as Speaker did [in the] course of nearly twenty-two big leag[ue sea-] sons."—Bob Broeg, Sporting News

Courtesy AP/Wide World

broke his right arm twice while taming Texas broncos did he switch. So successful was the change that Speaker actually began his base-ball career as a pitcher. As a minor leaguer with Cleburne in the North Texas League, Speaker lost his first 6 games, however, and the manager converted him to an outfielder. From Cleburne he progressed to Houston where his .315 average and 33 stolen bases in only 84 games attracted a $750 bid from Boston.

He came to the major leagues late in 1907. Management was unimpressed with the nineteen-year-old rookie who produced only 3 singles in 19 at bats. The following spring Speaker toured training camps look-ing for a job. No club showed interest and finally Speaker paid his own way to Little Rock where the Red Sox were preparing for 1908. When the major leaguers broke camp to head north, the Red Sox left Speaker with the Little Rock team in lieu of a $500 bill for use of the local grounds. However, Boston added a proviso that for an additional $500 it could reacquire Speaker. When he ravaged Southern Association pitching for a .350 av-erage, Boston retrieved its modest invest-ment. Speaker began slowly, but starting in 1909 he hit over .300 for eighteen of twenty seasons, the last thirteen with Cleveland, Washington, and finally Philadelphia.

Just shy of six feet tall and weighing 193 pounds, Speaker held his bat low, pumping it up and down before he cocked it about hip high. His technique limited his strikeouts to a total of 220, about 10 a season. The style also produced sharp line drives and Speaker leads the all-time doubles hitters list with 793.

During his Indian days, he also managed for six years. In his first full year as player/boss, the 1920 pennant race pitted the Yan-kees, the White Sox, and Speaker's crew. Late in the season, Chicago and Cleveland had split the first two of a 3-game set. In the last game, the White Sox loaded the bases with two out. Joe Jackson drove the ball to the deepest corner of right center. Speaker broke quickly and raced after it. He timed

his leap perfectly, soaring into the air to make the catch while crashing into an un-padded concrete wall. He lay unconscious for several minutes, still clutching the ball for the out. The Indians went on to win the pennant and then conquer Brooklyn in the World Series with Speaker hitting .320.

Like Cobb, he was devoted to his mother. After the final out in the 1920 Series, Speaker raced in from his center-field post, pausing long enough only to snatch the ball from shortstop Bill Wambsganss (who'd made the only unassisted triple play ever in a World Series), and climbed into the stands. Pushing aside the fans, he fell into the out-stretched arms of his mother who once had consulted lawyers about a suit to prevent baseball from selling her boy for $750 like "slavery."

A few years later, however, Speaker and his pal Cobb would be drenched by the fall-out from the Black Sox scandal, with the same Hub Leonard whom Cobb tried to lac-erate as a central figure (see Scandals). Speaker and Cobb would finish their careers together in the Athletic outfield. They were still able to hit but were creaky shadows of themselves when forced to chase balls.

But Speaker spent his first years centering a marvelous outfield. In 1909, a stocky, one-time pitcher and civil engineer from Califor-nia, Harry Hooper, came to Boston. Accord-ing to Hooper, he was persuaded to move East in 1909 by John J. Taylor, the Red Sox owner who dangled the possibility of Hooper practicing his profession while playing some ball. He quickly established himself as a fielding star, covering the turf in left. When Duffy Lewis arrived a year later, the triumvi-rate that kept the Sox contenders was in place. In 1914, they began to share some playing time with a hard-throwing left-handed pitcher who could also hit, George Herman Ruth. But the Babe did not become a serious outfielder until 1918, and it was another two years and another team before he was totally converted. Hooper claimed he had urged management in Boston to trans-form the pitcher into an everyday outfielder.

Speaker startled everyone after the final out of the 1920 World Series when he clambered into the box seats to buss his mother.

Courtesy NBL

"Harry B. Hooper, right-fielder of the Bos-ton Red Sox and one of the original 'Speed Boys' who will be the first man to toe the plate in the big fracas, is one of the very best men in the country to lead off a batting order."—Philadelphia Inquirer

Courtesy NBL

Baseball offered a way out of the drudgery of the mines, an escape from the farm, and a chance to work outdoors rather than in dank factories. Minuscule as the wages were in comparison with the pay of modern ball players, they were better than what most could earn off the diamond. But while the game promoted by A. G. Spalding, Ban Johnson, and other movers and shakers beckoned to white men, it barred those of color. The sport drew its strength from the Northeast and Midwest rather than the South, and black men were not welcome almost from the start.

In 1875, Congress, still flushed with emancipation zeal, passed a Civil Rights Bill. The measure decreed full and equal access to transportation, accommodations, and places of public amusement. But in 1883, the U.S. Supreme Court declared the act unconstitutional, thereby opening the way for the Jim Crow statutes of the South and the de facto discrimination in the remainder of the country. Not surprisingly, only a few years later, professional baseball firmly slammed the clubhouse door on black players.

Ironically, Cooperstown, the site designated by the Mills Committee as the cradle of baseball, also is the hometown of the first black professional, John W. (Bud) Fowler, born in 1854, who played for a team from New Castle, Pennsylvania. *Sporting Life* said of Fowler, "If he had a white face he would be playing with the best of them." A handful of other nonwhites also took the field. Sol White, a former third baseman in the Ohio State League, wrote a 1907 history of men of his race in the game and claimed that by the mid-1880s there were at least twenty in organized baseball.

Among these were Ohio-bred Moses Fleetwood Walker and his brother Welday. Sons of a physician and students at Oberlin College, the Walkers obviously were better educated than most of those who pursued the sport for pay. Fleet Walker distinguished himself as a catcher, and when a syndicate created a team based in Toledo, he was the second man recruited. Toledo took the Northwestern League championship in

1883, and on the strength of that record, the club was invited to join the American Association, then regarded as a major league. Thus Walker and his brother, who played the outfield, became the first black major leaguers.

His presence was not universally welcomed. During a game in Louisville he received more than his share of jeers, which the *Toledo Blade* attributed to outrage over his race. Perhaps unnerved, Walker committed an unusual 5 errors. When Toledo traveled to Richmond, the manager received a communique that threatened a mob assault on Walker. The possible confrontation was avoided when Walker was released before the Richmond trip because of injuries. However, according to Robert Peterson in *Only the Ball Was White,* Baltimore and Washington applauded Walker's appearance.

During the 1884 season, the first concerted effort to bar blacks came from Cap Anson and Spalding's Chicago White Stockings. The club journeyed to Toledo for an exhibition but Anson announced he would pull his team if Walker played. A. G. Spalding had written letters to the Toledo club supporting the position of his manager and warning of the consequences. However, Toledo refused to accede, and rather than forfeit its share of the gate, Chicago backed down. Three years later with Walker and black pitcher George Stovey as the battery for Newark in the International League, Anson seized the opportunity of another exhibition game to reiterate his stand. Newark bowed to the pressure; instead of the "African" battery as Stovey and Walker were known, a pair of whites faced Chicago. Later in the same year, Anson again forced Newark to keep its nonwhites out of the game.*

Other teams also balked at meeting blacks on the field. All but two of the St. Louis Browns petitioned against a contest with the Cuban Giants because of their racial makeup. (Charlie Comiskey was one of the pair who refused to sign the document.) Several teams experienced great internal strife fomented by whites. The Syracuse Stars recruited hands from the defunct Southern League and several players offered less than

Cap Anson threatened to withdraw h[...] cago White Stockings if Toledo insis[...] playing its catcher, Fleet Walker.

Courtesy NBL

(Opposite) *Oberlin College in Ohio [...] a baseball team in the early 188[...] included two blacks, Moses Fle[...] Walker (10) and his brother Welda[...]*

Courtesy NBL

---

*Because the white-owned press generally ignored the segregation of organized baseball and provided scant coverage of the Negro teams and leagues, and the limited nonwhite publications lacked resources for detailed reporting, facts are often uncertain. An excellent account of the early days was done by Jerry Malloy in the Fall 1983 issue of *The National Pastime.* Books packed with information on the subject include: *Only the Ball Was White* by Robert W. Peterson, *Voices from the Great Black Baseball Leagues* by John Holway, *Get that Nigger Off the Field* by Art Rust, Jr., and *Invisible Men* by Donn Rogosin. More recent events get detailed treatment in *Baseball's Great Experiment* by Jules Tygiel.

minimal support in the field to their black pitcher Robert Higgins. So blatant was the lack of effort that the Stars lost to Toronto 28–8, with 21 unearned runs. Newspapers carried tales of the "Ku Klux coterie" and the "boycott against Higgins." The troubles caused the League directors in a secret session to instruct the Secretary "to approve of no more contracts with colored men." Several newspapers excoriated the decision; the *Binghamton Daily Leader* said the league "made a monkey of itself when it undertook to draw the color line." The *Newark Call* editorialized:

> If anywhere in this world the social barriers are broken down it is on the ball field. . . . the best man is he who plays best. Even men of churlish dispositions and coarse hues are tolerated on the field. In view of these facts, the objection to colored men is ridiculous. . . .

Even in the game's first organized incarnation, the 1867 National Association of Base Ball Players specifically prohibited the signing of blacks because of "the possibility of any rupture being created on political grounds." (For eighty years baseball people hid behind the same rationale.) The International League directive was not rigidly enforced but gradually nonwhites were excluded. And in major league ball the color line was never inscribed in the National Agreement but it remained part of baseball's unwritten canon until 1946.

Although 1887 is regarded by such authorities as Sol White as the year in which the systematic exclusion of blacks from organized baseball began, some blacks foresaw their proscription. During 1886, the Southern League of Colored Base Ballists, with headquarters in Jacksonville, was announced but it was stillborn. However, that same year, a Pittsburgh entrepreneur formed the National Colored Base Ball League. Sol White and Welday Walker both played for the league but it died after only a matter of days. Dreams of separate but at least equal ball vanished completely.

In 1895, Booker T. Washington, as president of all-black Tuskegee Institute, proposed to avoid conflict through separation of the races "in all things that are purely social" and that struck most as applicable to baseball. The 1896 *Plessy* vs. *Ferguson* ruling of the U.S. Supreme Court held "separate but equal" acceptable. The United States now picked up the pace toward segregation and inequality and baseball fell into step without qualms.

There were several cases in which blacks sought to pass and play. Vincent Nava, born Irwin Sandy, allegedly was a nonwhite who held spots with Providence and Baltimore from 1882 to 1886. George Treadway, who took the field with Baltimore, Brooklyn, and Louisville from 1893 to 1896, may have been a black man posing as an Indian.

Black athletes formed independent teams that barnstormed through the country, meeting one another and on occasions in places such as Cuba, meeting traveling all-star major leaguers in pursuit of a few extra bucks after the regular season. For the outsiders, it was a difficult existence. Sol White figured the average salary of a black player in 1900 as $466—below the $571 earned by white minor leaguers and far beneath that of major leaguers paid about $2,000 a season.

Some managers and owners seemingly toyed with the idea of breaching the color barrier. A notable case involved John McGraw, then with the Orioles. Supposedly, while his team was in spring training in Hot Springs, Arkansas, in the spring of 1900, McGraw spotted Charlie Grant, a bellboy at the Eastland Hotel, in a sandlot game. Many young blacks doubled as menials for such establishments while playing in a hotel league during the winter and spring. Baseball historian Lee Allen claims McGraw informed Grant: "Charlie, I've been trying to think of some way to sign you for the Baltimore club and I think I've got it. On this map there's a creek called Tokohama. That's going to be your name from now on, Charlie Tokohama and you're a full blooded Cherokee."

American Indians were acceptable. But Charles Comiskey among others refused to fall for the deception. "I'm not going to stand for McGraw ringing in an Indian on the Baltimore team. Somebody told me that the Cherokee of McGraw's is really Grant, the crack Negro second baseman from Cincinnati, fixed up with war paint and a bunch of feathers."

McGraw protested his innocence but Charlie Grant never joined the Orioles and was condemned to a respectable career with

John McGraw unsuccessfully tried off Charlie Grant as an American "Grant, Stovey, Walker, and Higg are good players and behave like gen and it is a pity that the line shoul been drawn against them."—Sportin 1888

"If anywhere in this world the soc riers are broken down it is on the bal There, many men of low birth an breeding are the idols of the rich an tured; the best man is he who play Even men of churlish dispositions and hues are tolerated on the field. In these facts, the objection to colored ridiculous. If social distinctions are made, half the players in the country shut out. Better make character and pe habits the test. Weed out the toug intemperate men first, and then it ma order to draw the color line."—N Call, 1887

Courtesy NBL

the Negro teams of the period. (McGraw undoubtedly acted only out of a desire to win; some thirty years later he was the one notable baseball figure in an informal poll, taken at a dinner, who opposed the entry of blacks to the game. A prominent sportswriter of the time, Joe Vila, actually praised McGraw as the only fellow with "the guts to say that Negroes should not be permitted to play on teams with white men.")

The Negro teams of the early 1900s formed mainly in the Northeast. The status of clubs was precarious as entire leagues sometimes collapsed within a single season. Games often took place twenty-five to thirty miles from a railhead, necessitating travel on broken-down primitive buses, hay wagons, even drays with nothing but a few boards on a flatbed. Negro teams circumvented blue laws that kept major league teams from playing on Sundays. In New York, for example, the Lincoln Giants charged no admission but grandstand patrons were expected to pop for a half-dollar program and a quarter in the bleachers. The fans paid but no programs were issued.

H. Walter Schlicter, a white businessman, created a powerhouse team, the Philadelphia Giants. In 1906, Charlie Grant played for the club along with a burly Texan, pitcher Andrew "Rube" Foster. ★ An alleged member of the club was Jack Johnson, a massive first baseman from Galveston destined to achieve his fame as world heavyweight champion only a few years later. But the star of the club was Foster. Born in 1879, Foster quit school after the eighth grade to earn his living amid the rowdies of baseball, not an easy decision for the son of a church elder who enforced a strict code of behavior. He grew to 6'4", weighing well over 200 pounds, and relied solely on his heavy-muscled fastball. He had begun his career with the Waco Yellow Jackets but Frank Leland spotted his talent during a game in Hot Springs and recruited Foster for his Chicago Union Giants.

In the tradition of his home state, Foster packed a pistol, a habit that endured throughout his career. Coupled with his volatile temper, this gave him a fearsome reputation. Cautioned that he would now face the stiffest competition including occasional forays against whites, Foster allegedly answered, "If you play the best clubs in the land, white clubs . . . it will be a case of Greek meeting Greek. I fear nobody."

In Chicago, the newcomer scored an early triumph but then fell upon frustrating days as opponents learned to time the fastball. He bounced from club to club before realizing he would have to add to his repertoire and learn to exploit hitters' weaknesses. That expertise earned him Honus Wagner's encomium for his baseball smarts. After observing Foster on the mound, Frank Chance declared him "the most finished product I've ever seen in the pitcher's box."

By 1903, he was good enough to lead the Cuban X Giants to victory over the Philadelphia Giants in 4 of the 5 wins for the "colored championship" of the world. That in turn earned him a post with the losers. During an exhibition against the local white Athletics, Foster supposedly outpitched Waddell, and like a knight in an ancient joust, thus appropriated the loser's nickname. For all their success, the Philadelphia Giants received very little reward, and in 1906, Foster led a band of eight to Chicago and the Leland Giants.

He quickly demonstrated an ability as a showman that matched his skills on the mound. Foster substantially increased receipts through his bookings for the club; Leland agreed to give the field hands half the gate. According to John Holway, holiday doubleheaders that had brought a man $150 now put as much as $500 in his pocket. Three years after he emptied the Philadelphia Giants of their best he returned to the well and carried off the black Honus Wagner, John Henry "Pop" Lloyd, as well as a fine young catcher, Bruce Petway. Foster then managed the Leland Giants to an incredible 123 (or 126 by some accounts) wins in 129 games. Some were undoubtedly gained at the expense of ragtag sandlotters, but there were 22 consecutive victories against the best outfits in New York City, and 6 straight in Cuba where the top white players appeared in postseason all-star battles.

Foster duplicated the strategy of McGraw, playing for the single run with the walk, the stolen base, the bunt, and the hit and run. One opponent remembered a Foster team that bunted for 7 innings until it beat the

"Rube Foster is a pitcher with the tricks of a Radbourne, with the speed of a Rusie, and with the cool of a Cy Young. What does that make him? Why the greatest baseball pitcher in the country—that's what the great baseball players of white persuasion who have gone against him say."—Chicago Inter-Ocean

Foster became an entrepreneur who almost single-handedly kept the Negro Leagues alive.

Courtesy NBL

(Following page) John Henry "Pop" Lloyd, labeled "the black Honus Wagner," played in Havana among other cities.

Courtesy NBL

Frank C. Leland (in suit) *put together his Chicago Leland Giants early in the 1900s with Foster* (back row, far right) *as pitcher, manager, and booking chief. "Race prejudice exists in professional baseball ranks to a marked degree, and the unfortunate son of Africa who makes his living as a member of a team of White professionals has a rocky road to travel."*—Sporting News, *1889*

Courtesy NBL

enemy. And like his white counterpart with the Giants, Foster abrogated to himself the powers of decision—". . . push it here, hit by the first baseman, hit over there. He directed your play all the time," recalled third baseman Dave Malarcher.

After that sensational 1910 season, Foster broke with Leland and joined forces with a white tavern owner to create the Chicago Union Giants, which quickly became the best nonwhite team in the area. Aside from contests against similar outfits, Foster arranged games against white teams that featured such stars as Joe Tinker and Johnny Kling, the Chicago Cub catcher, recognized as organized baseball's first Jewish star. (He changed his name from Kline to avoid anti-Semitism.) For such exhibitions, Tinker and Kling picked up an extra $100 to $150.

The best of Foster's men, along with other U.S. black players, joined forces with a handful of Cubans for a Havana series against the 1910 World Champion Detroit Tigers, led by Ty Cobb. According to John Holway's research, catcher Bruce Petway threw out Cobb every time he attempted to steal. Furthermore, over the 11-game tour, which the Tigers won 7–4, Pop Lloyd, Grant Johnson, and Bruce Petway all hit for better averages than either Cobb or his redoubtable teammate Sam Crawford. Never again did Cobb play against nonwhites.

But ability to compete against the best in organized baseball was not enough. With the exception of boxing, where Jack Johnson thumbed his gloves in the eyes of outraged Caucasians, sports remained closed to men of color.

By the time the National and American leagues consummated their marriage through the 1903 World Series, with Honus Wagner and Fred Clarke in attendance for the losing Pittsburgh Pirates, and Cy Young and Jimmy Collins for the victorious Boston Red Sox, pitchers possessed a full armory. The overhand fastball evolved naturally as delivery gradually rose from its originally mandated underhand style. Candy Cummings had introduced the curveball; Edward "The Only" Nolan had perfected the overhand curve. Fred "Tricky" Nichols and Tommy Bond were credited with a drop or sinker. Bobby Mathews offered a variety of curves and some said he and Charles Sweeney threw an "indrop" or fadeaway, which was popularized by Christy Mathewson and was in reality a screwball. A. G. Spalding and then Tim Keefe had mastered the "slow ball" or change of pace and imparted the art to Amos Rusie. All of these relied only on grip and body mechanics. But the urge to improve on nature spawned baseball alchemists, scientists who through the addition of an alien substance to the ball cover, transformed a humdrum pitch into a golden phantom. Among the tinkerers was Elmer Stricklett, a less-than-mediocre thrower whose seminal discovery was the effect of moisture, in particular saliva, upon thrown balls.

Stricklett reached the major leagues with the White Sox as a twenty-eight-year-old rookie in 1904 and he lasted for only 7 innings there before plodding off to Brooklyn for three more unimpressive years. But while in Chicago, Stricklett passed on his knowledge to his roomie and fellow rookie, Big Ed Walsh, ★ a strapping former laborer in the Pennsylvania coal mines.

Until then, armed only with an undeviating fastball of which hitters grew increasingly fond, Walsh struggled to control his spitter. In midseason 1906, Walsh achieved mastery of the pitch. His club ran off a 19-game winning streak in August, with Walsh accounting for 7 wins, including 4 shutouts. The Sox went on to upset the favored Cubs led by Frank Chance in the World Series and Walsh tossed 2 of the victories.

He swaggered for 151 wins in the following six seasons—writer Charles Dryden described the confident Walsh as "the only man who could strut while standing still"—a spree marked by 40 wins in 1908. In a last-pitch, futile try to gain the pennant that year, Walsh even captured two complete games of a doubleheader 5–1 and 2–0 at the end of the season. During this performance he yielded a single walk, statistical proof of his spitful art. It was the second time in his career that Walsh won in a twin bill. (The more renowned 2-games-in-a-day pitcher, "Iron Man" Joe McGinnity, recorded 5 doubleheaders in which he took both games three times, splitting the other pairs, but he owed his nickname to his previous vocation in a foundry.)

Walsh contended that his wet ones arrived at the plate with four different breaks: "I could break the ball down and away, straight down, down and in and up. To get the rise I threw underhand but the other three pitches were thrown with the same motion as my fast one." Walsh explained his motions and tactics:

> When I loaded up the spitter I kept the glove in front of my mouth so I could bluff the pitch. I didn't throw the spitter on every pitch. I managed two or three to every hitter. The other times I relied on my fast ball which I threw with the same motion. I'd grip the ball with the fingers close together and the thumb underneath. I let the ball slip from under my wet fingertips. Learning the release is the trick.

How effective was the trick? Sam Crawford, whose lifetime batting average stands at .309, faced Walsh often: "I think that ball disintegrated on the way to the plate and the catcher put it back together again. I swear, when it went by the plate it was just the spit went by."

The spitter offended some players such as Frank Chance. He was particularly incensed after a visit to Buffalo where Bison pitcher George McConnell injured three catchers who tried to capture the wet ones. Chance also argued too much time was wasted while infielders tried to wipe off a ball before heaving it. Other officials and guardians of the game denounced it as unsanitary and as a menace to fielders because the ball would slip in their fingers as they tried to throw it. Both charges lack validity; by the time a spitter arrived for its meeting with bat or

"Walsh is one of the most wonderful p[...] *that the game has ever developed. Sho*[...] *become permanently crippled tomorr*[...] *crippled that he could never again wie*[...] *little white sphere through which he g*[...] *his fame, this remarkable athlete woul*[...] *down through history as one of the g*[...] *masters of his art. His name would be* [...] *with those of Christy Mathewson ar*[...] *Young, men who cheated time and con*[...] *their cunning through twice the span* [...] *ordinary pastimer's day of major leagu*[...] *fulness."*—Cincinnati Enquirer

Courtesy NBL

glove the moisture was long gone. The anti-spitter crowd officially dried up baseball in 1920, the very year in which Walsh finished his career with a stint as a minor leaguer in Bridgeport (Connecticut) of the Eastern League. After 1920, only pitchers still active that season and who had used the spitter before could continue to throw it.

Although he tossed a no-hitter against Boston in 1911, Walsh believed his best game was one he lost. On October 2, 1908, Walsh idled time before a game in Cleveland, supplying the tenor for a barbershop quartet. The quartet included Chicago teammates: lead singer Nick Altrock, an adequate left-hander who achieved fame as a baseball clown in partnership with Al Schacht (a bit-part major leaguer); baritone Doc White, who won 190 games as a pitcher, mostly with the White Sox; and the ace of the Indian staff, a long-armed righty bass, Addie Joss. ★ Suddenly, when it came time to warm up for the game, Walsh was surprised to see Joss preparing to pitch. The eponymously baptized White Sox manager, Fielder Jones, then ordered Walsh to get ready.

Walsh struck out fifteen Indians; he insisted he should have received credit for a sixteenth but the scorer took away one because of a dropped third strike. Indeed, the game turned on this pitch. In the Cleveland third inning, lead hitter Joe Birmingham singled. Walsh picked him off but when Birmingham desperately ran toward second, the throw from a fill-in first baseman hit the runner in the back and rolled away, allowing Birmingham to reach third. Walsh then whiffed the next two batters and he had two strikes on weak-hitting Wilbur Good. Walsh, still furious, threw an extra-strength spitter that fooled not only the hitter but also broke catcher Ossie Schreckengost's index finger and bounded back to the grandstand. By the time Schreckengost retrieved it, Birmingham had scored. It was the only run of the game, for Joss threw a perfect game to shut out the Sox. Two years later the unfortunate Joss died of pneumonia. In his relatively brief nine years in the majors, Joss produced 160 wins and the second best all-time earned run average of 1.88. His demise, incidentally, brought about baseball's first All-Star game, a 1911 charity affair for the benefit of his widow.

During Walsh's tenure with the White

Sox, Ring Lardner began his career as a Chicago sportswriter. In one memoir he recalled that the flinty Fielder Jones grunted: "We'll get along okay as long as you don't keep pestering me about who's gonna pitch the next day. Anything drives me crazy, it's the newspaper guys all the time wanting to know who's gonna pitch tomorrow." Lardner responded: "My paper will be satisfied if I'm right about half the time. I'll just pick Walsh every day."

Inasmuch as Big Ed set a record with 66 starts in that 1908 season, Lardner's answer was close to the mark. Walsh's brash, opinionated style and his lack of formal schooling—he entered the mines at age eleven—served as fodder for Lardner's creation of the great fictional ball player, Jack Keefe. (Other major league sources of inspiration for Lardner included Boston pitcher Hub Perdue and White Sox manager Kid Gleason.) In typical Jack Keefe fashion, Walsh once met a woman in a Pullman dining car who expressed admiration for his physique. He ingenuously answered, "Yes, but you should see me stripped."

In his own league, Walsh contended for pitching honors with Connie Mack's pair of aces, righty Charles Albert "Chief" Bender and the southpaw Eddie Plank. A Chippewa Indian, Bender left a reservation in Minnesota at age eight to attend a Philadelphia school operated by the Episcopal Church and funded by the federal government. Although the institution aimed to benefit destitute white and Indian kids, it was also designed to orient the American natives away from their traditional way of life. The youngsters learned the trades of shoemaker, baker, carpenter, and the like. In Bender's case, the effort to wean him away from his background succeeded. At age thirteen he returned to the reservation, but after two months fled to the Carlisle Indian School, later the alma mater of the great Olympian and brief major leaguer, Jim Thorpe. At Carlisle, Bender discovered baseball and as a nineteen-year-old graduate he joined the Athletics in 1903. Curiously, in a period when the likes of Ed Walsh would win as many as 40 in a season, Bender surpassed 20 only twice, but consistently finished seasons with a high ratio of wins to losses. His lifetime earned run average is 2.46.

But the best of them all journeyed to

Charles "Chief" Bender spent twelve years toiling for Connie Mack before jumping to the Federals in 1915. After an eight-year absence he made a brief final appearance in a White Sox uniform in 1925.

Courtesy NBL

(Following pages) *A benefit for the widow of Cleveland pitcher Addie Joss brought together an American League All-Star team in 1911. The back row, left to right:* Bobby Wallace, Frank Baker, Red Sox pitcher Smoky Joe Wood, Walter Johnson, Highlander first sacker Hal Chase, Washington outfielder Clyde Milan, Highlander pitcher Russ Ford, and Eddie Collins. *The front row, left to right:* Washington infielder Germany Schaefer, Tris Speaker, Sam Crawford, Joss's friend, former Cleveland outfielder Jimmy McAleer, Ty Cobb, Washington catcher Gabby Street, and Cleveland catcher Paddy Livingston.

Courtesy NBL

"*Beaten, held in check through eig[...] nings, helpless before the speed of [...] quard, the Red Sox rallied desperately [...] ninth, threw the Giants into panic, an[...] most routed Marquard. . . . And b[...] Marquard's excellent pitching the C[...] were playing clean, hard and fast ball great crowd of thirty-five thousand s[...] the situation, and with the seventh it r[...] thunders of cheers, howling its hope [...] Red Sox, urging them on. . . . It was a[...] ate work down there, and the players [...] beginning to show the pains and wour[...] fierce strife.*"—Hugh S. Fullerton, [...] York Times*

Rube Marquard left the Giants in [...] and, although he pitched another ten y[...] never achieved the success he enjoyed [...] McGraw.

Courtesy NBL

Labor Day, 1916, poster hyped face-o[...] tween Reds manager and pitcher Math[...] and the Cub marvel, "Three Finger" B[...]

Courtesy NBL

major league baseball from birth in Humboldt, Kansas, through a childhood in the wilds of Los Angeles, and finally a part-time career as a telephone company post hole-digger and pitcher for the Weiser, Idaho, minor circuit club. Walter Johnson first suited up as a Washington Senator in 1907. "Barney," or "The Big Train," in tribute to his sidearm fastball, Johnson labored his entire twenty-one major league seasons in Washington, and not until 1924 were his efforts crowned with a World Series appearance. Only Cy Young's 511 wins beat Johnson's total of 416; his 279 losing efforts, which put him third in that dubious derby, emphasize both the incredible number of games he pitched and the futility of pitching for his club.

The dominant figure of the National League pitchers was of course McGraw's pet, Christy Mathewson, with his career total of 373 wins. The Giants also muscled their way to honors via the strong arm of Richard William "Rube" Marquard. As a boy in Cleveland, Marquard hung out around the ballpark: "When I was about thirteen I used to carry bats for Napoleon Lajoie and Elmer Flick [an outfielder who hit .315 over thirteen years] and Terry Turner and a lot of the other Cleveland Indians. They weren't called the Indians then. They were called the Cleveland Bronchos and then the Naps. . . . sometimes I'd be their batboy."

Marquard's father was the city's chief engineer and like so many better educated parents of the period he regarded his son's fascination for baseball as rampant foolishness. By age sixteen, Marquard was determined to become a big leaguer. Although he'd never been away from home, he hopped a freight train, bummed rides, and slept in open fields for five days and nights in hopes of a shot with the Waterloo club in the Iowa State League. A day later he won his first pro game against Keokuk, but after the Waterloo manager refused to offer a contract, the homesick Marquard returned to the freight yard for a trip back to Cleveland.

There he worked for an ice cream business and pitched for the company team. The Cleveland team spotted his talent, but when they offered only $100 a month, as much as he earned from the ice creamery, Marquard negotiated a $200-a-month deal with Indianapolis in the American Association. Op-

tioned for a year to Canton, he returned to Indianapolis for the 1908 season. Opening day he outpitched another eighteen-year-old wunderkind, Smoky Joe Wood of Kansas City. According to Marquard, a sportswriter compared him to another famous lefty, Waddell, and thus originated his "Rube."

Cleveland now sought to buy his contract but Marquard, still stung by their earlier parsimony, said he'd quit before he'd play for them. After a brilliant season in Indianapolis with 28 wins, 47 complete games, including a perfect one, and leading the league in strikeouts, Marquard agreed to his sale to the Giants for $11,000, supposedly the top sum paid for a player at that time.

Marquard gave the club three consecutive seasons of more than 20 wins (1911–1913), the years the Giants represented the National League in the World Series. However, not even his 2 wins in 1912 could save the New Yorkers from dropping all three championships. His independent streak inevitably led to confrontations with McGraw and eventually, after a mediocre year, Marquard engineered his trade to Brooklyn where he helped win two pennants for the Dodgers.

The strongest contenders against the Giants, the Chicago Cubs, relied not only on Tinker, Evers, and Chance but also on a farm boy who surrendered the tips of two fingers of his right hand to a feed cutter and mangled several others. Mordecai Centennial "Three Finger" Brown ★ (born July 4, 1876, exactly one hundred years after the Declaration of Independence) exploited his handicap with a grip and release that saw the spin imparted mainly by his thumb, giving him one of the nastiest curveballs ever to frustrate hitters. His 100 victories helped put the Cubbies of 1906, 1907, 1908, and 1910 into the World Series, and his lifetime ERA of 2.06 is the game's third best.

The man who ranks third among major leaguers in total victories started his major league life in 1911. Named for the U.S. president at the time of his 1887 birth, Grover Cleveland Alexander ★ grew up on a farm near St. Paul, Nebraska, as one of twelve boys in a thirteen-child family. Legend holds that he honed his pitching skills bringing down chickens or turkeys with well-aimed rocks.

Alexander deserted the farm for a job

"Scribes throughout the country are just about convinced that Grover Alexander is the greatest pitcher in the world today. . . . Alexander is a greater pitcher than [Walter] Johnson, in the opinion of this writer, because there is more versatility to the Nebraskan. When in his prime Johnson was unhittable because of his terrific speed. When his fast ball was not working good Johnson was not hard to hit, as he never had much of a curve. Alexander, on the other hand, has a fast ball that has as much, if not more of a break to it, than that of Johnson, though not quite so fast; and added to this the Nebraskan has the best curve ball of any pitcher in the game today. Add to this Alexander's wonderful control, and a slow ball that is just as good as any pitcher possesses, and it will be easy to see that the Philly star is the king of pitchers."—Chandler D. Richter, Sporting Life

Courtesy Wayne Guthrie, *Indianapolis News*

stringing telephone lines, relying on semipro ball to supplement his income. He graduated to the minors at Galesburg, Illinois, where his career halted abruptly. On a day when he was not pitching but playing right field, he opened the eighth inning with a single. The next hitter hit a sharp grounder to the second baseman who flipped to the shortstop for the force. The subsequent throw to first smacked the onrushing Alexander squarely between the eyes. Unconscious for more than two full days, he awoke with double vision. When he returned to the baseball diamond, the superb control was gone. Galesburg fobbed him off on Indianapolis, and Indianapolis then shipped him home to the farm.

There Alexander stubbornly battled to overcome his visual defect, throwing to anyone willing to catch. Later he said that if he quit he knew he would "go to pieces." With the 1910 season on the horizon, Indianapolis dealt him to Syracuse. A few days before he was to report, his body finally yielded to his desire. Throwing in the St. Paul schoolyard, Alexander suddenly regained the power to focus. He toted up 29 wins for Syracuse and the Phillies bought his contract.

With pinpoint accuracy for his breaking fastball, his sidearm curve, and his change of pace, Alexander won 28 as a rookie and a total of 190 games in seven years with the Phils before World War I interrupted his career. His 31 victories in 1915 powered the club to its first World Series. He pitched the only game won against the Red Sox and lost 2–1 in another. The following season Alexander boosted his wins to 33 including 16 shutouts. And in 1917, "Old Low and Away," as a later teammate Jesse Haines ★ —himself a formidable pitcher—imaginatively dubbed him, had another 30 victories. Moreover, Phillie home games were played in Baker's Field with the right-field fence a mere 239 feet from home.

Among the qualities marveled at by colleagues was the all-business approach of Alexander. Said Rube Bressler: "An hour and a half, an hour and three-quarters and the game would be over. Game after game, he'd pitch in an hour and a half. No fussing around out there, no stalling, no waste motion, no catchers and infielders always running out to the mound to tell him he's in trouble and just making matters worse."

Supposedly, after Cleveland took the first game against the Reds in 1916, Phils manager Pat Moran apologetically asked him to handle the closer due to the imperatives of a train schedule. In fifty-eight minutes he shut out the Reds 4–0. Opponents were deceived by his seeming casualness; he barely warmed up before the start of a game. Said Frank Frisch: "He had such an effortless motion, his fast ball sneaked. You'd get set, but it would be by you, in the catcher's mitt. He mixed his pitches like nobody before or since, and if you tried to guess with him, you were a cinch to lose."

Achilles only had a flawed heel; the chinks in Alexander were more numerous. Perhaps from birth, or maybe after the accident with Galesburg, Old Pete suffered seizures. He would pass out on the bench and some accounts claim he once suffered an attack just as he threw a game-ending pitch. Teammate Hans Lobert remembered:

> Maybe two or three times a season he'd have an epileptic seizure on the bench. He'd froth at the mouth and shiver all over and thrash around and sort of lose consciousness. We'd hold him down and open his mouth and grab his tongue to keep him from choking himself. It was awful.
>
> After we'd gotten him down we'd pour some brandy down his throat and in a while he'd be all right. It always happened on the bench, though, never out on the pitching mound. We always kept a bottle of brandy handy because there was never any warning.

Other reports mention a bottle of ammonia kept for the purposes of restoring the stricken pitcher. Players aware of the condition protected him from publicity about the problem; the newspaper stories of the period occasionally refer to his lust for whiskey but never his illness. The brandy sluiced down his throat was hardly the right remedy in light of his flaming alcoholism. The intensity of his ailments increased after Alexander served in the trenches of World War I with an artillery unit, which blasted his hearing and added headaches to his troubles.

Bressler remarked: "Somebody said if Alex didn't drink he'd probably have won more games. I don't see how he could have been any *better*. My God, he won over 30 three years in a row. How much better can you get? Maybe drinking *helped* him. Maybe

In full kit, buck sergeant Grover Cleve Alexander sails for the trenches as a m of the American Expeditionary Force

Courtesy NBL

Captains Mathewson and Cobb serve gether with a chemical warfare unit. A gled practice for a gas attack dest Christy's health.

Courtesy NBL

it let him relax." (The mythology on the healing powers of alcohol is among the ingloriousness of the times.)

Alexander never apologized for his insobriety: "I don't feel sorry for myself, or excuse my drinking. I guess I just had two strikes on me when I came into the world. My father back in Nebraska was a hard drinker before me, and so was my grandfather before him. Sure, I tried to stop—but I just couldn't."

When he returned from World War I, Alexander found himself traded. He would still win more than 170 games and the most memorable performance of his career was yet to come. The Phillies also rid themselves of Eppa Jephtha Rixey ★ a few years later and he turned in 179 victories for Cincinnati. The Phillies by these measures self-destructed, leading to eons of wandering the deserts of the second division.

Other big leaguers also marched off to war. Christy Mathewson, already washed up as a pitcher and dished off to Cincinnati in 1916, enlisted. Along with Ty Cobb he received a captain's bars. During a chemical warfare training exercise in France, by error eight men died of gas and a number of others, including Matty, received severe doses. The accident weakened his lungs, leading to his death in 1925. Another former Giant, Harvard grad Eddie Grant, fell to enemy fire in the Argonne Forest. Navy blue and olive drab replaced gray and white uniforms on the likes of Casey Stengel, Harry Heilmann, ★ Eddie Collins, and Rabbit Maranville, ★ but on the whole, except that 1918 saw the season end a month earlier as a concession to the demands of the war effort, baseball incurred few wounds from World War I.

By the time the German armies and the Allies lay deadlocked in France, American baseball already was engaged in its own small war. It was, like the larger conflict, grounded in economics and the course of empire. For both wars, the right of self-determination served more as a tactic than as a true rallying point.

With attendance swollen to new heights and baseball frenzy producing handsome profits, several wealthy businessmen in 1913 sought to cash in with the organization of the Federal League of Professional Clubs. The tyro league president James Gilmore ap-

proached Ban Johnson to inquire whether organized baseball would admit his group to the National Agreement governing the sport. Johnson, now the insider rather than the parvenu of 1901, haughtily answered, "There was not room for three major leagues."

Operating on the principle that if you can't join 'em, lick 'em, the Federals declared war. They erected stadiums in their eight franchise cities—Baltimore, Brooklyn, Buffalo, Chicago, Indianapolis, Kansas City, Pittsburgh, and St. Louis. Far worse, in the eyes of the establishment, was an assault on the holiest of holies, the reserve clause of organized baseball. The new league announced that it was unenforceable under U.S. law and started to sign top players with lucrative inducements. The legal argument was a simple, logical one; the purpose of the reserve clause was to exert monopoly control over talent. To give teeth to its reserve provision, the National Agreement also stated that any player who signed with a club not covered or who even entered into negotiations would be ineligible to play in the majors for at least three years.

Lawyers busied themselves with briefs. Players cheered the inevitable consequences: bidding for their services. Establishment figures huffed dire warnings with Ban Johnson in the role held by A. G. Spalding during the aborted Players League uprising of 1890. In an interview with the *New York Evening Sun*, the head of the American League demanded unconditional surrender: "There can be no peace until the Federal League has been exterminated. . . . [We] will fight these pirates to the finish. There will be no quarter. . . . I've heard that peacemakers are at work, but they are wasting their time. The American League will tolerate no such interference."

Johnson pronounced the newcomers "a joke," ridiculing their ballparks, asserting they were broke, and scoffing: "They have many unknown players, taken off the lots . . . a bunch of Bush Leaguers with a sprinkling of big fellows."

The Feds actually hired eighty-one major leaguers and 140 from the minors, all covered by the National Agreement. But the biggest names were stars dimmed by age—Mordecai Brown and Joe Tinker from the Cubs, Eddie Plank and Chief Bender from the Athletics. Supernovas of the game ex-

In 1917, Brooklyn, the National League champs, trained at Hot Springs, Arkansas. The pyramid includes (middle row, right) *stellar outfielder Zach Wheat.*

Courtesy NBL

GIANTS vs. WHITE SO

WORLDS SERIES 1917

NEW YORK · CHICAGO

Brush Stad
Polo Grou

© UNDERWOOD & UNDERWOOD

PRESIDENT WILSON THROWING OUT BALL AT THE OPENING OF TH
AMERICAN LEAGUE SEASON AT WASHINGTON.
A BIG ENOUGH BOY TO ENJOY THE NATIONAL
GAME –AND– A MAN BIG ENOUGH TO GUIDE–

(Top) *The 1916 Phillies practiced in Florida. Notable fence sitters were Joe Oescheger (center) who went the distance in a 1919 20-inning marathon, 9–9 draw against Burleigh Grimes of Brooklyn. A year later Oescheger sweated a 26-inning, 1–1 tie against the Dodgers' Leon Cadore while with the Boston Braves. At extreme right lounges pitcher Eppa Jephtha Rixey, a 266-game winner over twenty-one seasons.*

Courtesy NBL

(Bottom) *Brooklyn owner Charles Ebbets, puffed with pride over his clean-shaven stalwarts, overextended himself building the park that bore his name, and lost control of the club to the McKeever brothers. Note the rookie shot of Charles Dillon Stengel directly beneath Ebbets's right.*

Courtesy NBL

(Opposite) *The United States entered World War I just as the 1917 baseball season began. Wilson, a devout fan, continued the tradition of throwing out the first ball begun by his predecessor, William Howard Taft.*

Courtesy NBL

ploited their advantage. Ty Cobb bumped his pay from $12,000 to $20,000 a season. Even the unassertive Walter Johnson was on the verge of accepting a deal that included a $10,000 bonus for his signature when Washington Senator owner Clark Griffith persuaded his wealthier compatriot, Charles Comiskey of the White Sox, that the loss of Johnson would diminish Chicago attendance. Comiskey agreed to match the prospective bonus and Johnson stayed put. Ban Johnson made no move to enforce the three-year suspension theoretically due the Big Train for dealing with the outlaw league.

The Federals played a full season in 1914, and while initial fan reaction was strong, the league fell well below the gates drawn by the rival leagues. Throughout the year, disputes about contracts bounced through various courts, eliciting conflicting decisions. The newcomers launched their biggest offensive, an antitrust suit. They were encouraged when the Chicago judge assigned to the case was Kenesaw Mountain Landis, ★ notoriously hostile to trusts. Landis deliberated slowly, so slowly in fact that events rendered the case moot.

Even though Indianapolis captured the Federal League title in its first year, owner Harry Sinclair, later a central figure in the Teapot Dome oil scandal of the Harding Administration, transferred the club to Newark for 1915. More than twenty-seven thousand attended the first game there but doom stalked the league. The Brooklyn entry ended the season $800,000 in the red; bankruptcy enveloped both Kansas City and Buffalo.

To salvage something from their investments, Federal League head Gilmore, Brooklyn owner R. B. Ward, and Sinclair concocted an audacious scheme. They rented offices in Manhattan, bought an option on vacant land, and hired a firm to draw plans for a 55,000-seat stadium in New York as a 1916 venue. The trio mounted an impressive enough bluff to decoy National League officials into a settlement offer. The terms allowed owners of Federal League players to sell the contracts to the highest bidders; the blacklist would not be enforced. Ward received a settlement that amounted to $400,-000 for his Brooklyn interests and Pitts-

burgh franchisees $50,000. Chicago Federal League owner Charles Wheegman obtained the right to buy the Cubs, and in St. Louis, Phil Ball purchased the St. Louis Browns.

Left out of the deliberations were the Baltimore investors who sought redress in the form of a major league club. Organized baseball dismissed the city for its pretensions. Comiskey declared it "a minor league city, and not a hell of a good one at that." Charles Ebbets, his National League colleague, seconded: ". . . it is a minor league city, positively and absolutely, and will never be anything else." He added some remarks about "too many colored population" who were too "cheap" to guarantee money at the gate.

The Baltimore stockholders refused to accept their exclusion and spurned a $75,000 settlement. Instead they too attacked through the courts on antitrust grounds. A jury awarded a total of $254,000 but baseball appealed to higher courts. The decision was reversed by a U.S. Court of Appeals on the basis that the activity was not interstate commerce and therefore not subject to the application of federal laws.

The U.S. Supreme Court upheld the reversal with an opinion written by Oliver Wendell Holmes who said:

> Exhibitions of baseball . . . are purely state affairs. It is true that . . . competitions must be arranged between clubs from different cities and states . . . that in order to give the exhibitions the League must induce free persons to cross state lines and must arrange and pay for their doing so is not enough to change the character of the business . . . transport is a mere incident, not the essential thing . . . the exhibition, although made for money would not be called trade or commerce in the commonly accepted use of these words.

The decision was announced in 1922, seven years after the Federal League had been interred. As attorney Gary Hailey noted in the *National Pastime,* it fit the prevailing legal doctrine of the period. The antitrust laws were "applied only to businesses engaged in the production, sale or transportation of tangible goods." Baseball was given a pass not because it was a sport, as some believe, but because it, like grand opera, law, and medicine, did not qualify as commerce.

ADIRONDACK BATS, INC.
Northern
White Ash

Adirondack
302
DOLGEVILLE, NEW YORK
MADE IN U.S.A.

Whip Action

LOUISVILLE SLUGGER
125
HILLERICH & BRADSBY CO
MADE IN U.S.A.
LOUISVILLE, KY.

LOUISVILLE SLUGGER
125
HILLERICH & BRADSBY CO
MADE IN U.S.A.
LOUISVILLE, KY.

Powerized

Roger Maris

LOUISV

LOUISVILLE SLUGGER
125
HILLERICH & BRADSBY CO

Powe

REG. U.S. PAT
McLAUGHLIN—M
Northern
White Ash

ADIROND
302
DOLGEVI

LOUISVILLE SLUGGER
125
HILLERICH & BRADSBY CO
MADE IN U.S.A.
LOUISVILLE, KY.

Powerized

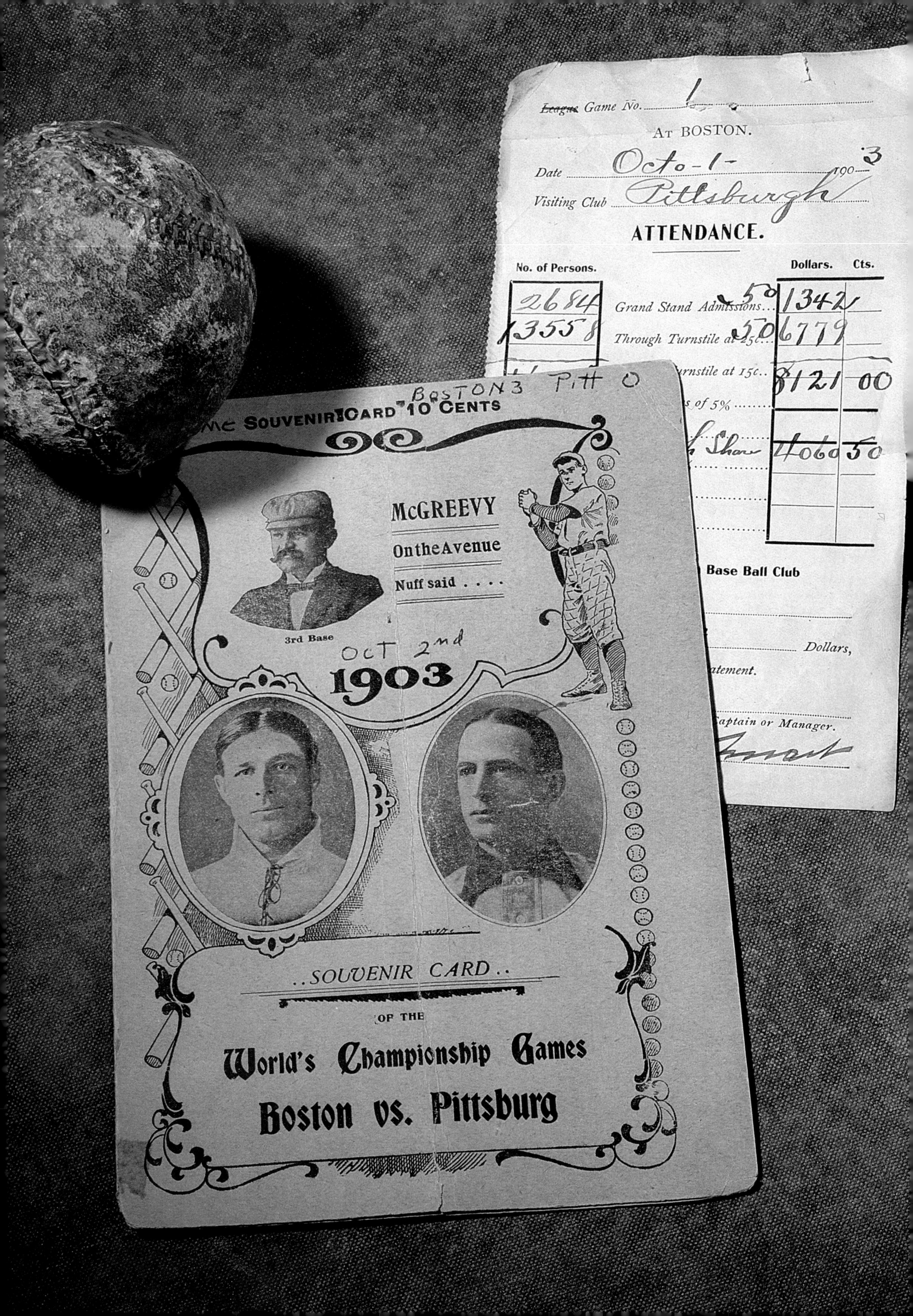

Game No. 1

AT BOSTON.

Date Octo-1- 190 3

Visiting Club Pittsburgh

ATTENDANCE.

No. of Persons.		Dollars.	Cts.
2684	Grand Stand Admissions... 50	1342	
1355 8	Through Turnstile at 25c..	506	77 9
Pitt 0	Turnstile at 15c..	8121	00
	of 5%		
	Share	4060	50

BOSTON 3 Pitt 0

Base Ball Club

Dollars,

atement.

aptain or Manager.

Souvenir Card 10 Cents

McGREEVY
On the Avenue
Nuff said . . . .

3rd Base

OCT 2nd

1903

..SOUVENIR CARD..

OF THE

World's Championship Games

Boston vs. Pittsburg

Bats, from top: *Bat used by Willie Mays to hit 4 home runs in 1 game; bat used by Babe Ruth to hit his 60th home run; bat used by Hank Aaron to hit his 714th home run, bat used by Roger Maris to hit his 61st home run; bat used by Mickey Mantle to hit his 565-foot homer; bat used by Bobby Thomson to hit his pennant-winning home run in 1951; bat used by Roberto Clemente for his 3,000th hit.*

Facing page: *Ball used in first World Series (1903), program from first World Series, attendance sheet from first World Series game (16,242 attended).*

Above: *"The Mighty Babe" by Robert Thom, 1976.*

Giants: *John McGraw's uniform from 1927.*

Chair from Forbes Field; on seat, clockwise from top: *Shoes worn by Lou Brock in stealing record 893rd base of his career, sheet music for "Take Me Out to the Ballgame" from 1917, first batting helmet used in major leagues (by Ralph Kiner in 1952), fingerless glove (1886), ball (1855), first catcher's mask (1876).*

World War I hardly touched baseball. Eddie Grant of the Giants died in combat and the life of Christy Mathewson was cut short. Otherwise, it was business as usual when Johnny came marching home. Far more menacing to baseball was the growing American predilection for betting. Gambling had never enjoyed general legal sanctification in the United States but it flourished almost from the moment Europeans began to colonize the New World. In the big cities, law enforcement, in return for its cut, winked at illegal wagering. Bookmakers openly plied their trade; anyone with a passion for a turn of the cards, the roll of the die, or the spin of the wheel could find gratification easily. Spas like Saratoga Springs, New York, and Hot Springs (Arkansas) openly catered to the sporting fancy. Readers relished Damon Runyon's accounts of lovable rogues engaged in the unlawful business of chance.

As clearly defined contests, with its long schedule of more than 1,200 games a season plus the frenzy of the World Series, baseball naturally attracted the betting community. The itch to risk was surpassed only by the hunger for the sure thing. So it was that the first act of the newly constituted National League in 1876 had been banishing for life four Louisville players who conspired to dump games. Men like A. G. Spalding, Ban Johnson, and John Heydler, National League head during the turbulent early years of the twentieth century, constantly fretted over the possible corruption of the sport.

When the redoubtable Frank Chance took over management of the New York Highlanders in 1913, his first baseman was Hal Chase, a graceful fielder and solid hitter with a dubious reputation. Almost immediately, Chance complained about him to newspapermen Fred Lieb and Heywood Broun: "Did you notice some of the balls that got away from Chase today? They weren't wild throws; they were only made to look that way. He's been doing that right along. He's throwing games on me."

Neither Lieb nor Broun printed Chance's indictment for fear of libel. Actually, Chance's predecessor with the Highlanders, George Stallings, accused Chase of tossing games but Ban Johnson scolded Stallings for

denigrating such a popular player instead of investigating the complaint. Chance simply traded Chase to the White Sox. Subsequently, he leaped to the Federal League for a season before coming to the Cincinnati Reds. In 1918, manager Christy Mathewson told Heydler he suspected Chase. The National League president sought evidence, but when Mathewson enlisted in the army, Heydler could not make his case. Off the record, however, he informed Lieb that he considered Chase guilty.

John McGraw, desperate to restore Giant fortunes, ignored the warnings of his spiritual son and hired both Chase and another reprobate, Heinie Zimmerman, a third baseman good enough to win the triple crown in 1912. Midway through the season McGraw suspended the pair. Heydler had finally obtained a copy of a canceled check for $500 paid to Chase by a known gambler. McGraw subsequently claimed that he and owner Charles Stoneham confronted Zimmerman, who confessed to a bribe offer of $250 to a pair of Giants. McGraw swore Zimmerman deliberately slacked off during the 1917 World Series against the White Sox. The Giant manager contended that "to avoid legal complications" he drove Chase and Zimmerman out of baseball by tending contracts for absurdly little money. The pair quit without protest and Chase bumped around semipro leagues in the Southwest.

The slow, delicate action against the two—and others who also came under suspicion—is partly explainable because of the absence of smoking guns. Undoubtedly, there was also a certain reluctance to admit publicly that money could weaken the game's integrity.

Meanwhile, Charles Comiskey had developed a powerhouse Chicago White Sox squad. With buys of Eddie Collins from the Athletics; Joe Jackson, the sensational outfielder from Cleveland, who is the only rookie ever to hit .400; and Eddie Cicotte, a master of the erratic knuckler, from Boston, Comiskey's club won the 1917 pennant by 9 games and struck down the Giants in the Series by 4–2. The pitching star for the champions was Urban "Red" Faber, ★ who cut up the New Yorkers in 2 starts and won a critical game with 2 innings of relief.

"The old Roman," Charles Comiskey, offered rewards to anyone who could prove malfeasance on the field.

Courtesy NBL

Joe Jackson. "From out of the hills of North Carolina [actually South Carolina] years ago there came a raw-boned, strong active youth. . . . Some scout . . . had discovered him up in the hills playing baseball. In two years he had risen from a poor mill boy to the rank of a player in the major leagues. . . . The ignorant mill boy had become the hero of millions. Out on the hot prairies teams of 'Joe Jacksons' battled desperately with the 'Ty Cobbs.'

"There came a day when a crook spread money before this ignorant idol, and he fell. For a few dollars . . . he sold his honor. . . ."—New York World

Courtesy NBL

The Sox slipped to fifth during the abbreviated 1918 season with the best hitters, Jackson and Collins, absent because of the war, but retrieved pennant honors in 1919.

It was a club full of potential Hall of Famers. Collins already had strung together eight .300 years in ten seasons. (He would add another six as a full-time player.) Jackson had eight .300 years, one .400, and Cicotte, who won 29 games, was at his peak. Lefty Williams won 23 games to complement the knuckleballer. First baseman Chick Gandil hit .290 and fielded .997 to lead the league for his position. Buck Weaver at third and Swede Risberg at short were strong performers, with Weaver a steadily improving hitter. In center field Happy Felsch covered turf on a par with Speaker and commanded a respectable batting average. Catcher Ray Schalk ★ finished the season with his best average, .282; he is recognized as the first receiver to back up plays at first and third and once made a putout at second. "Schalk was called 'Cracker,' a name derived from his whiplike manner," says Eliot Asinof in *Eight Men Out.* "He was a little man, five feet, nine inches tall, weighing less than 150 pounds. But there was nobody that size who made a bigger impact on a ball game."

Charles Comiskey, like his fellow industrialists, believed in capital investment—he had paid handsomely for such assets as Eddie Collins and Joe Jackson and the construction of the ballpark—but he exemplified the pattern of a tight monetary policy toward the workers. With the exception of Collins in the $12,000 to $15,000 range, the players received less than their opponents. Joe Jackson earned $8,000 per season and Cicotte only $6,000. The pitcher had been promised a bonus if he achieved 30 wins but believed management deliberately held him out of action after his twenty-ninth victory. Furthermore, the White Sox meal allowance fell short of the rest of the league. It was also a team riven by cliques; Gandil, Cicotte, and Risberg hung together, disdaining Cocky Collins's education and elevated salary.

Thus when the 1919 Series opened against Cincinnati, the White Sox were the odds-on favorites but not a happy crew. Red Faber had somewhat of an off year, managing only 11–9 and suffering an injury. Vague rumors of dark doings circulated but such gossip was common before any big sports event. When Cicotte's second pitch in the opener plunked Cincinnati second baseman Morrie Rath between the shoulders it was attributed to early wildness. But to a small coterie it signaled good times ahead, for by that act Cicotte passed the word that a conspiracy by the Sox to dump the Series was on. The knuckleballer was battered from the game before the end of the fourth inning. Catcher Ray Schalk, not a party to the corruption, could not understand why Cicotte paid no attention to his signs. After the Reds won 9–1, sportswriter Hughie Fullerton, covering the games with the technical assistance of Christy Mathewson, growled to a comrade, "I don't like what I saw out there. There is something smelly. Cicotte doesn't usually pitch that way." Matty concurred. And in fact Cicotte had completed all but 5 of his 35 starts and allowed only 1.82 earned runs per game. Another suspicious observer, Ring Lardner, caroled a parody of the song of the bubble creator, "I'm forever blowing ball games."

In the second game, another of the villains, Lefty Williams, walked three, gave up a triple, and then settled down behind the deficit to restrict the Reds to a total of 4 hits. But the Sox lost this one 4–2. In the aftermath, as the train rattled toward Chicago with the teams and officials aboard, Comiskey paid a midnight visit to the compartment of National League president John Heydler. The Old Roman informed Heydler that his manager, Kid Gleason, suspected calculated foul play. Comiskey, however, would not approach American League president Ban Johnson because of a long-standing feud. Nor did he feel it seemly to contact the other member of the National Commission governing the game, August Herrmann, because he happened to own the Reds. Heydler agreed to seek out Ban Johnson.

Unfortunately, Johnson, who had fought hard against the intrusion of alcoholic beverages in ballparks, was a less than temperate man himself. Heydler awakened him from a drunken stupor and the exasperated Johnson dismissed the accusations of his enemy, "That is the yelp of a beaten cur."

The third game in Chicago pitted honest Dickie Kerr against the Reds and it appeared that the talk of a fix was gossip only. Kerr

"I don't like what I saw out there There's something smelly. [Eddie] doesn't usually pitch like that."—[F] Fullerton

Courtesy NBL

Chick Gandil, first baseman for the [prime mover among the dumping [quit baseball after the 1919 Series.

Courtesy NBL

(Top, left) *Jackson (left) ranged the outfield with co-conspirator Happy Felsch.*

> *I'm forever blowing ball games,*
> *Pretty ball games in the air.*
> *I come from Chi*
> *Just go to bat and fade and die,*
> *Fortune's coming my way,*
> *That's why I don't care.*
> *I'm forever blowing ball games,*
> *And the gamblers treat us fair.*
> —*Ring Lardner*

Courtesy NBL

(Top, right) *Catcher Ray Schalk first accused his colleagues of throwing games, then recanted.*

Courtesy NBL

(Bottom, left) *"Take Dickie Kerr, now a wee hop o' my thumb. Not much taller than a walking stick . . . the tiniest of the baseball brood. Won't way [sic] 90 pounds soaking wet, an astute scout once reported after a look at Kerr. Too small for a pitcher, especially a left handed pitcher. Too small for much of anything, except, perhaps, a watch charm."*—*Damon Runyon*

Kerr, one of the uncorrupted, won a pair of games during the 1919 Series.

Courtesy NBL

(Bottom, right) *Another man who kept his Sox white was Eddie Collins, bought from Connie Mack at a premium price and whose salary and personality earned him envy and the nickname "Cocky."*

Courtesy NBL

shut out the visitors and Gandil, leader and chief beneficiary of the scheme, doubled home 2 runs in the 3–0 win.

But the fourth game was a farce, with Cicotte at center stage. The game was scoreless until the fifth. On a tap back to the box, the pitcher threw wildly to first, putting a runner on second. The next hitter singled to Joe Jackson, in on the plot, but so instinctively a great ball player that he made a perfect throw home. However, pretending to make a cutoff, Cicotte deflected the ball, permitting the run to score and the batter to take second. He scored on another single and the Reds won 2–0. Schalk complained openly about his battery mate's behavior.

Claude Williams then tossed another artful game, suffering only 1 bad inning and yielding only 4 hits. He still lost 5–0. Dickie Kerr restored some honor in the sixth game, going 10 innings for a 5–4 victory. Again it was Gandil who produced the winning run as the gang contrived to make its losing struggle seem genuine. And Cicotte took the seventh game (this was the first of a three-year trial of a best-of-nine World Series) to add further legitimacy. But word passed that the gamblers who suborned the players wanted no more mock heroics. Williams, perhaps warned of possible damage to his health, surrendered 4 runs in the first inning of the eighth game to wrap up the Series.

A day after the finale, Comiskey sought to squelch speculation: "I believe my boys fought the battles of the recent World Series on the level. . . . And I would be the first to want information to the contrary—if there be any. I would give $20,000 to anyone unearthing any information to that effect." Subsequently, he repeated his challenge, for some unknown reason lowering the reward for evidence of a fix to $10,000.

Other authoritative figures ignored the mutterings of a plot and the erratic play of the losers. The 1920 *Reach Guide,* in its review of the previous season, declared:

> Any man who knows anything at all about baseball and baseball players knows absolutely that both the game and its exemplars are absolutely honest so far as its public presentation is concerned, and any man who insinuates that the 1919 World Series was not honorably played by every participant therein not only does not know what he is talking about, but is a menace to the game quite as much as the

gamblers would be, if they had the ghost of a chance to get in their nefarious work.

The *Sporting News* also ridiculed the talk of a fix and referred to those who persisted in this vein as "slimy creatures." Even Ray Schalk, who had voiced suspicions about the integrity of his mates, backed off, saying he had been misquoted.

But as early as two weeks after his team was defeated, owner Comiskey was approached by a St. Louis businessman who reported that gamblers seeking an investment from him confided that the Series had been perverted. Later, Comiskey claimed he could not find any evidence to support the tale.

An ambitious Illinois state attorney secured testimony from a small-fry participant and then supposedly dragooned Cicotte, Williams, and Jackson into confessions of their roles. Felsch confided his guilt to newspapermen. The instigators of the operation were identified as a former featherweight boxing champion, Abe Attell; an erstwhile White Sox pitcher, Bill Burns; and New York City gambler Arnold Rothstein, fondly fictionalized by Damon Runyon as "The Brain."

Farce now intruded on drama. Occupancy of the office of the state attorney changed and the critical papers vanished, including the reputed confessions of the guilty ball players. But with the public disclosures, Ban Johnson pursued the case with the zeal of Inspector Javert. Some believed his Jean Valjean was not the actual miscreant but his enemy Comiskey. In any case he logged ten thousand miles searching for witnesses and convinced Bill Burns to appear before a grand jury that indicted players and gamblers on a charge of conspiracy.

With a little bit more venality, the 1919 Series could have been the one both sides tried to lose. Reds pitcher Hod Eller summarily rejected a $5,000 offer to ease up. And Edd Roush, the Cincinnati outfielder, later complained that on one occasion after he drove a ball between the enemy outfielders, the man ahead of him slowed up until Roush yelled, "Get running, you crooked son of a bitch." Roush was no man to defy; he spoke his piece even in the awesome presence of John J. McGraw. A lifetime batting average of .323 compensated for any ab-

Suspicions also fell upon the winn[ing?] cinnati Reds. Edd Roush, the cr[u fielder who had the temerity to tell McGraw, chased one dubious te[around the bases.

Courtesy NBL

sence of servility. In keeping with his char-acter, Roush swung a 48-ounce bat, the heaviest ever regularly used in the majors and four ounces more than Babe Ruth's for-midible bludgeon.

Well before the case came to trial in 1921, however, Johnson himself was a casualty. He had squabbled not only with Comiskey but also with the owners of the Yankees, the Colonels, Ruppert and Tillinghast L'Hom-medieu Huston, and Harry Frazee, the Red Sox proprietor. Aware that the National Commission had failed to function effec-tively—it had bumbled other affairs affect-ing contracts and disputes—the club owners were determined to create an effective gover-nor and protect the game from fallout due to the scandal. They settled on a federal judge with a known fondness for baseball, a repu-tation for rectitude, and a history of sympa-thy for the game's organization.

Kenesaw Mountain Landis, named for a site in Georgia where his father, a Union army surgeon, was wounded, never attended law school but learned his craft by working in law offices. He achieved a reputation for toughness when he slapped a $29,240,000 fine on John D. Rockefeller's Standard Oil Company, although the Supreme Court re-versed his decision. Landis attracted more attention when he attempted to extradite Germany's Kaiser Wilhelm I on a murder rap after a German U-boat torpedoed the *Lusitania* and a Chicago man died. Landis also smote labor leader Big Bill Haywood with a twenty-year term. (Possibly some own-ers thought that indicated a proper attitude toward the hired help, but Landis later disappointed some hopes in this respect.) He added to his reputation as a hanging judge by occasionally sentencing men to jail for minor violations of the Prohibition statutes, although Landis himself frequently enjoyed illicit beverages. The magnates of baseball remembered him best for having sat on the antitrust case of the Federal League in 1915 until the challenge died in bankruptcy.

Severe looking, with a shock of white hair, he provided a doughty image of baseball's determination to clean up its act. And in the summer of 1921, when a jury exonerated the accused players and gamblers of any crimi-nal charges—the players and their judgmen-

tal peers celebrated in a speakeasy—Landis banned the tainted athletes forever. He an-nounced: ". . . any player that throws a game, no player that entertains propositions or promises to throw a game, no player that sits in on a conference with a bunch of gam-blers in which ways and means of throwing a game are discussed and does not promptly tell his club about it, will ever play profes-sional baseball."

The final clause addressed itself to the case of Buck Weaver, who apparently was present during discussions of the plot but received no bribe money and indeed hit .324. Pocketing as much as $35,000, Gandil had abandoned baseball after 1919. Accord-ing to Eliot Asinof in *Eight Men Out,* Ris-berg received $15,000, Cicotte $10,000. Felsch, Williams, Jackson, and Fred McMul-lin received $5,000 apiece. Cicotte and cer-tainly Jackson, statistically, merit nomina-tion to the Hall of Fame but by betraying the game they forfeited any consideration.*

Ban Johnson remained chief of the Ameri-can League until 1927, but the power he wielded as a member of the National Com-mission was gone. He was succeeded as League chief for four years by Ernest Bar-nard, and then Will Harridge, ★ secretary to both, filled the office for nearly twenty-eight tranquil years.

The autocratic Landis quickly earned the unofficial title of "czar," demonstrating that obsession with the law cited by Lieb. He issued a ukase against the typical barnstorm-ing trips taken immediately after a World Series. When Babe Ruth defied the edict in 1921, Landis swatted him with a forty-day suspension for the start of the 1922 season.

In 1926, Hub Leonard, claimed that Tris Speaker and Joe Wood, while with the Indi-ans and Cobb in Detroit, conspired to fix a 1919 game enabling Detroit to win third-place money. Landis immediately opened an investigation; Joe Wood was a coach at Yale but Speaker was player-manager of the Indi-ans and Cobb the same for the Tigers. Released a year earlier by the Tigers, Leon-ard refused to personally confront the ac-cused before Landis. In their defense, Cobb argued that he had failed to get a hit that day but Speaker who supposedly was cast as a loser struck 2 triples and a single. Some

Once convinced of foul play, American League president Ban Johnson pursued the investigation with the zeal of an Inspector Javert.

"Professional baseball has reached a cri-sis. The Major Leagues, both owners and players, are on trial. Charges of crookedness among owners, accusations of cheating, of tampering with each other's teams, of at-tempting to syndicate and control ballplay-ers are bandied about openly. Charges that ballplayers are bribed and games are sold out are made without attempts at refutations by men who have made their fortunes in baseball.

"The National League met and ad-journed without even mentioning the subject. The American League, besmirched with scandal, wrangled, fought, and black-guarded each other, then separated without an effort to clear the good name of the sport. They keep silent hoping it will all blow over."—Hugh S. Fullerton, New York World

"Fullerton had picked up an ugly story that was kicking around in the gutter—a story that decent writers would refuse to han-dle—and blew it up into a muckraking tirade against organized baseball. There are two kinds of people in the world; one builds up, the other tears down. Hugh Fullerton, of course, belongs to the latter."—Baseball Magazine

Courtesy NBL

---

*The fullest account of the 1919 Series and the roles of those involved is Eliot Asinof's *Eight Men Out.*

"[Kenesaw Mountain] Landis had r[...] able charisma; he stood out in any gat[...] he attended. Along with all the virtue[...] honest federal judge, he had many [...] foibles of the ordinary man. He was e[...] dinarily patriotic and had loved be[...] since he was a small boy. I think [...] totally honest, but he was vain, egot[...] domineering, and a show-off. He swo[...] a trooper, chewed tobacco, and was f[...] bourbon whiskey. He had great resp[...] the law and for himself as a person en[...] with the enforcement of the law, whe[...] be that of government or of baseball[...] writers doubted his sincerity, think[...] contradictory that a man who could [...] bootleg liquor behind the scenes wou[...] tence a man for twenty years for viola[...] the Prohibition Amendment and th[...] stead Act as Landis had done. To [...] stand the seeming contradiction you [...] understand that Landis on the bench [...] totally different man from Landis in t[...] clubhouse."—Fred Lieb

"His career typifies the heights to [...] dramatic talent may carry a man in [...] ica if only he has the foresight not to [...] the stage."—Heywood Broun

Courtesy NBL

potentially incriminating correspondence was explained as a joint venture in a race-track bet.

Landis publicly dismissed the charges but the two stars lost their managerial slots, and when they laid down their bats two years later, they were never invited to remain in the game. Indeed, Landis hardened his heart against all forms of gambling and only a few men had the temerity to visit racetracks openly.

Owners who thought they had a czar for the players and a servitor for front-office matters suffered severe trauma when the commissioner cast his hard eye on their minor league practices. Landis disliked the extension of major league control down through the farm systems, which potentially restricted qualified men from coming up. Several times he penalized clubs for burying potential talent on the plantations. But the most important contribution of Landis was the restoration of baseball's reputation for integrity.

The Black Sox scandal broke wide open late in September 1920. The immediate suspension of the accused individuals cost the White Sox another pennant, but other events also shook up baseball.

Chicago, Cleveland, and New York were in contention for the American League pennant when August arrived. On August 16, 1920, the Indians were visiting New York. Starting for the Yankees was Carl Mays, a submarine pitcher with a mean reputation. Mays had been Red Sox property in 1919 but quit the club in the middle of a game. Subsequently traded to New York, Mays was the center of a battle between the Yankees and Ban Johnson who wanted the pitcher suspended. Johnson lost the skirmish, added Yankee owner Jake Ruppert to his enemies, and Mays pitched well for his new club.

Early in the game, Ray Chapman, the twenty-nine-year-old shortstop from Cleveland, came to bat. A near-.300 hitter, the right-handed Chapman hung over the plate. He was an excellent bunter and Mays, perhaps seeking to thwart him, fired high and inside. Wrote Joe Vila in the *Sporting News:*

Chapman seemed rooted to the spot. He made no move either with his head or feet to get out of the way and the ball, pitched with all of Mays' strength, struck him squarely on the left temple. The impact sounded as if the ball had hit the bat, but as it rolled back towards Mays, who threw it to Pipp, Chapman crumpled up and slowly went down on his knees, never uttering a sound.

A doctor from the grandstand administered first aid. Two Cleveland players lifted Chapman to his feet. He may have said something but he collapsed into unconsciousness and died the next morning.

There were brief threats to prosecute Mays, who had a reputation for bean balls. Reporters like Vila exonerated Mays, arguing that the pitch was not aimed at the victim's head, and Mays finished the season at 26–11. He remained in the majors for nine more years but could never escape the shadow cast by Chapman's death. In retirement he said: "I won over 200 big league games [208 to be exact] but no one remembers that. When they think of me, I'm the guy who killed Chapman with a fast ball."

The game's first major league fatality brought a change. The authorities agreed that the well-soiled balls allowed in play hampered vision. Umpires received instructions to use new balls when one became dirty. John Foster, editor of *The Spalding Guide,* suggested the use of protective headgear. But the idea was ignored.

The Indians replaced Chapman with Joe Sewell, ★ giving themselves a .300 hitter for the next ten seasons. In fourteen years, the last three with the Yankees as a third baseman, Sewell struck out a mere 114 times. In 1924 and 1932, he was a K in only 3 at bats, and twice in his career he whiffed on just four occasions. Furthermore, he led his league in fielding twice, topping rivals in putouts and assists four times.

Suspending the members of the Black Sox conspiracy just before the end of the season opened the way to the pennant for Cleveland. From the National League came the Brooklyn Dodgers under Manager Wilbert Robinson who'd also won in 1916. Brooklyn's best were outfielder Zach Wheat, ★ a .317 hitter in nineteen big league years; Rube Marquard, closing out his career; and pitcher Burleigh Grimes, ★ a spitball artist. Grimes thrived on his image as a hard case. Before his turns he neglected a razor, allowing a villainous-looking black stubble to grow. He perfected a malevolent glower as he peered in at hitters, invariably bringing ball and glove up to his face to convey the possibility of a wet one.

Burleigh Grimes was well schooled in the lessons of adversity. During his second year with the Pirates in 1917, Grimes started to lose. He lost and lost until May of the following year with Brooklyn when he ended his drought after 17 consecutive defeats.

Grimes told Red Smith:

Sometimes when I was pitching, the spitter was excellent. Sometimes I would be off by two inches and I'd have to come in with the fastball and curve.

How much I used it depended on how good my fastball was that day. If it was popping, I'd forget about trick deliveries. If it wasn't, I'd go for the spitter and the curve. I'd say the spitter was advantageous 75 percent of the time.

One day I went 18 innings against Chicago and used only three spitters all day. All the others were fastballs. We beat Jim Vaughn but I had to go 18 innings.

Zach Wheat covered the outfield for Brooklyn when they were the Superbas, then Robins, and finally Dodgers.

Courtesy NBL

"[Burleigh Grimes] always looked like a man who was about to commit assault and battery when he threw the ball."—John Kieran, New York Times

Courtesy NBL

Overall, Grimes would record 269 victories with seven different National League clubs.

The Indians of course had Speaker in center field but the show stopper was Stan Coveleski, ★ another spitball expert who used slippery elm, a sap-laden piece of tree bark, for lubrication. Coveleski also went to the mound with a gritty piece of sandpaper glued to his pants. With his spitter, emery pitch, knuckler, and fastball, Coveleski befuddled the Dodgers and won 3 games, surrendering only 2 runs over 27 innings. Cleveland took the Series 5–2.

Born Stanislaus Kowalewski in 1889 in Shamokin, Pennsylvania, Coveleski attended a Polish school for about a year and then joined his father in the coal mines. As a boy he separated slate from coal, and on Sundays or during the few daylight hours after work, he indulged his habit of throwing stones. He told interviewer Rod Roberts: "I'd tie a can on a tree, pick a pile of stones and see how many times I could hit it. That's where I got my control."

He and his five brothers all played ball whenever they could, making their own baseballs by wrapping a chunk of rubber with cord string and sewing on a canvas cover. By age eighteen he was pitching in the minors and Connie Mack signed him. Sent out for seasoning, he learned to throw the spitter in Portland, Oregon. Meanwhile, his older brother, Harry, had reached the major leagues and achieved fame with the Phillies as the "Giant Killer" after he beat the New Yorkers three times in the final week of the 1908 season to ruin their pennant hopes.

After a brief appearance with the Athletics in 1912, Stan Coveleski struggled until 1916 before he took up permanent status as a major leaguer with the Indians. Control marked Coveleski's style, in spite of such notoriously aberrant pitches as the spitter and knuckler. He theorized: "If you can hit [certain] spots you're a pitcher and if you can't hit them you're not. You've got to believe in yourself. [One time] Steve O'Neill [the Indian catcher] called for three balls. Cobb was on first base and I threw three waste balls. We picked him off. I know he was gonna go on the fourth one."

With that control and his variety of deliveries, Coveleski eventually finished with 215 victories, having led his league twice in

ERAs. In perhaps his best season he went 20–5 with the 1925 Washington Senators as he and Walter Johnson hurled the club into its first World Series.

Coveleski's performance in the 1920 World Series is often overlooked because of a single play by the journeyman Cleveland second sacker, Bill Wambsganss. In the fifth inning of the fifth game, with no outs, the Dodgers' Pete Kilduff led off second and Oscar Miller edged off first. Brooklyn pitcher Clarence Mitchell smacked a line drive, which Wambsganss snagged near second base. He stepped on the bag to double up Kilduff who had strayed too far and then tagged Miller, charging from first on the pitch, to complete an unassisted triple play, the only one ever in a World Series.

The other contender for American League honors during that season was the Yankees. As the Highlanders, the New York American League entry provided little competition to the Giants for the favor of the fans and not much competition against their opponents either. The best efforts amounted to a pair of second-place finishes.

For a change of luck, the name officially became the Yankees in 1913. As a gesture of good will, the Highlanders had offered the temporary use of their park to the Giants in 1911 after a Polo Grounds fire. In return, the Highlanders became tenants of the Giants in 1913.

Fortune began to warm the Yankees in 1915 when brewer Jacob Ruppert, eventually an honorary colonel, and Huston bought out Farrell and Devery for $460,000—a paltry sum by modern numbers but a less than niggardly 2,500 percent profit for the sellers who had anted up only $18,000 for the original franchise.

Ruppert and Huston labored to turn the Yankees into winners. A sartorial dandy, Ruppert mandated two uniforms for each player, enabling them to appear in freshly laundered suits daily. To add performance to style, the partners hired tiny Miller Huggins ★ as manager, a 5′6″, 140-pound, former second baseman with unimpressive credentials as a field foreman. Huggins arrived in 1918 and an ebb tide of talent buoyed the club.

First came pitcher Bob Shawkey, one of Connie Mack's fire sale items in 1915. He

Pitcher Harry Coveleski (left) while with the Phillies stifled the Giants in the last week of the 1908 season, forcing the playoff with the Cubs. Cleveland Indian brother Stan (right) tossed 216 wins in his career and beat the Dodgers three times in the 1920 World Series.

Courtesy NBL

would win 168 games for the Yanks. The owners also filled a hole at third base with a $37,500 payment to Connie Mack for Home Run Baker. Baker had sat out the 1915 season rather than accept the offers of the Athletics or the Federals. By 1920, the club was shuffling talent with large sums of cash to deal itself the first of a long string of winning hands. The principal person involved was Babe Ruth, who became a Yankee for the unheard-of sum of $125,000 plus a $300,-000 loan to the financially strapped Red Sox owner, Harry Frazee, a man with a penchant for investing in flop Broadway musicals. Frazee sold Ruth over the objections of his manager Ed Barrow.

"Cousin Ed" had improved on his discovery of Honus Wagner by turning Ruth, a fine left-handed pitcher, into an outfielder so that his bat could come to play every day. No one could have faulted Barrow's genius if he had permitted the kid from Baltimore to remain just a pitcher; Ruth's record for the Sox was 89 regular season wins against only 46 losses. He won a Series game for Boston in 1916, going 14 innings in a 2–1 struggle, and in 1918, he bested the Cubs twice. Sandwiched in those three World Series triumphs is a string of 29⅔ scoreless innings, unsurpassed until Whitey Ford ★ some forty years later recorded 33⅔ runless innings. When his new team occasionally ran short of pitchers, Ruth returned to the mound. In 1920, he went 4 innings, allowed 3 hits, 2 runs, and then moved to the outfield. His single and double helped him to a 14–7 victory. The following year he won again, yielding 4 runs but striking out Ty Cobb. In the same game he also walloped a pair of homers, including a 460-footer to center field in the Polo Grounds.

In 1921, the Yankees hired Barrow to run the front office and work with Huggins. Also on hand for the 1921 season were the twenty-two-year-old whiz-kid pitcher Waite Hoyt and a strong catcher, Wally Schang, both obtained through deals with the Red Sox. Bob Meusel, coming off a strong rookie year, added punch to the outfield. In the near future the Yankees bolstered their troops with such additions as pitchers Herb Pennock and Bullet Joe Bush, two more Boston recruits, and a raw-boned New Yorker, Henry Louis Gehrig.

But it was Babe Ruth, the "Sultan of Swat," who did the most to alter Yankee fortunes and baseball's as well. The club captured its first pennants in 1921 and 1922. Ruth socked an amazing 59 home runs in 1921, surpassing his old marks of 54 a year earlier and 29 while in his final year in Boston. The closest anyone previously came to his figures was Gavvy Cravath, the forgotten long-ball tycoon of the Phillies (with 19 in 1913 and 1914, 24 in 1915).

Some attributed Ruth's lurid achievements to the introduction of a rabbity quality to baseballs. The dead-ball era actually had ended with Ben Shibe's invention of the cork center in 1909 and the Reach Company manufacture of this design in 1911. After World War I, the resilience of the ball increased due to a finer grade of wool wrapped more tightly. By 1925, the livelier ball and the banishment of the spitter accounted for a 45-point increase in batting averages compared to 1915. By 1930, teams were scoring 3.5 more runs per game than in 1915 and homers had risen from a paltry 384 to a grand 1,565.

Fans flocked to witness the new phenomenon, baseball's act of violence, often stunning the crowd with its decisiveness, and also asserting that no matter how desperate the situation, defeat might yet be overcome. With Babe Ruth as the main attraction, Yankee attendance in 1920 doubled over the previous year. Charles Stoneham, unconsoled by the World Series wins of his Giants over the Yankees in 1921 and 1922, observed the passions and revenues engendered by his tenants and sought to evict them, piously explaining that with two separate play yards, more Sunday dates would be available to both clubs.

In 1922, the American Leaguers broke ground for Yankee Stadium with Huston supervising construction of the $2.3 million project. That year saw a World Series confined to a single park, as the tenants of the Polo Grounds met their landlords. The results were entirely satisfactory for McGraw; his pitchers limited the Yanks to 1.76 earned runs while his club batted .309, taking the Series 4–0 (a 3–3 tie after 10 innings had necessitated a fifth game but Landis ordered the receipts donated to charity). While none of the Giant pitchers ever achieved

(Top) *Brewery tycoon Jacob Ruppert used the profits from suds to create the New York Yankee dynasties, and his first straw boss was Miller Huggins.*

Courtesy NBL

(Bottom) *Ross Youngs, the brilliant and short-lived Giant outfielder, stretches a hit into a double.*

Courtesy NBL

(Following pages) *The first Yankee pennant club in 1921 featured outfielder-pitcher George Herman Ruth* (middle row, fourth from right) *who hit .378, with 59 homers, and hurled a pair of wins. Home Run Baker* (back row, eighth from left) *at third base was in his penultimate season while pitcher Waite Hoyt* (middle row, second from right), *barely twenty-two years old, was in his fourth major league season, winning 19 games. To Hoyt's right and next to Ruth is pitcher Carl Mays, more renowned for the only fatal beaning than his total 208 victories, including 27 in 1921.*

Courtesy NBL

enough for Hall of Fame election, McGraw enjoyed the services of shortstop Dave Bancroft, ★ second baseman Frank Frisch, first sacker George "High Pockets" Kelly, ★ and outfielders Ross Youngs ★ and Casey Stengel. The graceful-fielding Kelly stood a towering 6′4″ and offered power as well as consistency, hovering around .300. Ross Youngs streaked through baseball, a Roman candle, flashing a .322 average over ten seasons before dying suddenly of kidney disease at age thirty.

Yankee Stadium opened in 1923 with 74,-217 people, the largest crowd yet to see a game. It was altogether a most satisfactory year for the Yankee management. Ruppert bought out Huston for $1.5 million, then settled in to see his club finally whip the Giants in the World Series, despite a pair of homers, including an inside-the-park sprint, by Stengel.

Not the least of the year's accomplishments was the signing of the twenty-year-old Columbia student Lou Gehrig to a contract that specified a $1,500 bonus and a $3,000 salary. Scout Paul Krichell convinced Ed Barrow to invest in Gehrig by remarking, "I think I saw another Ruth today."

Little more than a year later, June 2, 1925, first baseman Wally Pipp made the mistake of complaining of a headache, the residue of a bean ball, and Huggins played Gehrig, up with the club after a season at Hartford. Gehrig did not sit down for another 2,129 games over almost fifteen seasons.

The Yankees sailed off on a brief hiatus following the triumphant 1923 year and American League honors went to Washington. Stanley "Bucky" Harris, ★ who broke into the majors as a rookie second baseman with the Senators, became the twenty-seven-year-old playing manager for the club in 1924. Walter Johnson, in a last gasp of supremacy at age thirty-seven, copped the Most Valuable Player award with 23 wins. Leon "Goose" Goslin ★ in left field played in all 154 games, hit .344, and topped the league with 129 RBIs.

Right fielder Sam Rice ★ was a man haunted by memories of personal disaster. His wife, two babies, and parents perished in 1912 when a tornado blew away their Illinois home while he was off for a minor

league tryout. Twenty-two-year-old Rice, shattered by his loss, wandered the bush leagues, labored in a distillery, toiled on a railroad section gang, and even tried to bury himself in the U.S. Navy. During a furlough, he earned himself a place on the Petersburg, Virginia, team and quit the military. Clark Griffith collected him to square a bad debt of $800 owed to the Senators by Petersburg. Originally a pitcher, Rice became a right fielder, and in 1924 he led the league with 216 hits, batting .334.

In the National League it was John McGraw's last pennant. The Giants beat out Brooklyn despite a 22–13 record for Grimes and an astonishing 28–6 for Arthur "Dazzy" Vance. ★ Oddly, Vance first reached the majors in 1915 with the Pirates for whom he lost 1 and three years later briefly served with the Yankees and lost 3 more. With Brooklyn in 1922, at age thirty-one, he picked up his first victory, and when he quit thirteen years later he had amassed 197 wins. A high kicker and a wit who helped earn the Dodgers their rep for daffiness, Vance, according to teammate Johnny Frederick, "could throw a cream puff through a battleship."

In the Series' first game Walter Johnson pitched 12 innings, fanned 12, and still lost 4–2. After 4 games, the Senators had tied up the Series at 2 apiece with homers and hits by Goslin and Harris. But the Giants battered Johnson to another loss before Manager Harris tied the Series anew in game six with a timely single. In the deciding match, the desperate Senators asked Walter Johnson to relieve starter Firpo Marberry at the start of the ninth, the score knotted at 3–3. He shut down the New Yorkers over the next 4 innings. In the bottom of the twelfth, luck once again savaged McGraw. With 1 away, Senator catcher Muddy Ruel lifted a simple pop foul. Giant receiver Hank Gowdy threw his mask down and started for the ball. But he tripped over the mask and muffed the play. Ruel doubled. Harris let Johnson, a good hitting pitcher (24 career home runs), swing for himself. He grounded to Travis Jackson ★ at shortstop. Ruel held second but Jackson fumbled the ball, leaving men at first and second, still only 1 out.

Bucky Harris came to the plate and bounced one toward third, a possible double-

Philadelphia police escort Giant outfielder Stengel to safety after an inside pitch from the Phillies' Lefty Weinert so ired Casey that he threw a punch at Weinert.

Courtesy NBL

Stengel beats the throw for a game-winning, inside-the-park homer with two out in the ninth inning of game one of the 1923 Series against the Yankees. Traded over the winter by McGraw to Boston, Stengel snarled, "Well, maybe I'm lucky. If I'd hit three homers McGraw might have sent me clear out of the country."

Courtesy NBL

(Top) *A strapping Columbia first base[m]
named Henry Louis Gehrig trades his [c]
for Yankee pinstripes at age twenty, aft[er his]
sophomore year. In 1925, he began h[is in]
credible streak of 2,130 consecutive g[ames.]*

Courtesy NBL

(Bottom) *Never touted for his speed, G[ehrig]
stole home against the White Sox. [In his]
career he managed to steal that base [15]
times. Ty Cobb's total was 46. Anothe[r mea]
sure of his competitive spirit: Umpires e[jected]
Gehrig at least half-a-dozen times.*

Courtesy *New York News*

(Opposite) *During the exhibition tou[r of the]
Bustin' Babes and Larrupin' Lous, th[e play]
ers presented cups to American Legio[n teams.]*

Courtesy NBL

126

play ball. A new McGraw protégé, nineteen-year-old Freddie Lindstrom (a .311 lifetime hitter), ★ set himself, and then the ball struck a pebble and bounded over the rookie's head. The winning run scored, giving Walter Johnson his first World Series victory after seventeen years.

The seeming goat was shortstop Jackson, then in his first full season as the Giant shortstop. But that season he batted .302 and in succeeding years hit for a near-.300 average with moderate power—135 career homers over fifteen seasons. The best clue to his intelligence and effectiveness is that McGraw named him field captain. But not even Jackson and newcomers Hubbell, Terry, and Ott seemed enough. McGraw teams lay becalmed in the doldrums; the Giants and the tactics of the hard-earned single run were a ship clinging to wind and sail while others sped ahead powered by the engine of the 3-run homer.

Washington and Johnson returned to the Series against the Pirates in 1925. Game three produced a controversy that literally followed Sam Rice into the grave. With the Series even at 1 apiece, Washington led 4–3 in the top of the eighth. Pittsburgh's Earl Smith lined a ball deep to right. Rice raced for the ball and caught up with it as it was about to reach the temporary bleachers. The ball met his glove just as he toppled over the low wall separating the fans from the playing field. Umpire Cy Rigler ran out as Rice emerged with the assistance of teammate Earl McNeely. Seeing the ball in Rice's mitt, Rigler signaled "out."

The Pirates, spearheaded by owner Barney Dreyfuss, stormed from the dugout protesting that Rice dropped the ball, then picked it up. But the decision stood. Over the years, when asked whether or not he had made the catch, Rice would only add to the mystery with the answer: "The umpires called him out, didn't they?" Fellow Senator Ossie Bluege kept the question alive years later, claiming, "Sam told me . . . that he never did catch the ball."

Rice, in an strange gesture, wrote a letter in 1965 which he mailed to the Hall of Fame with instructions that it remain sealed until after his death. When Rice died in 1974, the contents were made public. Testifying from the tomb, Rice said:

> I . . . had the ball in view all the way, going at top speed and about 15 feet from the bleachers jumped as high as I could and back handed and the ball hit the center of the pocket in the glove (I had a death grip on it).
>
> I hit the ground about 5 feet from a barrier about 4 feet high in front of the bleachers with all the brakes on but couldn't stop so I tried to jump it . . . but my feet hit the barrier about a foot from the top and I toppled over on my stomach into the first row of bleachers. I hit my adams apple on something which sort of knocked me out for a few seconds but McNeely arrived about that time and grabbed me by my shirt and pulled me out. I remember trotting back towards the infield, carrying the ball. . . . At no time did I lose possession of the ball.

Publication of the note brought further clarification from Norman Budesheim, a seventeen-year-old fan in those temporary bleachers. He recalled:

> Sam . . . hurtled the barrier hitting it with the ball definitely in his outstretched glove. . . . I caught Sam full across the chest and arms as did my friend. I was not hurt in any way, though Sam's cleats tore the trouser legs of my companion. When Sam went out of the park (over the barrier) he had the ball in his glove, definitely.
>
> However, upon hitting us, he definitely dropped the ball . . . he rolled off our laps and was flat on the ground in the tight space between our legs and feet and the barrier he and I frantically trying to get the ball—me to give it to him and he to get it himself naturally. . . . Sam beat me to the ball but we both heaved him over the barrier onto the field.

Budesheim insisted he believed Rice held the ball long enough in his glove to justify the umpire's decision.

Despite the loss, the Pirates overrode the Senators, withstanding 3 Goslin homers and 2 more Johnson wins. However, the aged veteran lost the finale. The blow that scrapped the Big Train was a base-loaded double by Hazen "Kiki" Cuyler ★ in the eighth inning at a moment when Washington led 7–6. Cuyler had a .321 lifetime average during his eighteen major league seasons and headed the class in steals four times.

The top Pirate average for the season belonged to Cuyler at .357 but a thirty-five-year-old speed vendor, Maximilian Car-

Washington outfielder Sam Rice end dreadful disaster, spoke from the about a long-disputed play.

Courtesy NBL

(Opposite) *Hitting behind Ruth, fought a losing battle for headlines. Louis Gehrig, the records show, is a able to the New York Yankees as Herman Ruth but Gehrig has not be one-third the salary that Ruth has The difference in their wages repre difference in color. Ruth has it in go rig is almost totally devoid of it. Ru showman of the highest type. Gehri had any showmanship and probabl will have. Ruth is always on para Gehrig never is. Gehrig is a steady pendable laborer. He has nothing of ist in him. He cannot dramatize si as Ty Cobb did and as Ruth has do Cobb's departure."—H. G. Salsing troit News*

Courtesy NBL

narius (translated into Max Carey ★ to boost fan appeal), finished with a .343. Between 1910 and 1925, he outstole everyone else ten times. Rounding out a trio of outstanding performers was third baseman Harold "Pie" Traynor. ★ Two explanations for the nickname exist. Traynor's father, a printer, supposedly took a look at his grimy youngster and remarked, "You look like pied type." Another version says that as a boy in Somerville, Massachusetts, Traynor shopped for his mother and inevitably the final item on the grocery list was a pie.

Traynor played even with the bag and his quickness into the hole led some to call him a second shortstop. Because he moved so swiftly to his right, writers were fond of saying, "[So and so] doubled down the line but Traynor threw him out at first." Charley Grimm, who played first for the Pirates with Traynor and then against him as a Chicago Cub, claimed Traynor often fielded the balls down the line with his bare hands. "He had the quickest hands and quickest arms of any third baseman I ever saw." During his thirteen full seasons he batted better than .300 nine times. His lifetime .320 is the best of any third baseman in the Hall of Fame.

Traynor started out as a shortstop and when the Pirates determined they needed him at third he said:

Nobody taught me how to play third base. . . . The way I learned was simply to tackle each situation as it arose and master it before going on to something else. I think I learned more about playing third base in the morning bull sessions in the hotel lobby than I did out on the field . . . the hardest thing in making the switch from short was learning to play that much closer to the hitter. A shortstop can always gamble a little because he can see the ball better and gets a better jump . . . I learned to play third base wide. When I was young and had good legs, I could play in closer and take more chances. But as I grew older and found my reflexes slowing I found I was second-guessing myself. That's when I started over again, playing back and relying more on my positioning.

The year 1926 proved to be the high-water mark of the playing manager. In the National League, Rogers Hornsby ★ starred at second base in his first (and last) year running that club, and shortstop Dave Bancroft held the dual roles for the Boston Braves. In the American League, Tris Speaker with Cleveland, Ty Cobb in Detroit, Bucky Harris at Washington, Eddie Collins for Chicago, and George Sisler ★ on the St. Louis Browns all doubled, although Cobb restricted himself to playing 79 games. A year later five of the seven were gone; only Bancroft and Harris remained in their combined posts.

In the heart of the Great Depression, from 1930 to 1939, the player-manager syndrome briefly flourished again as much for economic as for tactical reasons, but then quickly disappeared. Not even the shortage of able-bodied men during World War II could reverse the trend of separating field hands from straw bosses. Pete Rose's double duty for Cincinnati in 1986 was a singular atavism.

It is notable that during the peak doubling years, the managers almost invariably brought with them outstanding credentials as players; every last one of the class of 1926 made the Hall of Fame as a player. That, however, was no guarantee of success as a manager. Consider, for example, George Sisler. That most exacting and least generous of experts, Ty Cobb, declared: "He could do everything. He could hit, hit with power, field, run and throw. And in his early years in the major leagues, he was a pitcher, and a great one."

As an Ohio schoolboy and sandlot star in 1911, the seventeen-year-old Sisler quickly became a target of minor league recruiters. The Akron club signed him to a contract but the moment the boy's father heard of the deal he repudiated it because his son was underage. Young George went off for an education at the University of Michigan.

According to legend, the Wolverines were coached by a former failed major leaguer catcher and student named Wesley Branch Rickey. One day while Rickey sat gabbing with the athletic director, a student burst in with the news that a freshman was fanning everyone who came to bat. Rickey rushed to the scene and beheld a vision that remained with him. Only one ball reached the outfield as the kid blew the ball past twenty of his fellow collegians in a 7-inning game.

Four years later, Rickey had abandoned torts to conduct the affairs of the St. Louis Browns, while Sisler collected a degree in

Max Carey choked far up on the bat, National League ten times in stolen

Courtesy NBL

mechanical engineering and a superb record as a pitcher, fielder, and hitter. He made Sisler a Brownie. Rickey used his new hand as a pitcher, outfielder, and first baseman. On the mound he won 4 and lost 4, but 2 of his victories were against Walter Johnson, 2–1 and 1–0. He hit a respectable .285. The following year, his first full season, Sisler pitched only 27 innings before Rickey decided to use him as an everyday player. First base became his basic post, although he was so agile that occasionally he filled in at second and third, albeit a lefty.

Sisler's batting average kept climbing. It peaked at .407 in 1920 and .420 in 1922, a season that saw him hit safely in 41 straight games. Lifetime he batted .340. He was the consummate fielder. Rickey delighted in recalling a squeeze play attempt where Sisler was holding a man at first. He timed his rush perfectly, charging the bunt swiftly enough to tag the batter and then throw home to nip a sliding runner from third.

A sinus infection afflicted Sisler's eyesight after his .420 season and he sat out the entire 1923 year. He struggled to reach .305 when he returned to the club, which also named him manager. Over the rest of his career he batted as high as .345 but he never matched his earlier achievements.

Contemporary critics compared Sisler to Cobb as a scholar of the game and for his skill with the bat. However, as one observer put it, "He had none of the raging fire in him that Cobb had. Sisler, instead, was a cold flame."

In fact, neither a blazing conflagration of spirit nor cool ardor could turn the pair into winning managers. No pennants accrued for either Cobb or Sisler. For that matter, Dave Bancroft and Eddie Collins both came up empty as field bosses. Tris Speaker boasted a single pennant, the victory in 1920 somewhat tarnished by the dubious collapse of Chicago.

Perhaps the most curious figure who sought to combine superb playing skills with the presumptions of management was Rogers Hornsby, dubbed "Rajah" as a corruption of his name and in deference to his imperious manner. In performance on the field, Hornsby matched Cobb, Sisler, or any other player with the possible exception of Ruth. His lifetime average of .358 is second

only to Cobb; his .424 in 1924 stands as the highest of the twentieth century, and for six consecutive seasons he topped the league in average. He led all players with homers for 1922 and 1925, 42 and 39, respectively. While not a base stealer, Hornsby covered the ninety feet from home to first as swiftly as anyone. Christy Mathewson called him the fastest man in baseball. His quickness at second base and the sureness of his glove were diminished only by a mild weakness backing up for pop flies. J. Roy Stockton of the *St. Louis Post-Dispatch* explained: "Hornsby was unfamiliar with pop flies because he hit so few of them himself."

Indeed, backing up was something Hornsby resisted throughout his baseball life. Unlike Cobb who restricted his assertiveness and aggression toward those he considered his lessers, Hornsby refused to grant an inch to anyone. He brought the same cold, analytical eye to every confrontation. Only occasionally, as when he knocked out rival manager Art Fletcher with a single punch because "I couldn't make any headway against him talking," did he resort to his fists. His stiff-necked attitude with subordinates and owners sent his show on the road often; he played for five different clubs and managed a similar number. Supposedly he once growled: "It don't make no difference where I go or what happens, so long as I can play the full nine."

Detractors usually complained that Hornsby insisted his way was the only way. But he knew when to listen. As a nineteen-year-old rural stripling, Hornsby batted in the mid-.200s, hardly making him a treasure. The St. Louis Cardinals offered him to Little Rock of the Southern Association in 1915 for a mere $500. Little Rock refused to meet the price and the Cards seemed stuck with their acquisition.

Hornsby then took the advice of those like Miller Huggins who counseled him to abandon his bush-league crouch. He stood more upright, dug in, and fully extended his arms in his swing. "I learned by standing in the extreme left corner of the batter's box I had better control of the situation. I could pull inside pitches to left and drive the outside pitches to right."

Scrappy and unwilling to digest the guff of veterans, Hornsby recognized a need to improve his physique. He spent a winter on an

Harold "Pie" Traynor was among the first to show third base need not be reserved for those with stout chests and a hot bat. He not only hit well but fielded spectacularly.

Courtesy NBL

uncle's farm, building muscles through hard labor, and when he returned to the Cardinals in 1916 he packed an added 25 pounds. He switched to the heaviest bat in the rack, 35 ounces, adding both power and regularity to his hits.

For all of his apparent contentiousness, Hornsby treated umpires gently. On a called strike, Hornsby would inquire politely, "What was that one, exactly?" Informed it cut the outside corner he could remark, "Did it? I'll have to watch those, looked a little high to me." That flattery brought him the good will of the officials. They seldom called a third strike on him, honoring both his judgment and his respect for them.

Hornsby was as obsessive about the game as Cobb, but as a contest of skills, not a personal, bloody war. "I don't fight with umpires and I'm not going to. I don't run wild on the basepaths spiking other players. If I had to play dirty baseball, I would rather not play at all."

He made few friends; his obsession with baseball excellence allowed no margin for error. Billy Herman ★ was a rookie under Hornsby:

> He was a real hard-nosed guy. He ran the clubhouse like a gestapo camp. You couldn't smoke, drink a soft drink, eat a sandwich. Couldn't read a paper. When you walked in the clubhouse, you put your uniform on and got ready to play. That was *it!* No more kidding around, no joking, no laughing. . . . Very cold man. He was liable to go a month and never even say hello to you. . . . When you *would* hear from him is if you made a play he didn't think was quite up to his standards. It still burns me up just a little bit to remember some of his sarcastic remarks.

Other managers like McGraw, Huggins, and later Joe McCarthy ★ similarly insisted on a tightly disciplined attitude in the ballpark. But away from it they relaxed and in some instances offered guidance and even the affection of a surrogate father. Hornsby remained aloof.

He avoided cigarettes, coffee, and whiskey as possible inhibitors of his reflexes. He never watched a movie; as a man who grew up when films truly flickered, he protected a primary asset, his eyesight.

His one vice was the racetrack. Late in Hornsby's playing career, Judge Landis, anxious to preserve baseball's image of purity, warned him about his wagering on horses (a vice quietly shared by John McGraw among others). Undaunted, Hornsby snapped that he did not consider betting at the track any more of a gamble than investing in the stock market. Hornsby reportedly lost $100,000 in the 1929 Crash. In the confrontation between Hornsby and Landis it was the judge who blinked.

During the 1925 season, Branch Rickey managed the Cardinals and owned shares in the team but he increasingly came into conflict with the principal proprietor, Sam Breadon. Rickey and Hornsby were hardly the best of friends. The styles of the fiercely profane second baseman and the Sunday-school devotee clashed. Still, Hornsby realized Rickey's enormous contribution: "Because he's played the game and knows it, he would have been the greatest manager in baseball, if he had been able to explain his ideas to players in language they understood."

Hornsby was reluctant to replace Rickey but once he was convinced that Breadon intended to dismiss Rickey anyway, he accepted the job, also buying out Rickey's interest in the club. Hornsby improved the Cardinal record for the remainder of 1925 and then drove them to the pennant in 1926. At first base he had Sunny Jim Bottomley, ★ a man of such congeniality that his constancy with bat and glove seemed almost a bonus. Bottomley hit .299 that season, 11 points under his eventual lifetime figure, but he drove in a league-leading 120 runs and smacked 40 doubles. The three outfielders, Ray Blades, Taylor Douthit, and Billy Southworth, all topped .300. Behind them roamed a coming star, Chick Hafey, ★ who would become a fixture the following season. Hornsby himself contributed a subpar .317. Flint Rhem, a young right-hander, won 20 games; Jess Haines, whose major league pitching career extended through his forty-fourth birthday, added 13 wins at age thirty-three. Lefty Bill Sherdel accounted for another 17. A surprise pickup from the Chicago Cubs, the thirty-nine-year-old physical wreck, Grover Cleveland Alexander, posted a 2.91 ERA with his 9 victories.

The Yankees reasserted their strength in 1926. In addition to Ruth, Gehrig, Meusel, and Earle Combs, ★ the power increased

"Rogers Hornsby, baseball's Mr. Blunt, must have thought that diplomacy was a respiratory disease. . . . They called him Rajah, and the lofty nickname fit him quite well and only partly because he was handsome and hazel-eyed, dimple-cheeked and with a glowing complexion. He also was majestically aloof and taciturn, independent and a loner.

"He was, however, too rough-cut in speech, manner and background to be truly regal, but the image of majesty was there. In fact, to be as honest as Hornsby, he was a petty, prejudiced person, though a frank, outspoken man who hated hypocrisy almost as much as he did baseball general managers."—Bob Broeg, Sporting News

Courtesy NBL

considerably with rookie second baseman Tony Lazzeri. An ideal lead-off hitter, Combs batted from a deep crouch, averaging nearly 200 hits and 70 walks a season. Herb Pennock's record stood at 23–11, Urban Shocker's 19–11, and Hoyt, with nine seasons tucked in his glove at age twenty-seven, was a 16-game winner.

The stage was set for one of baseball's most memorable scenes. Pennock outpitched Sherdel in game one of the 1926 Series with a single by Gehrig driving home Ruth for the winning run. Bottomley collected 2 of the 3 hits yielded by Pennock. Alexander lurched out to the mound for game two and he struck out ten Yankees, retiring the last twenty-one men for an easy 6–2 St. Louis win. Game three was another triumph for the Cardinals and Jess Haines. Game four went to New York with Hoyt the beneficiary of 3 Ruth homers. Pennock pitched 10 innings to again beat Sherdel in game five, but old-man Alexander captured game six 10–2.

Game seven began with Hoyt and Haines as the adversaries. In the fourth inning, Yankee shortstop Mark Koenig erred and so did outfielder Bob Meusel. The Cardinals exploited the mistakes for 3 tainted runs off Waite Hoyt. Haines gave up a homer to Ruth and 1 more run to take a 3–2 lead into the seventh. It was a raw, rain-sodden afternoon and Haines now weakened. He managed to get 2 outs but yielded a single and a pair of walks, loading the bases.

Hornsby, afraid Haines no longer had control, signaled from his post at second base for relief. In from the bullpen ambled the ancient Alexander, his cap, which always seemed a size too small, high on his head, his red warm-up sweater over his arm. The hard-boiled school of revisionist journalism alleges Alexander had been dozing, the residue of a hangover from celebrating his win in game six. His wife and others deny it.

In any event, Hornsby met him and reportedly reminded Alexander, "There ain't no room." Alexander grunted acknowledgment and threw a few pitches to loosen up.

Into the batter's box stepped Lazzeri, coming off an excellent first year, .275 with 18 homers, 14 triples, and 28 doubles. The opening pitch was vintage Alexander, low and away, an unhittable strike. The second delivery has been somewhat a matter of debate; it too was a strike but on the inside of the plate. Lazzeri pulled a vicious long foul. "A few feet more and he'd have been a hero and I'd have been a bum," said Alexander later. One account insists the ball was deliberately inside where Lazzeri could not possibly drive it fair. Another version claims Alexander made the pitch fatter than he intended. With 2 strikes on Lazzeri, Alexander wasted one and then struck with his meat and potatoes, the low and away curve. Lazzeri swung and missed, ending the inning.

Alexander shut out the Yanks in the eighth and ninth, surviving a 2-out walk to Ruth in the final round. Bob Meusel came to bat and Ruth suddenly tried to steal second. Catcher Bob O'Farrell gunned him down and the Cardinals had the Series with 2 victories and a save for Alexander. Ruth's attempted steal has been called one of the few bad plays the Babe ever made, but in his defense he argued that with Old Pete as effective as he appeared, the only hope was to get into scoring position.

Alexander, nearing his baseball dotage, demonstrated he could pitch with fuzz-faced boys in 1927, winning 21 games for the Cardinals. But Rogers Hornsby was not on the premises to witness the continuing vindication of his faith in Old Pete. Although his club had captured the championship, Sam Breadon resented Hornsby's attitude. Late in the 1926 season, when approached about a potentially lucrative exhibition game, the manager apparently told his employer to play that game in a place where no baseball has ever been.

Hornsby felt insulted by Breadon's tender of a one-year contract without a raise. When the two could not agree on terms, Hornsby shuffled off to the Giants for Fordham University's slick second baseman Frank Frisch and a less-than-illustrious pitcher, Jimmy Ring. Cardinal fans were outraged. They swathed the doors of Breadon enterprises with black crepe, hung Breadon in effigy, and forced him to disconnect his home telephone because of crank calls.

Hornsby could do nothing about the swap and indeed may have seen an opportunity to succeed McGraw. However, before he could report, the shares he held in the Cardinals posed a problem. He certainly could not play for the Giants and own a piece of a rival team. Yet, Sam Breadon only wanted to pay less than $80 a share while Hornsby set his

"The Yankees can get along withou Pennock like an automobile without oline, like a hunk of liver without its of bacon, like a mud-turtle without it Pennock is the best left-hander in th ness, not excluding the phenomena Grove, who is not yet matured. If (Ruppert thinks the Yankees can get without Herbie, he is kidding himsel bie wants $20,000 and he's cheap price."—Jack Conway, New York Mirror

Courtesy NBL

price at $105 for his 1,167 shares. League president John Heydler resolved the dispute with a compromise of $100 per share; Breadon agreed to chip in $80,000, the Giants $17,500, and the League advanced $19,200.

Hornsby lasted only a year in New York, substituting for McGraw as manager during the season and leading the Giants to a better finish than anticipated. But once McGraw recovered from an illness, he swapped his second baseman to the Boston Braves for the tubby, good-hitting catcher, Shanty Hogan, and outfielder Jimmy Welsh. Hornsby could only manage the feeble Braves to seventh place. The Chicago Cubs, seeking to improve their lot for 1929, offered five players and $200,000 to Boston for Hornsby. Showing a rare appreciation for an owner's fiscal pre-dicament, Hornsby then encouraged Boston proprietor Judge Emil Fuchs to consummate the deal: "If you don't take it," he tactfully told Fuchs, "You are a . . . fool."

Working for Cub manager Joe McCarthy, Hornsby slumped from his Boston average of .387 to a mere .380. He led the league at his position in both assists and double plays and the Cubs won the pennant. He remained in Chicago several more years. Inevitably, the years eroded the splendid skills. As a dugout manager for the St. Louis Browns and then Cincinnati, age could not soften his bluntness. He offered his epitaph: "Baseball is the best. But it's like everything else, I guess, some players for you, some against you. I'm a tough guy, a gambler on horses, a slave driver and in general a disgrace to the game. I wish I knew why. I only wanted to win."

(Above) *"Like an old gunfighter, summoned from time past, riding slowly into town for one last rendezvous, Alex moved slowly across the outfield grass."*—Donald Honig

Courtesy NBL

(Left) *The Hornsby grip helped carry him to seven batting titles.*

Courtesy NBL

In late fall of 1986, my son and I went to look at a couple of colleges in Boston, which was still recuperating from the sudden reversal in the World Series. The loss of the last two games had been so staggering that I had referred to it in print as "The Curse of Babe Ruth," a reference to the Red Sox not having won a World Series since Ruth was shipped away to the lowly New York Yankees early in 1920.

In my fevered mind, Babe Ruth had loomed over the 1986 Series the way the left-field wall looms over the playing field of Fenway Park. One of my colleagues even ran across an eighty-eight-year-old fan named Bill Morrissey who could remember the "general grumbling" by the fans when the Babe departed.

Now the Babe even extended into a couple of colleges in his first major-league town. Our first stop was Boston University, that long strip of urban campus that begins behind Kenmore Square, a few blocks from Fenway Park. After the tour, my son and I decided to visit a friend who lives in Miles Standish Hall, a wonderful Pilgrim name for a college dormitory.

"This is really the old Sheraton Hotel," our friend said, gesturing at the lobby. "The Yankees used to stay here. In fact, Babe Ruth used to order the same room all the time. We're not sure what room it was, but it was on the eighth floor."

The three of us smiled at the thought of Babe Ruth's room, the buckets of beer that must have been carried up there during Prohibition, the tubs of ribs and fried chicken, the women visiting the room in platoons. Babe Ruth's room. Imagine trying to write a term paper on symbolism in the modern novel, or study for a psychology test, while hearing echoes of Babe Ruth cavorting.

"Is he ever, uh, seen?" I asked. I don't believe in ghosts, but I like the idea of them, at least in other people's residences.

"Not really," our student friend said.

It was a stimulating thought, however—the Babe rambling around his old hotel room, wishing for just one more coldie, to quench a thirst that hasn't gotten any better since his rambunctious soul left his cancer-ridden body on that muggy day in August 1948.

The three of us smiled again at the thought of Babe Ruth, gone from this earth for thirty-eight years, before either of the two young men had been born, yet a living persona, bigger than the Buckners and the Wilsons who had played in the 1986 World Series, bigger than anybody in the game today, bigger than anybody who ever played this game. The Babe.

My son and I left Boston University and walked across Kenmore

"The myth celebrates American in in a good lost time, and Babe Ruth w than a man. He was a parade all by a burst of dazzle and jingle, Sant drinking his whiskey straight and g with a bellyache caused by glutto Jimmy Cannon, New York Post

Courtesy Ted Astor

As a boy, George Herman Ruth spent much of his time at St. Mary's Industrial School for "incorrigibles," in Baltimore where he learned his baseball.

Courtesy NBL

At nineteen, Ruth went directly from St. Mary's to organized baseball. He signed with the Baltimore Orioles of the International League under the watchful eyes of the proprietors, Jack Dunn (left) and Neal Hanlon (right).

Courtesy NBL

Square, headed for Northeastern University. I assured my son that the shortest route just happened to take us past Fenway Park, so we crossed over the Mass Pike, truck drivers blaring their diesel horns underneath. We descended a few steps to the edge of the old ball yard, Jersey Street nearly deserted, with no hordes bulging from the beer joints and the souvenir stands.

"The last time I was here, people were happy," I told my son, remembering the night of October 23, when Bruce Hurst had put the Sox ahead, 3 games to 2.

I could remember the fans lurching in the streets, celebrating another fine game by Hurst, the polite, conservative family man of the Red Sox. With the Mets' right-handed hitters taking dead aim at the famed Left Field Wall, the Green Monster, Hurst became the first Red Sox left-hander to win a World Series game in Fenway Park since Babe Ruth.

Hurst knew that Ruth had beaten the Cubs in the fourth game of the 1918 World Series, when Ruth was still one of the best pitchers in the game, before Ed Barrow of the Red Sox decided to make Babe Ruth a full-time outfielder, before the sale that devastated the Red Sox for decades, before the Yankees changed the game of baseball forever.

Sixty-eight years after Babe Ruth's victory over the Cubs, he was still a tangible presence on the Fenway Park mound, peering over Bruce Hurst's left shoulder.

"Way to go, keed," the Babe might have been saying on that nippy night in Fenway. He never could remember names, old-timers tell me. I couldn't believe Ruth would not root for his fellow lefty on his first team, in his old ballpark, even though the Red Sox may be jinxed for eternity for shuffling him off.

In the late-autumn mist, my son and I walked along the irregular contour of Fenway Park, noting the screen atop the left-field wall, the offices behind home plate, and then the long straight line down the right-field foul line, just about the way it was when Ruth came up in 1914.

The few old stadiums are among baseball's greatest treasures today: In Fenway Park and Wrigley Field and Tiger Stadium and White Sox Park and Municipal Stadium in Cleveland and even in refurbished Yankee Stadium, you can visualize the old heroes—Hack Wilson, Hank Greenberg, Lou Gehrig—hitting home runs into the unique nooks and crannies, not like the neutral, circular, carpeted multipurpose nonentities of today.

Even walking outside Fenway Park on that misty morning, my son and I could feel the challenge to a left-handed hitter: Home plate seemed a thousand miles away from the right-field stands.

Boston bought his contract in mid[...] gave him several starts, and then farm[...] out to Providence in the Intern[...] League.

Courtesy NBL

138

This is the same ballpark in which Babe Ruth, a pitcher, a barrel-chested busher just out of the orphanage in Baltimore, propelled baseballs into the right-field stands. He came to this town a pitcher and he left a slugger. You couldn't sit him down three days out of four. It would be a crime against nature.

We thought about Babe Ruth's home runs as we passed the right-field stands. We giggled at the idea of spunky little Len Dykstra emerging from the Mets' dugout and hitting a leadoff home run in the third game of the Series, right into Ruth's right-field stands, and we imagined Dykstra running around the bases, muttering to himself, just as Japanese soldiers had screamed what they imagined to be the ultimate insult to American soldiers in World War II: "Nuts to Babe Ruth," or words to that effect.

Refreshed from our walk outside the ballpark, my son and I then crossed the communal gardens in the Fenway, and walked over to Northeastern, where we were meeting another friend. Richard Lapchick is one of the last visible 1960s civil-rights activists, a teacher and writer who operates something called the Center for the Study of Sport in Society.

He is also the son of Joe Lapchick, a famous basketball player, one of the original Celtics of New York, who later coached the New York Knickerbockers and St. John's University. Richard Lapchick is extremely proud of his late father; he keeps photographs of him on his office walls.

In one of the photographs, angular Joe Lapchick was a few inches taller than a robust, slick-haired, broad-nosed beaming moose of a man: Babe Ruth. They had played in an exhibition during the off-season and had posed together.

Reports from that era indicate that the Babe's athletic prowess did not extend to basketball, that he was a clutcher and a grabber in a sport he had never played, except for exercise or a few barnstorming bucks. He and Joe Lapchick had stood side by side, giants of their respective sports, instinctive friends despite their opposing temperaments. On Richard Lapchick's wall, his father and Babe Ruth were smiling from more than half a century ago. In the fall of 1986, George Herman Ruth was everywhere.

Babe Ruth endures. His appeal is beyond numbers, beyond detail. The greatest of the other players tend to become museum pieces, as historic as the wrinkled photographs and the bulky uniforms, but Babe Ruth's contagious grin, his legend, and his records—even the broken ones—keep pace with each generation.

I will always remember Babe Ruth's career total of 714 home runs, but for the purposes of this article, I had to go to the *Baseball Encyclopedia*

to look up the number of home runs by that excellent player, Henry Aaron. (It was 755; did you have it?)

The legend reinforces the numbers. Growing up as a newspaper junkie in New York in the 1940s and 1950s, I read Jimmy Cannon and Arthur Daley and Red Smith and Frank Graham resurrecting the Babe Ruth anecdotes—Ruth hitting a homer for a dying boy, Ruth's famous "stomachache heard round the world," Ruth dangling his manager, Miller Huggins, out of the observation deck of the train. Some of these legends were even true.

Did Ruth point out a spot in the Wrigley Field bleachers during the 1932 World Series, or did he just hold up a finger or two to Charlie Root? Forty-one years later, Red Smith wrote: "I was there, but I have never been dead sure of what I saw."

In his definitive biography, *Babe Ruth: The Legend Comes to Life*, Robert Creamer examines all the legends, and Babe Ruth manages to grow bigger, not smaller, for all the scrutiny. He was too flamboyant, too good, to be merely a Yankee. Babe Ruth belonged to all of us.

I think of the baseball players who have given me the most excitement since I discovered the sport as a child in 1946—Ted Williams and Stan Musial, the two left-handed stars of that World Series, slashing line drives to all corners of the memory; Jackie Robinson, dancing off third base for my beloved Brooklyn Dodgers, helping to carry black and white America toward the second half of the century; Bob Gibson, glowering and claiming the mound as his; and Pete Rose, chesty, blunt, driven.

I think of all the great players of my four decades as fan and journalist—the smooth DiMaggio, the fluid Mays, the complete Aaron, the forceful Frank Robinson, the gallant Clemente, the graceful Koufax, the turbulent Mantle, the natural Valenzuela, the disciplined Seaver.

Having seen all the great players of the past four decades, I will take the word of my elders that Babe Ruth could pitch and field and throw and run—yes, even run—with the best of them. And I fully accept that the sum of his ability made him the most exciting, the most dominant player the game has ever known.

In 1969, during the celebration of baseball's centennial, the baseball writers and broadcasters voted Babe Ruth "The Greatest Player Ever"—a title so Twentyish, so circus-posterish, that it was Ruthian in its sweep. The man even had an adjective in his honor.

Fortunately, there are still people around to remind us of what Babe Ruth meant in his time, from his first game in 1914 to that last 3-homer splurge with the Boston Braves in 1935, a career that spanned a world

(Opposite) In 1915, Ruth became a starter for the Sox, winning 18, dropping only 8. Except for a handful of pinch-hit appearances, he served exclusively as a pitcher.

Courtesy NBL

Married to his first wife, squire Ruth in a knickered tweed suit with cap posed at the doorway to "Home Plate," a farmhouse in Sudbury, Massachusetts.

Courtesy NBL

war and a depression, Woodrow Wilson to Franklin Delano Roosevelt.

My father used to tell me stories of being a fourteen-year-old, either playing hookey or already dropped out of school, going up to Yankee Stadium for the first game on April 18, 1923. The new stadium in the Bronx would be known as The House That Ruth Built, since no one player had ever turned around a franchise and inspired a stadium.

My father was hardly a Yankee sympathizer but he talked with awe of the crowd, estimated at more than seventy-four thousand fans inside and perhaps another twenty-five thousand outside, the expectation, the immediate majesty of the huge open-air cathedral in the Bronx. And my father recalled how Ruth produced his trademark, a home run, in the first game in the stadium he had "built."

By now, the elderly are the caretakers of the Ruthian legend. They must guard against foolish youths making any misjudgments about The Babe. A few years ago, a just-born sportswriter in New York made the unfortunate reference to Babe Ruth as, and I paraphrase, "a fat guy who hit home runs." I cannot lay my hands on the letter, but I remember how an elderly fan flogged the young whelp with words:

*Traded to the Yankees for the 1920 se
Ruth played for diminutive Miller Hu
who sought to impose discipline on his
living outfielder.*

Courtesy NBL

> Didn't the young boob know that Babe Ruth was a fine base runner for much of his career, opportunistic and quick, pitty-patting from first to third on almost any single, even with those skinny ankles? Didn't the young boob know that Ruth could reach and catch more than the normal share of drives to his field? Didn't the young boob know that Ruth had an arm that matched anything of the Furillo-Clemente-Evans-Parker post-war crowd?
>
> Didn't the young boob know that Babe Ruth was a marvelous pitcher who won 94 games and lost only 46 with an exquisite earned run average of 2.28? We must always be on guard against young boobs, and against being boobs ourselves. Never mind the pictures of Babe Ruth, with his Falstaffian/Ruthian belly of later years. Until his appetites totally got the better of him, he was a fine athlete, even though it was the home runs that made him one of a kind.

There are still fans who remember Babe Ruth. We happened to hear about one during the World Series of 1986. More than two hundred members of the overflow press corps were placed in excellent seats, only twenty-five rows up from the field, staring straight down at home plate and the left-field line.

Showing the intrepid qualities that had won him the Pulitzer Prize a few years earlier, my colleague, Dave Anderson, asked a few fans near us what had happened to the season ticket holders we had obviously displaced. They pointed out eighty-eight-year-old William Francis Morrissey from South Boston, who had been going to games since he was a child.

A real-estate assessor who was still working at the age of eighty-eight, Bill Morrissey told Dave Anderson that he had seen approximately 3,500 games, so far, including many of the Braves' games in Back Bay until they left town in 1953. He remembered Tris Speaker and Cy Young, and he praised Don Mattingly, the contemporary star of the Yankees. But most of all he raved about the robust young pitcher, George Herman Ruth, coming up from Baltimore in 1914, costing the Red Sox all of $2,900, impressing everybody with his left arm, his power, and his raw behavior in and out of uniform.

Bill Morrissey could remember the 1916 Series when Ruth beat the Brooklyn Dodgers, and he could remember 1918 when Ruth beat the Cubs in the first and fourth games, and in the process put together 29⅔ scoreless innings, the World Series record until another fair left-hander, Whitey Ford of the Yankees, broke it in 1961.

"Babe Ruth was the best pitcher the Red Sox ever had," Bill Morrissey said on the night Bruce Hurst won his second game of the 1986 Series. "But he hit so well, I suppose he had to become an outfielder. And he knew what base to throw to."

The record books attest to the 714 home runs and the 17 shutouts in 148 major-league starts. I take the word of Bill Morrissey about the complete way Babe Ruth played the game. I never had the pleasure of seeing the man in uniform, although I once had a distant glimpse of a dying man in a camel-hair coat, rasping into a microphone in Yankee Stadium.

It was a sunny day, but chilly in the recesses of the right-field stands, once known as Ruthville. I was only eight years old, and I remember the day through a screen of elbows and topcoats.

We were Brooklyn Dodger fans in my household, and a trip to Yankee Stadium was basically a maneuver on enemy soil, but since my father had been to the first game in The House That Ruth Built, he thought we ought to be there for this one.

We could rationalize crossing the borders because Babe Ruth loomed larger than team loyalties. He was a Red Sox, a Yankee, a Boston Brave, and he had even "coached" for our beloved Dodgers. Babe Ruth was public domain.

Besides, we were going to pay homage to a dying man. No need to

"The Ruth is mighty and shall prevail. He did yesterday. Babe Ruth made two home runs and the Yankees won from the Giants at the Polo Grounds by a score of 4 to 2. . . . Victory came to the American League champions through a change of tactics. Miller Huggins could hardly fail to have observed Wednesday that terrible things were almost certain to happen to his men if they paused any place along the line from first to home. In order to prevent blunders in base running he wisely decided to eliminate it. The batter who hits a ball into the stands cannot possibly be caught napping off any base. . . .

"Why shouldn't we pitch to Ruth? [said John McGraw]. 'I've said before and I'll say again, we pitch to better hitters than Ruth in the National League.' Ere the sun had set on McGraw's rash and presumptuous words, the Babe had flashed across the sky fiery portents which should have been sufficient to strike terror and conviction into the hearts of all infidels. But John McGraw clung to his heresy with a courage worthy of a better cause."—Heywood Broun, New York World, 1923

Courtesy NBL

apologize for that. It had been in the papers that he was in and out of the hospitals, losing weight, losing his voice. Baseball had staged an appreciation for Babe Ruth on April 27, and 58,339 fans had clogged Yankee Stadium to applaud the Babe, who had stood up there in his camel-hair topcoat and made a quavering speech over the rudimentary public address system, and people had wiped their eyes.

Then he managed to survive the entire 1947 season, and was honored again on the final day. The Yankees had already sewed up the pennant—they had gone three seasons without one, for goodness' sakes—and were not objecting to the sound of turnstiles.

George Weiss, the general manager, even arranged the first old-timers game, starring Ruth's contemporaries, and there was a rumor that Ruth might get into uniform and pitch an inning, but that talk evaporated when people saw the faded man. He was barely well enough to trudge onto the field, again in that camel-hair coat, and make another speech.

There are two things I remember from that day—although, the way memory works, they may not actually have happened that way. I distinctly remember Ty Cobb, nineteen seasons past his last game, squaring around to bunt, pushing the catcher, Wally Schang, backward, and people laughing at that typical Cobb maneuver.

My microfilm copy of the *New York Times* does not confirm that semi-friendly shove, but it does note that Cobb "deftly dumped a bunt in the infield" but that the "old gentleman of 61 was tossed out. He registered disgust, and then broke out in a broad grin. That also wasn't like the Cobb of old."

The other thing I remember is the broken, distant voice of Babe Ruth squawking on the public address system. I can remember myself hunkered among adults, smelling the cigarettes and the hair spray, and the mothballs from the winter coats just out of the closet, hearing the Babe talking about baseball as the greatest game for young boys.

The only problem is, the speech I remember Ruth delivering in late September is the speech he gave in his April farewell:

Thank you very much, ladies and gentlemen. You know how bad my voice sounds. Well, it feels just as bad. You know, this baseball game of ours comes up from the youth. That means the boys. And after you've been a boy, and grow up to know how to play ball, then you come to the boys you see representing themselves today in our national pastime. The only real game in the world, I think, is baseball. As a rule, some people think if you give them a football or a baseball or something like that, naturally, they're

"Supposedly 'over the hill,' slipping down the steps of Time, stumbling toward the discard, six years past his peak, Babe Ruth stepped out and hung up a new home-run record at which all the sports world may stand and wonder. What Big Bill Tilden couldn't do on the tennis court, Babe Ruth has done on the diamond. What Dempsey couldn't do with his fists, Ruth has done with his bat. He came back. Put it in the book in letters of gold. It will be a long time before anyone else betters that home-run mark, and a still longer time before any aging athlete makes such a gallant and glorious charge over the comeback trail."—John Kieran, New York Times

Courtesy NBL

Courtesy UPI/Bettmann News photos

athletes right away. But you can't do that in baseball. You've got to start from way down, at the bottom, when you're six or seven years old. You can't wait until you're fifteen or sixteen. You've got to let it grow up with you, and if you're successful and you try hard enough, you're bound to come out on top, just like these boys have come to the top now.

There's been so many lovely things said about me, I'm glad I had the opportunity to thank everybody. Thank you.

My assumption is that I have seen Babe Ruth making this talk so often, either in old film clips shown on new-fangled message boards in the modern stadiums, or on television, or perhaps it was Bill Bendix croaking his farewell speech in the movie of Babe Ruth's life, that the events have merged. It is also possible that Ruth repeated the same theme in his autumn farewell, it having been so well received in his spring farewell.

Faithful to his reputation as a man of excesses, Ruth made yet another farewell performance at Yankee Stadium, this one on June 13, 1948, as the Yankees celebrated the twenty-fifth anniversary of The House That Ruth Built. Carrying a bat for a cane, he trudged onto the field and gave yet another speech, and the old-timers staged another game, but by that time Ruth had repaired to the clubhouse for a beer with his old pal, Jumping Joe Dugan.

He died two months later, on August 16. My father called from his newspaper office to tell us, just as he had called to tell us that Franklin Delano Roosevelt had died, early in 1945. Ruth's illness had been more publicized, more protracted, than the president's, but that is a strange side value of athletes. They not only teach us how to live, how to play a game in some isolated, pure fashion, but they also teach us how to die.

Athletes are the most accessible gods we have, performing unrehearsed miracles on grass or hardwood or ice or the canvas ring. Presidents make speeches, dancers follow a choreography, astronauts work in teams, but athletes improvise, in public. Their strengths and their weaknesses become a public struggle, a morality play before our eyes.

Their foibles and their aging, their illnesses and their deaths, seem always to be greeted with surprise. How could Chris Evert Lloyd possibly turn thirty and have a bad knee? How could Joe Louis lose? How could such-and-such a player have an alcohol problem, just like the man down the block?

We were surprised to see Babe Ruth wasting away in front of our eyes, surprised to hear of his death. Impossible, we said. Not the Babe. Not the man who ate a dozen hot dogs, drank buckets of beer, wenched conspicu-

Lou Gehrig hitting behind Ruth gave the Yanks awesome power for a decade. Poles apart in personality, they worked together as teammates and for promotions.

Courtesy AP/Wide World

147

ously, and survived scrapes and suspensions and stomachaches. If the Babe can be reduced to a whispering, withered old man of fifty-three, it can happen to any of us.

Still, we were shocked at Ruth's passing because he had seemed larger than life. His contemporaries, now fast disappearing, have left a legacy of quotes about the man—"awesome" and "animal" and "unbelievable."

He set such a formidable shadow that it soured men who had to labor in it. Roger Maris was vilified by some fans and some members of the sporting press because he had the audacity to play right field in Yankee Stadium and hit enough home runs into Ruthville to challenge and surpass Ruth's record of 60 home runs in the 1927 season.

The times were different by 1961, the year of Maris. The country was bigger and electrified, bombarded by television and radio, connected by jet planes and fast interstate highways, and Maris was pursued by more furies than Ruth could have imagined.

Gone were Ruth's amiable companions of the long sleeper trains; now the furies carried tape recorders and popped in for the quick psychological plumbing of Roger Maris's depths. How would Ruth have taken to questions about his inner motivation, his personal dualities, his mixed feelings, his yin and his yang?

In a pilgrimage to the Babe Ruth Birthplace Museum in the old "Pigtown" section of Baltimore during the 1982 World Series, the perceptive Stan Hochman of the *Philadelphia Daily News* mused about simpler times:

> Nobody hung around to ask him how he got the nickname Babe. And nobody asked him the derivation of Pigtown. And nobody asked him what he'd eaten for breakfast that day or if a typical breakfast consisted of 14 hotcakes smothered in pure maple syrup. . . . Nobody asked him to name the last book he'd read or the last movie he'd seen. Or what he weighed. Or if he slept in silk pajamas.

Somebody must have been keeping tabs on such details, because Bob Creamer gets right down to the bare facts in the *Babe* biography. But Hochman is absolutely correct: Babe Ruth was able to remain this intuitive, uninhibited force because the furies were not there in regular swarms in those days.

Asked to dig into his own psyche too often, by all the evidence, Ruth would have belched or giggled or thrown the amateur shrinks out of the

(Opposite) *Before an exhibition game at Brooklyn's Dexter Park, the fellows wore cowboy suits to herald a rodeo. Gehrig also donned chaps, spurs, and a ten-gallon hat for a movie role in* Rawhide.

Courtesy AP/Wide World

His major league career running out, the Babe put on a beard for a game with the hirsute House of David semipros.

Courtesy AP/Wide World

clubhouse, depending on his mood. He would not have submitted to analysis easily. I was a rookie reporter in 1961, and I can attest that Roger Maris was reasonably decent during his chase of Ruth's record, at least until his hair started falling out in patches.

The legend of Babe Ruth seemed to stalk Roger Maris in 1961, when the American League had just expanded from eight teams to ten, and the schedule had been enlarged from 154 games to 162.

The Baseball Commissioner was Ford Frick, a former newspaperman, occasional ghostwriter, and enough of a friend to have been a deathbed visitor of Ruth. Roger Maris could not win this one. Frick ruled that if Maris broke Ruth's record in anything more than 154 games, the two accomplishments would be accorded separate but equal credit. Somebody else used the word "asterisk," but Frick was given the credit or the blame for the word.

Maris hit his sixty-first homer on the last day of a 162-game season, and had the asterisk branded on him for eternity. He also died in 1985 at the age of fifty-one, two years younger than Ruth had been when he died.

To this day, people talk about Maris as a freak, a one-dimensional athlete who happened to have a looping uppercut swing that could reach the inviting target of Ruthville. There are younger boobs who forget that Maris was a complete player, a fitting tenant of Ruthville, but it was never easy to stand in Babe Ruth's footprints.

Henry Aaron, a marvelous ball player with speed, power, arm, competitiveness, and athletic intelligence, ran smack into the Curse of Babe Ruth as he chased the all-time home run record in 1973 and 1974. Aaron felt racial prejudice was the motive for many people not wanting to see him catch Ruth—a special irony since Ruth had often been taunted by rivals for his broad nose and large lips.

This had been the only insult that could really distress Ruth, who once invaded an enemy clubhouse and warned the other players they could call him a blankety-blank or a so-and-so, but that they shouldn't "get personal," as he put it. There was no evidence Ruth had any black ancestry, but more than a few Negro fans were glad to think one of them had slipped through the net of discrimination and was hitting all those home runs.

Whether Aaron was right or wrong, it was an uncomfortable legacy of America that he should have felt that way. This superb ball player socked a pitch by Al Downing of the Los Angeles Dodgers for his 715th career homer early in the 1974 season, and he widened his total to 755 before

"Ruth did everything big. His appe food was enormous. I've seen him eat dog sandwiches, washing them dow beer, and then ask for more. He coul the same way, since he had an ab capacity for handling beer and While I never attended any of hi known debauches, neither did I ever years as a player, see him stinking I've seen players on the field who we ously carrying hangovers from big before—Ray Caldwell, Rabbit Mar Paul Waner, Grover Alexander, Ha son—and it affected their play, bu Ruth during a season. In addition t the greatest home-run hitter, he also game's foremost showman. He sizzle charisma. He was worshipped by the tudes, and boys followed him in drove ever he went. He may have been d some things, but he knew he was goo athlete and as the center of attract glorified in it and he acted according Fred Lieb, My Life in Baseball

Courtesy NBL

he retired after 1976, but he never gave any indication that he had truly passed Babe Ruth.

The memory of Babe Ruth does not fool around. His spirit has rumbled in historic Fenway Park like the Loch Ness Monster or Big Foot, ever since the World Series of 1918, when Ruth won 2 games. He played one more season for the Red Sox, setting a record of 29 home runs, still shifting between the outfield and the mound. He was the greatest player in the game—and then his owner sold him for $100,000.

"I think the Yankees are taking a gamble. While Ruth is undoubtedly the greatest hitter the game has ever seen, he is likewise the most selfish and inconsiderate man ever to put on a baseball uniform," Harry Frazee said.

Back in Boston in 1986, William Francis Morrissey still remembered Harry Frazee. "He was a showman," Morrissey said in his strong South Boston accent. "Needed the money to finance a show, *No, No, Nanette,* am I correct?" I was in college at the time, and I wasn't going to all the games the way I did later, but I remember the general resentment.

"People thought Frazee was a ham-and-egger, you know, he needed the dough. He sold other good ball players, too, but when he sold Ruth, people were upset. I don't remember the fans organizing a boycott, but the press talked it up. We saw a lot of bad baseball in Boston after that."

Ruth had been glad to escape the Red Sox for a bigger salary on the Yankees, the lowly New York Yankees, who were trying to build themselves into a first-division outfit like the Philadelphia Athletics of Connie Mack, the Detroit Tigers with slashing Ty Cobb, and the Boston Red Sox of Tris Speaker and then Babe Ruth.

Ruth never uttered any farewell curse; he knew opportunity when he saw it. But his departure cast a spell that festered in the crevices and eaves of Fenway Park. In the dark of night at Fenway Park, the lonely, haunted spirit of the Red Sox howls: "No, No, Harry Frazee."

What else do you do after a team wins five of the first fifteen World Series, then sells off its best player? The Red Sox slipped below .500 in Ruth's last season, and did not reach it again until 1934, and even when they won, they lost.

In 1946, their best player, Ted Williams, batted .200 and drove in only 1 run, and Enos Slaughter of the Cardinals raced home from first base with the winning run of the Series. In 1948, they lost a playoff to the Cleveland Indians. In 1949, they led the dreaded Yankees—lowly no more—by 1 game with 2 to play in Fenway, and lost them both.

In 1967, their ace pitcher, Jim Lonborg, couldn't make it on two days

(Following pages) *The farewell appearance of 1948. "To paraphrase Abraham Lincoln's remark about another deity, Ruth must have admired records because he created so many of them. Yet he was sublimely aware that he transcended records and his place in the American scene was no mere matter of statistics. It wasn't just that he hit more home runs than anybody else, he hit them better, higher, farther, and with more theatrical timing and a more flamboyant flourish. Nobody could strike out like Babe Ruth. Nobody circled the bases with the same pigeon-toed majesty."*—Red Smith, New York Times

Courtesy AP/Wide World

of rest, and they lost the seventh game of the Series to the Cardinals again. In 1975, they won the classic Carlton Fisk body-english sixth game, but manager Darrell Johnson changed pitchers, and Cincinnati's Joe Morgan blooped a wrong-field single to win the Series.

In 1978, they struggled to tie the Yankees in the Eastern Division, but Bucky Dent lofted a 3-run homer over the left-field screen to put the Yankees ahead. Then in 1986, after Bruce Hurst had put them ahead, they lost both games in New York in agonizing late-inning fashion to bring on yet another grim winter in New England.

"I don't want to hear about that jinx crap," said John McNamara, the manager of the Red Sox, but of course it was too late for that. We princes and princesses of the word-processor set had already been to work on the Curse of Babe Ruth.

Whether we were inventing it, resurrecting it, solidifying it, or exaggerating it is almost beside the point. If you can talk about it, it already exists. How many other baseball players have left their own jinx on a ball club, without even meaning it? But then again, nobody ever said Babe Ruth was any other ball player.

A publicity stunt to hype the Notre D
Southern California football rivalry
the boys in less familiar uniforms. Th
iron notables at the dais include
"Pop" Warner, famous for his Univer
Pittsburgh elevens (far left), Knute
of Notre Dame (third from left),
Walsh, a former reporter and Ruth
ness manager (center), and the coach
Howard Jones (second from right).

Courtesy UPI/Bettmann News photos

Murderers' Row they called the New York Yankees of 1927 and that roster is cited whenever arguments of the best team arise. Actually, the one significant addition over the team that lost the World Series to the Cardinals in 1926 was pitcher Wilcy Moore. There was no change either in the infield or outfield. However, the tandem of Ruth and Gehrig sacked and pillaged pitchers with unprecedented ferocity. To Babe's 60 home runs, Gehrig added 47. Undoubtedly, the trepidation that led to 138 walks for Ruth helped Gehrig to drive in 175 runs. Babe knocked in 164 himself. Tony Lazzeri matched his rookie output of 18 home runs but no other Yankee reached double figures. Consistency, though, marked the entire outfit. Ruth finished the year at .356 and Gehrig at .373. (The league leader was Harry Heilmann of Detroit at .398.) Combs in center field hit .356 and Meusel in left hit .337. Lazzeri batted .309 and the club average was .307.

Their opponents for the Series figured to give a fair measure of themselves. The Pittsburgh Pirates as a club batted .305, a bare 2 points below their foes. Aside from Pie Traynor and his .342, there were the Waner brothers, Paul ★ and Lloyd, ★ outfielders who checked in at .380 and .355. However, the entire team hit only 54 home runs versus the Yankees' 158; Pittsburgh totaled 258 doubles and 78 triples against New York's 291 and 103 in these categories.

The mismatch extended to the pitchers. During the 1920s, Firpo Marberry of the Washington Senators was one of the first true specialists in relief, although Bill James notes some appeared earlier. Miller Huggins in 1927 decided his team could profit under such an arrangement and nominated thirty-year-old rookie Wilcy Moore, an occasional starter, as his chief painkiller. Moore performed brilliantly, saving 13, ending the season with a 19–7 record. Undoubtedly, the crashing bats of Ruth and Gehrig assisted him in 13 tie-breaker or come-from-behind wins. Moore, who never approached this efficiency in his remaining five big-league seasons, recorded a 2.28 ERA.

The one pitcher who surpassed Moore for best season percentage was Waite Hoyt at 22–7. He notched a 2.63 ERA. A street-smart Brooklyn kid, Hoyt spoke up whether it was to John McGraw who first discovered

him, Jacob Ruppert who paid him, or Miller Huggins who managed him. Hoyt claimed that after the disappointment of 1926, he went to spring training in St. Petersburg, Florida, troubled by the vicissitudes of his career. He walked the length of a pier jutting into the bay, stared up at a sky brilliant with stars, gazed upon the riding lights of the boats in the harbor, and looked down into the black water.

"I could actually feel as if a hand had touched me on the shoulder and that made me realize there was a God," Hoyt recalled. He was inspired to take "a personal inventory" and the goods came up short. Hoyt resolved to mend his ways, to accept the advice of Miller Huggins. He credited his new attitude with 45 victories and only 14 defeats in the following two years.

But religion was not very much in style during the Roaring Twenties. At the time, Hoyt counseled wives of his fellow players to instruct their children to pray: "God bless Mommy, God bless Daddy, God bless Babe Ruth. Babe has upped Daddy's paycheck by 15 to 40 percent."

The Series opened in Pittsburgh and Huggins, says the legend, applied psychology. He instructed his big men to swing for the seats during batting practice. Ruth obliged and his cannon shots were followed by barrages from Gehrig, Meusel, and Lazzeri. The Pittsburgh players watched in awe. Lloyd Waner, a rookie, supposedly turned to his brother Paul, himself only in his second year, and said, "Jesus, they're big." (The brothers weighed barely 150 pounds each.)

Historians claim the Pirates folded from fear. But in truth, they lost 2 games by a single run and Yankee pitching overcame them in the other pair. Hoyt eked out a 5–4 win. Moore saved Hoyt's game and started game four, which he won after a Pirate wild pitch in the bottom of the ninth. Only Ruth delivered home runs, bashing a pair. He batted .400 and drove in 7 runs. Gehrig contributed pairs of doubles and triples and 5 RBIs. The Waners acquitted themselves well, Lloyd at .400 and Paul at .333.

The Yankees seemed intent on a repeat performance in 1928 as the team swaggered to a 13½-game lead by July 1. But Lazzeri and Joe Dugan, the fine Irish wit at third base, both missed games because of injuries. Ruth blasted another 54 homers and Gehrig

"Waite Hoyt is about ripe, and he is seventeen and has never been kissed by a safety razor or any other kind."—O. B. Keeler, New York American

Hoyt attracted the attention of John McGraw while a schoolboy wiz at Erasmus High in Brooklyn but his prowess with the 1920s Yankees earned him fame.

Courtesy NBL

27, impressive but 26 fewer than the pair produced in 1927. Hoyt won another 23 while dropping only 7, but Wilcy Moore faded to 4-4 and Herb Pennock had begun to slip. However, George Pipgras, who had shown promise in 1927, amazed with an iron arm, 300.2 innings, 24 victories. The Yanks barely fended off a stretch drive from a spanking new contender forged by Connie Mack in Philadelphia, as the extravagant July 1 lead wasted away to a bare 2½.

John McGraw's Giants, packed with the likes of Bill Terry ★ at first, Mel Ott in right field, shortstop Travis Jackson, third sacker Fred Lindstrom, and a rookie pitcher with a most persuasive screwball, Carl Hubbell, all of whom would reach the Hall of Fame, nevertheless lost out to the St. Louis Cardinals. Bill McKechnie, ★ whose spectacles and mild demeanor earned him the nickname of Deacon, ran the club. The Cardinals fielded six future Hall of Famers themselves. Jim Bottomley, the blacksmith-trained first baseman, muscled a league-leading 31 homers and hit .325. Frankie Frisch showed high style at second, with his .300 average and league-topping fielding percentage of .976. Rabbit Maranville batted only .240 but his glove at shortstop held the center of the diamond together. In left field Chick Hafey, converted from pitcher to outfielder by Rickey, was good for .337. The pitchers had excellent credentials. Old Pete at age forty-one still befuddled hitters for a 16–9 record plus a pair of saves. Jess Haines won 20, and Bill Sherdel was good for 21 in the best season of his career.

With the Yanks seemingly on a decline, the 1928 Series figured to be close. Hoyt opened for New York with a 3-hitter to defeat Sherdel 4–1. Meusel and Bottomley both homered, but the Yankee blast came with two on and Bottomley only spoiled a shutout. In game two, the Yanks revenged themselves on Alexander, shelling him from the mound in the third. Gehrig homered with two on for a 9–3 finish. Huggins surprised the experts, choosing a late pickup from the Senators, Tom Zachary, as his starter for the third contest. Gehrig made the job easier with a pair of homers, good for 3 runs, and Haines was the loser, 7–3.

Hoyt reappeared to start game four. The Cardinals led 2–1 in the seventh as Ruth, who had accounted for the Yanks' lone run

with a homer, came to bat against Sherdel. The Cardinal lefty ran up 2 strikes and then fired another ball through the strike zone, seemingly chalking up a strikeout. But the umpire, going by the rules for the Series, voided it as a quick pitch; Ruth had not set himself when Sherdel delivered. At the time the quick pitch was quite common and allowed during regular season play. In this instance, the umpire's decision, not surprisingly, caused a great but futile row.

Ruth stepped back in to hit, supposedly taunting Sherdel. The pitcher then threw two out of the strike zone. He came back with a fastball, which Ruth swatted into the seats. The discomfiture of the Cardinals soared as Gehrig followed with a homer, and then the Yanks battered Sherdel and Alexander in relief, for 2 more. Ruth hit his third home run in the eighth and the game ended 7–3 with 4 straight for New York.

Connie Mack's new collection of stouthearted men with strong arms and potent bats stomped the 1929 Yankees. Demoralized by the midseason death of Miller Huggins, the New Yorkers finished 18 games behind. The Athletic powerhouse featured four genuine superstars: first baseman Jimmie Foxx, ★ catcher Mickey Cochrane, ★ left fielder Al Simmons, ★ and left-handed pitcher Robert Moses Grove.

Although Frank (Home Run) Baker had quit baseball for a year rather than accept Connie Mack's terms in 1915, and finally became a Yankee, he maintained high regard for his old mentor. While minding the store of the Easton, Maryland, club in 1924, Baker recruited a sixteen-year-old farm lad who could pitch, play first, second, or third, as well as catch and hit. Impressed with young James Emory Foxx's talent, Baker wrote to Mack, describing his fine, broad-shouldered merchandise.

Mack put the boy under contract. "Double X," as he became known, spent 1925 with Providence, but as a husky eighteen-year-old he joined the Athletics a year later. Foxx started slowly; the first of his career 534 homers did not reach the stands until 1927 when he was still a utility man, at first base and behind the plate. The next year he performed mostly at third, but once settled more or less permanently at first, he fulfilled the great expectations of Baker and Mack. For the pennant winners he stroked 33 homers

*Lloyd "Little Poison" Waner (le[f]
brother Paul "Big Poison" Waner u[n]
tummies of foes for fourteen years
side in the Pittsburgh outfield.*

Courtesy NBL

156

as part of his .354 average. He repeated that sort of performance year after year, leading the league in four-baggers four times and in slugging percentage five times. Ted Lyons, ★ fated to spend his entire twenty-one years as a major leaguer with a White Sox club ravaged by the scandal, and who nevertheless won 260 games, said that Foxx's biceps "seemed to carry 35 psi air in them."

Foxx possessed extraordinary upper body strength. He walloped four balls completely over the left-field stands at Comiskey Park and put one in the center-field bleachers, over a 35-foot-high wall 440 feet from the plate. One of his smashes at Philadelphia's old Shibe Park measured out at 500 feet, and in a game at Yankee Stadium, he blasted a pitch from Lefty Gomez into the upper left-field corner of Yankee Stadium, barely missing the never-accomplished feat of driving a fair ball out of that park.

When Foxx came to the Athletics as a catcher he became discouraged because of Gordon "Mickey" Cochrane, his competition for the position. Bred on a Massachusetts farm, Cochrane starred as a halfback for Boston University's football squad. He minored in basketball, hockey, boxing, and baseball where he served as a shortstop, outfielder, even pitcher, catching only a game or two when the regular receiver broke his finger.

Cochrane said he became aware of the big-league baseball life as a BU student:

Across the street from Boston University is the old Brunswick Hotel. At that time, the Yankees with Babe Ruth and the Tigers with Ty Cobb—well, nearly all the major league teams stopped there. The players would sit outside the hotel on summer evenings and pick their teeth after fine dinners. They would sit around and kid each other in the morning, while we slaved in our classrooms. It looked like an alluring life and I figured it was something to dream about.

While still a student Cochrane joined a semipro team for a summer at Saranac Lake, New York, and caught a few more games. After he returned to the classroom in the fall, a Saranac Lake teammate told Cochrane of an opening for a catcher on the Dover club in the Eastern Shore League. Cochrane disliked the position but he wanted to play so badly he talked himself and the manager into the job. The Eastern Shore statistics do

not list Cochrane. He protected his amateur status with the alias of "Frank King."

Cochrane spent 1924 with Portland in the Pacific Coast League. He continued to hit well, finishing the season at .338, and showed speed on the bases. But he was a reluctant catcher, hoping to escape to the outfield. Connie Mack swapped five players and $50,000 on paper to his Portland franchise for Cochrane's services and only then did the Athletics' manager realize why Cochrane yearned for the outfield. Said Mack: "I liked him on the train; he listened so eagerly. But was I in for a shock at camp! After the polished [Cy] Perkins [the regular catcher] Mickey was awful! He was crude at receiving the ball. His stance and crouch were both wrong. And on foul balls he was simply pathetic."

Mack considered shifting him to the outfield, but by now Cochrane himself decided his best opportunity lay behind the plate. He started to study catchers, talk to them, and listen intently to Cy Perkins, although Perkins knew his instruction would cost him his job. Cochrane said he modeled himself after Perkins, particularly in avoiding rigid fingers. He boasted that between Perkins and himself there were 2,500 games without a single broken finger.

As a rookie in 1925, Cochrane caught 134 games for Mack and batted .331. In 1928, he was chosen the American League's Most Valuable Player. During the years of the Second Mack Dynasty, from 1929 to 1931, the fiery Cochrane led the troops on the field. A later teammate, Doc Cramer, called Cochrane "tough as a piece of flint" and most formidable when a runner tried to outrace a peg home. "Because home plate was his . . . you had to take it away from him."

Cochrane's combative spirit was matched by the premier pitcher for the club, Robert Moses Grove. Maryland-bred, like Foxx, Grove grew up in the coal mining area around Lonaconing in the Allegheny Mountains. A baseball cost 25 cents in the early 1900s, ordinarily well beyond the means of Grove and his chums. On the rare times when the youths acquired a "25-cent rocket" the cover would quickly be knocked off and it would be recovered with layers of thick black tape. More often, recalled Grove, "We made our own. We'd get some old wool socks, unravel them and, using a cork stop-

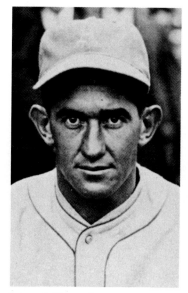

Jug-eared Mickey Cochrane sparked the 1929–1931 Philadelphia Athletic champions and his .320 lifetime beats all other catchers.

Courtesy UPI/Bettmann News photos

per for a center, wind ourselves a ball.''

The hero of the locals was Walter Johnson, and Grove remembered as a youth traveling by train from Lonaconing to Washington to see ''that bugger pitch. . . . Down around the knees—whoosh! One after another. I pitched against a lot of guys and saw a lot of guys throw and I haven't seen one yet come close to as fast as he was.''

Grove dropped out of school after the eighth grade, tasted the coal dust of the mines, drove spikes for the railroad crews, and worked in glass and silk factories. In 1920, the lanky nineteen-year-old won a tryout with Martinsburg in the Blue Ridge League. He started as a first baseman but switched to the mound. Sixty strikeouts in 59 innings were enough to attract talent scouts. Jack Dunn of the Baltimore Orioles carried off his contract for $3,100.

Grove finished the year in Baltimore, then remained with the International League outfit for four years, striking out more than 1,100, winning a total of 109 games. Dunn shrewdly refused to sell his star with the first flush of success, confident that the market would rise. Indeed it did; when Connie Mack decided he wanted the big lefty, he paid $100,600. The odd figure supposedly was designed to make Grove the most expensive purchase ever; Ruth went for $100,500 (though scholars of baseball finance say that other considerations in the Ruth sale pushed that deal to $135,000).

The money brought the expected headlines and also added an ''s'' to Grove. In fact, to the end of his days, Mack referred to him as Groves. At his major league debut, a mature twenty-five-year-old, standing 6'3", Grove threw only fast, faster, and fastest. Not until he established himself as a major leaguer did he develop a curve.

Joe Sewell, who whiffed so rarely, said: ''Sometimes when the sun was out, really bright, he would throw that baseball in there and it looked like a flash of white sewing thread coming up at you. . . . Inning after inning, he never slowed up. He could stand out there for a week and barrel it in at you.''

Paul Richards, the one-time catcher and later manager, claimed Grove threw so hard his ball did not have time to tail away. Hitters, said Richards, thought it would pass waist-high but it was actually up around the letters, making them think it jumped.

Never ''Robert'' but either ''Lefty'' or ''Mose,'' ''churlish,'' ''mean,'' ''surly,'' and ''crabby'' were the polite adjectives heaped upon Grove throughout his career and his volcanic temper scourged infielders guilty of a misplay as well as sportswriters and photographers. Grove ripped his uniform after a tough loss, splintered wooden doors that blocked him during a clubhouse rampage, and even lashed out at the soft-spoken Mack. His most memorable tantrum occurred in 1931 after he had won 16 straight games. Outfielder Al Simmons begged off the day to visit a doctor about his sore ankles. Simmons's rookie replacement missed a routine fly ball, allowing a run, and Grove lost 1–0. Grove went berserk after the game, tearing up his baseball suit and the clubhouse. Most of all he wanted to destroy Simmons for having cost him the game by his absence.

Late in life Grove defended his angry man stance: ''I had a reason. Everybody was mean to me. It was rough on a kid trying to make it in baseball in those days. I was with the Baltimore club for two weeks before anybody spoke to me.''

He was a man as hard on himself as others, punishing himself with a 10-cent cigar if he lost, rewarding a win with a 25-cent smoke. Whatever motivated him, Grove won an even 300 games over his seventeen major league seasons. In his prime he was so fast that excellent hitters like Gehringer and Heilmann confessed an inability to pull against him. In an era without stadium lights and with 3 P.M. starting times, Grove frequently came in to relieve with his blazer during the final minutes. His record during the Second Mack Dynasty was 128–33, a .795 percentage. For his entire career, which included eight years with the Red Sox, whose Fenway Park supposedly dooms lefties, Grove led the league in ERAs nine times.

In left field, the Athletics displayed Aloysius Szymanki, or Al Simmons. The son of Polish immigrants in Milwaukee, Simmons appropriated his box score name from a hardware company ad. A right-handed hitter, Simmons defied form and seemingly lacked courage by bringing his left foot away from the pitcher and toward the dugout. He was called a ''bucket stepper'' by early appraisers of his style, who were contemptuous of batters who pulled away from pitches and toward the water pail that once sat beside

Catching and managing for the Detroit Tigers after Mack broke up his club, Cochrane was victimized by a near-fatal beaning and the emotional stress of his job.

''[Lefty Grove] could throw a lamb chop past a wolf.''—Arthur ''Bugs'' Baer

Courtesy *Rochester Times Union*

159

every dugout. Yet somehow Simmons managed to move hips and mass toward the ball for good power, including the low outside curve that he would knock against the right-field fences.

He started out in 1920 playing amateur ball for Milwaukee's Right Laundry team. An instant success, he progressed to semipro outfits for $8 and $12 a game. He wrote a letter to Connie Mack asking for a tryout and Mack politely rebuffed him, saying he received a thousand similar volunteers. But after Simmons demolished minor league pitching, Mack purchased his contract for $50,000.

Simmons debuted in Philadelphia in 1924, a year before Foxx, Cochrane, and Grove all made the roster. In his second season he collected 253 hits, 43 doubles, 12 triples, 24 homers, 129 RBIs, and a batting average of .384, which earned him only third place behind Harry Heilmann, a pupil of Cobb in Detroit and Speaker. In succeeding years he posted similarly robust figures.

In personality, Simmons fell into the same category as Cochrane and Grove (although the catcher was a congenial man off the field). With the trio in the game, the Athletics offered one of the most cantankerous of teams, mellowed only by the friendly spirits of Foxx and Jimmy Dykes at third. Connie Mack, always sensitive to the personalities of his field hands, would announce the day's battle plan and then turn to Simmons, "Is that all right with you, Al?" The question did not seek his approval but instead politely informed Simmons of his responsibilities.

Simmons was the victim of Mack's experiment with the patriarchs Speaker and Cobb in his 1928 outfield. Growled Simmons after an afternoon of chasing balls, ordinarily the privileges of the others, "If this keeps up, by the end of the season I'll be an old man myself."

Perhaps his most impressive one-day performance occurred during a morning–afternoon Memorial Day show against Washington. The Senators led 6–3 in the bottom of the ninth. With two out and two on, Simmons smacked a game-tying home run. During the early extra innings, he doubled and singled to no avail. But in the fifteenth, Simmons belted a double for his fourth straight hit. Foxx then dribbled a slow grounder and Simmons became hung up between third and

home. He dove back to the bag, safely, but hurt his knee badly. When the next batter singled, Simmons could barely hobble in with the winning run. Between the games, the knee swelled. A doctor advised Mack that Simmons could not play and if he pinch hit, he would need to hit the ball out of the park in order to reach base. Simmons sat on the bench in the afternoon contest as the Athletics again fell behind, 7–4. But when Philadelphia loaded the bases, the manager beckoned to his crippled warrior. Simmons, never short on confidence, drove a pitch into the seats for a grand slam and a leisurely limp around the bases.

The next year, Simmons refused to sign a contract until Mack met his demand of a total of $100,000 for the next three seasons. The owner held out literally until minutes before the opening game. Then the managerial desires conquered his proprietary restraint. Without a moment of spring training, Simmons suited up and on the very first pitch he saw that spring, cracked a homer.

In the twilight of his career Simmons played for a number of clubs. His simmering temper kept him packing and thinned his wallet. While with the Senators he fought with Clark Griffith over a bonus promised for a .300 season. Griffith then fined him $200 for calling a spectator "a God damn son-of-a-bitch." Simmons appealed to Landis and the Commissioner held a hearing that solemnly sought to discern whether Simmons cursed a fan or only engaged in self-criticism. The fine stood.

Although Mack himself hardly ever used language unacceptable in a convent, his players, like Simmons, spoke a ruder tongue. During the 1929 Series, both benches freely and loudly indulged in invectives. From his box seat Commissioner Landis and other nearby spectators heard it all. The czar issued a ukase: further profanity meant large fines. Just before the next game, Cochrane swaggered over in front of the Cub dugout and with his eye on Landis, yelled, "Hello, sweethearts, we're going to serve tea this afternoon, come on out and get your share." The Commissioner stared stonily as if he had heard nothing.

After the Athletics won, Landis visited the victors in the locker room and offered congratulations to all but Cochrane. The catcher decided Landis was still in a swivet over his

"Unquestionably, [Al] Simmons [he Connie Mack] was the worst lookin top hitters. His style was atrocious. should have been a sucker for an pitch. He wasn't. . . . Curves shou troubled him. They didn't. In fact, the deadliest clutch hitter on the gre letics team."—Arthur Daley, New Times

Courtesy AP/Wide World

stunt but just as he was ready to leave he stepped in front of Cochrane: "Hello, sweetheart, I came in after my tea, will you pour?"

The Chicago Cubs, under manager Joe McCarthy, beat out the National League competition almost as badly as the Athletics did their rivals. The club won by 10½ games; Rogers Hornsby batted .380 and the sulky Cuyler .360. The team averaged .303, 7 points better than the American Leaguers. Hornsby also had 39 homers, more than the Athletics leaders, Foxx and Simmons.

Another Chicagoan matched Hornsby in homers and also drove in 159 runs. Lewis Robert "Hack" Wilson ★ had toiled for McGraw from 1923 to 1925 without notable success. Traded to the Cubs, he emerged as a power hitter, leading the league in home runs from 1926 to 1928 and maintaining an average well over .300. At 5'6" and 190 pounds, with tiny feet (a size 5½ shoe), Hack Wilson looked more like a regular on a bar stool than a center fielder.

Born in 1900, Wilson grew up in the Pennsylvania steel country. He quit school in the sixth grade, went to work for a print shop, pulling twelve-hour days for $4 a week. He moved on to a harder regimen: "I reported at the Baldwin Locomotive Works and got a job with a finishing gang, swinging a sledge hammer, driving rivets and doing other jobs that required strength. I followed my father into the Tindle & Marsh steel mill as a hammer man, working on huge pieces of white hot steel with a steam hammer."

During his time away from the mills, Wilson played ball, usually catching. The manager of a silk-mill industrial-league team offered to put him on the payroll with baseball as his vocation. Wilson achieved enough to receive a minor league contract. However, he broke his leg sliding into home, and on recovery, the leg initially was too stiff for a catcher so Wilson shifted to the outfield.

By the spring of 1924, Wilson proudly wore the uniform of the New York Giants. He remembered: "But John J. [McGraw] was not so proud of me. I was awkward. I was built like a hack. I didn't bat right. My stance was wrong. I'd have to change it. Sure I was fast on my feet, but I didn't look like an outfielder. I looked like a hack." (A low pile of bricks and an old-fashioned cab both are known as a "hack." Wilson once remarked that a fellow Giant gave him the name because of a resemblance to another squatty major leaguer, Hack Miller.)

Discounted by McGraw, Wilson nevertheless spent the season with the Giants and played in the Series against Washington. But midway in 1925, he returned to the minors where he remained until the Cubs secured his services. The short, stout man led his league in homers for 1926, and tied for honors the following two seasons. His figures climbed steadily, rising to 39 for 1929 and 56 in 1930, the best for a National Leaguer through 1987. That year he knocked in an incredible 190 runs, the highest total ever.

Wilson figured prominently, for both sides, in the 1929 Series with the Athletics. He outhit everyone with a .471 average for the 5 games but his performance in game four is the one in the book of memory. The Philadelphians, bolstered by Foxx's homers, captured the first two contests. The Cubs, behind Guy Bush, won game three. The following afternoon, the Chicagoans rapped out an early 8–0 advantage. In the fifth inning, Wilson had dropped a fly ball for an error but no damage ensued, thanks to his subsequent excellent grab of a long fly.

The Athletics came to bat in the bottom of the seventh, about ready to concede. Al Simmons spoiled Charlie Root's shutout with a blast onto the left-field roof. Foxx then singled to right. Outfielder Bing Miller, a .312 lifetime hitter over sixteen years, lifted a ball to center. Wilson lost it in the sun and it was scored a single. Third sacker Jimmy Dykes singled to left and Foxx trotted in with the second Athletic run. Shortstop Joe Boley dropped one into right field and it was now 8–3. Pinch hitter George Burns popped to short for a brief respite. But second baseman Max Bishop smacked a hit past Root's head, driving in another run and forcing Root out of the game. Art Nehf relieved. Outfielder Mule Haas lined the ball to center. Wilson tracked it, then lost it completely. It bounced under his last-ditch bare-hand grab, rolling to the wall. Haas raced around the bases behind two other men to make the score 8–7. Cochrane walked. The Cubs replaced Nehf with Sheriff Blake. Simmons smashed a ball, barely foul, just missing a second homer for the inning. He then rapped a grounder toward third. Some claim infielder Norm McMillan misplayed it, turning a double play into a single. Foxx then picked up his second hit of the inning, tying the score. The Sheriff fled, yielding to Pat Malone. He quickly loaded the bases by plinking Miller with a pitch. Dykes then doubled off the left-field wall, ending the scoring at 10 runs. Mack summoned Lefty Grove who whiffed four of the six Cubs he faced and instead of the expected 2–2 in games, the Cubs trailed 3–1. The Chicagoans refused to fold after the disaster. They led in game five, 2–0 in the bottom of the ninth. But Haas tied it with a 2-run shot and doubles by Simmons and Miller brought victory.

Cub manager Joe McCarthy refused to blame Wilson for the game-four disaster: "You can't fasten it on him. The poor kid lost the ball in the sun, and he didn't put the sun there." Several years later Wilson informed a reporter he had broken his regular sunglasses. "My sunglasses were nothing but window glass that day. If that fly had been hit two minutes sooner or two minutes later, I'd have stuck it in my pocket. But it got dead in the sun and I didn't have a chance."

The collapse hardly dimmed his free-wheeling spirit for it was the next year that Wilson racked up his 56 homers and 190 RBIs. But he had also developed a fondness for forbidden spirits.

Wilson and pitcher Pat Malone, a boozing buddy, were hardly the only baseball stars who lit up speakeasies. The Yankees were notorious for their partying; Babe Ruth tippled readily, albeit mostly beer. Alexander, McGraw, Cochrane, and Foxx enjoyed liquor—an illegal substance during the 1920s. There is no record of any members of the baseball establishment calling for specimen analyses and penalties for such transgressions. But then, Prohibition was a phenomenon visited upon the sporting interests by an alien segment of society. And, with even the Commissioner a partisan of good whiskey, the athletes could hardly be disciplined on this score.

Wilson's drinking took its toll, swiftly. He slumped badly in 1931; his average fell to .261 and his home runs totaled only 13. In 1932, he wore a Brooklyn Dodger uniform and struggled to .297 and 23 homers. But by 1934 he was through.

Wilson left behind not only his record and his unfortunate encounter in the seventh in-

ning of the 1929 Series but also the stuff of legend. Joe Judge, like Wilson finishing out his career in Brooklyn, recalled a game in which the manager wanted Wilson to pinch hit but he was not on the bench. Sent to locate the slugger, Judge found him in the clubhouse surrounded by empty beer bottles. "They want you, two out in the ninth, and two on. They want you to hit," Judge related. While Wilson staggered away to the field, Judge frantically tried to clean up the mess to protect Hack. Before he could finish his housekeeping, however, the team poured into the locker room. Judge feared the worst; the evidence was palpable. But no one cared, for Wilson had hit one out of the park.

Arthur Daley of the *New York Times* delighted in recounting a torrid afternoon with the badly hung-over Wilson suffering in the outfield, chasing ball after ball as they clanged against the metal wall of Philadelphia's Baker Bowl. When then Dodger manager Casey Stengel plodded to the mound to yank the pitcher, Wilson bowed his head, striving to rest. The abused pitcher, Walter "Boom Boom" Beck, however, in disgust fired the ball in the direction of the fence. The drowsing Wilson heard the clang of ball against metal wall. He instinctively retrieved it and fired it on a line to second base. Only then did he realize that the ball had been heaved by a disgusted Beck.

Volatile by temperament, Wilson would explode with fury on striking out, slamming his bat to the ground with great force. "It ain't no show with me. I blow up pretty easy." Indeed, he emulated Cobb on one occasion, leaping the wall to throttle a heckler. He was equally pugnacious with other players. After singling against Cincinnati, Wilson left the bag without benefit of time-out to punch heckling Redleg Ray Kolp. That same evening he bumped into Cincinnati pitcher Pete Donohue at the railroad depot. One or two words led to stitches for the pitcher's chin. Aboard a train, Wilson and Malone once boasted their intent to intimidate Manager Rogers Hornsby. Hearing of the threat, Hornsby showed himself, wearing only his shorts and his glower. It was enough to send the intoxicated warriors in search of less formidable foes. Wilson died a victim of his alcoholism and a pauper, although he earned as much as $250,000 playing baseball.

"[Hack Wilson] was built along the [lines of?] a beer keg and not unfamiliar with [its con?]tents."—*Shirley Povich*, Washing[ton]

Courtesy NBL

162

Two weeks after the fall of the Chicago Cubs, Wall Street struck out, leaving the national economy in shambles. The collapse of commerce and industry failed to affect baseball immediately. In fact, baseball during the 1930 season soared with inflationary figures. Chuck Klein ★ as an outfielder with the Phillies hit .386, smacked 40 home runs, and knocked in 170 runs, but failed to be first in any of these categories, trailing Bill Terry's .401 and Babe Herman's .393, behind Hack Wilson's 56 homers and 190 RBIs. His standing would have improved little in the American League with Ruth and Gehrig rapping more homers (49 and 41) and Gehrig beating him with 176 RBIs. A .320 hitter with 300 homers for seventeen years, Klein became seventh on the all-time list when he retired in 1944.

Connie Mack's Athletics carried off the pennant in 1930 as well as the following season. And in the National League, the St. Louis Cardinals matched the achievement. The Athletics beat their rivals 4 games to 2 in their first encounter, with 2 homers each for Simmons and Cochrane, 1 for Foxx, and 1 for Jimmy Dykes. Grove won a pair as did George Earnshaw. The Cards gained revenge in 1931 in a 6-game World Series during which Johnny Leonard Roosevelt Martin, born during the first term of Teddy's presidency, and otherwise known as "Pepper" or "the Wild Hoss of the Osage" (a river that flows through Kansas and Missouri as well as an American Indian dialect), stole 5 bases and batted .500. Burleigh Grimes, bestubbled jowls aglower, and spewing his spitter, limited the Mack men to 2.04 earned runs in his two victories. Another free spirit, "Wild Bill" Hallahan (he led his league in walks three times), yielded 1 run in 2 games.

The second Mack dynasty and the new Cardinal kingdom failed to exert hegemony over the nation-states of baseball in 1932. Instead, with a venerable Babe Ruth, a prime Lou Gehrig, a clever southpaw named Vernon Lefty Gomez, ★ and another jewel plucked from Boston, Charlie Red Ruffing, ★ the Yankees ran away to a 13-game lead over Philadelphia. As a Red Sox, Ruffing won a mere 39 while losing 96, compiling such dismal records as 10–25 in 1928 and 9–22 in 1929. Originally an outfielder,

Ruffing lacked several toes due to a boyhood accident, rendering him too immobile for fly chasing. But he never lost his talent with a bat, socking 36 career homers and occasionally serving as a pinch hitter. However, his most impressive credentials are the 231 victories in pin stripes and 7 World Series wins.

The 1932 Series pitted the Yanks against the Chicago Cubs. During the third game the moment occurred that magnified the already gargantuan legend of Babe Ruth. In the first inning he had clouted a 3-run smash against Charlie Root. The Cubs, like most teams, dearly enjoyed ragging Ruth, and when he came to the plate in the fifth inning, they loosed a stream of invectives that swelled to a torrent as Root poured in a called strike, wasted a pair, and then threw a second strike past the Babe. On the next pitch Ruth hammered the ball into the Wrigley Field bleachers, farther than anyone had ever done before.

These facts are indisputable but acres of newsprint have been devoted to the question of whether Ruth called his home run. At some point in this time at bat, Ruth gestured; the eyewitnesses and the mythopoeic community differ on its details. Some say he held up a single finger to denote it takes only one swing for a hit; others report two fingers to indicate just a pair of strikes; another school insists he actually pointed to center field whereas the idol smashers assert Ruth only lifted his arm to adjust his shirt. According to Robert Creamer in his encyclopedic *Babe*, only Joe Williams in the *New York World Telegram* declared Ruth actually pointed to center field for his home run. Other stories backing the "called" blow only said Ruth indicated a home run without specifying location.

Victim Charlie Root growled that if Ruth had pointed to the fence he "would have ended up on his ass." Billy Herman backed this version: "He didn't point. . . . Ruth would've been sitting in the dirt, maybe rubbing himself where it hurt," an opinion seconded by the manager of the day, Charlie Grimm. Maybe, but a duster, with a 2–2 count in a World Series game and Lou Gehrig next to hit, is a massive risk. (Ruth hit an outside pitch, according to Root.)

Burleigh Grimes, on the Cub bench, said his colleagues, notably Guy Bush and Bob

While the Dow Jones of the day headed for zero, 1930 batting averages continued to boom. Chuck Klein with the Phils hit .386, good only for third place in the National League.

Courtesy UPI/Bettmann News photos

(Following page) *Babe Ruth cheered colleague Lou Gehrig's slide home and the Yankee pair demolished the Chicago Cubs in the 1932 Series with 3 homers for Gehrig, 2 for Ruth, including the one that allegedly was called.*

Courtesy UPI/Bettmann News photos

Smith, rode Ruth as "a big ape and a lot worse." He remembered "Ruth held up his finger to say he had one strike left, and the next thing you know everybody's saying he called his shot."

Ruth himself equivocated. Ford Frick, ★ a newspaperman before serving as president of the National League and ultimately commissioner, questioned the Babe later. "Did you really point to the bleachers?" asked Frick.

"It's in the papers isn't it?" parried Ruth.

Frick persisted, "Yeah, it's in the papers. But did you really point to the stands?"

"Why don't you read the papers? It's all there in the papers."

In 1945 Ruth confessed, "I didn't exactly point to any spot, like the flagpole. . . . I just sort of waved at the whole fence. All I wanted to do was give that ball a ride . . . anywhere."

A footnote to the alleged beau geste— Gehrig followed with a homer, giving him 3 for the Series and a .529 average and 8 RBIs in 4 games. But typically he had been upstaged. During the regular season he smacked 4 homers in a single game, missing a fifth only through a superb catch by Al Simmons. Unfortunately, he performed his heroics the same day John J. McGraw stepped down as manager of the Giants and that swept the sports page headlines.

McGraw's midseason replacement, first sacker Bill Terry, the last National Leaguer to bat .400 (.401 in 1930), guided the club to the 1933 pennant. A school dropout at thirteen, husband and father while still in his teens, Terry said: "When I was 15 I was doing a man's work. I unloaded freight cars, throwing sacks of flour into trucks at the railroad yards in Atlanta."

As an adolescent he pitched for the low minors, clubs in towns like Thomasville and Newman. "I played baseball because I could make more money doing that than I could anything else. I quit the Southern League because I got tired of all that tramping around to cities with a minor-league team. I was married and had a baby and I wanted to settle down."

Many of the young men of his time saw baseball as a way out: Coveleski said, ". . . before I knew what hit me, I was signed to a contract with Lancaster, and I was out of those damn mines for good." Grimes said,

"Compared to farming or working in the lumber woods or in a steel mill, baseball was a picnic." Edd Roush said, "I didn't expect to make it all the way to the big leagues, but I didn't care. I just had to get away from them damn cows." Terry regarded baseball less as an escape than a vocation, with financial gain his dominant concern. He took a job with Standard Oil in Tennessee and the Standard Oil Polareines dominated industrial team competition. Alerted by the Memphis Chicks to Terry's superb bat work, McGraw interviewed Terry. He stunned McGraw, rejecting the initial offer and demanding a sum that bettered his salary with the oil company.

Carl Hubbell, a left-handed reincarnation of Matty and his fadeaway, and whose screwball boosted him to a 26-game winning streak (over two seasons) and helped Terry club to three World Series, remarked: "Bill played the game and managed as if he were running a business. There's some question in my mind whether Bill ever enjoyed baseball as the All-American boy enjoys it. I don't think he ever played for fun but for what he could get out of it."

Happily for the Giants, Terry got those World Series shares. The 1933 team easily overcame Washington in 5 games. Mel Ott, who would succeed Terry as manager nine years later, batted .389 and contributed a pair of homers.

Ott had come to the Giants as a seventeen-year-old kid with a freaky batting style, dropping his hands below his belt, then hoisting his right leg, almost emulating a pitcher. McGraw resisted farming him out where someone might mistakenly try to change his style. McGraw refrained from tinkering himself, but the heavy-legged Ott, 5'9", 172 pounds, muscled like a middleweight fighter, constantly broke down with charley horses.

Ott remembered:

[Bernie] Wefers was brought in to get me off my heels and up on my toes. He damn near killed me. He had me sprinting up and down, for hours at a time I was supposed to run with my knees high, almost touching my chin. After a couple of weeks, I was ready to try it on the bases and Mr. McGraw was there to watch. I got as far as second base—going great guns— and then I kicked myself in the chin, tripped on the bag and fell flat on my face.

New York Giant first sacker Bill Terry regarded baseball as a job but his art with the bat made him the National League's last .400 man. As manager of the team Terry flew three pennants, winning also the 1933 Series.

Courtesy UPI/Bettmann News photos

Giant outfielder Mel Ott stepped out in an odd fashion but the short right field of the Polo Grounds served him well (511 home runs). John McGraw never farmed out the seventeen-year-old kid. "No minor-league manager is going to have a chance to ruin him."

Courtesy NBL

McGraw allegedly growled, "Well, he'll never go to the Olympics, but at least he'll be able to come in on a ground ball." Ott practiced his sliding in hotel rooms, using pillows for bases. He employed his newly created ability to run bases for his first homer, an inside-the-park job after Hack Wilson slipped on the grass and the ball rolled to the fence. Over the years, Ott more than justified McGraw's faith. Pie Traynor called him the best ball player he ever saw.

The decade listened to a revival of the argument for and against the lively ball. Writers bemoaned the apparent hike in 4-base hits. A 1934 column by Garry Schumacher in New York grumbled: "The new, dynamite-laden pellet has made a travesty of baseball. It has taken the science and skill from the game."

His contemporary, John E. Wray of the *St. Louis Post*, cried:

> It is the prevailing belief that the public worships at the shrine of the Big Wallop and the High Batting Average. As regards the Knot Hole Gang attendance and the free ladies' day patronage* this is true. With many of these, the climax of a game is not a steal of home but a knock over the wall. Whether the lively ball or the batter's prowess accomplishes this doesn't concern them. But the old "die hard" boys who like to see a run earned will never be reconciled to seeing a tally gained by intelligence and planning offset by a rubber cored wallop over the roofs.

Actually, 1929 and 1930 stood as high-water marks for total homers with succeeding years dropping to lower plateaus. The Depression deepened during these years and, although baseball remained one of the few activities to bring joy to Americans, the box office suffered. Attendance overall dipped to 60 percent of the booming 1920s,

although a critical meeting between the Giants and Cardinals in 1934 drew 62,573 paid fans and 15,000 were denied entry. The Polo Grounds accommodated roughly 55,000; the added customers packed the aisles or shared seats. Yankee Stadium crammed in 77,000 for a doubleheader with Detroit.

Still, the owners cinched their belts a notch or two. In 1931, officials slashed rosters from twenty-five to twenty-three men. The cut was restored eight years later, lasting until 1986 when teams went down to twenty-four players. The New Deal of President Franklin Delano Roosevelt wrought the National Recovery Act that sought to regulate the economy. Lawmakers proposed to include baseball under the NRA, dictating wages and working conditions. However, the Supreme Court ejected the NRA from national play, eliminating the threat to baseball's way of business.

As in the past, owner Mack ignored his managerial desires and sold off his stars. First Al Simmons, Jimmy Dykes, and Mule Haas departed for Chicago in exchange for $150,000. Millionaire Thomas Yawkey ★ had bought the Boston Red Sox, sailing them out of the financial doldrums. He invested $275,000 in Jimmie Foxx and Lefty Grove and several lesser figures.

To field-boss his club, Yawkey bought Clark Griffith's son-in-law, the gifted manager-shortstop of the Washington Senators, Joe Cronin. ★ Only twenty-six when Griffith put him in charge, Cronin followed the pattern of Bucky Harris, the playing manager named nine years earlier by the Senators, and brought home a winner in his initial season. But although Cronin continued to star in the infield and at bat for Yawkey, he could never lead the Red Sox to a pennant. When he finally hung up his glove and quit managing, Cronin served Yawkey as front-

Joe Cronin as Washington shortstop ... American League MVP award in 19... as rookie player-manager in 1933 co... pennant. Traded to Boston in 1935, ... tinued to hit and field well, but not u... had hung up his glove in 1946 co... produce another championship team...

Courtesy AP/Wide World

(Opposite, top) *The tradition of A... games began in 1933 as a benefit ar... by columnist Arch Ward of the C... Tribune. John McGraw served as m... of the National League entry that in... the likes of Frank Frisch, Carl Hubbe... Dizzy Dean (back row, third fro... fourth from left, extreme right).*

Courtesy NBL

---

*The phenomenon dates back as early as 1867 when the Knickerbockers of New York set aside the last Thursday of each month as Ladies Day. Wives, daughters, and feminine friends were provided with "suitable seats or settees." A pre-twentieth-century observer explained: "[it] purifies the moral atmosphere of a base ball gathering, repressing . . . all outbursts of intemperate language which the excitement of a contest so frequently induces." To curry favor with women, the owners arranged special passages to enable them to reach their seats without mingling with the regular and often rowdy crowd. Called "charming deadheads" by some, installed sometimes in the best seats and on other occasions relegated to hard bleacher benches, the female fan was known as a "cranklet." Sportswriters sought to introduce levity to their accounts with references to female dress and deportment.

Consider this from I. E. Sanborn: "But only one of the three tallies would stand on account of the ground rules, for an ever-curious daughter of Eve had picked up the ball, perhaps thinking it was another apple from the garden of Eden, and her act left no doubt that the hit had gone into the crowd. If she can be identified that woman will be barred from the park forever, as relentlessly as her primeval ancestress was shut out from that other paradise."

Ladies Days succumbed to the rising interest of women in the sport and their willingness to pay full price in the 1970s.

(Following page, top) *"If [Frank] Frisch wasn't the best second baseman that ever lived, then Eddie Collins or Rogers Hornsby was. . . . Frisch could do everything on the field, and most of all he could compete."—Red Smith,* New York Herald Tribune

In this incarnation, Frisch was newly arrived at a New York Giants spring encampment where he examined new bats along with an equally contentious teammate, Casey Stengel (center).

Courtesy NBL

(Following page, bottom) *"They can say what they want about Frisch slowing up, but not many second basemen could turn in the play Frisch made on Ralph 'Buzz' Boyle's shot in the third. Frisch raced back of second, scooped up the ball with one hand and still had time to toss out the fastest man on the Dodgers."—Murray Tynan,* New York Herald Tribune, *May 25, 1934.*

Courtesy NBL

(Left) *Connie Mack guided the American Leaguers to a 4–2 win in the first All-Star game. Babe Ruth (back row, fourth from left) homered with one on. To Mack's right, stand a parade of Hall of Famers: Joe Cronin, Lefty Grove, Bill Dickey, Al Simmons, and Lefty Gomez, the winning pitcher.*

Courtesy AP/Wide World

office chief and then became American League president.

No doubt the batter-friendly green monster in left field of Fenway Park made the transition easier for slugger Jimmie Foxx, who posted more than 200 of his 534 career-total homers with Boston. Lefty Grove notched only one 20-win year in Boston but still collected 105 there.

Mack shipped Mickey Cochrane to Detroit for $100,000. Catcher-manager Cochrane brought the 1934 and 1935 Tigers home as pennant winners. But "Iron Mike" melted under pressure; twice he left the team to recuperate from unspecified "nervous" or "physical" ailments. And in May 1937, his career and nearly his life suffered a grievous injury when Yankee pitcher Irving "Bump" Hadley fractured his skull with an errant pitch. Another twenty years passed before players began to wear helmets.

In the nadir of the Depression, Chicago sought to uplift spirits with a gaudy World's Fair. Arch Ward, columnist for the *Chicago Tribune*, campaigned for a sporting contribution, an all-star baseball game with the profits consigned to charity. John J. McGraw and Connie Mack managed the two squads; Ruth appropriately provided the winning margin with a 2-run homer as the American Leaguers triumphed 4–2. More important, what Ward begat as a one-time show grew into a tradition and over the years produced its own magnificent moments.

Claimants to the supremacy yielded by the Athletics included the St. Louis Cardinals. The man most responsible for the Redbird pretensions was Branch Rickey. A 1914 listener recorded a sample of Rickey's sermonizing: "Every man must be at bat in this world and he is called upon to make clean hits. 'P.O.' means put out the evil in your lives. 'A' means assist the other fellow every chance you get. Keep the errors down as best you can and you will win your game. Sacrifice hits are a valuable asset."

Rickey brought to the game not only one of the shrewdest eyes for talent and the knowledge of how to exploit it but also a keen sense of baseball husbandry. Under Rickey, the Cardinals developed a massive farm system designed to breed stock for service on the parent club and as a cash crop through sales.

Other organizations, notably the New York Yankees and later the Brooklyn Dodgers when Rickey transferred his operations there, emulated the farm network he created. The only resistance came from a surprising quarter, Commissioner Landis. He freed seventy-four Cardinal serfs in 1938 and ninety-one Tiger cubs in 1940 because he felt the players were unfairly denied an opportunity to reach the majors. Landis, chosen by the owners and hardly a radical, never lost his distrust of monopolies. He seemed to regard the burgeoning empires built by the likes of Rickey as akin to the Standard Oil monster he sought to slay with an enormous fine.

The Cardinal network started in 1920, with Fort Smith in the Western League, and Syracuse in the International League a year later. By 1928, St. Louis owned seven minor-league franchises and controlled 203 players on the "Rickey plantation." Ten years later, there were thirty-eight clubs who owed allegiance to the Cards. Some operated as wholly owned subsidiaries, others under working agreements. To stock his chain, Rickey inaugurated baseball tryout camps. Between 1920 and 1945, the Cardinals won eight pennants and five World Series.

Pepper Martin, the terror of the 1931 Series, Chick Hafey, Joe Medwick, ★ John Mize, ★ Enos Slaughter, ★ Stan Musial, and Jay Hanna Dean ★ all grew up in the Cardinal organization. Such stalwarts were aided and abetted by only slightly lesser performers, such as outfielders Terry Moore, Johnny Hopp, shortstop Marty Marion, the brother battery of catcher Walker Cooper and pitcher Mort, and a host of short-term sensations, such as catcher Don Padgett, third baseman Whitey Kurowski, pitchers Tex Carleton, Paul Dean, Max Lanier, and Harry Brecheen.

Rickey also improved the club through trades. For Rogers Hornsby he obtained Frankie Frisch. Frisch studied chemistry at Fordham and earned nomination as a second-string all-American halfback. He went directly from the campus to the Giants. There John McGraw schooled him in the arts of baseball:

I might never have become known as the "Fordham Flash" but for the training I received from McGraw. I could have flopped as

"He [Branch Rickey] was steeped in the old style religion, and because he was a razor-sharp operator who refused to play ball or even visit the park on Sunday, he was often pictured as a sanctimonious fraud. His observance of the Sabbath was not a pose and was not, as was widely believed, due to a promise to his mother, nor did he consider Sunday baseball sinful. When his devout and devoted mother raised no objection to his seeking a career in professional baseball— the equivalent in rural Ohio in 1902 of selling his soul to the devil—he promised himself that this was the very least he could do to show his respect and love. He kept his promise to himself even when it got him fired from his first major league job as a catcher for Cincinnati."—Red Smith, New York Herald Tribune

Courtesy NBL

a ball player under any other teacher. No one was permitted to disagree with McGraw. He let us know that he did not care for suggestions from players. At the same time he impressed upon us the value of team play over individual play. It didn't matter with McGraw how we got the winning run or who got it, so long as we won. The player who scored the winning run wasn't permitted to brag. McGraw would come back with, "The Giants got it."

During his nineteen years at second base, Frisch compiled a .316 average and his slick glove work strengthened his clubs in the vital middle.

By mid-1933, Rickey had elevated Frisch to player-manager. In that dual role, Frisch also demonstrated a keen sense of McGraw's posture toward umpires, adding a few grace notes of his own. Jimmy Powers of the *New York Daily News* described a performance:

> Frisch immediately skied his glove. It was an elegant motion. He seized the chocolate mitt between a thumb and forefinger and flipped it into the air. The leather had a great spin, and it soared up until the relentless law of gravity broke its headlong flight. Then it stopped . . . like a wounded bird, fluttered gently down to the grass . . . Off came the Frisch cap. Bingo! He hurled it to the earth. He looked at Barr [the umpire]. Still no response. Frisch took a running start . . . 20 full strides. He leaped upon his recumbent headgear. He stomped it viciously with his spikes. Like a man "scotching" a loathsome snake he beat the ground, churning up a smoking volcanic eruption of clay. . . . The cap is the umpire. Frisch is battering him. He is driving out the perverse devil that causes decisions to go willy, nilly against his beloved Cardinals. Ah, what a master . . . Frisch began declaiming to the Roman Senate. He threw his arms about and used all manner of charming adjectives, adverbs, superlatives and invectives.

Ejected several times for such declamations, Frisch protested to columnist Sid Keener of the *St. Louis Post Dispatch*:

> Something must be done with these temperamental umpires. They refuse to listen to a fair discussion. They insist they are always right and the manager or player who is arguing is wrong. One word from us and we're out of the game. . . . The club owners should convince President Heydler [National League head] that his system is making a "sissy" game out of baseball.

And, in fact, one protest by Frisch actually caused the league to reverse an ump's decision, forcing a replay of a game.

Outstanding on the 1930s Cardinal teams was Joe Medwick, a husky recruit from New Jersey who broke into the lineup during the 1932 season. He abhorred his nickname, "Ducky," supplied by a female observer of his gait, and his style of play resembled more of an angry water buffalo than a squawky waterfowl. In spite of the urgings of Manager Frank Frisch to show patience, Medwick was notorious for preying on bad balls. Dodger Buzz Boyle whined: "The only way to fool that guy is to throw right over the heart of the plate. He hits wild pitches farther than he does good balls." Indeed, Medwick seemed to regard a base on balls as an affront to decency and labored hard to avoid such easy passage. Jimmie Foxx, during comparable seasons, collected four times as many walks.

Opposing pitchers moaned about Medwick's tenacity. Van Mungo, who posted excellent records with the cellar-trapped Dodgers of the period, said: "I'd rather pitch to any other hitter in the league. He's bad news all the time. No game is ever won against the Cardinals until Medwick is out in the ninth. I'd rather face nine left handed hitters all day than face Joe twice. He can do more harm with one swing than nine other guys." (Like Medwick, Mungo was a righty.)

Dutch Leonard (no kin to the Dutch Leonard who accused Cobb and Speaker of crimes against baseball), who also threw for Brooklyn, complained:

> He's a baseball murderer. You can't let up on him for a second. And the harder you bear down, the harder he hits. I fooled him twice with knucklers . . . last month and Sunday he hit the same pitch out into the street. I think the club should forbid his carrying a bat to the plate. Make Medwick use his fist to swing against us. Then he'd hit only singles.

In 1934, he paced the Cardinals with an early hitting spree, explaining his success in Ring Lardnerese: "I just smell the lettuce. I have two good friends in this world. Buckerinos and base hits. If I get base hits I will get buckerinos. I smell World Series lettuce, and I'll get my two or three a day."

During his eight-year tenure with St.

"Big John Mize is a 'whale' in every
of the definition. He can pull the ba
he also has power in all directions. H
sharp eyes and enough 'plate intellige
be a consistent hitter. The pitchers
league fear no man as much, and that
ultimate tribute.

"There are other potential 'whales
National League. . . . But just for no
this department's doubloons, the onl
and ripened specimen of Physeter
rocephalus outside the American Lea
J. Robert Mize."—John Lardner,
week.

Courtesy AP/Wide World

Louis, Medwick never dipped below .306, soared as high as .374, led the league in doubles thrice, and triples, homers, and slugging averages once. He won the National League triple crown in 1937, a feat unaccomplished over the next fifty seasons.

Johnny Mize, "the Big Cat," typified the Rickey apparatus. A burly kid, Mize grew up in Demorest, Georgia, a town so small, said Mize, that a good-size crowd would cause the place to tilt. As a high-school sophomore, he impressed the coach of nearby Piedmont College enough to be invited to play on that school's team. He played three years of college ball while still in high school, and as his reputation grew, Mize was invited to take the field with half a dozen clubs within a thirty-mile radius. An executive with a local lumber company tipped off its headquarters of the prospect. Rickey personally inspected the goods and signed up the seventeen-year-old for Greensboro in the Piedmont League.

In 1931, outfielder Mize hit .337, whacked 9 homers, and batted in 64 runs in only 94 games. He hit his way ever higher, advancing to Elmira and then three seasons with Rochester of the International League, the highest of the minors, before joining the Cardinals in 1936. He never hit less than .300 and twice led the league in homers in his five St. Louis seasons. Among his career achievements, Mize smashed 3 homers in 6 different games, a major league record.

Mize, a mild-mannered fellow, joined an outfit that had earned a reputation for raucous behavior and exciting play. Frank Graham of the *New York Sun* wrote:

They may not be the greatest team that ever played . . . although surely they are one of the best but . . . they capture your imagination and inspire your respect. They don't look like a major league ball club or as major league ball clubs are supposed to look in this era of the well dressed athlete. Their uniforms are stained and dirty and patched and ill fitting. They don't shave before a game and most of them chew tobacco. They have thick necks and knotty muscles, and they spit out of the sides of their mouths and then wipe the backs of their hands across their shirt fronts. They fight among themselves and use quaint and picturesque oaths. They are not afraid of anybody, enemy ballplayers, fans, umpires, club owners, league officials, not even the august Judge Landis himself. They don't make much money, and they work hard for it. They will risk arms, legs, and necks, their own or the other fellow's to get it. But they also have a lot of fun playing baseball.

And they did entertain, not only with their hell-for-leather game tactics but even while warming up. Fans paid to see the Cards put on a show, pepper exercises with balls flipped from behind the back, antics with a bat and an earthy repartee. They formed a hillbilly band, and enlivened the routine for a hotel manager by dressing up in painter's overalls to disrupt proceedings in the grand ballroom.

Towering above all Cardinals in the 1930s was Rickey's ace pitcher and constant problem child, Jay Hanna Dean.* More than anyone he personified the Gashouse Gang. Born in rural Arkansas in 1911, Dean quit school after the second grade. He once remarked, "I didn't do so well in the first grade either." He took to the sultry fields as an itinerant cotton picker. Wandering to Texas, Dean sought escape from farm drudgery by enlisting in the army at sixteen. He escaped from the military by virtue of being underage and subsequently was discovered on a Texas sandlot in 1929. His first contract bound him to the Cardinal subsidiary in St. Joseph, Missouri, where he performed so well he moved up to Houston and by Labor Day had won 25 games as a minor leaguer. Promoted to the parent club that same season, he was allowed a single start in which he permitted a scant 3 hits and 1 run.

During the winter of 1930–1931 he visited the offices of Rickey to talk terms. According to Red Smith, several hours passed. Then while Dean slipped out a rear door, the Cardinal vice-president and general manager emerged from his executive session with the twenty-year-old tyro of one pro season's experience.

The Mahatma† was coatless, his collar was unbuttoned and his necktie hung loose. His

"As a ballplayer, [Dizzy] Dean was a natural phenomenon, like the Grand Canyon or the Great Barrier Reef. Nobody ever taught him baseball and he never had to learn. He was just doing what came naturally . . . when a scout discovered him."—Red Smith, New York Herald Tribune

"Mr. Dizzy would be getting twice as much, or close to it, pitching for the Giants, and he would be worth it. As a matter of truth, he is worth it in St. Louis, but because salaries have never been high there he doesn't get it. Mr. Nutsey [Paul Dean] was started out at a beginner's pay, as it is figured in St. Louis. By now it is apparent that he is a real pitcher and worth much more than $3,000. I am glad the pitching Deans struck and I think this sort of striking in baseball should be encouraged. I see no reason why a young ball player should be expected to wait a full year for adequate recognition at the cashier's window once he has established his class . . . they are the greatest brother act since the Barrymores were juveniles."—Joe Williams, New York World Telegram

Courtesy NBL

---

*For years he was known as Jerome Herman until he revealed that he had taken the names from a catcher Jerome Herman Harris who resembled him.

†Tom Meany of the newspaper *PM* dubbed Rickey "Mahatma" after reading John Gunther's *Inside Asia* in which the author described India's Gandhi as a "combination of your father and Tammany Hall."

hair looked as though it had been slept in. He was sweating, and over the half-glasses on the end of his nose, his eyes were glassy. "By Judas Priest! By Judas Priest! If there were one more like him in baseball, just one, as God is my judge I'd get out of the game!"

Apparently, the gangling Dean insisted on substantially more than the $3,000 considered appropriate for a fellow with one major league game to his credit. The incredulous Rickey added: "He told me, after one game this busher told me, 'Mr. Rickey, I'll put more people in the park than anybody since Babe Ruth.'"

Rickey consigned Dean to Houston for 1931, refusing to accept the slim evidence of major-league stuff in the country-boy braggart. Another 26-win year overcame any doubts and in 1932 Dizzy went 18–15 for the Cardinals, leading the league in innings and strikeouts, a category he dominated for three consecutive seasons. And just as he predicted, Dean put fans in the stadium seats. Billboards plastered with posters advertised the days Dean was to pitch. On one occasion, the heat forced Dean to beg off. The Cardinals, still using megaphones instead of a public address system, apologized to the fans. Substitute Bill Hallahan suffered the boos of the disappointed.

Diz naturally pitched for the National League in the 1934 All-Star game but the headlines rightfully belonged to Hubbell. In the first inning, Charlie Gehringer singled and Heinie Manush ★ (lifetime BA .330), a well-traveled outfielder then with Washington, walked. To the plate came the fading Babe Ruth, a sentimental choice as an all-star. Hubbell set him down with 3 called strikes. Lou Gehrig dug in at the plate. He struck out swinging, but Gehringer and Manush executed a double steal, placing runners at second and third. The next hitter was Jimmie Foxx and Paul Gallico gushed:

By that time Hubbell's magic had become too potent. It filmed Foxx's eye and slowed his muscles. The old dipsie doodle ball was swooping and dipping. There was red hot magic on it. It was turning into a rabbit, or a humming bird, or a bunch of flowers on its way to the plate. It would come up in front of Foxx's eyes and then vanish completely. Foxx struck out swinging. The crowd [Hubbell's hometown fans] lifted the Polo Grounds six feet off the ground with a roar and then set it down again.

The wizardry extended into the second inning as Hubbell whiffed the first pair, Al Simmons and Joe Cronin, giving him consecutive Ks against five of the most potent batsmen ever to grace a field. The coup lost some of its immediate glitter as the American Leaguers pounded out 9 runs against Lon Warneke and Van Mungo (Dean's stint permitted no runs).

The main rivals to the Cardinals were the Giants. During the season, Bill Terry, while being questioned about the chances of other teams, committed an unfortunate gaffe. Asked about the potential of the forlorn Dodgers he remarked, "Is Brooklyn still in the league?" The innocent insult provoked Casey Stengel and his wards to David-like heroics against the Goliath across the river as the Dodgers beat the Giants in several critical encounters at the end of the season.

But a substantial threat to the Cardinals came from within, from Dizzy Dean and his rookie brother Paul. Inside the unlettered twenty-three-year-old lay a man acutely conscious of the Dean worth and determined to get it. Early in the 1934 season, with 6 wins by Dizzy and 5 for Paul (sometimes referred to in the press as "Daffy" or "Nutsey"), the brothers demanded an increase in Paul's $3,000 salary. Dizzy was earning $7,500 and declared: "I'm underpaid, but my brother is worse underpaid. I'll take the rap for myself, but my brother must have $2,000 more or we don't pitch."

Management balked; the Deans went on strike like other working folk of the times. The standoff ended quickly, and although neither side proclaimed victory, columnist Joe Williams assumed the pair gained some concessions. Said Enos Slaughter of Rickey, "He'd go into the vault to get a nickel change."

In August, with 33 wins credited to them, the Deans skipped out on an exhibition game. Manager Frisch, insisting on team discipline, fined Diz $100 and Paul $50. They refused to accept the punishment and Frisch immediately suspended both. Diz erupted in a locker-room tirade, rending his uniforms in his passion. The suspensions and fines stood until a hearing before Landis brought an apology from Diz and his return to good

"During the reign of [Carl] Hubbell base itself is a Marathon route."—He, Broun

"The most charming feature of t All-Star game if Hubbell is right a arm red hot will be the spectacle of Am League sluggers snapping their spina in an attempt to hit his screwball."– Gallico, New York Daily News

Courtesy AP/Wide World

In prehelmet days, Medwick hung ov
plate a moment too long while wit
Dodgers and absorbed a pitch in the
from Cardinal hurler Bob Bowman.

Courtesy *New York Daily News*

Joe Medwick remained calm and c
while Cardinal vice-president and g
manager Branch Rickey appeared
during a salary holdout discussion.

Courtesy UPI/Bettmann News photos

174

graces. Although he missed a number of starts because of his tantrums, Dean still finished the year a 30-game winner, while Paul captured 19 including a no-hitter.

The Series against Cochrane and his Tigers went 7 games and opened a new era in baseball commerce. For the first time, a sponsor—the Ford Motor Co.—paid $100,000 for the exclusive broadcast rights. In game one, with Dizzy pitching, Medwick led the Cardinals to an 8–3 victory with 4 hits including a homer. Dean appeared on network radio that evening with the broadcast shortwaved to Admiral Richard E. Byrd and his expedition at Little America in the Antarctic. Confided Dean: "I didn't have a thing out there on my fast ball or my curve ball; I finally staggered through and won. . . . I can pitch better than that." Not one to let sleeping dogs lie, Dean continued: "The Tigers are not as good a ball team as I had them figured out to be, because I could take four National League baseball clubs over here this year and win the American League pennant with them."

Nevertheless, the Series lasted a full 7 games, with Dizzy accounting for 2 Cardinal wins and a loss while Paul won twice. In the final confrontation, the Cardinals scored 7 runs in the third, allowing Diz to win easily. The frustrated Detroit crowd turned ugly during the sixth inning. Joe Medwick slid into third base on a triple. Medwick, apparently miffed by third sacker Marvin Owen's footwork as he approached, lashed out with his own spiked shoe while still supine. The two squared off but were separated. However, when Medwick went to left field for the bottom of the sixth, the fans bombarded him with bottles, fruit, and seat cushions. Not until Frisch consented to remove Medwick from the game did the uproar cease but the game was beyond Tiger reach.

Pitcher Kirby Higbe defended Dean's frequent excursions in praise of himself: "A lot of people said he bragged but as far as I'm concerned, he didn't brag. He just told you what he was going to do and then went out and did it. If he said he was going to shut them out, he shut them out. I don't call that bragging."

Dean enjoyed excellent seasons in 1935 and 1936 with 28 and 24 wins. He exploited his reputation with a byline newspaper col-

umn entitled "Poppin' Off," and continued to squabble with Manager Frisch as the Cardinals unsuccessfully struggled to repeat as pennant winners.

In the All-Star game of 1937, a line drive off the bat of Earl Averill, ★ Cleveland's fine outfielder (a lifetime .318 hitter), smashed the big toe on Diz's left foot. With his toe still in a splint, he tried to pitch too soon, succeeding only in straining his right shoulder. Arm trouble followed; Rickey peddled him to the Chicago Cubs for $185,000 and several lesser players. Relying mainly on guile, he won 16 games over three seasons for Chicago but never again did he confound the enemy with his speed and big curve. He retired in 1941. The Browns used him to draw a crowd in 1947 with a 1-game, 4-inning appearance to complete his twelve major league years but he really played only five full seasons.

He professed a simple philosophy of pitching. In *The Dizziest Season* by G. H. Fleming, Dean explained:

Power and more power. Smart pitching, this so-called pitching to weaknesses of hitters is the bunk. You finally get so that you're outsmarting yourself. I got myself in a jam trying to be smart against the Giants Monday. With a couple of men on base, guys flocked all around me giving advice. I listened and tried to do as I was told. And I only got in more trouble. Then I says to myself, "Phooey on that smart stuff." I just reared back and let 'er go. I struck out George Watkins and Hughie Critz, and we were out of that jam.

If you can get the ball over with something on it, there's no call to be smart and try to get it to certain parts of the plate. That plate's only a few inches wide and the ball park is as big as all get out. . . .

I think pitchers are a better judge of what to throw than catchers. The pitcher's throwing it, ain't he?

There was in the baseball Dean the primitive human cited in another context by Jean Jacques Rousseau. Red Smith celebrated him: "As a ballplayer, Dean was a natural phenomenon, like the Grand Canyon or Great Barrier Reef. Nobody ever taught him baseball and he never had to learn."

Joe Medwick slides into third base on a triple in the seventh game of the 1934 World Series. Third baseman Marv Owen of the Tigers objected to Medwick's technique and the pair grappled briefly. Detroit fans, outraged as much by their club being routed as Medwick's action, deluged him with debris forcing his removal from the game.

Courtesy AP/Wide World

In that 1934 season, Dean faced a new slugging threat, Henry Louis Greenberg. ★ The Tiger first baseman was only in his second season and in origins he was from another planet than Dean. A child of New York City's Lower East Side, the first American homeland for tens of thousands of European Jews, Greenberg grew up in the Bronx as his father opened a shirt shrink plant (before a process to prevent shrinkage was incorporated into garment manufacturing).

David Greenberg could not understand his son's passion for a game when he should have been educating himself for a vocation. He despaired after arriving home from a long sweaty day in the garment center to find a pile of sawdust littering the small green patch of grass. Hank told writer Joe Falls that as a kid he would spread out the sawdust and practice his slides until his knees bled. "We didn't have a very big lawn. I'd have to go down the alleyway, between the house and garage, and here I'd come—running up the alley, making a lefthand turn and sliding."

The Yankees showed an interest in the strapping youth but he reasoned Lou Gehrig on first base would block his advancement. He decided his best opportunities lay elsewhere and signed with the Tigers for $9,000. In 1933, he put in close to a full season with Detroit, batting .301 and knocking 12 homers. In 1934, his average climbed to .339 with 26 home runs. The 1934 pennant drive confronted him with a moral dilemma. A critical series with the Red Sox fell on Rosh Hashanah, a high holy day for Jews. Greenberg resolved the situation by attending religious services in the morning and smacking a pair of homers in the afternoon for a 2–1 Tiger win. Delighted with the achievement by a man of the faith, Rabbi Leo Franklin congratulated him and Greenberg said: "I guess I didn't do anything wrong. Tonight I'm going home and pray to God and thank him for those home runs."

Greenberg quietly won the hearts of Detroiters with his exploits on the field and by reaching out to local youth. He sometimes showed up on a Sunday morning to play in pickup games with residents of Belle Isle. On other occasions he invited kids working as ushers to shag balls for him. When he suggested to management that he shift to the outfield to make room for slugger Rudy York at first, Greenberg hired popcorn vendors and ushers to hit to him so that he could improve his skills. At his own expense he traveled around the spring training circuit to consult veteran outfielders on techniques. During batting practice he would take his licks, and instead of lounging around the cage gassing with other players, he would race to the outfield and insist on chasing down every drive. Writer Art Hill remembered sitting in the ballpark for three hours while Greenberg "endlessly . . . would hurl a ball against the outfield wall and field it on the hop, like a kid in his own backyard who has no one to play catch with."

Fred Haney, who managed the Browns and later would lead Milwaukee to its 1950s pennants, remarked: "Greenberg puts more thought, effort and conscientiousness into his work than any other player in the league and to my mind he's the best competitor in the league."

But with a bat he required no instruction. He led the league in home runs for 1935, driving in 170 runs for the winning Tigers. A broken wrist sidelined him most of the following season, but he returned to terrorize American League pitchers with 40 four-baggers in 1937 plus 183 RBIs, third best in the history of the game (behind Hack Wilson's 190 and Lou Gehrig's 184). In 1938, he made a determined run on Ruth's 60 and fell 2 shy at 58. His productivity earned him Most Valuable Player in 1935 and 1940.

He became the first major league star to enter the military service, snared by the peacetime draft in May 1941. Discharged December 5, he enlisted two days later upon the bombing of Pearl Harbor.

As a first baseman, Greenberg usually suffered from comparisons with Lou Gehrig, still a potent figure when Hank arrived in Detroit and of course a beneficiary of New York City's dominance in print and broadcasting. And even as Greenberg first cast an evanescent glow in 1934, a star of even greater magnitude ascended in San Francisco. John Kieran, the savant of the *New York Times* sports pages and a resident wit on the new radio sensation "Information Please," appended a small note to one column about talk of the best player in the game, "Joe DeMaggio [sic]" with the San Francisco Seals. At seventeen, DiMaggio ★

"Even from this distance—maybe 5 from the plate—I could see how to powerful he [Hank Greenberg] was stood at the plate. He had the big house swing, a tremendous arc, an knew if he ever connected, watch ot Sam Greene used to tell me about berg's homers. They were never line d high flies; they were towering sho scrapers, majestic blasts that would deep into the upper deck in left. Falls, Detroit News

Courtesy UPI/Bettmann News photos

broke in with the Seals as a shortstop. Management was persuaded that was not his best position after he committed 11 wild throws in a single exhibition game. "And I mean they were wild throws," recalled DiMaggio. "They went clear into the stands. It got so that every time a ball was hit to me, the people sitting in the stands back of first base got up and ran, and when I say this I'm not kidding."

His manager, Jim Caveney, exiled him to center field. DiMaggio said: "On the very first ball hit to me I was lucky enough to make one of those circus catches, and when I came back to the bench, Caveney said to me, 'Why didn't you tell me you were an outfielder in the first place?' How could I tell him? I didn't know what I was."

When the eighteen-year-old rattled off hits in 61 straight games during the 1934 season everyone took notice. But talk of a trick knee diminished his market price. The Yankees bought his contract for the bargain price of $25,000 with delivery set for the 1936 season. DiMaggio then lit up the Bay Area with a .398 average for his final minor league season.

His Yankee Stadium debut was delayed by a diathermy burn—aches and pains and salary disputes kept DiMaggio out of opening day lineups for most of his career—but he quickly lived up to press notices. As a rookie he batted .323, drove in 125 runs in only 138 games, and amassed 206 hits including 15 triples and 44 doubles, testaments to his ground-gobbling long strides. The shortstop scatter arm had turned into a powerful defensive weapon; DiMaggio led the league with 22 assists, first in left field, and finally in his career groove of center.

Impressive as the rookie's figures seem, he did not even rate in the top five American League hitters for average. The highest honors, thanks to a .388 percentage, went to Luke Appling, ★ the Chicago shortstop who, with his similarly luckless teammate, pitcher Ted Lyons, spent a lifetime plugging away for the White Sox without ever seeing a pennant fly from Comiskey Park. Appling's bat control enabled him to foul off pitch after pitch, 19 on one occasion. He ended his twenty years with a lifetime .310. Appling and Lyons, both superior performers, should have been the nucleus of an outstanding club but instead remained a pair of glittering

atoms whirling through a White Sox era that never approached critical mass.

The 1936 Yankees with DiMaggio, however, compared favorably with the Colossus of 1927. The twenties Murderers' Row compiled 158 homers; the descendants, 182. At .307 the earlier club outhit the new version by 7 points but DiMaggio and company scored 90 more runs.

Lou Gehrig and Tony Lazzeri were the only holdovers from the Ruthian gang, which numbered six Hall of Famers; the Yankees who dominated their league and took four straight World Series from 1936 to 1939 included five such stellar figures.

Perhaps because fans had become so accustomed to Gehrig, DiMaggio's marvelous displays in the outfield and his prodigious work with the bat soaked up the ink. Actually, the Iron Horse outshone the newcomer in his initial season. Gehrig socked 49 homers, hit .354, and drove in 152 runs, aided no doubt by the constant presence of DiMaggio on bases. In 1937, Gehrig's 37 four-baggers fell behind DiMaggio's 46, although the first sacker outhit his younger teammate, .351 to .346. By 1938, Gehrig's production had slipped moderately to a .295 average and 29 homers. The following season, after 8 games, unable to run and clumsy even when tying his shoelaces, Gehrig told Manager McCarthy to remove him from the lineup. Within a few days, specialists diagnosed a terminal form of creeping paralysis, now frequently referred to as "Lou Gehrig" disease rather than amyotrophic lateral sclerosis.

There was no question that DiMaggio was now the premier Yankee. In honor of the new transoceanic-flying boats, he was nicknamed "the Yankee Clipper." He kept his name before the public not only through his feats but also in a series of salary wrangles with owner Jake Ruppert and general manager Barrow. As a rookie he received $8,500. The Yanks were already deep in spring training for 1937 before a compromise of $15,000 brought him to camp. When he demanded $35,000 for 1938, the haggling extended well into April, beyond opening day. The shadow of the Depression still lay over the nation and the front office sought to use it to shame DiMaggio into surrender. Dan Daniel of the *World Telegram* was shown a box purportedly filled with fan mail,

"Joe DiMaggio batting sometimes gave the . . . impression—the suggestion that the old rules and dimensions of baseball no longer applied to him, and that the game had at last grown unfairly easy."—Donald Hall, Fathers and Sons Playing Catch

Courtesy AP/Wide World

(Following page) "I believe DiMaggio to be a model for all ballplayers. It goes for all of them, past or present. I don't make Ruth or Cobb or Wagner exceptions. Baseball is still a game played nine men to a side. As one of the nine, DiMaggio has never had a superior. No one ever contributed more to the whole. It is the most unselfish skill possessed by any man who ever played the game for a living. It is an accidental gift, I believe."—Jimmy Cannon, Sport

Courtesy AP/Wide World

(Top) *"Instead of olive oil or smelly bear grease he [Joe DiMaggio] keeps his hair slick with water. He never reeks of garlic and prefers chicken chow mein to spaghetti."*— Life

Almost from the start of his major-league career, contract signing for DiMaggio became a sports page drama; salary squabbles and injuries kept him away from most opening days.

Courtesy AP/Wide World

(Bottom) *"Joe hasn't been the greatest hitter that baseball has known, either. He'll not match Ty Cobb's lifetime average, he'll never threaten Babe Ruth's home-run record, nor will he ever grip the imagination of the crowds as the Babe did. . . . That explains why the contract that he signed the other day calls for an estimated $65,000 instead of the $80,000 that Ruth got. If he were not such a matchless craftsman, he might be a more spectacular player. . . . And so more highly regarded.*

"But you don't rate a great ballplayer according to his separate special talents. You must rank him off the sum total of his component parts, and on this basis there has not been during Joe's big-league existence, a rival close to him. None other in his time has combined such savvy and fielding and hitting and throwing. Because he does so many other things so well and makes no specialty of stealing, DiMaggio rarely has received full credit for his work on the bases. But travel with a second-division club in the league for a few seasons and count the times when DiMaggio, representing the tying or winning run, whips you by coming home on the unforeseen gamble and either beats the play or knocks the catcher into the dugout."—Red Smith, New York Herald Tribune

Courtesy UPI/Bettmann News photos

179

panning the holdout. "The public is with us," Daniel quoted Barrow.

Meanwhile, the more liberal *New York Post* declared, "Public sentiment will be behind Joe's efforts to get himself the largest share of the Colonel's ready money." He eventually settled for $25,000, but for the third year in a row he was not on hand for opening day. Injury restricted him for 1939 but he approached the ethereal heights of .400 before a September slump dropped him to a mere .381, including 30 home runs. It was during this season that he accomplished his best-remembered catch. With Earl Averill on first, and one out, Greenberg blasted a ball into the deepest area of the stadium. "I started running, hoping that if the ball didn't go into the bleachers I could hold it to a triple and keep Greenberg from getting an inside-the-park homer. I ran at top speed with my back to the infield. I managed to get behind the flagpole and I couldn't have been more than two feet from the bleacher wall [just shy of the 461-foot mark]. Don't know yet how I made it," DiMaggio reminisced twelve years later. "Just stuck my glove up at the last moment and there was the ball. But actually I also pulled a rock on that one. When I caught the ball, Averill was almost to third and I should have doubled him up easily. But in the excitement, I thought the catch retired the side and before I woke up Averill was back on first."

So much for the vaunted phlegmatic attitude attributed to DiMaggio. Actually, as a neophyte, DiMaggio liked to emulate Tris Speaker and play shallow. He once boasted to Lefty Gomez he would make people forget Speaker. Gomez retorted, "You keep playing guys like Greenberg shallow and you're going to make 'em forget Gomez."

Although he was the idol of New York and other cities, DiMaggio was not immune to ethnic slurs. The Yankees among themselves referred to Lazzeri as "Big Dago," shortstop Frank Crosetti as "Little Dago," and DiMaggio simply as "Dago."

The first four years of DiMaggio, the Yankees stormed through the Series, knocking off the Giants in 1936 and 1937, wiping out the Cubs in 1938 and the Cincinnati Reds in 1939. They lost only 3 games to the crosstown rivals in their two confrontations and shut out both of the western teams.

Chicago's appearance in 1938 followed a spectacular stretch drive to overtake Pittsburgh. The decisive moment came as darkness lowered over Wrigley Field late in September. The Pirates led by half a game; the two teams grappled in a 5–5 tie while the umpires pondered whether to halt play. The arbiters agreed on 1 more inning, the ninth. Veteran Charlie Root stifled the visitors in the first half; the Pirates brought on Mace Brown, their relief ace who finished with a 15–9 record. Brown got 2 outs, then faced the thirty-eight-year-old catcher-manager Charles "Gabby" Hartnett. ★ Dismissed as a prospect by a Giant scout in 1918 because "his hands are too small," Hartnett, a refugee from a steel-wire mill in Worcester, Massachusetts, signed with the Cubs. Like Yankee catcher Bill Dickey, ★ he was slow afoot but durable, surviving twenty seasons during which he chattered incessantly with batters and umpires while squatting behind the plate.

Now, manager Hartnett came to bat with two down, the autumn twilight hiding Mace Brown's curves more than ever. Hartnett missed the first pitch and barely nicked the second. Brown, perhaps anxious to end the long day, decided not to waste one. He launched another curve but dropped it between the belt and knees. Hartnett connected; in the gloom, many spectators could not even see the ball but Gabby knew: "I got the kind of feeling you get when blood rushes to your head and you get dizzy." Indeed, the ball sailed into the left-field stands. He circled the bases with an entourage of fans and ushers.

The 1930s abounded with first-rate catchers. For the Yankees, Bill Dickey posted excellent stats, collecting 102 homers over the 1936–1939 period, keeping his average well over .300 and guiding the likes of Red Ruffing, Lefty Gomez, Spurgeon Chandler, and Joe McCarthy's increasingly used relief pitchers (first Pat Malone and then Johnny Murphy). Dickey, who roomed with Gehrig, epitomized the quiet professional; in fact, he was so unobtrusive that he shocked followers of the game in 1932 when he rose from the dirt at home plate after being bumped by Washington runner Carl Reynolds and smashed his fist flush on Reynolds's chin, breaking Reynolds's jawbone in two places.

"[Gabby] Hartnett's smash, against Brown with the count two strikes ar balls, probably saved the Cub pe chances."—Associated Press

Indeed, the homer in the ninth agair Pirates put the 1938 Cubs ahead for

"[Hartnett] was so good that he last years in spite of the fact that he co run. All other skills were refined in him the greatest of these was his throwing. ting behind plate, he could whistle th down to second base on a trajectory c as his feet."—Red Smith, New York ald Tribune

Courtesy AP/Wide World

A day earlier a charging runner had hurt Dickey, apparently putting him in a disagreeable mood. Reynolds had been on third when a pitch escaped from Dickey, who then threw to trap Reynolds off the base. The ball sailed into short left. Reynolds headed home, beating the throw, and bowling over Dickey to loose the beast in the frustrated catcher.

Dickey was a model baseball citizen after the incident, which cost him a thirty-day suspension and a $1,000 fine. He was unflappable whether dealing with the all-business Red Ruffing—"the best pitcher I've ever caught" said Dickey—or the idiosyncratic Gomez. Facing Jimmie Foxx on one occasion, Gomez shook off every sign until Dickey visited him and inquired: "Just what do you want to throw, anyway?" The pitcher responded, "I don't like the way he's looking at me. If it's all the same to you I'll just hold on to the ball."

Only Johnny Bench matched his durability, in thirteen seasons catching 100 or more games. His finest single moment graced the 1943 World Series. Spavined, able to catch only 71 games in the season, about to enlist in the navy at age thirty-six, Dickey won the final game of the Series from the Cardinals with a 2-run homer.

Aside from Dickey, Cochrane, and Hartnett, three other backstops from the 1930s achieved Hall of Fame status. Josh Gibson from the Negro Leagues broke in as an eighteen-year-old with the Homestead Grays in 1930; Rick Ferrell played his first full season that same year and Ernie Lombardi began his tour of the majors in 1931.

During his eighteen years, in which he hit .281, Ferrell ricocheted among the St. Louis Browns, Boston Red Sox, and Washington Senators. No American Leaguer ever caught more than his 1,805 games and he demonstrated his defensive skills by adroitly handling four knuckleballers in the Washington starting rotation.

At 5'10" and 170 pounds, Ferrell was one of the lightest men to put on the mask. Perhaps the most massive ever was Ernie Lombardi, a 6'3", 230-pound behemoth who did his best work behind the plate with the Cincinnati Reds. Like DiMaggio, he was a product of the Bay Area, growing up in Oakland.

Brooklyn actually brought him to the National League but the Dodgers already had Al Lopez, ★ a catcher who would enter the Hall of Fame for his managerial guile. Lombardi was traded in 1932 to Cincinnati. Blessed with an enormous honker, Lombardi bore the nickname "Schnozz." A publicity stunt brought a meeting with comedian Jimmy Durante, also gifted with a prominent nose. Durante announced, "Lom's is bigger, but mine is more educated."

At bat Lombardi wielded tremendous line-drive power but his position, which tends to restrict running muscles, combined with his bulk, allowed infielders to back up twenty-five feet on the grass and throw him out on what ordinarily would go as a base hit. As age diminished him from slow to slowest, foes took increasing advantage. Sighed Lombardi, "It took me four years to find out [Dodger shortstop] Pee Wee Reese ★ was an infielder." Wits in the press box would giggle, "Lombardi doubled to left and beat out a single."

In 1938, the Reds already had clinched the pennant by the final game and Lombardi held a 2-point lead for the batting title over Johnny Mize. Manager Bill McKechnie told Lombardi he could sit out the finale but Red Barber remembered: "Lom said, 'I'm playing.' He did and got two hits, so it was really his batting title. He earned it." Harold Rosenthal, writing for the *New York City Tribune,* saw Lombardi in his last years with the Giants. With men on base, a pitch appeared about to get away, curving to the catcher's right, and "there was no time to get the glove over. Lombardi merely stuck out his bare hand, caught the ball, and flipped it back to the mound."

While a minor leaguer in Oakland, a persistent blister on his pinky obliged Lombardi to adopt a unique grip, interlocking his fingers like a golfer. Still he connected safely enough to compile a .306 lifetime average and capture two batting titles.

Teammates regarded him with affection. Bucky Walters, a pitcher who ran up a 27–11 record for the pennant-winning Reds in 1939, remarked, "He did everything but run good. And he was a helluva guy on the club. Everybody loved him."

The veteran spent his 1942 season with the Boston Braves. Tommy Holmes, an outfielder, told Donald Honig:

Cincinnati catcher Ernie Lombardi's hand was big enough to palm seven baseballs; occasionally Lom caught errant pitches with that meaty hand.

Courtesy UPI/Bettmann News photos

We had a few rookies on the team . . . and they weren't making much money. . . . They were pretty excited about making their first Western trip. Lombardi—bless him—went around to all the kids and said, "Hey, kid, got enough money?" And without waiting for an answer he'd push a twenty on them. Just wanted them to be able to feel like big leaguers.

In 1938, Lombardi occupied the best seat in the house for the unmatched performance of a hard-throwing, erratic lefty, Johnny Vander Meer. Said Lombardi: "You could sit in a rocking chair and catch them guys [Bucky Walters and Paul Derringer]. Vandy was real hard to catch because he was so wild."

But on June 11, with Lombardi signaling mainly for fastballs, Vander Meer shut out the Braves 3–0 in a no-hitter. Four days later, at the first night game held in Ebbets Field, with Lombardi calling the shots, Vander Meer threw his second consecutive no-hitter, a 6–0 victory.

During the 1939 World Series, in the tenth inning of the fourth and final game, with Frank Crosetti and Charlie Keller on base, DiMaggio singled to right. Crosetti broke the tie and when the ball was fumbled both Keller and DiMaggio continued to run. Keller bounded by Lombardi just as the throw arrived and the catcher toppled onto his back. With Lombardi still flat on his back, DiMaggio raced home for the third score of the inning. For years Lombardi was accused of falling asleep, although DiMaggio's run hardly mattered. In fact, Keller said he had never bumped Lombardi. Vander Meer, on the mound, later said: "The throw from the outfield came in a short hop and hit Lom in the cup. You just don't get up too quick from that. . . . He was paralyzed. He couldn't move. Anybody but Lombardi, they'd have had to carry him off the field."

In 1940, Lombardi's .319 average aided the Reds to a second pennant. But a late season injury curtailed his World Series participation as Cincinnati overcame the Tigers in 7 games.

Detroit had barely squeaked past a resurgent Cleveland club by the margin of a single game. Much of the Indian success was due to the right arm of a twenty-two-year-old pitcher already in his fifth year of major league competition. Bob Feller, a Van Meter, Iowa, farm boy, switched from shortstop to pitcher at the suggestion of his father William, a semipro himself. According to the Feller lore, the farm grew wheat and Bill Feller invested in a tractor with a combine instead of raising the more time-consuming crops of oats and corn, thereby enabling the parent to cultivate the prodigy son. The beneficiary of this parental enthusiasm remembered:

He pitched batting practice to me, even built me a batting cage out of leftover lumber and chicken wire. Later he caught me when I pitched. This was every night practically, after our farm chores were done. During cold or rainy weather, we'd play in the barn. He'd have me pitching under game conditions with a dummy batter.

He bought me proper equipment too; uniform, spikes, a good glove always and official league balls, not the nickel rocket variety that a lot of my friends had to use.

And we talked and talked about baseball, studied books on the fine points of the game, sitting around our big warm kitchen.

Probably the greatest thing he did for me was when I was twelve, we built a complete ball field on our farm. We called it Oakview 'cause it was up a hill overlooking the Raccoon River and a beautiful view of a grove of oak trees. . . . We had a complete diamond with an outfield fence and scoreboard and even a grandstand behind first base.

We charged a small admission to cover our expenses—my father transported the players and my mother fed them. . . . Our team of farm boys played teams from as far west as Omaha, some pretty fast teams too. We drew some pretty fair-sized crowds on certain weekends. I was the only real "kid" on our team.

As a high schooler in 1934, he threw 5 no-hitters in the 7 games he pitched. Progressing to the semipro Farmers Union team, Feller fanned 21, allowed no hits in his first start, slumping in his second outing to 1 hit although he whiffed 23. He averaged 19 Ks per game throughout 1935 with 5 no-hitters.

Scouts flocked about but the boy journeyed to Cleveland where he worked out with the big leaguers before home games and then sold peanuts in the grandstand. When the Indians went on the road, the youth wrapped packages in a clothing store. At

When Johnny Vander Meer (left) *tos pair of consecutive no-hitters, Lo caught them.*

Courtesy NBL

(Opposite, top) *Lombardi lies stunne dirt while Joe DiMaggio slides hom final game of the 1939 Series. For y catcher was unfairly accused of mali on the play.*

Courtesy AP/Wide World

(Opposite, bottom) *Seventeen-year-c Feller for Cleveland started his firs league game in 1936, fanned sevente letics a year later, and eighteen T 1938, although he lost the game 4*

Courtesy AP/Wide World

some point Bill Feller signed a $60-a-month contract for his son. In July 1936, the Cardinals met the Indians for an exhibition. After the third inning, Manager Steve O'Neill, preserving his regular staff, inserted the seventeen-year-old. The gawky Feller threw 5 warm-up pitches, then whizzed his fastball by eight Redbirds in his 3-inning stint, giving up 2 hits and 1 unearned run. Recalled Feller:*

> The first batter up was Leo Durocher. I threw one ball over his head, two behind him and got two in the strike zone. Then O'Neill said to him, "You'd better watch yourself, Leo. This kid hasn't got the best control in the world." So Leo dropped his bat, ran into the dugout, and hid behind the water cooler.
>
> Everybody was laughing except for Cal Hubbard the umpire and me of course.
>
> Hubbard said, "Get back out here and hit. You're making a travesty of this game. You still have one strike left."
>
> Leo said, "You take it, Cal. I don't want it." Finally, he came back and stood in the back of the box and waved at one. That was my first big league strikeout.

Feller made several relief appearances and finally received a starting assignment. He instantly fulfilled the greatest of expectations, fanning fifteen St. Louis Browns. Several weeks later he broke Waddell's American League record when he whiffed seventeen Athletics. By the end of his abbreviated season, no one doubted his prowess.

Cleveland handled him gingerly, spotting his appearances in 1937 when he pitched in 26 games for a 9–7 record with 150 strikeouts, averaging 1 per inning. As a regular starter in 1938, he was 17–11 and racked up the first of four consecutive seasons with 240 or more Ks. World War II cut three years off his career but nevertheless Feller amassed 2,581 strikeouts with a game high of 18 against the Tigers in 1938—a game he lost 4–1. During his career he threw 3 no-hitters, a record until Sandy Koufax ★ showed up ten years later, and 12 one-hitters.

One other Hall of Famer started his career in the 1930s. Theodore Samuel Williams, a twenty-year-old San Diegan, a skinny 6'3", 150-pound stripling, took to the Red Sox

outfield in 1939 and stayed through 1960, except for two separate tours of military duty. "The Splendid Splinter" would thicken into a solid oaklike figure and "The Kid" would grow gray around the temples, but constant was his awesome skill with the bat. He hit .327 that first season and .316 the year he quit. In between he soared as high as .406 and .388, dipping below .300 only in his penultimate season. His lifetime .344 is sixth on the all-time charts. In this category, the closest to Williams among his contemporaries, Stan Musial, ranks twenty-third with a .331 average.

The man whom Jimmy Cannon called "the greatest hitter of his time" first attracted notice as a pitcher. But when Ted's mother, a dedicated soldier in the Salvation Army, asked for a $1,000 bonus, the Yankees passed. Williams signed with the new San Diego Padres of the Pacific Coast League as a pitcher and part-time outfielder. The Padres already owned a seventeen-year-old second-base sensation, Bobby Doerr, ★ who remembered: "All of us were singles hitters. We took one look at that tall skinny kid belting balls into the right field stands, and we all knew he'd be signed."

After Ted threw a home-run ball to the first man he faced, the Padres shifted his priorities from throwing to hitting. Eddie Collins, now general manager of the Red Sox, traveled west to inspect Doerr, on whom the club held an option. (Doerr proved to be the finest second sacker ever to play for the Sox, completing his career with 223 homers and an average of .288.) Collins watched Williams wield a bat and quickly claimed him. As a minor leaguer with the Sox during a spring in Sarasota, he rapidly established credentials as an original. One observer remembered his unique fielding style. When a fly ball headed in his direction, the teenager would slap his backside and yodel: "Hi-ho Silver, awa-a-ay."

Assigned to Minneapolis, he smote 43 homers, hit .366, debated with fans, occasionally ignored his outfield duties, and displayed his volatile temper by tearing up his locker and punching out the water jug. He initially delighted Red Sox patrons in 1939 as he cavorted about right field, his first position. After a homer Williams would run to

Power and consistency in the face birds and the unknowing: "They shift on me in '46. . . . I led the A League four times after that, and i led it six years. They changed the account of me." Indeed, because pitchers walked Williams rather him hit, he was disqualified for batt until the rules were changed.

Courtesy NBL

(Opposite) "The Kid," Ted Wil gangling twenty-year-old in 1939, his inimitable style and a scientifica trolled passion for hitting to the f

Said pitcher Spud Chandler of kees after a meeting on what to Williams: "I'll tell you what I High and tight is ball 1, and low a is ball 2."

Pitcher Bobby Schantz, after si struction: "Did they tell me how to Williams? Sure they did. It was vice, very encouraging. They said h weakness, won't swing at a bad ball best eyes in the business, and can with one swing; he won't hit at bad, but don't give him anything

Courtesy UPI/Bettmann News photos

184

Night turned into day for the first time
major leagues as Crossley Field in C
nati lit up the diamond during the
season. President Franklin D. Roo
from the White House threw the switc
turned on the arcs. Said Ed Barrow,
office boss of the Yankees, "Night ba
is a passing attraction which will ne
long enough to make it wise for the
York Club to spend $250,000 on a lig
system for the Stadium." Baseball
night game was in 1883 either ir
Wayne, Indiana, where the profess
from Quincy met the mideastern c
team or at Chambersburg, Pennsylvan
tween George Pensinger's Paint Sho
Clay Henninger's Nine. The minor le
had made night games a regular feat
1930.

Courtesy AP/Wide World

While newcomers Feller and W
shined in individual roles, the Yanke
dominated the American League a
last four World Series of the deca
youthful DiMaggio, the aging Gehr
Bill Dickey, the catcher in his prir
stroyed the opposition.

Courtesy NBL

right field and when the locals cheered he would take off his cap and, flashing that huge grin, swing it high in the air to tumultuous cheers. On post, Ted paced the grass, seemingly always moving, pulling off his glove, taking a few murderous practice swings.

It was Williams who hung "The Kid" on himself and he amused press and public with his third-person references to "The Kid." Youthful mood swings with occasional fielding lapses and failures to run out high pops eroded the relationship with some writers and a handful of fans. But as he aged Williams taught himself to be more than adequate in the outfield and his passion for hitting turned him into one of the foremost practitioners of the art.

As the decade drew to a close, there was one other notable starter, the Baseball Hall of Fame. Residents of Cooperstown, New York, the hamlet on the shores of Lake Otsego, occasionally had tried to make capital of the Mills Commission conclusion that in 1839 baseball sprang from the mind of native son Abner Doubleday. They managed to build Doubleday Field, allegedly on the site of Abner's first demonstration, but while National League President John Heydler showed for the dedication, the diamond served only townies and an occasional visiting semipro or minor-league outfits.

Cooperstown's idyllic setting had attracted a fair number of summer citizens, including Edward Clark, whose wife was a native. In 1848, three years after Alexander Cartwright explained his vision, lawyer Clark rendered expert counsel to Isaac Singer, inventor of the sewing machine. Further efforts on behalf of Singer and his manufacturing company brought Clark half ownership and then control of the business. Clark prospered mightily and the family interest in Cooperstown expanded proportionately. Clark eventually built a community gymnasium on Main Street, which was replaced by even larger edifices in 1930 and then in 1986. A hefty scholarship fund enables qualified area high-school grads to attend the colleges of their choice. Clark money funded a farmers' museum and, in conjunction with the New York State Historical Association, a handsome folk-art museum housed in a mansion once occupied by Clark ancestors, and a large regional medical center.

In 1935, Stephen Clark, grandson of Edward, was apprised of a rare archeological find. Recalled Clark years later, "I was talking to Walter Littell, the local newspaper editor. I used to talk things over with him from time to time. He mentioned that a man over in Fly Creek had found an old baseball and was offering to sell it. I bought it for five dollars."

Clark had no intention of anything so grand as a Hall of Fame or even a museum. He simply thought it might be appropriate to set up a small, temporary exhibition of artifacts. Alexander Cleland, an official of another Clark charity, scrounged some additional items and the materials went on display in the village library. When Cleland suggested that an all-time all-star team be selected for baseball's centennial—1939, in accord with the Doubleday legend—Ford Frick, then president of the National League, recognized the germ of an institution. Frick proposed a permanent Hall of Fame.

In 1936, the Baseball Writers of America chose the first five members of the Hall, electing Ty Cobb, Walter Johnson, Christy Mathewson, Babe Ruth, and Honus Wagner. With a $40,000 advance from the Clark family a building was constructed on Main Street to house the growing collection. The first visitors were admitted in 1938 but the formal opening was held June 12, 1939.

At the start, William Beattie, supervisor of the community gym next door, doubled as director of the Hall, which operated with three temporary paid employees. (The staff currently numbers twenty-five.) During its first year 25,332 people paid 25 cents to tour the National Baseball Hall of Fame and Museum, its official monicker.

The Hall expanded regularly to accommodate its increasing treasures and the growing number of visitors. The first addition came in 1951 and then the Hall of Fame Gallery followed seven years later. In 1968, on a plot behind the Hall, rose the library, housing every book written on baseball, complete files of such nineteenth-century publications as the *New York Clipper* and *Sporting Life* and twentieth-century periodicals devoted to sport and baseball, thousands of clippings, letters, photographs, tapes, films, scrapbooks, and other memorabilia. In 1980 the Hall gained another wing. And in the late

1980s, the old community gym was renovated to expand museum facilities.

By the close of World War II, the Hall obviously required a full-time director. Bob Quinn, a former executive with the Boston Braves, assumed the post with the two major leagues contributing $5,000 each to his salary and the Commissioner's office donating a similar amount. Sid Keener, a former St. Louis newspaperman, and then New York City reporter Ken Smith, succeeded Quinn. Howard Talbot became director in 1976.

Stephen Clark, although hardly a baseball fan, served as president of the institution until his death in 1960, when Paul S. Kerr, a Clark Estates executive, took charge. In 1977, Edward W. Stack, who manages Clark family interests, assumed the office.

The Hall still receives $15,000 a year from major league baseball. For the most part, however, it depends on admissions (roughly 250,000 a year, with a record 281,000 in 1987), sales from the gift shop, a modest income from licensing programs, and a share in the gate receipts from the annual exhibition game at Doubleday Field.

Clubs, players, and fans all freely contribute items for exhibition. The first fingerless gloves, the mitt that graced John McGraw's hand, rough-hewn, handmade bats, and the sleek ones used by the likes of Aaron and Mantle, Babe Ruth's bowling ball and his locker, balls from every celebrated game,

medallions, trophies, tickets, contracts, statues, photographs, paintings, gadgets and games, uniforms of long-gone franchises as well as contemporary ones, crates of artifacts from the Negro Leagues—truly a Smithsonian-style collection comprises "baseball's attic."

In the Hall of Fame Gallery hang the plaques of those elected: 164 major league players, 11 from the Negro Leagues, 10 managers, 5 umpires, and 20 pioneers and executives. Members of the Baseball Writers Association on active duty for a minimum of ten years vote on a ballot of thirty names supplied by a screening committee. All candidates must have played in ten major league seasons and been active within twenty years before the election but retired for a minimum of five years. An otherwise qualified player who dies before the five-year waiting period may be nominated six months after his death.

Electors vote for a maximum of ten individuals. Anyone receiving a vote on a total of 75 percent of the ballots cast becomes a member of the Hall of Fame.

A special group, the Baseball Hall of Fame Committee on Veterans, is drawn from members of the Hall and individuals connected with baseball, the writers' organization, and broadcasting. It is responsible for electing old-timers, managers, pioneers and executives, umpires, and men from the Negro Baseball Leagues.

(Opposite) "You've been reading about my bad break for weeks now. But today I think I'm the luckiest man alive. I now feel more than ever that I have much to live for."—Lou Gehrig, 1939.

Two years later he was dead of amyotrophic lateral sclerosis, the disease that is now commonly referred to by the Iron Horse's name.

Courtesy AP/Wide World

The National Baseball Hall of Fame and Museum, Cooperstown, New York, opened its doors in 1939.

Courtesy NBL

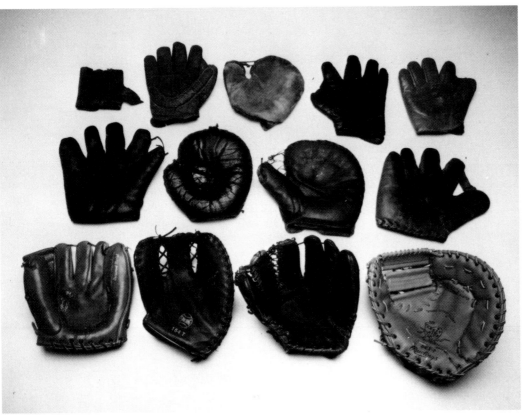

"Bar big gloves from baseball and bat
averages will bob up. The real artist
play without gloves or mitts. The old tir
worked without gloves. Take the mitt
present players and see how many great s
are left. The big mitt has made the
player. Men break into the game simply
cause they can hit. The big mitt does the
Sporting goods manufacturers are respo
ble for the big gloves. Outfielders shoul
compelled to catch in their bare hands or
very small gloves. The only except
should be the catcher and perhaps the
baseman."—Tim Murname, Boston Gl
1908

"We have no desire to revert to the g
less game, but there is a wide margin
tween no gloves and the present huge r
which enable the veriest dub to face a
non shot. The big mitt should be confine
the catcher; the pitcher and infielders she
wear only small gloves; and the outfiel
should wear no gloves at all."—Spor
Life, 1908

Courtesy Ted Astor

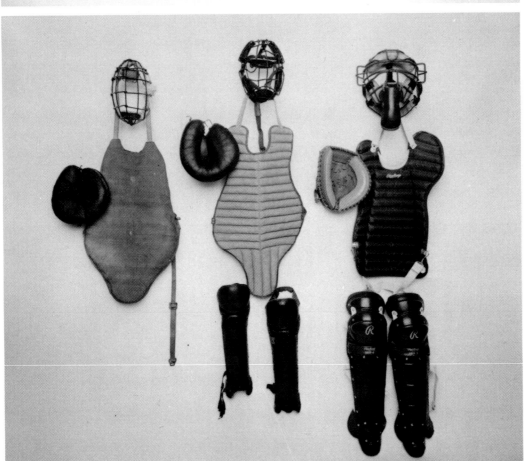

First came the glove, then a bird-cage-s
mask that was redesigned to allow for b
vision. Next catchers donned chest prote
and Roger Bresnahan innovated the
guards. The latest gear includes steel-pl
shoe tips, skull caps to protect the h
dangling throat guards, and waist-le
chest protectors supplemented by hard ru
cups covering the crotch.

Courtesy Ted Astor

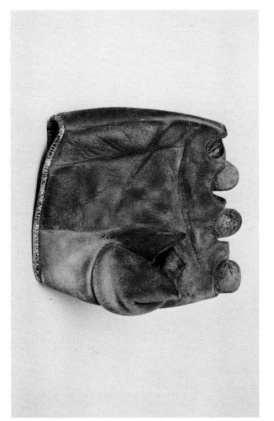

(Left) *"The catcher will find it advantageous when facing swift pitching to wear tough leather gloves, with the fingers cut off near the joint, as they will prevent his having his hands split and puffed up."*—Henry Chadwick

The last man to play without a glove, according to historian Bill James, was ambidextrous third baseman Jerry Denny of Louisville in 1894.

Courtesy Ted Astor

(Right) *John McGraw's glove, barely bigger than what a man uses ordinarily for cold weather, measures a mere nine inches from thumb tip to pinky end, compared to a modern tool that stretches a full fifteen inches.*

Courtesy Ted Astor

"The bat was round, not more than two and one half inches in diameter and could be of any length to suit the striker."—Jacob Morse, Sphere and Ash *(an 1888 history of baseball)*

Custom-made bats by Hillerich started to appear before the end of the nineteenth century. Heinie Groh employed the bottle bat with its six-inch handle and forty-one-ounce weight for curveball pitchers.

Courtesy Ted Astor

When World War II exploded in Europe in 1939, the initial effect on baseball was minimal. The American economy surged out of the Depression, thanks to orders for war goods, and people could afford to spend money on tickets. Overall attendance in 1938 was 9,006,521, but by 1940 it climbed to 9,823,484. However, the deepening threat to the United States posed by Germany's Nazi armies and the increased belligerence of imperial Japan intruded on the game. The first peacetime draft of young American men carried off a handful of big leaguers, most notably Hank Greenberg, already twenty-eight years old.

The last season before the nation became totally enveloped in World War II provided ample material to divert American attention from the stunning victories of German *blitzkriegs*. Foremost was the amazing feat of Joe DiMaggio, who hit safely in 56 consecutive games before, as the song "Jolting Joe DiMaggio" wailed,

> One night in Cleveland, oh, oh, oh,
> Goodbye streak, DiMaggio.

It had begun May 15 with a mere single against the White Sox. The streak seemed in jeopardy after 35 games when DiMaggio went hitless in his first three tries against the St. Louis Browns, but in his final opportunity he came through with a base hit. Enemy pitcher Bob Muncrief brushed off postgame queries on why he did not walk DiMaggio: "That wouldn't have been fair—to him or to me. Hell, he's the greatest player I ever saw."

Another adversary, Johnny Babich of the Athletics, sought to pitch around him but DiMaggio reached out and poked a hit. On July 4 at Yankee Stadium, DiMaggio surpassed Willie Keeler's string of 44 straight with a 3-run homer.

DiMaggio, a 6'2", 200 pounder, swung a long heavy club with a thick end. He stood with feet wide apart, the stride of his left leg as little as three inches. Keeler, the proponent of "Hit 'em where they ain't," was a bare 5'4" and 138 pounds, choking up on a short fat bat that Ed Barrow described as "like a paddle."

The end came in Cleveland on July 17 before a crowd of 67,468. Both Ken Keltner at third and Lou Boudreau ★ at short snuffed

out potential hits with brilliant fielding plays. During the spree DiMaggio had 4 4-hit games, 5 in which he connected thrice. Included in his 91 hits were 15 homers, 16 doubles, and 3 triples for an average of .402.

Meanwhile, Ted Williams also had been busy with his bat. On the last day of the season his average stood at .39955, guaranteeing him, when rounded off, the first .400 year since Bill Terry. With Boston firmly in second place and some 15 games behind New York, manager Cronin invited Williams to spend the day on the bench protecting his figures. Ted declined and declared if he couldn't hit .400 swinging the bat he did not deserve the mark.

As The Kid approached the plate for the first time, Athletics catcher Frankie Hayes said: "I wish you all the luck in the world, Ted, but Mr. Mack told us he'd run us out of baseball if we let up on you. You're going to have to earn it."

Williams dug in without any ritual spike tapping, head twisting, or stretchy squats. He was always all business, bat cocked high, prepared for the fluid swing with its massive weight shift through the hips, all practiced hours on end before a hotel room mirror or in the batting cage. He assiduously cultivated the stroke, pruning away superfluous head movement, lopping off torso tics that sapped power. In the first appearance of the doubleheader he lashed a single. He followed with a home run and went 4 for 5. Not content to rest even then, Williams went 2 for 3 in the final game to give him a .406 average. He also led the league with 37 homers and a .735 slugging average.

This was the first of six straight years (with time out for military service) that the Williams eye and discipline drew more walks than any other American Leaguer (and better than National Leaguers five of the six seasons). He had demonstrated his incredible restraint even as a rookie. Yankee pitcher Spud Chandler, after his first encounter with Williams in 1939, recalled a Yankee meeting on what they had learned about him. "I'll tell you what I learned," growled Chandler. "High and tight is ball one. Low and away is ball two."

Because he received so many walks, the 400 official at bats he needed to authentically lead the league was threatened. Recognition of Ted's fanatical faith in the strike

"Picked off a Louisville sandlot team, same that produced Billy Herman of [Chi]cago Cub fame, in the fall of 1937 [and] signed to a Colonel [Louisville Club] [con]tract for $200, Harold (Pee Wee) [Reese,] sensational 19-year-old shortstop, has [been] sold to the Brooklyn Dodgers in a [deal] which Larry McPhail, general manag[er of] the Flatbushers, says will approx[imate] $75,000."—Tommy Fitzgerald, Loui[sville] Courier Journal

Courtesy UPI/Bettmann News photos

(Opposite) *As the 1941 Ted Wil[liams] thumped the ball at a better than .400 [clip, becoming the last major leaguer to [hit] that figure, fellow Red Sox Jimmie [Foxx] fingered the musculature.*

Courtesy UPI/Bettmann News photos

zone caused officials to include walks when considering times at bat in the future.

Perhaps because Williams already was feuding with the press, he lost some votes for Most Valuable Player. However, DiMaggio's streak, his 30 homers, and his 125 RBIs, which led the Yankees to an easy pennant, also heavily influenced the jury.

The World Series of 1941 featured a new subway rivalry; the Brooklyn Dodgers, winners after twenty-one long years deep in the National League wasteland, had overcome the Cardinals. The Dodgers featured batting champion Pete Reiser, one of the stars of the Rickey plantation freed by Landis; Joe Medwick, sold to Brooklyn in 1940; and a number of quality players obtained from other clubs—Billy Herman from Chicago, homer leader Dolf Camilli and 22-game winner Kirby Higbe, both from the Phillies, and American League castoffs outfielder Dixie Walker and, another 22-game victor, Whitlow Wyatt. A lifetime .304 hitter, Herman brought the experience of three World Series as a Cub and a vacuum cleaner approach for balls hit to his position.

The increasingly solid cement of the infield was a second-year man, Harold "Pee Wee" Reese, bought from the Red Sox minor-league franchise in Louisville. Reese, whose nickname came from a marbles tournament—at 5'10" he was hardly short stuff—only batted .229 but the Dodgers believed in him.

Red Ruffing took the first game for the Yanks but Wyatt evened matters the next day. Fred Fitzsimmons, forty years old, with a strange style in which he faced second base before throwing, started game three for Brooklyn. He had a shutout when a wicked drive from pitcher Marius Russo bounced off his knee. Reliever Hugh Casey, who suffered even more catastrophic events in game four, allowed 2 runs for a Yankee win.

In the climactic game four, the Dodgers clung to a 4–3 lead in the ninth with two away. Tommy Henrich was down to his final strike against Casey, who apparently fooled Henrich with what some insist was a spitter. But the third strike also confounded catcher Mickey Own (who denied Casey loaded the ball) and it skidded out of his mitt and rolled far enough for the alert Henrich to scamper to first.

Swiftly, the Yanks exploited the error. Di-

Maggio singled. Casey picked up a pair of strikes on Charlie Keller before "King Kong" whacked the ball against the right-field screen, barely missing a homer but driving home both Henrich and DiMaggio. Dickey walked, and with 2 strikes on him, second baseman Joe Gordon smacked a double to put New York ahead 7–4. The Yankees went on to a 3–1 closer in game five.

Two months later the Japanese rained bombs on Pearl Harbor and, in contrast to World War I, World War II greatly affected baseball, although President Franklin D. Roosevelt declared: "I honestly feel that it would be best for the country to keep baseball going. There will be fewer people unemployed and everybody will work longer hours and harder than ever before. And that means they ought to have a chance for recreation and for taking their minds off their work even more than before."

FDR, however, reaffirmed that there would be no special exemption from military service. Players could not opt to work in a defense plant, as they had in 1918. Hank Greenberg had enlisted while the fires of smashed U.S. ships still burned. DiMaggio, Williams, Cochrane, Gehringer, Reese, Feller, Musial, Mize, Lyons, Herman, among a galaxy of Hall of Famers, swapped flannel knickers for olive drab, navy blue, and marine green. Hundreds of lesser-known major and minor leaguers did likewise. Some saw combat; others served as recreation and physical training instructors or played exhibitions designed to keep spirits high. Left to carry on the game were a handful of men deferred because of family responsibilities, age, or physical impairment.

Rosters were padded with old-timers like the Waners, who postponed retirement, and a handful of underage phenoms, like fifteen-year-old Joe Nuxall who came on for Cincinnati in 1944, threw two-thirds of an inning, and left with an ERA of 67.50 before returning eight years later to resume his career. Perhaps the most widely publicized fill-in was Pete Gray, a one-armed outfielder who appeared in 77 games for the St. Louis Browns during 1945. Babe Herman, celebrated for zaniness instead of his .324 average, emerged at 42 for 37 games in the Brooklyn outfield. The Dodgers got two wartime seasons out of a former Pittsburgh star, Floyd "Arky" Vaughan, ★ a lifetime .318

(Previous pages) "Two were out, was on, the Yanks looked throttled j second time in the series. The Br horde scarcely could contain itself as pared to hail the feat with a tumu outburst. Casey worked carefully on H and ran the count to three balls an strikes. Then he snapped over a low, breaking curve. Henrich swung and n A great Flatbush triumph ap clenched. But in the twinkling of an e victory was to become an even greate sion.

"As the ball skidded out of Owen and rolled toward the Dodger bench Mickey in mad pursuit, police guards rushing out of the dugout to hold ba crowd which was preparing to dash out on the field. Owen retrieved the b in front of the steps, but Henrich was t like wild for first and he made the bag out a play.

"The Yanks, of course, had not i the game. They were still a run behin though they had a man on first, needed to collect only one more out to his margin. But there was an o ring to DiMaggio's line-drive sin left. . . ."—John Drebinger, New Times, 1941

Courtesy NBL

Baseball went military along with the rest of the United States in World War II. Hank Greenberg (far left) had been drafted in 1940, hardly demobilized before bombs fell on Pearl Harbor, and along with other Americans enlisted for the duration.

Courtesy UPI/Bettmann News photos

The shortage of able-bodied men caused the St. Louis Browns to put one-armed Pete Gray in the outfield.

Courtesy AP/Wide World

197

shortstop, occasional third sacker, and outfielder. Others who sought to carry on included Leo Durocher, Joe Cronin, Pepper Martin, and even Jimmie Foxx, who tried his hand as a pitcher.

Although the clubs managed to eke out the regular 154-game schedules, they were forced to curtail spring training and prepare for the baseball wars in such inhospitable climbs as Bear Mountain, New York, Muncie, Indiana, and Asbury Park, New Jersey. To save further on travel, the 1945 All-Star game was canceled. At least the players were spared the World War I indignity of close order drill with bats supervised by army sergeants. However, White Sox pitchers posed throwing at a poster-size target of a Japanese soldier.

Exhibition games over a four-year period raised $2.5 million for Army and Navy relief groups, the USO, and the Red Cross. Furthermore, with receipts from All-Star games and other promotions, baseball contributed $328,000 to buy sports equipment for the armed services.

Joe DiMaggio made his final civilian appearance in the 1942 World Series but in a losing cause as St. Louis, with Slaughter and a bright newcomer named Stan Musial, defeated New York in 5 games. The DiMaggio-less Yanks revenged themselves the following year in similar fashion.

The diminution of talent allowed the once-hapless St. Louis Browns to capture a pennant in 1944 with a club batting average of .252. This was the only pennant in the fifty-three-year life of the franchise, which moved to Baltimore in 1954. Their local National League counterparts, the Cardinals, in their third straight Series downed the Brownies in a 6-game set.

The surrender of Germany early in the spring of 1945 started an exodus of players from military service. Hank Greenberg, discharged as a captain, returned to continue his heroics as a Tiger. In his very first appearance, July 1, he smacked a homer. The race between the Tigers and the Washington Senators was not decided until the final day and again Greenberg provided the victory margin, a grand slam. He continued to shine with 2 homers, 7 RBIs, and a .304 average as Detroit scuttled Chicago in 7 games.

With the world temporarily at peace, the genuine stalwarts of the game took over in 1946—Greenberg was the only Hall of Famer in the 1945 Series. Joining him on the Tigers after the championship was third baseman George Kell. ★ A less-than-.300 hitter during the war, he apparently required top pitching in order to hit, for he later racked up nine seasons over .300. He led American League fielders seven times.

And some new faces strode onto the stage. Most notably, in Pittsburgh, a free-swinging outfielder named Ralph Kiner ★ socked 23 homers to give the rookie the league leadership; in Boston twenty-five-year-old southpaw Warren Spahn, who put in a token appearance in 1942, began to meet great expectations.

Pittsburgh signed Kiner as an eighteen-year-old for a $3,000 bonus and a promise of an additional $5,000 if he reached the majors. With nearly three minor-league years tucked into his experience he entered the navy, serving as a bomber pilot in the Pacific. The Pirates took him to spring training in 1946, planning to season him further in the minors. But 14 exhibition-game homers changed Manager Frank Frisch's mind and Kiner stayed with the parent club.

Kiner's 23 homers were accompanied by a miserable .247 average and a league-leading 109 strikeouts. But he doggedly strove to refine his art. During his first two seasons he recorded on index cards every pitch thrown to him. He thus studied the pitching strategy used against him and how he coped with each pitch. He also invested in a movie camera to provide visual evidence of his rights and wrongs. With a colleague, he spent so much time in extra batting practice that the pair chipped in to buy a car for their pitcher. He also benefited enormously from a deal that brought Hank Greenberg to Pittsburgh for his last active year where he encouraged and counseled Kiner. All of the effort paid off, as Kiner more than doubled his rookie home-run output for the next five years, leading the league a total of seven consecutive seasons and accumulating a total of 369 homers in his ten-year career. He cut his Ks by 25 percent and boosted his average by roughly the same margin. All the while he labored for a club almost exclusively in the second division, making it easy for rivals to pitch around him.

The Waner brothers, thirty-eight-Lloyd and forty-one-year-old Pau Dodger ranks in 1944.

Courtesy UPI/Bettmann News photos

Sergeant Joe DiMaggio of the army and Chief Specialist Pee Wee R tained ball teams playing for the file in Hawaii.

Courtesy NBL

Wrongly smeared as a slacker, liams flew navy fighter planes, an called a few years later to pilot je the Korean War.

Courtesy NBL

At twenty-five, Warren Spahn was two years older than Kiner and coming off an even tougher war when he joined the Boston Braves in 1946. Casey Stengel had managed the club when Spahn arrived fresh from two minor-league years in 1942. Irate because he thought the Dodgers were onto the Boston signals, Stengel reversed the code; the previous sign for a fastball now meant curve and vice versa. Recalled Spahn:

Pee Wee Reese was at bat with a runner on second who could see our catcher's signals. Casey called for a brush back pitch. I threw three straight inside fast balls that never fazed Reese. He merely leaned back and took them for balls. Casey stormed out to the mound, lifted me because I hadn't decked Reese. In the dugout he stopped me and told me to pick up my railroad ticket to Hartford. "Young man," he said, "you've got no guts."

For Stengel, it was a rare and monumental misjudgment. The allegedly gutless young pitcher entered the army shortly afterward. He served with a combat engineers unit that participated in the bloody Battle of the Bulge, the critical Rhine crossing, and the desperate fight to conquer central Germany. When the authorities handed him his honorable discharge he held three battle stars, a purple heart for shrapnel in his foot, and a battlefield commission as a lieutenant.

His first year's 8–5 was followed by one of his thirteen 20-or-better-win seasons and suddenly the futile Braves had become a contender. In 1948, injuries plagued Spahn and he started slowly. Veterans Johnny Sain and Vern Bickford and a Giant castoff, Bill Voiselle, carried the club early but then Spahn began delivering his fastball and curve most assertively. For the September stretch drive, Manager Billy Southworth relied almost exclusively on Spahn and Sain, starting them almost every other day. Describing the abbreviated rotation, Beantown fans took up the chant, "Spahn, Sain, and pray for rain." The pair started 11 out of 16 games beginning with a Labor Day doubleheader against the Dodgers. They swept Brooklyn, gratefully recuperated with two days of scheduled rest plus a lucky couple of rainouts, and went on to win 7 more while dropping 2. Bickford, however, with help in relief, clinched the pennant.

During the same season, Cleveland, managed by Lou Boudreau who led the league at shortstop with a .975 fielding percentage and batted .355, boasted a pair of 20-gamers in Bob Lemon ★ and Gene Bearden, while Feller won 19. For all of that superior pitching, owner Bill Veeck heard the spiked shoes of the Red Sox, Athletics, and Yankees as the summer began. Veeck searched for a reliever and spot starter, then remembered a 13-inning exhibition game in 1934 that pitted Dizzy Dean against the already legendary black wizard, Satchel Paige. ★

A year after Jackie Robinson had broken the color line, Veeck surreptitiously brought the aged wonder of Negro baseball to the ballpark and inveigled Boudreau into batting practice against him. Boudreau caught the forty-two-year-old rookie as he warmed up. He was impressed by Paige's ability to put the ball where he desired. Boudreau then picked up a bat, took nineteen swings, failed to put adequate wood on anything offered, and Paige was signed up immediately. The news brought denunciations of Veeck as "crude" and "in quest of publicity." Actually, thanks to the feverish pennant race, Cleveland attendance was already on a record-setting pace.

Two days later, Paige relieved and shut out the St. Louis Browns for 2 innings using "my single wind-up, my triple wind-up, my hesitation wind-up and my no wind-up. I used my step-and-pitch-it, my sidearm throw and my bat dodger." Veeck could not have been dismayed when sixty-five thousand, almost half of them black, paid to see an exhibition contest in which Paige faced the Dodgers in relief.

When the Indians announced Paige would start August 3, Municipal Stadium sold out. In front of seventy-two thousand fans, the biggest night game crowd ever, the Indians won with 7 innings from Paige. Ten days later he filled Comiskey Park, shutting out the White Sox. His performance faltered in September but the others on the staff carried the club to the Series. Paige was bitter that he did not start a championship game. He appeared only briefly in relief as the Indians overcame the Braves. Spahn won one, lost another.

After the Braves shifted to Milwaukee,

Fresh out of the navy, free-swinger Ralph Kiner (right) *stuck with the Pirates, aided greatly by advice from Hank Greenberg, who came home from the war a captain in time to club the Tigers into the 1945 Series, and a year later found himself in a Pittsburgh uniform.*

Courtesy NBL

"On the night of June 17, 1946, Dizzy Dean, while broadcasting the Red Sox–Browns game in St. Louis, informed his listeners that the Cardinals were ahead in their night game in Boston. 'Spahn is now pitching for the Braves,' said Dizzy and then added, 'Who in the world is Spahn?' "—Joe Reichler, **Associated Press**

Courtesy Mark Kauffman, *Sports Illustrated*

Spahn, Lou Burdette, and a pair of sensational young sluggers, third sacker Eddie Mathews ★ and outfielder Henry Aaron, powered the club to pennants in 1957 and 1958. Milwaukee beat the Yankees in the first World Series but dropped the second one to the same rivals.

Neither age nor three knee operations that required painful rehabilitation could conquer Spahn. As the seasons rolled by, someone inquired about the concessions forced on him. "You don't make concessions," snapped Spahn. "If you concede one little thing, pretty soon you find yourself conceding another, then another. I can't admit that I'm old. I'm competing in a business against younger arms, younger legs, but I have to do all the things they do and do them better."

When the years banked the fires of his heater, he improved his curve, then perfected a change-up, added a slider, and introduced an occasional screwball.

Stan Musial declared:

He was one of the great athletes as well as the best National League pitcher of my era. He could have been a hitter or an outfielder. Spahnie not only knew everything about his profession, but he was smart enough to change before he had to. Even while he still had the good high fast ball to go with his change-up, only fair curve and great control, he began to tinker with the screwball. The screwjie became a great pitch when he lost something off the fast ball. He had the nerve to throw it down and in on left handed batters, as well as low and away from right handed batters. . . . He's the only pitcher ever to walk a batter to face me.* Back in 1957 when the Cardinals were threatening Milwaukee's league lead, Fred Haney [Braves manager] brought Spahn from the bullpen in the ninth inning to protect a one-run lead. He walked the batter in front of me to set up an inning-ending double play. I obliged.

At age thirty-nine, he threw his first no-hitter and repeated the trick a year later. At forty-two, he became the oldest pitcher ever to win 20 games as he tossed 7 shutouts for a 23–7 record. When he finally retired in 1967, following two seasons of minor-league efforts, Spahn had 363 wins, the highest ever by a lefty.

The glory of 1946, however, belonged to Enos Slaughter. He stood only 5′9″ but played as if he were a tight end run amok. As an eighteen-year-old kid from a North Carolina farm, Slaughter drifted onto one of Rickey's plantations in Columbus, Georgia. During a slump he moped in from his outfield post to be met by Manager Eddie Dyer, who snarled: "If you're tired, kid, I'll get some help for you."

Slaughter brooded over the reprimand and decided: "I realized that here it was, Depression times and I was letting down people putting up their hard-earned pennies, dimes and quarters for me to help them out of their problems. I vowed never to walk on a ballfield again."

And so he developed a habit of running to and from his position, of running to first base even on a walk. Among the impressed observers was a rough kid from Cincinnati. Subsequently, Peter Edward Rose copied Slaughter's style.

After joining the parent club in 1938, Slaughter, who chose the nickname "Country" from several candidates, entered the .300 ranks his next five seasons. He was chosen for a total of ten All-Star teams. But he is most celebrated for his World Series antics.

In 1946, the St. Louis Cardinals faced off against the Boston Red Sox, propelled into the championship by Ted Williams. Slaughter hit .320 in the 7-game set, contributing a homer and 2 RBIs. In game four, Rudy York was at third base when Hal Wagner lifted a ball that backed Slaughter to the bullpen fence. York tagged up and lumbered home, secure in the knowledge that even a man as slow as he could beat a throw from that far. Slaughter's peg cut him down. "Country" once insisted his accuracy and power came from hours of practice, throwing rocks at jackrabbits while on his way to milk the cows. In game five, a ball struck him on the elbow causing a fearful blood clot. Physician Robert Hyland cautioned that another blow to that elbow could force amputation. Slaughter insisted on gambling.

It was 3–3 in the eighth inning of the finale and he was on first base with two gone. Harry Walker blooped one into center field that fell in front of Leon Culberson, sub-

The biggest event of the 1940s was the appearance of blacks in major league uniforms. Jackie Robinson was the first, in 1947, but the oldest and most famous among blacks was a forty-six-year-old, rubber-armed wizard named Leroy "Satchel" Paige who surfaced with Cleveland in 1948. Here he is pictured with Tribe owner, Bill Veeck.

Courtesy NBL

Enos Slaughter slides across the plate for the decisive run of the seventh game of the 1946 World Series, giving the Cardinals the championship. Slaughter beat the Red Sox, scoring from first base on a bloop single to center field.

Courtesy AP/Wide World

---

*Spahn intentionally passed Del Ennis, pinch hitting for Wally Moon.

Al Gionfriddo, a throw-in from Pitt
which gave the Dodgers $100,000
men, ranged to the bullpen barn
Yankee Stadium left field to hau
game-tying home-run bid by DiM
Gionfriddo's catch forced the Yanks
games before subduing Brooklyn in
Films of the play show the rarely em
DiMaggio kicking the dirt as he pu
after rounding second.

Courtesy NBL

stituting for an injured Dom DiMaggio. Slaughter, off with the pitch, kept running as shortstop Johnny Pesky, his back to the plate, hustled out to take the relay. Pesky started to turn to hold Walker at first but his peripheral vision caught Slaughter cutting inside third to save ground and tearing for home. The shortstop whirled and threw but Slaughter slid safely for the decisive run. "I would have needed a rifle to nail Slaughter," moaned Pesky, who took the rap for the play although the real boner was the failure of anyone on the Sox to alert Pesky to Slaughter's daring.

Ten years later, donning the uniform of the New York Yankees late in the season, Slaughter hit .350 in the World Series as a forty-year-old.

The modest beginnings of Kiner and Spahn and Enos Slaughter's heroics in the first year after the Allies' victories were dwarfed by the precedent-shattering breach of baseball's color line by Branch Rickey, then chief of the Brooklyn Dodgers.

The deliverance of Brooklyn after wandering more than twenty years in the National League wasteland actually preceded the arrival of Rickey. In 1938, a rambunctious, redheaded, one-time department store executive, lawyer, and real estate investor, mastermind of a nearly successful plot to kidnap the German Kaiser at the close of World War I, first came to baseball as a minor-league owner at age forty. Leland Stanford Mac-Phail ★ introduced air travel to the game and inaugurated night ball for the majors in 1935 while with Cincinnati. As general manager, MacPhail had been responsible for the acquisition of much of the talent that brought the Reds their 1939 and 1940 pennants. During his four years with Brooklyn he bought, traded, and drafted the people who carried the Dodgers to the 1941 World Series. But in mid-1942, Larry MacPhail joined the military; he would return to baseball in the Bronx for a tempestuous term with the Yankees.

Rickey and Cardinal owner Sam Breadon had grown estranged. Breadon no longer deferred to Rickey's knowledge of the game. Ostensibly, the ultimate quarrel arose over Rickey's resistance to radio sponsorship by breweries although later he allowed beer companies to pay for Dodger broadcasts. So the Mahatma jumped at the opportunity to operate Brooklyn and promptly began building a farm system. His Class D outfit, Newport of the Piedmont League, evaded the limitations of the military draft with fifteen boys age seventeen or younger. Among the youths were Clem Labine and a free-swinging outfielder, Edwin "Duke" Snider. ★ Manager Jake Pitler, later a coach for Brooklyn, remarked: "When we took off in our bus on a road trip we were loaded with comic books and candy bars, but we carried practically no shaving cream."

Quite possibly the dearth of available bodies turned Rickey toward the huge pool of hitherto, untapped talent: black athletes. As early as 1940, Gabby Harnett, managing the Chicago Cubs, remarked: "If managers were given permission, there'd be a mad rush to sign up Negroes." Jimmy Dykes of the White Sox, Bill McKechnie in Cincinnati, and Leo Durocher voiced similar sentiments. *Washington Post* columnist Shirley Povich wrote:

> There's a couple of million dollars worth of baseball talent on the loose, ready for the big leagues, yet unsigned by any major league . . . pitchers who could win 20 games . . . outfielders who could hit .350. . . . Only one thing is keeping them out of the big leagues— the pigmentation of their skins. . . . It's a tight little boycott that the majors have set up against colored players.

Rickey's memoirs state: "The very first thing I did when I came into Brooklyn in late 1942 was to investigate approval of ownership for a Negro player. There was a timeliness about the notion. The Negro in America was legally but never morally free. I thought: if the right man with control of himself could be found. . . ."

Rickey raised the issue with George V. McLaughlin of the Brooklyn Trust, which controlled a large block of stock, and with members of the board of directors like Joseph Gilleaudeau and Jim Mulvey (whose daughter would marry Ralph Branca, the Dodger pitcher to be cursed with the memory of the home run struck by Bobby Thomson in the celebrated 1951 playoff). All agreed Rickey could proceed as long as his purpose was not a crusade but the economics of strengthening the roster and widening the fan market.

Certainly Rickey could justify his actions on these grounds but also he must have been motivated by his painful memories as coach of Ohio Wesleyan University four decades earlier. During a trip to play Notre Dame, a hotel in South Bend refused to house Charles Thomas, one of the few blacks in the school. Rickey often recalled Thomas rubbing his huge hands against one another while weeping, "Black skin, black skin. If I could only make 'em white." Rickey also heard the cry, "Get that nigger boy off the field," during a game against Kentucky. There were also genuine Christian beliefs in Rickey that refused to accept the denigration of a human being because of color.

A few abortive efforts to break the color line had marked the war years. Entrepreneur

William "Judy" Johnson wore the uniforms of the Philadelphia Hilldales, the Homestead Grays, and the Pittsburgh Crawfords while starring at third base during the 1920s and 1930s.

Courtesy NBL

and gadfly-owner Bill Veeck, who was plagued by his wounds as a marine, sought to buy the Phillies and stock the club with stars from the Negro Leagues. He claimed that as soon as Commissioner Landis heard of his scheme the sale of the franchise to him was blocked and the club given to other investors.

Pittsburgh owner Bill Benswanger declared: "Colored men are American citizens with American rights. I know there are many problems, but after all, somebody has to make the first move." However, he dropped his plan to use nonwhites in the face of opposition.

Officially, baseball insisted it was color-blind. John Heydler, as president of the National League in 1933, sanctimoniously announced: "I do not recall one instance where baseball has allowed either race, creed or color to enter into its selection of players."

Ford Frick, Heydler's successor, argued the League could not play nonwhites because the public "has not been educated to the point where they will accept them." He added: "Baseball is biding its time and waiting for the social change which is inevitable. Times are changing."*

Landis reiterated this position after Durocher remarked he would leap at an opportunity to sign up blacks but was forbidden. Said the Commissioner, after Leo visited the Judge's woodshed and discovered he had been misquoted: "There is no rule, formal or informal, no understanding, subterranean or otherwise against black ball players in the majors."

Still, no nonwhite skins graced either the major- or minor-league fields of what was known as organized baseball. Yet, there were black men with whippy arms, swift feet, and awesome bat power, traveling the western hemisphere and demonstrating remarkable skills. They were enrolled in the Negro Leagues, a loose university of the sport marked by highly individual philosophies, arcane—often self-generated—knowledge, spontaneity, mostly minimal rewards, and an inordinate affection for the game.

Rube Foster sired the Negro National League in 1920 with clubs in Kansas City (the Monarchs), Indianapolis (the ABCs), the Cuban All Stars (no home city), Chicago (housing both the American Giants and plain Giants), Detroit and St. Louis (Giants in both cities). The Eastern Colored League appeared three years later with outfits in New York (Lincoln Giants), Atlantic City (Bacharachs), Baltimore (Black Sox), Philadelphia (Hilldales), and Brooklyn (Royals). After the Eastern Colored League folded, the Negro American League emerged along with a facsimile of the all-white World Series. Scratching to survive, the teams played clubs in and out of their leagues, including such unaffiliated powerhouses as the Homestead Grays. Foster spent his own money to keep shaky franchises alive. He guaranteed hotel bills when rained-out games shut off income and he bullied and coaxed associates into a professional presentation. A brief flirtation with prosperity ended with the Great Depression, which suspended regular league play for several seasons. Teams and field hands continued at bare subsistence levels. Frequently, salaries were suspended and the only receipts for a game came from passing the hat.

John Henry Lloyd, whose career dated back to Rube Foster's days as an active player, was a playing manager for Hilldale. His star pupil was William Judy Johnson. ★ An outstanding third baseman who applied a scientific approach at the plate, Johnson was known as "the black Pie Traynor." Like many of his contemporaries, Johnson rightfully resented his exclusion from the majors: "The question of ever playing in the big leagues never occurred to me until I was twenty or so and playing ball already. Then it occurred to me that I should be playing. Often I've wished I could've played at the time Jackie Robinson came up. I feel as though I could've given something to help my race along."

Johnson told Art Rust, Jr. that most of the Negro teams of the day were of "triple A quality" and an all-star outfit could probably "beat hell out of any of the white major leagues any day."

Indeed, many white major leaguers enjoyed playing against the nonwhites after

Improvised buses like this one, used Kansas City Monarchs in 1934, stu men and equipment, ferried Negro players about the country on ten- an hour trips.

Courtesy NBL

The Homestead Grays in 1937 i Buck Leonard (standing, far left) legendary catcher Josh Gibson (st third from right). Vic Harris (k third from right) managed the te patrolled left field.

Courtesy NBL

---

*Men with Italian or Polish backgrounds, Jews, and other ethnic minorities also endured hostility from some players, fans, and reporters. But unlike blacks, these groups were never barred from organized baseball.

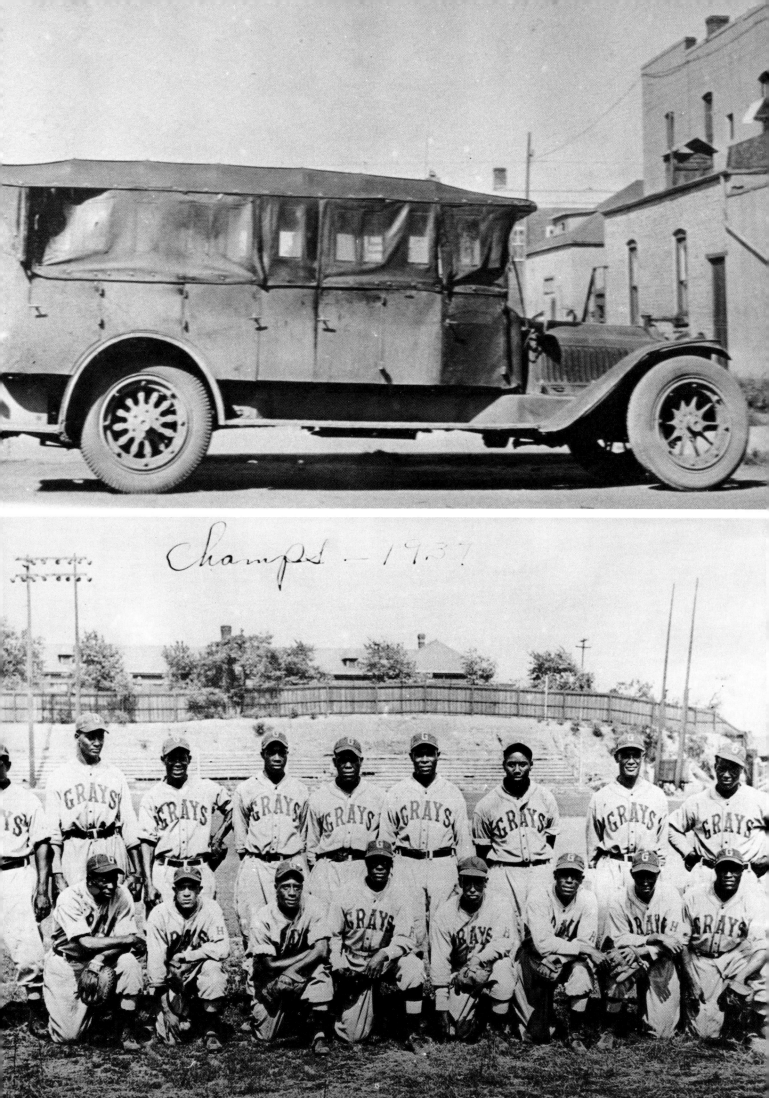

Champs - 1937

their season ended.* Johnson reminisced: "The big-league boys always liked to come out there [Hilldale Field] and play because they could make big money. They would never take a guarantee. They'd take sixty or forty percent—sixty for winning, forty for losing. They were willing to take it because of the crowds we were having." Particularly during the Depression, the $200 to $750 a man from such contests amounted to significant money, especially for the poverty-ridden nonwhites.

Relations with the white major leaguers generally were congenial. Said Newt Allen of the Kansas City Monarchs: "We had good friends during those times before integration came. We had Paul and Dizzy Dean, the Waner brothers, the DiMaggio brothers, Bob Feller, Pepper Martin, Lon Warneke, Mike Ryba. Dizzy Dean was just a prince of a guy."

Top players like Mickey Cochrane, Jimmie Foxx, George Earnshaw, and Bob Feller all urged their black counterparts to demand more money for their appearances. Feller even threatened to cancel a game unless the nonwhite opposition received its due.

The players sorely needed extra revenue; life in the Negro Leagues was often desperate for all but a few headliners. Everyone suffered from the endless travel, the frequently miserable accommodations, and the vicissitudes of the operations. Bill Drake said his weekly pay ran to $12.50 before Rube Foster tried to improve the lot of players.

Newt Allen, serving with the Kansas City Monarchs, earned as much as $900 a month during the boom years from 1927 to 1929. But the Monarchs drew the line at luxury travel. The players rode coaches or buses and carried their playing clothes in hand: "You wrapped your uniform, your sweatshirt, your stockings, your shoes and your bats. You've got your hand bag, you've got your suit-roll with your uniform in it and you've got your bat bag. You've got to go to the train or bus and get on the thing with that."

Judy Johnson jounced on a bus during a nonstop journey of 880 miles between Chicago and Philadelphia after a doubleheader.

Catnaps, sandwiches, and soda pop sustained him, although on his arrival his ankles had swelled to twice normal size. He played a doubleheader. Dave Malarcher remembered his longest bus trip, 1,700 miles from Monroe, Louisiana, to Winnipeg. During the 1930s the New York Black Yankees finished a doubleheader in Pittsburgh and then embarked for South Orange, New Jersey, site of 2 games the following day. They loaded sixteen men with luggage and equipment aboard two cars at 10 P.M. Saturday. One vehicle broke down in the Allegheny Mountains en route. The other arrived with nine men in South Orange minutes before the game. While they played, the second contingent motored to the park. They napped on the field and in the dressing room before the second game. The Black Yankees won both contests.

Perhaps the most strenuous schedule was that of the Homestead Grays, who claimed both Pittsburgh and Washington as their base during World War II. That put them in Forbes Field whenever the Pirates went on the road and in Griffith Stadium when the Senators left town. The Grays would leave Pittsburgh after midnight on a Sunday and drive 263 miles over the turnpikes to reach Washington by 11:00 A.M. Gulping down sandwiches, they would be on the field half an hour later, ready to play. On one occasion, a bus breakdown required three cabs from Hagerstown, Maryland. Gas rationing during World War II forced them into the baggage cars of trains when other space was unavailable.

Always there was the shortage of money. Walter "Buck" Leonard, ★ the great Grays first baseman (naturally, "the black Lou Gehrig"), remembered:

We'd play a semi pro team, say in Rockville, Maryland in the afternoon and a league game in Griffith Stadium that night. Or we'd play semi pro teams around Pittsburgh. We'd play the Edgar Thomas Steel Mill Team, and over in Braddock they had a team. We'd start at 6:30 and play as many innings as we could get in before dark. The Grays would get $75 to $100 for the whole team. But Sundays and weekends were the days you really expected to pay off your players. Those were the games

Buck Leonard, first baseman of the Gr 1938 clouts one before a large cr Griffith Stadium.

Courtesy NBL

---

*For the men in the Negro Leagues the season stretched for close to a full year. When they finished their league schedules (with all exhibition games on off dates), they would tour, taking on challengers in such places as Saskatoon and Moose Jaw, Canada, the Dominican Republic, Mexico, and Venezuela.

you played in Forbes Field, Griffith Stadium, Yankee Stadium and those parks. They were called "getting out of the hole days."

All-Star games aided depleted coffers immensely. Crowds of forty to fifty thousand packed Comiskey Park, matching or bettering the best the White Sox could attract.

In 1934, Leonard received 60 cents a day as meal money. It was enough during the Depression for two decent repasts. Ham and eggs plus toast and coffee took a quarter; the dinner tabs ran 30 to 35 cents. As the economy slowly improved, the food stipend rose to 75 cents, then an entire dollar. He lived in a $6-a-week room in Homestead.

On the road where they could not afford decent hotels, even if management would have permitted blacks to register, the players inserted newspapers between mattresses and sheets to foil the omnipresent bedbugs. Usually they took three rooms, which gave them use of a bath. Sometimes a YMCA admitted them; outside of the biggest cities the players changed into their working clothes at the hotel or YMCA. There was no trainer; they rubbed one another. The parks themselves ranged from the major-league quality available when the locals were traveling to rock-strewn, cow pattie–dusted pastures or high-school fields.

Baseball provided more than sport for its customers. Some teams served up minstrel shows along with their games. Patrons were treated to spectacles like the meeting between the Chicago American Giants and Kansas City in 1937; this featured 500 decorated cars, the precision drills of the Lincoln High School cadets, and a pair of fifty-piece marching bands. Baseball was a social event. Effa Manley, who carried on with the Newark club after her husband died, said: "Oh boy, did they dress. People came out who didn't know the ball from the bat."

The Negro Leagues pioneered night ball, as the Kansas City Monarchs played the first contest under the lights in 1930, a few months before white minor-league outfits introduced lights. The illumination was portable, with traveling poles, banks of lights powered by a truck-borne generator parked in the deepest part of the outfield. Players occasionally slammed into the poles or guy wires while pursuing balls. Lights might flicker as a belt on the dynamo slipped. The

candlepower was relatively feeble; in 1930, Smokey Joe Williams, age fifty-four, struck out twenty-seven men in a 12-inning game for the Grays, while opponent Chet Brewer of the Monarchs whiffed 19, including 10 in a row.

As dark as the living and playing conditions were, genuine stars lit up the game. James Bell, ★ a Mississippi native, demonstrated such aplomb as a nineteen-year-old that a teammate described him as a "Cool Papa" and the nickname stuck for his twenty-seven years in the Negro Leagues. Eddie Gottlieb, an owner and promoter of Negro baseball as well as a founding father of pro basketball, pumped up Bell as "the black Willie Keeler at bat and the black Tris Speaker in center field." Cool Papa wore the uniform of a number of teams—the St. Louis Stars, Detroit Senators, Homestead Grays, Kansas City Monarchs, Pittsburgh Crawfords, and even the Trujillo Giants during a Santo Domingo sojourn.

A switch-hitter, according to one source Bell hit .480 over a 200-game year—admittedly against some substandard opposition. Still, no one could deny his speed, especially after his 175 stolen bases in 1933. And in an exhibition game with white major leaguer Roy Partee catching, and future Hall of Famer Bob Lemon on the mound, Bell broke from first on the pitch as the batter bunted. Partee fielded the ball as Bell sprinted past him to score. Partee supposedly kept shouting "Time, time," but the umpire responded, "I can't call time, the ball's still in play." And in those games where he faced barnstorming white stars, Cool Papa hit in the neighborhood of .350. He coupled a sure glove with his speed. Paul Waner called the squeaky-voiced, bespectacled Bell "the smoothest center fielder I've ever seen."

In the tradition of all baseball, Bell engendered tall tales and hyperbole. One observer swore Cool Papa swiped 2 bases on a single pitch. It was Satchel Paige who insisted, "That man was so fast he could turn out the light and jump into bed before it was dark."

Paige, of course, was the best known of all Negro League stars. He told one interviewer that as a youngster in Mobile, Alabama, he hustled baggage at the railroad depot and to increase his capacity contrived a unique contraption: "I rigged up ropes around my shoulders and my waist, and I carried a

The speed demon of the outcasts w[as] Papa Bell, who allegedly scored fr[om first] on a bunt against white major leagu[ers dur]ing an exhibition game. When umpi[res gave] him slack, Bell would cut inside seco[nd base] by a yard or so to save seconds while [headed] to third.

Courtesy NBL

satchel in each hand and one under each arm. I carried so many satchels that all you could see were satchels." The result of his ingenuity, aside from more tips, was his nickname. On another occasion Paige insisted "Satchel" derived from a bag in which he toted his glove, baseballs, and his triple A–width shoes.

Tall, skinny, sleepy-eyed, the right-handed Paige projected an indolence totally contradicted by the velocity of his "bee ball," and control that enabled him to split a gum wrapper placed lengthwise on the plate. He developed that control as a kid, through long hours throwing bricks and stones at bottles placed between a pair of cans.

Buck Leonard, one of the best hitters to grace the Negro Leagues, said:

> Satchel Paige was the toughest pitcher I ever faced. I couldn't do much with him. All the years I played there, I never got a hit off him. He threw *fire*. That's what he threw. Satchel had an exceptional fast ball. That was his main pitch. It would get up to the plate and just rise a little, just enough for you to miss it. If you finally did get a piece of it, it wasn't much.

Asked whom he considered the best he ever saw, Dizzy Dean responded, "It's that old Satchel Paige, that big, lanky colored boy." Joe DiMaggio called him "the best I ever faced, and the fastest."

He was comfortable overhand, sidearm, or submarine style. He threw with a high kick, like Dizzy Dean's, and the ball seemed to suddenly appear from behind his foot. When arm troubles afflicted him, Paige developed a curve, knuckler, and a "hesitation pitch" that confounded hitters with a pause in mid-motion, just as his left foot struck the ground. The American League banned the delivery.

Paige was the Negro Leagues' greatest attraction almost from the start of his career in 1924. He showed a flair for the dramatic, appearing as little as fifteen minutes before game time. He would warm up, fielding balls at third base, clowning with players and spectators. He would promise to fan the first nine batters and make good on the pledge. Aware of his talents, he sold his services to the highest bidders, jumping clubs several times and earning suspensions that could not

be enforced. He earned as much as $25,000 to $30,000 during his best years in nonwhite baseball. Not until 1967 did Paige quit for good; six years earlier he estimated he'd participated in 2,500 games, won 2,000, and worked for 250 teams.

According to Paige, the two best hitters he ever saw were Ted Williams and Josh Gibson, the mighty catcher who played with Satchel for many years. Gibson was burly even at eighteen. He grew into a 6'1", 215 pounder, with broad shoulders and a tapered waist. He was still in his teens and a star with the Pittsburgh area semipro outfits when the Homestead Grays' catcher split a finger. Legend says Owner Cum Posey called Gibson out of the stands to sub; in reality, when Posey found both of his catchers injured he sent a taxi to bring Gibson to the field. He was an instant success with the bat but an unschooled receiver. Others, like Bruce Petway, Biz Mackey, and Frank Duncan, held better reputations as nonwhite catchers but Gibson developed more than passably at his post. (Roy Campanella, ★ who saw Gibson play, felt he was an excellent catcher.)

Walter Johnson remarked: "There is a catcher that any big league club would like to buy for $200,000. His name is Gibson. . . . he can do everything. He hits the ball a mile. And he catches so easy he might be in a rocking chair. Bill Dickey isn't as good a catcher. Too bad this Gibson is a colored fellow."

Next to Paige, Gibson pulled down the best money in the Negro Leagues as people paid to see him blast the ball farther than anyone else. He was credited with 71 or 75 homers for the Grays in 1931. (Unfortunately, statistics for the Negro Leagues were poorly kept.) Those who were on the scene talk of 4 home runs in a game at Griffith Stadium; monster 580-foot jobs to the deepest and loftiest crannies of Yankee Stadium; a ball he wedged in the loudspeakers at Comiskey Park, 435 feet to dead center; and a liner that shortstop Willie Wells speared with his glove, only to suffer a split web of flesh between his thumb and forefinger. In tandem with Buck Leonard (42 homers in 1942), Gibson was half of as formidable a hitting pair as Ruth and Gehrig.

Four others from the Negro Leagues were elected to the Hall of Fame. Oscar Charleston, ★ an outfielder like Ruth with a barrel

Newt Allen, who played with Satchel Paige on the Kansas City Monarchs, told John Holway: "Satchel kicked his foot way up here like Dizzy Dean, then'd throw around that foot. Half the guys were hitting at that foot coming up. He'd strike out 18 or 19 men at three o'clock in the afternoon."

Courtesy NBL

chest, preceded Bell as the best in center field. By the time the major leagues opened their locker rooms to nonwhites, Charleston was too old. Martin Dihigo, ★ 6'3", sailed out of Cuba as one of the most versatile men in the game. He was equally adept in the infield, outfield, and on the mound. Said Buck Leonard: "I say he was the best ballplayer of all time, black or white. He could do it all. He is my ideal ballplayer. . . . You take your Ruths, Cobbs or DiMaggios, give me Dihigo. Bet I'd beat you almost everytime."

Ray Dandridge ★ lingered on the cusp. In 1933, he was the nineteen-year-old captain of his hometown Portsmouth (Virginia) Fire Fighters. The Negro League Detroit Stars, barnstorming the territory, paused for a game. Dandridge homered and fielded so extraordinarily that after the game, Detroit's manager "Candy" Jim Taylor detoured the Stars bus to the teenager's home and convinced him to join the club. "When I went to Detroit," says Dandridge, "I didn't have enough to come back."

Over the following years he performed spectacularly as a third baseman for Detroit. Then he played with the "million dollar infield" of the Newark Eagles before Jorge Pascual lured him to the Mexican League in 1940. When Jackie Robinson suited up as a Dodger in 1947, Dandridge was player-manager for Vera Cruz. Two years later, pretending to be only twenty-nine, Ray accepted a contract from the New York Giants, who assigned him to their Minneapolis, Triple A club.

Short, stocky, even bowlegged, Dandridge dazzled fans with his quickness at his position, and at .364 finished the year 2 points behind the league leader. The following season he was named Most Valuable Player and in 1951 he continued to hammer the ball with a .324 average. That season he saw his young roommate, Willie Mays, ★ graduate to the majors but Dandridge apparently was now as much a victim of age discrimination as race. He was forty years old and the Giants had both Henry Thompson, a black, and Bobby Thomson at third.

Aside from Paige, the one other Hall of Famer named from the Negro Leagues to reach the majors was Monte Irvin, ★ a soft-spoken, former New Jersey high-school four-letter man. Described as "a kid who looked

a little like Josh Gibson at the plate," he was desired by four different clubs before he chose the local outfit, the Newark Eagles. Turning pro at age seventeen, he compiled an average of about .350 for ten years before he joined the New York Giants as a twenty-eight-year-old rookie in 1949.

However successful the Negro Leagues and monumental the achievements of the best players, the enterprise still lay outside mainstream America. And as the World War II propaganda of the United States reiterated the principle of the equality of men, politicians and civic leaders turned up the heat on baseball magnates. The Red Sox gave a perfunctory tryout to three men, Sam Jethroe of the Cleveland Buckeyes, Marvin Williams of the Philadelphia Stars, and a rookie with the Kansas City Monarchs, Jackie Robinson. Committees formed in New York City; newspapers castigated the absence of nonwhites.

Branch Rickey used the cover of the Negro Leagues to plot his breakthrough of the color line. A change in the baseball hierarchy encouraged him most; Judge Landis had died in 1944 and the owners chose as the new commissioner a Kentucky governor and senator, Albert B. Chandler. ★ His nickname, "Happy," connoted a bon vivant rather than an iron-willed replica of his predecessor. When a committee of blacks called on the new commissioner in 1945, Chandler was quoted in the *Pittsburgh Courier:* "I'm for the Four Freedoms. If a black boy can make it on Okinawa and Guadalcanal, hell he can make it in baseball."

Rickey read the papers and, with the tacit approval of his principal owners, claimed to want to help organize a "legitimate Negro league." While the entrepreneurs of nonwhite baseball choked on his effrontery, Rickey serenely instructed his scouts to look over the black talent required to man the "Brown Dodgers."

Later, Rickey declared that talent was but one quality sought.

> I had to get a man who would carry the burden on the field. I needed a man to carry the badge of martyrdom. The press had to accept him. He had to stimulate a good reaction of the Negro race itself for an unfortunate one might have solidified the antagonism of other colors. And I had to consider the attitude of the man's teammates.

"Scores of school kids turned out r just to see Oscar [Charleston] per, was to them what Babe Ruth is to lighter hue."—Chester L. Wa Pittsburgh Courier

Courtesy NBL

Toward the end of his career in 19 Gibson of the Grays rounds third w ton Snow, third baseman for the E Elite Giants, watches an outfielde the ball. "The old fan can bring Josh Gibson standing loose and at right-hand batter's box at Yankee during a Negro league doubleh 1934 and almost effortlessly prope ball over the third tier next to the bull pen, the only fair ball ever hit Stadium. He cannot go to a record find Gibson's career home-run tota in 17 years in black baseball prob passed Ruth's 714. He cannot eve tain about the top figure for a sin, which was reported to be 89. . . . A legends have grown, fed in the a reliable statistics by the stop-time men who remember."—Robert New York Times

Courtesy NBL

The names of Gibson, Paige, Leonard, and Bell, among others, filtered to Rickey. But for the most part, they were already beyond their primes. According to Rickey biographer Murray Polner, the Mahatma asked *Pittsburgh Courier* reporter Wendell Smith whom he might recommend and the journalist suggested Jackie Robinson.

The background on Robinson indicated intelligence, education, and maturity but willingness to accept "the badge of martyrdom" was not obvious. As an officer candidate in the army, Robinson once punched out a white superior for a racial slur. Only the intercession of heavyweight champion Joe Louis, boxing promoter Truman Gibson, and Judge William Hastie, the first black to sit on the federal bench, brought an investigation that cleared him. Jimmie Crutchfield, who played in an exhibition game against the Monarchs, recalled a close play in which Crutchfield beat Robinson's throw.

> Jackie raved and I told the umpire, "Throw him out of the ball game! He's just a young busher, he hasn't been up here two weeks." And boy, he left second base and started toward me, and I started toward him—but he was around 225 pounds then—and I started to laugh and he turned around and went back to his position.

Robinson was a shortstop for the Monarchs with a weakness going to his right. Club executive Dizzy Dismukes instructed Cool Papa Bell to hit there, giving Robinson practice. Remembered Bell:

> . . . the first time I hit the ball . . . Jackie caught the ball all right but you have to backhand it, you can't take an extra step, you have to catch it and throw. But when Jackie goes over to the right to catch the ball, he's got to take two steps before he pivots. So I beat the throw. Then I stole second base. He caught the ball just as I slid under him. . . .

Bell repeated his tactics with similar results. Indeed, Jackie's problem in going to his right eventually transformed him into a second baseman. Buck Leonard initially rated Robinson less than spectacular: "He was a hustler but other than that he wasn't a top shortstop."

When scout Clyde Sukeforth brought Robinson to Brooklyn for a meeting with Rickey, the ball player was still under the impression he was being auditioned for the Brown Dodgers. Rickey quickly disabused him: "You were brought here to play for the Brooklyn organization—perhaps as a start for Montreal."

Then, in one of the most extraordinary interviews an employee ever had with a prospective boss, the candidate was questioned about his personal life, queried on his contractual obligations to the Monarchs, lectured on the failure of Prohibition and on the potential harm to "the Negro race" if the first nonwhite player caused serious incidents on or off the field, read to from Giovanni Papini's *Life of Christ* (which speaks of the courage and achievements of martyrdom), and finally subjected to a minitorrent of abuse—a test to determine whether Robinson understood and accepted Rickey's strategy.

When Robinson responded to the hectoring with, "I've got two cheeks. Is that it?" Rickey proposed a contract with Montreal. Although the New York press lined up solidly behind Rickey and the cracking of the barrier, the *Sporting News,* which during the 1920s disparaged the color line, criticized him for "piracy" against the Negro Leagues. Owners of those operations also railed against Rickey, correctly foreseeing the threat to their future. But most of the nonwhite community wanted men of color in the major leagues and supported the move. Far more challenges lay ahead, but beginning in the spring of 1946 organized baseball could no longer be called all-white.

With Robinson starring in Montreal, a committee of major league executives drafted a secret report that acknowledged, "Every American boy, without regard to his race or his color or his creed, should have a fair chance in Baseball." However, the officials then declared few blacks qualified for acceptance in the major leagues because they lacked the "technique, the coordination, the competitive attitude, and the discipline, which is usually acquired only after years of training in the minor leagues. The minor league experience of players on the major league rosters, for instance, averages 7 years."

In support of the position, the executives

Cuban-born Martin Dihigo, lacking the white-skin passport for others from his birthplace to play major league ball, pitched and played outfield.

Courtesy NBL

Ray Dandridge won MVP while with Minneapolis of the American Association in 1950 but his age cost him a shot at the major leagues. "He astounded veteran observers with his moves. . . . The bowlegged Dandridge moves like a cat."—Sporting News

Courtesy NBL

cited a sports editor of black newspapers who declared there was not a single individual "in the ranks of colored baseball who could step into the major league uniform and disport himself after the fashion of a big leaguer."

To be sure, one of the weaknesses of the Negro Leagues was the absence of a farm system where players could learn and develop skills. In the Negro Leagues one either succeeded against the best or disappeared. But the long seasons, the often terrible conditions, and the camaraderie of those involved substituted for the lack of formal baseball schooling. The quick success of blacks, once admitted to major league play, disproved all subterfuges.

Rickey considered the document an attempt to frustrate his program; he had already signed up other promising black athletes. He met with Chandler who assured the Mahatma he meant what he said: that baseball was open to all.

Robinson's great year at Montreal, where he led the International League with a .349 average and stole 40 bases, guaranteed his promotion to the parent team in 1947. Teammates Pee Wee Reese and Gil Hodges squelched Dodger resistance to their new colleague. Phillies' owner Bob Carpenter warned his club might refuse to take the field against Robinson but backed off. When the Phillies subjected Robinson to obscene, vicious baiting, Brooklyn second sacker and Alabama-raised Eddie Stanky became outraged and challenged the Phils.

Gossip claimed the Cardinals intended to walk out if Robinson played and National League President Ford Frick warned the Cardinals against a strike. Author Jules Tygiel, in his book *Baseball's Great Experiment*, could not find evidence of any organized conspiracy by Cardinal players but the parties were not the sort to record their sentiments on paper. There is some question of whether Frick actually uttered the eloquent words attributed to him; one school believes *Herald Tribune* editor Stanley Woodward was the real author. (See Roger Kahn on Jackie Robinson.)

Robinson not only endured the season of torment but he also vindicated Rickey's faith in him both as the ideal pioneer and as a major league–caliber player. He hit .297,

stole 29 bases, led the league with 125 runs, tied for club honors with 12 homers, and helped his team reach the World Series. The *Sporting News* named him rookie of the year, solely for his achievements on the field. And Buck Leonard admitted he'd been mistaken: "You can be wrong about a ballplayer. . . . There were other players we thought were better players, but they got the right man after all."

In Robinson's first major league season, sixteen blacks, half in the Dodger organization, were scattered through organized baseball. The numbers increased rapidly with the palpable contribution of Robinson to Brooklyn. Nasty bumps marred the road to total integration. For several years nonwhites with some clubs could not stay in the same hotel during spring training. In 1953, the Cotton League expelled the Hot Springs, Arkansas, entry for using a black against a team from Jackson, Mississippi. As late as 1954, headlines still trumpeted, "Cards Sign First Negro." While organized baseball survived the dire and unfulfilled predictions of trouble that preceded the end of the color line, one prophecy proved true. The Negro Leagues vanished as their customers now flocked to see blacks in the majors.

A year later, Roy Campanella, the second of Rickey's black recruits, arrived in Brooklyn. Buck Leonard first saw him in 1936 when he was in his midteens, catching batting practice for the Baltimore Elite Giants. Campanella digested the complete curriculum of a ball player, mastering the art of swatting curves, guiding pitchers, and coping with all deliveries. He served as a fine accomplice to hurler Preacher Roe when the latter resorted to the spitter. Said Roe:

He'd handle most of them as smooth as if I was throwing a fastball. Once in a while, one of them would do a whole lot and get away from him. But Campy was always ready. He figured the umpire would ask for the ball, or the batter would call for the umpire to look at it. Campy'd toe the ball, sly, like, as he bent over to pick it up, and that would roll it dry. He'd do that if nobody was on base. If there were men on, he'd step on it, grind it into the dirt, hard, . . . where he could grab it if he had to.

In his brief ten years with Brooklyn, before an auto accident crippled him, Cam-

A bush-league player himself, Harva cated, and a former Senator, the folks tuckian Albert "Happy" Chand Commissioner helped nudge the door nonwhites. "Iron willed, unbelievab est, he conducted his commissioner's without fear of consequences."- Grimsley, Associated Press

Courtesy NBL

Pee Wee Reese and Rickey: The Mahatma brought Robinson to the Dodgers but Reese was the man who supported him on the field and in the locker room.

Courtesy Brooklyn Public Library, Eagle Collection

panella averaged almost 25 home runs a season, with 41 in 1953 and a league-leading 142 RBIs. During his tenure behind the plate, his club won five pennants.

Jackie Robinson dressed in Dodger blue one year before southern Democrats deserted the party over a platform plank calling for modest civil rights reforms; seven years before the U.S. Supreme Court ruled school segregation unconstitutional in *Brown vs. Board of Education;* sixteen years before the U.S. Congress, responding to the pressure of blacks and whites, passed significant legislation dealing with discrimination, voting rights, and the redress of wrongs against nonwhites. Still, forty years after Robinson's appearance in the major leagues, while many blacks and Hispanics star on the diamonds, few have been hired as field managers or even as third-base coaches, and in the high echelons of the front office they are almost nonexistent.

He was big—a bit overweight for most of his career—pigeon-toed, aggressive, and when something roused him, he could be loud, cutting the ears of sportswriters and umpires with a knifing tenor. Once in an almost empty Braves Field in Boston, I heard him ride an umpire named Frank Dascoli into the sod.

The Braves were batting against the Brooklyn Dodgers and Dascoli called the first pitch a ball. "Do the best you can, Frank," Jackie Robinson cried from his position near second base. The Boston franchise was dying. The grandstands were empty. You could have heard a hiccup from the field.

Ball two. Another close pitch. Again Robinson shouted, "Do the best you can." Ball three. Now Robinson piped shrilly: "Forget that, Frank. Just do the *worst* you can."

We all laughed, but Dascoli didn't laugh, and it may be superfluous to point out that the umpire called the next Dodger pitch ball four.

"Why does Robinson have to do that?" one of the reporters said in the press box. "Why is he opening his mouth all the time. Why can't he be like the others? You know. A good guy."

"What others?"

"Roy Campanella," the reporter said.

Robinson was, as the years would inform me, more than just a "good guy"; he was among the kindest and most compassionate of men. But that bit of umpire-baiting in Boston, and the response it drew, goes a long way, at least for me, in explaining apparent contradictions in the personality of a towering man.

Baseball integration did not blossom in an instant, with the signing of a contract, a few strokes from Branch Rickey's fountain pen. Of course Rickey hired Robinson for Montreal in the International League in 1946, shattering, as the reporters wrote, baseball's color line. And then, a year later, Robinson moved up to the Brooklyn Dodgers and played in a rousing World Series against the Yankees. But war with segregationists did not end with Jackie Robinson's minor league appearance or even with his major league success. I think, and Robinson tended to agree, that the extended nature of the war he had to fight was critical to his ball playing, his life, and—here the view can only be my own—his early death.

Major league baseball had been an all-white redoubt since the season of 1884 when two black brothers from Ohio played for the Toledo club in the American Association, which was then regarded as a major league. Welday Wilberforce Walker played 5 games in the Toledo outfield and Moses Fleetwood Walker, called Fleet, caught in 42 games and batted

"He charged at ball games. . . . His
his steals and his fake bunts and fak
humiliated a legion of visiting play
bore the burden of a pioneer and the
made him more strong. If one can be
of anything in baseball, it is that w
not look upon his like again."—
Kahn

Courtesy Mark Kauffman, *Sports Illustr*

.263. The Walker brothers then vanished from organized ball and, as baseball developed and matured across five decades and two centuries, it was persistently, defiantly, arrogantly, monochromic. White.

As far as anyone knows, there never was a written agreement among club owners barring blacks, no reverse Emancipation Proclamation, so to speak. But the discrimination was real and ardent. Baseball was a white man's game. The players were white, the coaches were white, the front-office people were white, and all of the sportswriters who chronicled the game were as white as the players they described. Blacks could buy tickets, although in some major league parks they were required to sit in segregated sections. They could pay their way in but, it became an article of baseball faith, blacks must never be permitted to play in organized ball.

A few individuals, and very few journalists, offered protests during the late 1930s. A Los Angeles sportscaster named Sam Balter asked repeatedly on network radio how baseball could advertise itself as the national game while excluding a significant portion of the nation. The *Daily Worker,* the official organ of the American Communist Party, raised the same point, which, given the country's general attitude toward communism, probably did more harm than good.

The leaders of the game did not feel that they had to defend themselves in public. After all, they literally owned the ball. Once Bill Veeck told me that he tried to sign a few blacks for the minor league franchise he ran in Milwaukee and was told by Commissioner Kenesaw Mountain Landis to go no further. If he went ahead, Landis said, Veeck himself would be barred from baseball. Racism reigned silently, omnipresent and supreme.

When Branch Rickey announced in the fall of 1945 that he was signing Jack Roosevelt Robinson to a contract with Montreal, howls rose from just about every baseball office in the land. The head of the minor leagues, W. G. Brabham, said with laborious sarcasm that he expected a "temple to Rickey to be erected in Harlem," near the one for Father Divine, a discredited and semicomic black evangelist. Albert B. (Happy) Chandler, the commissioner who succeeded Landis, maintains that every one of the fifteen other owners—there were then sixteen major league teams—opposed Branch Rickey's decision. "The only people who seemed to recognize that giving Robinson a chance was right, or even fair, were Rickey and me," Chandler says, "and believe me I had to do a lot of talking to make sure the other owners didn't do something really stupid. Some actually wanted me to throw Rickey, great as he was, out of the game."

The *Sporting News* mocked and growled. One of its columnists wrote that with Robinson signed "first thing you know we'll have Old Black Joe McCarthy managing the Yankees." A pompous editorial pretended to sympathize with Robinson, while actually deploring his opportunity. The *Sporting News* editorialist wrote that Robinson:

1. Is thrown into competition with a vast number of younger, more skilled and more experienced players . . .

2. Is six years too old for a chance with a club [even] two classifications below Montreal . . .

3. Is confronted with sweat and tears of toil, with social rebuffs and competitive heartaches . . .

4. Is thrown into the spotlight . . .

Granted that Robinson can take it, the first factor alone [competition] appears likely to beat him down.

Robinson went off to Montreal where at the age of twenty-six he batted a league-leading .349, stole 40 bases, and scored 113 runs in 124 games. He was voted Rookie of the Year. With Robinson, Montreal won the International League pennant by 18½ games and won the Junior World Series—all that there was to win in minor league ball—by defeating Louisville of the American Association, 4 games to 2.

Rickey did not at once advance Robinson from Montreal to the Dodger roster. He knew that he would, to be sure, and spent many winter days counseling with black civic and church leaders in Brooklyn. He wanted them to preach that in the season of 1947, black fans, like Jackie Robinson, would be on trial. No drinking, no scuffling, no rowdiness. The country would be judging black fans as well as big, black number 42.

Ideally, Rickey theorized, Dodger veterans would see Robinson's great skills in spring training and come clamoring to demand his promotion. The Dodgers had lost the pennant to the St. Louis Cardinals in a playoff series in 1946 and clearly Robinson could carry them to the World Series in 1947. "Most players," Rickey said, "have a healthy appreciation of money and it was my thought that they would see in Jackie not a Negro who was in some way threatening, but a five-figure World Series check." Rickey paused, made a small sigh, and said, as he said seldom, "I was wrong."

Rickey arranged a set of exhibition games between Montreal and Brooklyn, and Robinson became an arrow of dark fire. He ran the bases in his magical way: "Adventure," Rickey said. "Jack had such a sense of adventure." He won 1 game with a bunt single off Hugh Casey, the Dodgers' great veteran relief pitcher. A runner flashed home from third. The baseball stopped rolling. The game was over. Casey seized the ball

California-raised Robinson starred [in foot]*ball, track, and baseball at Pasaden*[a] *College, winning an athletic schola*[rship to] *UCLA. At the big school he impro*[ved as a] *four-letter man, adding basketball to* [his rep]*ertoire.*

Courtesy Metromedia, Los Angeles

and threw it over the roof of the stands. In the spring training against the Dodgers, Robinson batted over .500. The Brooklyn Dodgers clamored, but not in the way Rickey hoped. A petition was organized demanding that Robinson be kept off the team.

I knew Fred (Dixie) Walker in his later years, enjoyed his company, and we corresponded during his final struggle against cancer. His interests ranged from baseball to the architecture of English cathedrals, a ranging, soft-voiced, gentle fellow. "That Robinson thing back in the Forties," Walker said one night across a glass of red wine, "can I tell you about it?

"I didn't have anything against Jackie, but you know ball players back then didn't make much money and I had this wholesale hardware business in Montgomery, Alabama, that was important to me. And people were telling me, and I listened to them, that if I played with a Negro, nobody in Montgomery would buy my hardware . . . and . . ." Walker stopped. "Stupidest thing I ever did was that petition."

In the long-ago spring of 1947, Walker prepared a petition to Rickey that stated in effect: Promote Robinson and we won't play for Brooklyn. Walker, of course, signed it. So did Hugh Casey and a few others. Pee Wee Reese refused to sign. The idea lost momentum and the ill-born petition found its way to a Havana dump.

Robinson himself said he didn't really know much about the petition. The incident surely wounded him and he preferred to dwell on moments of acceptance and the color-blind friendships he developed. But once, after Casey's death by suicide, Robinson recounted a horrible moment he endured in the club car of a train. Several white Dodgers were playing poker. Robinson was reading a magazine. Casey had a bad run of cards and suddenly got up, walked over to Robinson, and rubbed Jack's head, an enactment of the baseball superstition: "Rub a nigger's head and change your luck."

"What did you do?" I asked Robinson.

"I suppose I could have decked Casey. But this was 1947. I wasn't supposed to respond, just take what happened. So Casey went back to his card game and I kept looking at the magazine."

Stories conflict on the most famous episode of opposition. Rud Rennie of the *New York Herald Tribune* was covering the Giants in 1947 when, by accident of schedule, the Giants made their first trip into St. Louis one series ahead of the Dodgers. Rennie liked St. Louis. He was visiting members of a barbershop quartet there that included Dr. Robert Hyland, team physician to the Cardinals, whose skilled hands won him acclaim as "baseball's surgeon general."

In 1939, he led the nation in ground gainers. His weakest sport was baseball.

Courtesy Metromedia, Los Angeles

When the amateur singers gathered and drank in the spring of 1947, Hyland said to Rennie, "It's a shame you're coming in with the wrong team. If you were coming in with the Dodgers, you'd have a helluva story."

While Rennie sipped, Hyland told him that the Cardinals had no intention of playing against Jackie Robinson and the Dodgers. The St. Louis players intended to strike. Rennie eased back on his drinking and when the singing was finally done he telephoned Stanley Woodward, his sports editor. He provided the names of a shortstop and two outfielders who were the Cardinal ringleaders, according to Bob Hyland. Rennie said he could not write the story himself—he had to protect his source—but Woodward could surely write it. "Doc Hyland says this thing is driving him nuts and he'd write it himself, if he was a writer."

Woodward gathered all he could through Rennie and then contacted Ford Frick, the president of the National League. Frick, in his most glorious moment, issued an eloquent statement to the Cardinal players:

> If you do this you will be suspended from the league. You will find that the friends you think you have in the press box will not support you, that you will be outcasts. I do not care if half the league strikes. . . . This is the United States of America and one citizen has as much right to play as another.

The story attracted national attention and the Cardinals never went on strike. A few revisionists insist that the Cardinals were not close to striking and that Hyland, Rennie, and Woodward took a bit of racist dugout chatter—but chatter and nothing more—and exaggerated it beyond reason. Having known Rennie and Woodward, I can only say that exaggeration was not their style. But conflict about the 1947 Cardinals still persists. Whatever, this was the last attempt to boot Robinson out of baseball.

He would go on to play for the Dodgers for a decade, from 1947 through 1956, and lead great Brooklyn teams to six pennants. While the most blatant opposition died in his rookie year, another shade of hostility persisted throughout his major league career. Certain sportswriters and rival players found him loud and combative and opinionated, which is not surprising because he could be all of those. These same people praise such qualities in Eddie Stanky and Leo Durocher. Stanky and Durocher were fiery competitors. Robinson? He was "uppity." He didn't know his place. He failed to fawn with gratitude toward baseball for giving him a chance. This second stage of prejudice did not presume to deny Robinson his right to make a living playing ball. Rather it demanded that Robinson, and after him all black players, conduct themselves as genial, passive charac-

"The Mahatma had given careful th about the type of man he required. . . candidate did not have to be the best ball player, though he naturally nee[d] perior skills. Rather, he had to be th[e] likely to maintain his talents at a co tive peak while withstanding pressur abuse. He needed the self-control to reacting to his tormentors without sacr his dignity."—Jules Tygiel, Base Great Experiment

Courtesy UPI/Bettmann News photos

218

ters. In short, this second stage fully appreciated blacks as second-class citizens, as Uncle Toms. That approach infuriated Robinson, conflicted him, and drove him to be louder and more aggressive than he truly was. He was nobody's field hand, nobody's Tom, and he made that clear right out front in every baseball relationship. In time he would sour on the game although near the end of his life he made a reconciliation.

He was born in Georgia, but raised in Pasadena where his mother went to work as a domestic while Jackie was still an infant. He admired his mother profoundly, for making a home for five children on a salary of $8 a week, but felt little warmth for the Pasadena of his boyhood. He remembered a white child jeering at him from across the street:

Soda cracker's good to eat;
Nigger's only good to beat.

Once he and some friends went swimming in a local reservoir in violation of a municipal ordinance. Somebody summoned the sheriff. The man surveyed the scene, pulled out a gun, and shouted to his deputy: "Looka here! Niggers in my drinking water."

Robinson told those stories with pain, rather than fury, and remarked that for a time he ran "with a pretty rough crowd." Sports, or rather his excellence at sports, stabilized him and he went on to Pasadena Junior College and UCLA, where he played baseball, football, basketball, and ran track. He was a wonderful football player, called "Lighting Jack," a record-breaking long-jumper, and, curiously, baseball seemed to be his poorest sport. Playing shortstop for UCLA in 1940, he batted only .097, 6 hits in 62 turns at bat. He said he concentrated more on the other sports and when I pressed him a bit, he shook me off. His late son, Jackie, Jr., was with us and Robinson was uncomfortable discussing a terrible year at bat in the presence of a troubled offspring.

I first encountered him in 1952—he was by then a well-established star—when the *Herald Tribune* sent me to spring training to cover the Dodgers. I admired what he had done and indeed what he was still doing and I suppose it showed because gradually he accepted me as a friend. Ball clubs traveled by train in those days and often we'd sit in a roomette and I would try to draw stories from him.

He didn't like to dwell on the bad times he'd gone through—racial abuse, bean balls, and the rest. Instead, he talked about good times that lightened his heart. He appreciated the friendship of his teammates, men

Bases loaded, opening game of the 1955 Series against the Yankees. Robinson nears the halfway point from third; ultimately he swiped home despite bitter protest on the call from catcher Yogi Berra.

Courtesy Hy Peskin, *Sports Illustrated*

Jackie on third base engaged in a war of nerves; no one dared pitchers more. "Dancing off the base, Robinson ran down the third-base line about ten yards towards home plate, and then ran back to third. 'Then he went down about fifteen yards, and when he ran back he slid into the bag and dusted himself off,' recalls Mal Goode. 'Ostermueller probably said to himself, I know that nigger isn't gonna steal home now.' He turned his head and went into a full wind-up position. Jackie broke for home and stole it."—Harvey Frommer, Rickey and Robinson

Courtesy Mark Kauffman, *Sports Illustrated*

221

like Pee Wee Reese and Carl Erskine. He said that the first opposing player who wished him well was Jeep Handley, who played infield for the Phillies in 1947. "Hank Greenberg talked to me too, but Handley was the first."

"You've had your wars with the press," I said.

"That's the way I am. I say what I think. They don't always like it when you do that."

"Dick Young [the noted baseball reporter] says that when he's with you, for some reason, he can never forget the color of your skin."

Robinson laughed a high, militant laugh, then called me by name. "Did it occur to you," he said, "that I don't *want* Dick Young to forget?"

A year later, Robinson hired me to ghostwrite columns for him in a short-lived black magazine called *Our Sports.* I say ghostwrite but ghost-type would be accurate. The ideas and most of the words were Robinson's.

Typically, he wanted to do a piece called "My Feud with Leo Durocher Is Over." Robinson explained that in his rookie season, Durocher, who'd been managing the Dodgers, was suspended for reasons never fully explained. The Dodgers won the 1947 pennant for Burt Shotton but in 1948 Durocher returned to the team.

Robinson had gained weight during the winter and Durocher took to needling him sharply. A skirmish began that continued ever more fiercely when Durocher switched boroughs and went on to manage the New York Giants. At length, Durocher called for a cease-fire by telling platoons of reporters that Robinson was a wonderful, winning ball player. Robinson said that he thought Durocher was a fine, winning manager and would I please go and set this down in English.

Reaching at the conclusion, I had Robinson write: "Leo says I'm his kind of ball player. Well, he's my kind of man." A day later I showed Robinson the handiwork. "Okay," he said, "except for one thing. Got a pen?"

I did.

Jack changed only one word, the last one. As printed, the column ended, "Well, he's my kind of manager."

The magazine folded after four issues, owing me a fee of $75. "Let's go up and see the publisher," Robinson said, "if you've got the time."

The publisher asked me if I'd take $37.50. Robinson glared. I settled for $50, which left Robinson uncomfortable. "They said $75; you should get $75," he said. He then took me to a men's clothing store, in which he had a small interest, and forced them to sell me a sports jacket below cost.

"I remember my father turned to friends at The Store one day and obs 'Well, you can say what you want abou nigger Robinson, but he's got guts. Willie Morris

Preacher Roe looks on against a against the Cubs.

Courtesy UPI/Bettmann News photos

"There's no one I respect more than J Robinson. This was the loneliest ma. ever seen during his first season wi. Dodgers."—Jimmy Cannon, New Post

But then there was Reese (right) Hodges (14), and Campanella (39) to for heroics.

Courtesy AP/Wide World

In the years I covered the Dodgers, Robinson sometimes fed me inside stuff—what went on at a clubhouse meeting—making me appear to be a better reporter than I was. Once or twice he said, "I thought you were a little rough on the team yesterday. I heard some of the fellows asking if you were anti-Dodger." The tone was friendly, not censorious. When we disagreed, he always heard me out, and when I asked a question I always got an answer.

Best manager you ever played for?

"Charley Dressen."

Worst?

"This fella now [Walt Alston] isn't too great."

How do you feel about Walter O'Malley?

"He'll never be the man that Mr. Rickey is."

I didn't use all that stuff at the time. I was trying to cover a ball club, not incite riots. But his dislike for O'Malley and Alston were significant in Robinson's final deed as a ball player. After the 1956 season, the Dodgers traded Robinson to the Giants for a journeyman left-hander named Dick Littlefield and $35,000. Jack by then was a Dodger institution, still attracting crowds, and the deal makes sense only as an act of denigration.

The idea of Robinson in a Giants uniform was jarring but Jack didn't say much for about six weeks. Then in an exclusive article for *Look* magazine, he announced that he would not play for the Giants. He was retiring.

"You could have let me know," I told him once.

"Sorry," he said, "but you didn't have $50,000. *Look* did."

Red Smith attacked him sharply for "peddling" a news story. Robinson refused to join the debate in print. He told me privately that he felt it was his retirement, his right to make some money, and didn't Red Smith realize he was trying to raise three kids and that his knees were killing him and that he couldn't play baseball the way he liked to anymore.

How did he play? In ways that defy statistical analysis. He not only stole bases, he goaded pitchers with his feet and with his taunts, and always took an extra base and several times went from first to third on sacrifice bunts.

He was at third base once with 1 out when someone hit a bouncer to Eddie Mathews of the Braves. Mathews made the textbook play. He gloved the ball, looked at Robinson, and threw to first. Robinson burst down the line like a quarter horse and scored.

"Helluva play," I said at dinner.

Walter O'Malley shoved Rickey out of the Brooklyn scene. Robinson disapproved of the maneuver and his relationship with the club started to fall apart.

Courtesy NBL

JACK ROOSEVELT ROBINSON
BROOKLYN N.L. 1947 TO 1956
LEADING N.L. BATTER IN 1949. HOLDS
FIELDING MARK FOR SECOND BASEMAN
PLAYING IN 150 OR MORE GAMES WITH .992.
LEAD N.L. IN STOLEN BASES IN 1947 AND
1949. MOST VALUABLE PLAYER IN 1949.
LIFETIME BATTING AVERAGE .311. JOINT
RECORD HOLDER FOR MOST DOUBLE PLAYS
BY SECOND BASEMAN 137 IN 1951.

"No," Robinson said. "Just the play."

"I don't get you."

"Look," Jack said. "I'm gonna move up the line with Mathews, staying about a step behind him. If he goes for me, I can beat him back to third. But he isn't likely to go for me, because he knows what will happen and it will make him look bush. So as soon as he throws to first, I'm going for home and there's no way they're gonna get me out."

He was a wonderful second baseman, impossible to take out on a double play, a line-drive hitter, capable of clutch home runs, a dominant, winning athlete, and, although he didn't like to admit it, a student of the tactics and strategies of victory.

He conquered the first stage of baseball prejudice but the second—the patronizing tolerance—left him disinclined to discuss the game. We'd meet for lunch after the peddled retirement and he'd steer the conversation to politics or ghetto housing or toward our various children. He supported Richard Nixon against John Kennedy because he told me Kennedy said, "Growing up where I did, Mr. Robinson, I didn't have a chance to meet many Negroes."

"And?"

"And," Jackie said, "if you've been a congressman and a senator, make it your business to meet Negroes, dammit."

The times were changing quickly. Negroes became blacks. Martin Luther King supplanted Robinson as a symbol. A few black extremists came to see Jackie himself as a "Tom." Still, there were moments.

We met often as I was preparing *The Boys of Summer* and when I had finished, I threw a large party for myself in the apartment I rented on Riverside Drive. Jackie came, with his wife Rachel, and asked me to stay close to him because he didn't think he knew anyone there. I did, then drifted when he began explaining very kindly how one lived with diabetes to the parents of a diabetic child. (Robinson had lived with diabetes for many years.)

Suddenly a bellow rose in the living room. It was Zero Mostel, the great-voiced actor, and he was shouting: "Mister Jackie Robinson!"

Jack actually cringed. Then he turned slowly—remember Hugh Casey—to see who was approaching him at a white man's party. He looked at Mostel and nodded. The room fell silent.

"You," Zero roared, "are my hero!" Then the Fiddler on the Roof hugged the ball player, the great integrator.

I don't think my eyes were the only ones to mist.

Rickey and Robinson survived long enough to reunite in 1962 for Jack's induction into the Hall of Fame. Rachel Robinson joined them.

Courtesy NBL

The 1949 All-Star game, held at Ebbets Field in Brooklyn, admitted the first blacks to the classic: Robinson, Campanella, pitcher Don Newcombe of the Dodgers, and Larry Doby, the Cleveland outfielder for the American League. A fortnight earlier, an aging star, Joe DiMaggio, had demonstrated his dazzling ability. In the previous season he had batted .320, stroked 39 homers (his best since 1937), and driven in 155 runs, although the Yanks lost the pennant to the Indians, managed by Lou Boudreau whose .355 average, 18 homers, and 106 RBIs brought him a well-deserved Most Valuable Player. The Yankee outfielder knocked the Red Sox out of their chance on the final day of the 1948 season with 4 hits. But both knees, a sore right heel, and a deep muscle pull forced him to limp off after his last single, with cheers from a gracious Boston crowd.

Over the 1948–1949 winter, DiMaggio failed to recover from a foot operation. The pain forced him to forgo spring training and another surgeon sought to repair the damage. Even without him, the club broke on top. Yogi Berra, ★ a graduate of a crash course in catching under Bill Dickey, picked up the power slack, eventually connecting for 20 homers. Tommy Henrich contributed 24 more in only 115 games and the infielders, shortstop Phil Rizzuto, second baseman Jerry Coleman (both league leaders in fielding), and medical student Bobby Brown* at third, hit consistently. Four fine starters—Vic Raschi, Ed Lopat, Tommy Byrne, and Allie Reynolds—were backed by a devastating reliever, Joe Page. Nevertheless, as the season ground into mid-June, the footsteps of the Red Sox pounded ever closer to the DiMaggio-less Yanks.

Holed up in a New York City hotel, a fugitive from the game and the press, DiMaggio awoke one day to discover the crippling pain in his heel gone. He worked out for a week at the Stadium, blistering, then callusing his fingers with long batting practice sessions. He tested himself in an exhibition against the Giants, producing no hits but also no soreness.

While the club prepared for a critical 3-game set with the Sox, DiMaggio visited an orthopedic supply shop that fitted him with a special shoe that bore no spikes on its built-up heel. He flew to Boston, put on a uniform, and stepped into the box against Bill Dickey, the batting practice thrower. He whammed the first ball high off the Green Monster, lined one to center, bounced a ball down third, and then cleared the left-field screen. A few moments later, he took 5 more authoritative cuts.

DiMaggio, Henrich, and Rizzuto represented the pre–World War II club. But there was a new order for the Yankees. The tumult of Larry McPhail had come and gone. He sold out to his partners Dan Topping and Del Webb. Off-field management had been tendered to George Weiss, ★ formerly director of the Yankee farm system. In that capacity, Weiss had worked with Charles Dillon Stengel, then a man of faded reputation, a once colorful, scrappy outfielder and clownish manager who presided over cellar denizens in Brooklyn and Boston. Weiss believed Casey was his type of manager. In 1949, shuttling players with increasing desperation,† Stengel looked to the elder statesman of the club for both inspiration and power.

When DiMaggio pronounced himself ready to play that night, Stengel quickly included him in the lineup. He batted first in the top of the second and fouled off a number of balls from a young lefty, Mickey McDermott. Finally, he singled to left center and following a walk to Johnny Lindell, Hank Bauer homered.

Rizzuto was at first when DiMaggio came to the plate for his second appearance against McDermott. This time DiMaggio reached the left-field screen for a homer. The final score was 5–4, Yanks. In game two, the New Yorkers fell behind 7–1 until the Yankee Clipper moved them closer with a 3-run homer. They tied it at 7 apiece before DiMaggio walloped one out of the park and into the street for a 9–7 victory. In the seventh inning of the final game, the Yanks held a slim 3–2 advantage when DiMaggio settled into his familiar stance, feet spread wide, bat

The first black all-stars took the f[...] 1949. From left to right: Dodger [...] Roy Campanella, Cleveland ou[...] Larry Doby, Dodger pitcher Don New[...] and Jackie Robinson.

Courtesy UPI/Bettmann News photos

Surgery on his foot prevented Di[...] from appearing in more than 76 gam[...] ing the 1949 season.

Courtesy AP/Wide World

---

*After a career as a cardiologist Brown became president of the American League in 1985.

†While Stengel has been credited with popularizing platooning, Bill James and Jim Baker trace the phenomenon as far back as 1914. The *Reach Guide*, reviewing that season, noted: "In accordance with his season-long policy Manager Stallings shifted his outfield to meet southpaw pitching." The Miracle Braves under Stallings used a total of fourteen men in the outfield.

held high. The count went to three and two as Mel Parnell, under instructions from Red Sox manager Joe McCarthy, worked very carefully. But when he tried to whip a fast-ball by, DiMaggio rode it into a light tower, eighty feet above the fence. He called it "the greatest series of my career," and with 5 hits in 11 at bats, 4 home runs, and 9 RBIs, who could argue?

Playing only 76 games, DiMaggio could not qualify for Most Valuable Player even though his club went on to win the World Series from Brooklyn. Ted Williams, in his prime, took the honors on the strength of top figures for slugging percentage, RBIs, runs, homers (43 and his best), and doubles, along with a .343 average. In the National League Robinson was MVP with 203 hits, 37 steals, and the league's best batting average at .342.

Impressive as Robinson's efforts were, the premier hitter in the National League and the closest to Williams in both consistency and power was Stan Musial. Like a number of his baseball forebears, Musial grew up in the Pennsylvania coal country. His father, a Polish immigrant who spoke no English, met his mother in the wire mill factory where they worked. Young Stanislaus hauled coal from the pit in the backyard of the family home to fuel the kitchen stove. He began pitching for the semipro Donora Zincs at age fifteen. In high school he fanned 17 in a 7-inning game and one of Rickey's bird dogs spotted him. Scout Wid Matthews wrote: "Arm good. Good fast ball, good curve. Poise. Good hitter. A real prospect."

He finished high school but arm trouble indicated an early frost in his career. Musial doggedly hung on, showing promise as a hitter. Any possibility of pitching ended after he dove for a ball and landed on his shoulder. Given an opportunity to learn the outfield he blossomed, producing so well that the Cardinals brought him up for the final two weeks of 1941.

During a Sunday doubleheader against Chicago, his first major league appearance, he rapped out 4 straight hits. The last of these found him at second following an infield out. After an intentional base on balls, Coaker Triplett nubbed one in front of the plate. Cub catcher Clyde McCullough pounced on it and fired to first baseman Babe Dahlgren (notable mainly for having re-

placed Lou Gehrig when the Iron Horse finally switched to the siding). Triplett, according to the umpire, beat the throw but both Dahlgren and McCullough took exception. Meanwhile, Musial rounded third and kept running. He crossed the plate before the Cubs could recover, scoring from second on a ball that traveled at best fifteen feet.

After he finished his day with 2 more hits, Cub manager Jimmy Wilson groused, "Nobody can be that good." But Casey Stengel, handling the Braves, recognized the germ of greatness. "You'll be looking at him a long, long while . . . ten . . . fifteen . . . maybe twenty years." (It was twenty-two, in fact.)

Ironically, during spring training, two of Musial's teammates, Johnny Mize and Terry Moore, had banged long home runs off him while he was still trying to succeed as a pitcher. Even Branch Rickey was impressed by the newcomer and the following spring he summoned Musial to his office and grandly announced: "I'm tearing it up [the contract] my boy. We're going to pay you $700 a month [instead of the $400 previously determined]."

In 1946, money nearly led Musial to abandon the Cardinals. The freewheeling Pascual brothers from Mexico had created the Mexican League and offered extravagant bounties to émigrés from the majors. A number of major leaguers, including pitchers Sal Maglie and Max Lanier and catcher Mickey Owen, opted for the cash and competition south of the border. Jorge Pascual visited Musial and allegedly dumped $75,000 cash on the kitchen table, promising $125,000 more over the next five years. Musial, earning $15,000 a season in St. Louis, was tempted, but he took his manager Eddie Dyer's advice: "Like Eddie said, people might point to Dicky or Gerry [Musial's sons] later and say, 'There go the kids of a guy whose word was no good.' I couldn't stand that."

For five of the next nine years, Stan the Man led the league in batting average. Of post–World War II hitters only Ted Williams registered a higher lifetime percentage (.344 to .331). Musial is ninth on the all-time list of slugging averages and fifth in RBIs. Although he racked up 475 homers, he fanned only about 30 times a year. His stance was unique: feet close together far

"From 1910 through 1960, Casey Stengel knew only one job. He happened to know that job about five hundred percent better than most."—Harold Rosenthal

By the time Casey's wunderkind Mickey Mantle arrived as a nineteen-year-old in 1951, the Stengel Yankees already had tucked away the last two World Series. Three more would follow.

Courtesy UPI/Bettmann News photos

Billy Martin delighted Stengel with his scrappy style, a mirror of the old man's youth. But the front office saw disaster in Martin as Mantle's party companion and traded him away.

Courtesy UPI/Bettmann News photos

back in the box, head slightly bent, the bat farther out than usual. Ted Lyons, the White Sox pitcher who won 260 games and subsequently coached for the Dodgers, described the Musial approach: "He looks like a kid peeking around the corner to see if the cops are coming."

But when the coiled Musial snapped into action, he lashed the ball to all fields with stunning efficiency. In 1948, he tied Cobb's record of 4 5-for-5 games. (Pete Rose eclipsed the mark with his fifth such feat in 1986.) In the fourth game he succeeded in spite of a jammed left wrist from a tumbling catch and a badly bruised right one from being hit by an errant pitch. Then there was a 5-homer day during a 1954 doubleheader, a .376 average in 1948, and a game-winning homer in the twelfth inning of the 1955 All-Star contest.

But the era of Cardinal domination was over early in Musial's long career and his last World Series was in 1946. Meanwhile, after so many years of frantic pumpery with rusted-out bodies and callow youths, Stengel now found himself awash in superb athletes and en route to a record five straight pennants and world championships. George Weiss purchased thirty-six-year-old John Mize from the Giants for $40,000 in 1949 and a year later Mize contributed 25 homers. That same season a boy from the streets of New York, Ed "Whitey" Ford, graduated from the farm system in midseason. The cocky lefty won 9, lost only a single game, and then shut out the Philadelphia "Whiz Kids" in his first World Series start.

The Phils earned their label at the start of the season chiefly from three men: center fielder Richie Ashburn, pitcher Curt Simmons, and pitcher Robin Roberts. ★ A sore arm stopped Simmons late in the season after 17 wins and he sat out the Series. The spray-hitting Ashburn finished at .303 in 1950 while Roberts, a righty, who had spent less than one full term in the minors, won 20 games for the 1950 Phils, the first of six consecutive seasons in which he would reach or surpass that figure.

Roberts said he became a pitcher by default:

As a kid I was mainly a third baseman and played some first base and a little outfield. I

never pitched seriously until I was in college at Michigan State. I was actually there on a basketball scholarship, a six-foot-one-inch forward, . . . when the spring rolled around. . . . I went out for the baseball team. They asked me, "Well, what do you play?" And I said, "What do you need?" And they said, "Pitchers." So I said, "Well, I'm a pitcher."

On the spur-of-the-moment decision rested Roberts' nineteen-year major league career and 286 wins.

Meanwhile, reinforcements continued to bolster the Yanks. Joe DiMaggio would retire at the end of 1951, but during spring training Stengel discovered a prodigy and protégé, a scatter-armed, switch-hitting shortstop who smashed the ball right and left to faraway places. Mickey Charles Mantle, ★ baptized by his father in honor of Cochrane and trained from childhood as a switch-hitter, stuck with the club on Stengel's insistence, although Weiss preferred to give him another minor league season. When the nineteen-year-old slumped early, he returned to the minors at Kansas City. But he recovered his confidence and his swing in time to rejoin the club for the World Series, only to suffer the first of numerous serious injuries when his foot caught in an outfield drain. Once DiMaggio left the scene, Mantle took permanent possession of center field.

His prodigious home runs inspired tape-measure encomiums. Photographs of ballparks with dotted lines illustrated the lengths to which Mantle would go. A right-handed blast at Griffith Stadium in Washington soared over the outer bleacher wall 457 feet from home. The total distance was estimated at 565 feet. From his left-handed stance he twice crashed a ball off the upper facade of Yankee Stadium, coming closer than anyone to driving a fair ball out of that park. Four times he won the American League home-run title and led in slugging three seasons, three times he was MVP, and in 1956 he captured the Triple Crown.

Like his predecessor, Mantle suffered a series of injuries that hampered his performance and shortened his career. He carried on without complaint, however. Early Wynn ★ remarked:

I played with him in an all-star game and I watched him dress, watched him bandage that

(Opposite) Cardinal Stan Musial, bat snapping around with a springlike force, terrorized enemy pitchers for twenty-two years. Of post–World War II players, only Ted Williams holds a higher lifetime average.

Courtesy NBL

Robin Roberts was a premier member of the Philadelphia Phillies' Whiz Kids.

Courtesy AP/Wide World

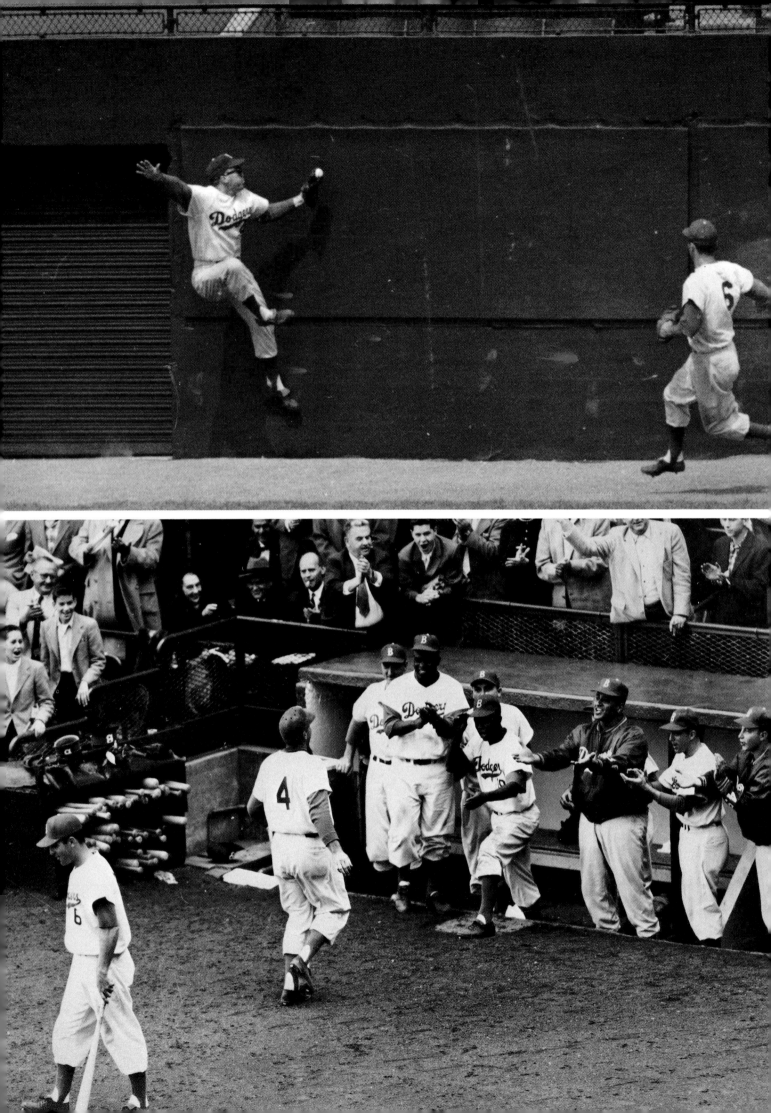

knee—that whole leg—and now I saw what he had to go through in order to play, and now I'll never be able to say enough in praise of him. Seeing those legs, his power becomes unbelievable.

Across the rivers that divide New York City into its boroughs of the Bronx, Manhattan, and Brooklyn, the other resident organizations boasted their own phenoms in center. The senior fellow, Edwin Donald Snider, the ineffable Duke, first suited up as a Dodger in 1947 to start an eighteen-year career. As in the case of Mickey Mantle, a semipro father molded the boy into a hitter. Young Edwin was right-handed but learned to swing from the other side of the plate. "My father kept telling me: 'There's a gold mine in baseball for left-handed hitters. Most of the pitchers are right-handed, the ball parks are built for left-handers, the fences are closer and you have a two-step advantage going to first base.' "

The Duke, as his father nicknamed him, played softball before he first encountered hardball at age fourteen. A high-school no-hitter attracted scouts but the Rickey brain trust took him on for his bat and converted him into an outfielder. No one doubted his power but he suffered from a total disdain for the strike zone.

Anything that came to the plate and looked good I had a whack at it. Missed it a lot, in the dirt, over my head, what have you. Mr. Rickey put me in that cage with an umpire; in back of the cage, himself and George Sisler. I was up there without a bat, a catcher and an umpire with me and a pitcher. And it was amazing how wrong I was. I had to call every pitch, where it was. Then they put a bat in my hand, I was able to swing at each pitch and I had to do the same thing all over again, tell the umpire and tell Mr. Rickey and everybody where it was.

Snider spent hours in the spring of 1948 in this Vero Beach, Florida, academy-for-one, tutored also in how to hit off-speed stuff to the opposite field. He absorbed the lessons well enough to notch 407 homers and run up a .295 lifetime average over his career. Twice, Snider cracked out 4 homers during World Series against the Yankees, most satisfyingly in 1955 when the Dodgers, for the first time, beat their cross-two-rivers rivals.

Unlike New York's other pair of highly celebrated center fielders, Snider competed for attention against better-known teammates. Pee Wee Reese captained a squad that gained six league titles in his final dozen years and the Dodgers never finished worse than third during that period. He varied his offensive contributions: 104 walks in 1947, 132 runs in 1949, 176 hits in 1951, 30 stolen bases in 1952, a .309 average for 1954 with 35 doubles. But according to teammates, his greatest contribution was his capacity to lead.

Duke Snider: "You can go to any player, ask him about Pee Wee, and he'll tell you how Pee Wee helped him become a better player and a better person."

Don Newcombe: "There was a point in time when you didn't know who your friends were. But we knew to a man—Jackie, Dan Bankhead [a black pitcher], Campy and I, the four of us—that Pee Wee was a friend."

Preacher Roe: "It just seemed like everything depended upon Pee Wee. He was very aware and very intelligent. He wouldn't go into a situation half knowledgeable. He'd do anything to sacrifice himself to move a runner along."

Roy Campanella: "He was one of the best bunters I ever played with. He was a hit-and-run man. He could steal bases. I had so much confidence in Pee Wee in the field, hitting behind the runner, calming down players in the dugouts, straightening out umpires. He is the greatest shortstop I've ever played with and a top gentleman who molded our team together from the word go."

Campanella himself arrived in the major leagues after close to nine years of seasoning in Negro baseball. He too had been approached by Rickey in 1945 about the prospect of joining the Brown Dodgers. Campy recalled:

I told him right off the bat that I was with an established Negro team and I wasn't taking no chance on a new one. He didn't say anything, just asked me what I was going to do that winter. I told him I was going to Venezuela to play ball and he said would I do him a favor and not sign any contract for next year until he had a chance to talk to me again. I said sure and left.

While the citizens of the Bronx and Manhattan raved about their center fielders, the denizens of Brooklyn bragged of their own Duke, here leaping for a drive by the Phillies' Willie Jones.

Courtesy AP/Wide World

Fellow players cheered Snider at the bat, as with his 4 homers against the Yankees in the 1955 Series he helped the Dodgers finally win one against their nemesis.

Courtesy AP/Wide World

Some weeks later, Campanella learned Robinson had signed not with the Brown Dodgers but with Montreal. The catcher received a firsthand account of Jackie's contract when he and Robinson played together in Venezuela. Rickey then telegraphed him in March 1946, asking him to sign up. Initially, plans called for a stint with an Illinois Three-Eye League team but the outfit refused to accept a black. Eventually, with Don Newcombe, he was assigned to Nashua (New Hampshire), a Class B entry.

When the Dodgers chose Havana for the 1947 rites of spring, neither the Havana Military Academy where Montreal stayed nor the Hotel Nacional where the Dodgers were housed would accept the black players. Campanella spent 1947 in Montreal, following Robinson's footsteps, then shifted to St. Paul at the beginning of 1948. Called up in midseason, Campy was an instant success. He debuted in a doubleheader against the Giants, rapping 3 hits including a double and triple in game one and 2 homers and a single in the nightcap. His performance behind the plate shunted Gil Hodges to first base.

Campanella appeared tubby but he moved with the grace of a sleek cat. During the 1949 Series against the Yankees he picked off both Henrich and Rizzuto.

Although the Dodgers, with four Hall of Famers in their prime, won far more National League pennants than any other club during the period, they will also be remembered for the decline and stunning fall of 1951. As of August 11, the Dodgers held a 13-game lead over the Giants, a solid but unspectacular club with half the number of Hall of Famers the Dodgers had. One, Monte Irvin, accrued his credentials in Negro baseball before coming to the team as a thirty-year-old rookie. The other was an unproven rookie of great promise, Willie Howard Mays.

But starting that second week in August, Manager Leo Durocher's troops won and won and then won some more. During the final weeks they triumphed in 37 while losing only 7, a bogglesome .841 percentage, while the Dodgers floundered around .500. As a consequence, the teams finished the regular season in a tie, necessitating a 3-game playoff.

The Giants took the first 3–1 but the Dodgers hammered a 10–0 victory to even matters. In those pre-TV days, when night ball was still an occasional affair, the deciding game was on a midafternoon Wednesday. It was not even a sellout; twenty-seven thousand came to the Polo Grounds that could seat more than double the number. The temperature in early October climbed to the high sixties but the sky lowered with gray rain clouds.

The seventh inning ended with the teams locked in a 1–1 struggle. Roger Kahn reported that Dodger starter Newcombe returned to the dugout to announce: "I got nothing left, nothing. My arm's tight."

His teammates, Robinson and Campanella, who was unable to play because of a thigh muscle pull, got on his case. "Bullshit," Kahn quoted Robinson. "You go out there and pitch until your goddamned arm falls off." "Roomie," added Campanella, "you ain't gonna quit on us now. You gonna hum that pea for us, roomie."

Newcombe received more tangible encouragement when the Dodgers rallied for 3 runs to take a 4–1 lead. Newcombe set down the enemy in the eighth. Larry Jansen, relieving Maglie, kept the Dodgers from doing further damage in the top of the ninth.

In the bottom half, Alvin Dark, the Giant shortstop, bounced one into the hole on the right side of the infield. Hodges broke to his right, Robinson to his left; Newcombe ran to cover the bag. The ball deflected off Hodges's glove, ending the outside chance for Robinson to make the play, and Dark was credited with a single. Manager Charlie Dressen now opted for a curious strategy. He instructed Hodges to hold the bag, limiting Dark's opportunity to steal. But Alvin's run meant nothing and when the next hitter, Don Mueller, grounded through the spot where Hodges would have ordinarily played, Giants occupied first and third.

Newcombe bore down. Irvin fouled out to Hodges. He threw an outside fastball to left-handed Whitey Lockman, who went with the pitch, knocking a double into left field. Dark scored, while Mueller jammed his ankle sliding into third and had to be carried off the field. Still, the Dodgers enjoyed a 4–2 lead with one away.

Into the batter's box stepped New York

Roy Campanella, already a star in[ ]ing Negro Leagues, arrived in [ ]after Robinson, quickly attracting [ ]ing for his exploits behind and at t[ ]While Yankee Hank Bauer vainly h[ ]a muff, Campy camped under the f[ ]ing the 1956 Series.

Courtesy AP/Wide World

third baseman Bobby Thomson. He had 32 homers and a .293 average and was a definite threat. Dressen summoned relief, right-hander Ralph Branca, tall, heavyset, and a very deliberate pitcher. Branca took the mound, coolly aware of the situation. He decided to start off with a strike and succeeded with a waist-high fastball that nipped the outside edge of the plate. Thomson scolded himself for having failed to swing.

Now Branca's strategy called for something on the nasty side, an inside pitch difficult to hit, yet close enough to tempt the eager. The Brooklyn pitcher chose high and tight; pitch three would then be low and away, an effective strategy. Branca fired, just where he wanted it. But Thomson swung and connected solidly. Third baseman Billy Cox said he screamed, "Get down, get down!" as it sailed overhead. Left-fielder Andy Pafko ran back thinking he had a chance. The Polo Grounds was deceptive, even to the expert eye. The facade of the upper grandstand in left projected outward several yards; many a prosaic fly ball suddenly transubstantiated into a homer when it glanced off the scoreboard mounted on the facade. In this case, however, Pafko was dead wrong, for Thomson's drive was no simple fly but shot deep into the deck.

While radio announcer Russ Hodges repeatedly shouted "The Giants win the pennant!" Thomson toured the bases, leaping and turning in an ecstatic dance. The stunned Dodgers straggled off the field, except for Robinson who stubbornly stayed at his post hoping to spot the failure of Thomson to touch second base.

Unnoticed in the hoopla, the twenty-year-old rookie on deck mingled joy with relief. Many years later, in an autobiography ghosted by Charles Einstein, Willie Mays said: "I was so scared . . . when Thomson went up to hit, scared I'd have to go up there with the game depending on me, that I was shaking, near sick to my stomach." (Still later, Mays told Ron Fimrite that he was never really fazed by major league baseball challenges.)

Manager Durocher insisted his protégé's season-long performance was as important as the homer: "The spark was Mays. When it looked like we couldn't win, he carried us on his back."

Certainly it was a season of monumental despair and soaring glory. Baseball fairly oozed through the genes of Willie Mays. His father, nicknamed "Kitty-Kat," was an Alabama legend for his slick efforts on semipro clubs and his mother held local women's records for sprints. Kitty-Kat Mays started to train his son while he was a toddler, rolling a ball to him, teaching him to throw it back. Later lessons included balls that bounced just in front of the ten-year-old, forcing him to learn to scoop. He became adept at the technique; Mays admitted to twice fooling umpires with traps that passed as catches.

A Giant scout, Eddie Montague, discovered the eighteen-year-old Mays playing with the Birmingham Black Barons. Montague wrote: "My eyes almost popped out of my head when I saw a young colored boy swing the bat with great speed and power and with hands that had the quickness of a young Joe Louis throwing punches."

As was customary in Negro ball, the Barons had no valid contract with Mays and the Giants obtained his services for $5,000. Assigned to Trenton for his first experience in "white" baseball, Mays, who had played against the best in the Negro Leagues, faced lesser competition than he'd previously confronted. Manager Bill McKechnie taught him to think tactics and strategy and he developed his own approaches to positioning for hitters, adjusting for the condition of outfield, speed of runner, and power of hitter.

Promoted to Minneapolis for 1950 and hitting .477, Mays was summoned by the Giants in May as Brooklyn began to stretch its lead. He started slowly, going 0–12 before a long home run off Warren Spahn, and then going through another 0–13 drought. A tearful Mays pleaded to be sent back to the minors.

Durocher, however, kept his faith: ". . . you're going to be playing center field tomorrow, and the day after that, and the day after that. So get used to the idea." He concluded his pep talk with instructions for Mays to pull up his pants instead of blousing them down to the ankles, thereby widening the umpires' perception of his strike zone. From that day on, Mays was a star. His infectious grin, his squeaky voice, and the media's accounts of his small-boy enthusiasm for the game instantly endeared him to fans.

Nobody blocked home better than Campanella, tagging out Yankee Ed Lopat in the 1949 Series.

Courtesy UPI/Bettmann News photos

235

During 1952, as a consequence of the Korean War draft, Mays played most of his ball for the U.S. Army. His call-up at the start of his career was far less injurious than that suffered by marine reservist Ted Williams, who lost prime time in 1952 and 1953 flying combat missions. Mays actually improved his baseball technique in the service. He had been appalled when he observed a teammate who "thought the way to catch a fly ball was to hold his glove like he was taking out an old railroad watch and looking at it." But when Mays tried the method he found it was "the most comfortable stance. I could never be off balance that way." Thus he adopted his famous basket-style catch.

Robin Roberts said he recognized Mays's greatness before he ever played a game:

I went out early to see him in batting practice. And he hit about five balls in the upper deck. Then he went out in the outfield and he could just run like the wind and throw like hell. And I remember thinking this has got to be as good looking a baseball player as I ever saw. And it turned out he was the best player I ever saw.

Stan Musial told writer Bob Broeg:

Willie ranks with DiMaggio as the best I ever saw. He's a perfect ball player, too. Mays can beat a ball club with his bat, his glove, his arm and his legs. He has stolen more bases than any other home-run hitter who ever lived and hit more homers than any base-stealer, past or present. The guy plays with a contagious enthusiasm. Why he can run better and faster, looking back over his shoulder to see where the ball is, than most players can digging for the next base with head down.

With Mays cracking 41 homers, driving in 110 runs, and batting .345 to top the league, the Giants reached the World Series in 1954. Opposing them was a club that set a record for American League wins; the Cleveland Indians with Early Wynn (23–11), Bob Lemon (23–7), Mike Garcia (19–8), and an aging Bob Feller (13–3) were 111–43. Wynn and Lemon held ERAs of 2.73 and 2.72 but best in the league was Garcia's 2.64. Much of the pitching staff's success was owed to Manager Al Lopez, a former catcher. This would be his only Cleveland pennant but he drove the Tribe to five second-place finishes before moving to Chicago. There, he led the White Sox to a pennant after forty years in the wilderness of the second division.

In 1954, Lopez's most overtly ferocious warrior was Early Wynn. Thickset, gristle-bearded, 200 pounds of malevolence toward all who entered the batter's box, he endured twenty-three years in the majors and collected an even 300 victories. He proudly holds a reputation as an exponent of total war in the duel between the pitcher and hitter, but he had to be taught to hate:

When I came into the majors as a 19-year-old kid, Bucky Harris [managing Washington] said to me, "If you get two strikes on a batter he's got to hit the dirt on the next pitch. That's the way we play the game. If you don't knock him down, it'll cost you $25." We even had a sign for the knockdown. It was a thumb.
I'm talking about the knockdown, not a brushback. If you brushed the guy back instead of making him hit the dirt, it cost you $25. It didn't matter if the hitter was DiMaggio or Ted Williams. I was making $350 a month. I couldn't afford giving up $25.

He learned the lesson well:

That space between the white lines—that's my office. That's where I conduct my business. You take a look at the batter's box and part of it belongs to the hitter. But when he crowds in just that hair . . . he's stepping into my office, and nobody comes into my office without an invitation when I'm going to work.

In 1956, while with Cleveland, Wynn faced the Senators' Jose Valdivielso who lined a shot directly at him. The pitcher never saw it; the ball, traveling faster than a hundred miles an hour, rocketed off his chin and rolled away. Wynn staggered, then in a daze, blinded by the shock, groped for the ball. He never found it and when Manager Al Lopez rushed to inspect the damage, Wynn shook him off: "I'm fine." But he kept his chin down on his chest. Lopez demanded to look at the jaw or he would summarily remove Wynn from the game. Early lifted his head to disclose a deep, bloody gash. Sixteen stitches closed the wound and a dentist removed seven loose teeth. Perhaps the one person relieved to see Lopez remove Wynn was Valdivielso, who knew only too well how Wynn would deal with him on his next at bat. Or even before—Wynn was not above plunking miscreants who sullied his office while earning first base with well-aimed pickoffs.

Writers cited Wynn's willingness to knock

(Opposite, top) *"Now it is done. The story ends. And there is no way to tell it. The art of fiction is dead. Reality has strangled invention. Only the utterly impossible, the inexpressibly fantastic, can ever be plausible again."—Red Smith,* New York Times, *after Bobby Thomson's 1951 homer that won the playoff for the Giants.*

Courtesy NBL

(Opposite, bottom) *On deck was a frightened, then relieved, rookie named Willie Mays as the Giants celebrated Thomson.*

Courtesy AP/Wide World

Fiercest of the Indians was Early Wynn, who hung on until he was forty-three when he collected his 300th victory.

Courtesy UPI/Bettmann News photos

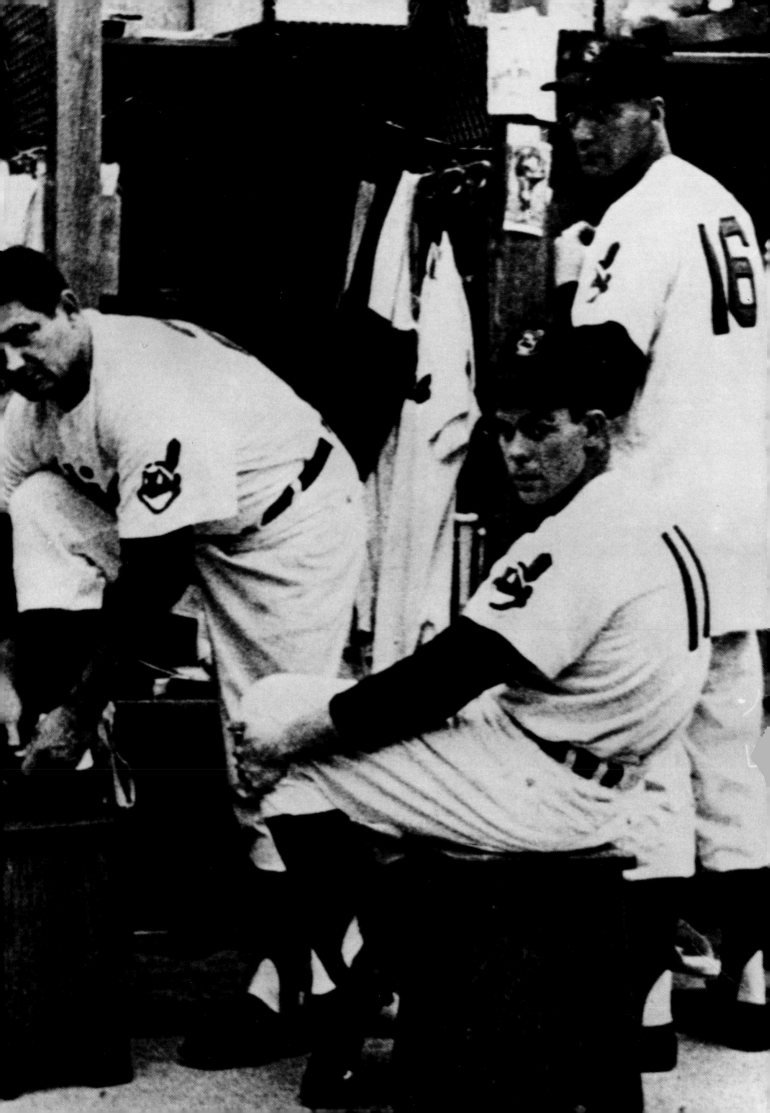

down his mother if she dug in at home plate. He equivocated: "It all depends on how much she was hitting." Once he was tossing balls to his son, who responded with a sharp rap up the middle. Wynn decked him on the next pitch.

He was a doleful 72–87 when the Indians procured his services. Coach Mel Harder instructed Wynn in the art of the curve, location, and patterns. He learned to throw everything with the same motion. For all of his fierceness, he controlled his "rage and tension," even talking to himself. And he went from a 19-game loser to a habitual 20-game winner.

"Early Wynn was the toughest pitcher I ever faced," said Ted Williams. Wynn returned the compliment: "With Williams and DiMaggio, I always conceded hits."

Bob Lemon broke into the majors in 1941 as a weak-hitting third baseman for the Indians. Following three years in the military he returned as a pitching prospect, becoming a 20-game winner by 1948, the year Wynn joined the club. He would have six more seasons of 20 or better for the Indians, posting top marks for total innings on four occasions and for complete games five times. When he finally quit he was 207–128 for a splendid .618 percentage.

To the surprise of most experts, however, the Giants trampled the Indians 4–0 in the 1954 Series. In the first game, with the score 2–2 in the eighth and two men on, Vic Wertz of Cleveland hammered a "homer" to center field, or at least what would have been a home run in almost every ballpark except the elongated Polo Grounds. In a high arc, the ball traveled 440 feet. Mays turned his back to the plate and galloped under it as his cap fell off. He gloved the ball, whirled, and threw in a single motion to prevent Larry Doby from scoring. Lemon then yielded a pinch-hit homer to Dusty Rhodes in the tenth. In game two, a bloop hit by Rhodes off Wynn in the fifth inning and his homer in the seventh defeated the Indians. Rhodes continued his magic with a pinch-hit single to drive in a pair in the third game as the Giants beat Garcia. Lemon dropped the finale even though Rhodes was not a factor.

Willie's grab on Wertz became known as "the catch" but there were witnesses who touted other feats. Broadcaster Russ Hodges swore Mays intercepted a Roberto Clemente ★ shot headed for a Forbes Field light tower. Mays himself argued his best robbed Bobby Morgan of the Dodgers. Mays remembered running far to his right, leaping into the air to stretch his body parallel to the ground before he snagged the ball in the tip of the glove. He slammed into the ground and his right elbow hammered him in the solar plexus, leaving him windless and unconscious, but the glove with the ball tucked in it lay upon his chest.

A small but important role in the Series belonged to a young New York pitcher who relieved starter Ruben Gomez in the third game and snuffed out the last five Indians for a save. Hoyt Wilhelm ★ began his career with the Giants in 1952 as a reliever and he was still coming out of the bullpen twenty years later, amassing a record 1,070 games and 123 wins as a nonstarter. (As an occasional starter he collected an additional 20 victories, including a no-hitter.) Wilhelm relied almost exclusively on the most mysterious of pitches, the knuckler.

In 1955, the Dodgers won their first World Series, avenging themselves against their frequent tormentors, the Yankees. It was a 7-game struggle in which Johnny Podres outshone Ford. Both won a pair but Podres kept the Yanks to 2 earned runs over 18 innings while Ford gave up twice that number. In the sixth inning of the final game Sandy Amoros made a spectacular grab of a critical fly by Berra to preserve Podres's 2–0 shutout.

A year later the same teams met in the postseason championship and again it lasted 7 games. This time New York triumphed, with 3 homers apiece from Berra and Mantle. But the high point was game five, as Don Larsen of the Yanks tossed the only perfect game in World Series history. Three fielding gems saved him. In the second inning, Jackie Robinson ripped a drive that third baseman Andy Carey could only deflect with his glove. It bounded to shortstop Gil McDougald who threw the forty-year-old Robinson out by half a step. In the fifth, Mantle sprinted to deep left center to haul in a shot from Gil Hodges with a backhand, shoe-top snatch. Hodges was again frustrated in the eighth as Carey speared his line drive.

(Previous pages) *The Cleveland Ind[ians]* 1954 racked up 111 victories thanks [to the] arms of (left to right) *Mike Garci[a,]* Lemon, Bob Feller, Early Wyn[n,] Houtteman, and Hal Newhouser. [Behind] are the fire fighters, Don Mossi an[d Ray] Narleski.

Courtesy AP/Wide World

"The million-to-one shot came in. He [wrote it] over. . . . Don Larsen today pitched [a no-] hit, no-run, no-man-reach-first gam[e in the] World Series. . . . He did it with a [tremen-] dous assortment of pitches that see[med to] have five forward speeds, including [the] one that ought to have been equipp[ed with] back-up lights."—Shirley Povich, [Wash-] ington Post

Courtesy UPI/Bettmann News photos

Just before Yogi Berra could hug La[rsen the] umpire called a questionable third s[trike on] the final hitter, Dale Mitchell. Yea[rs later,] when asked about the pitch, Mickey [Mantle] laughed, "I was too far away to see [it, but] Yogi had to jump for it."

Courtesy UPI/Bettmann News photos

Mickey Mantle came out of the West in 1951, a golden teenager with milker's forearms and a country-fresh grin. It was the springtime of the American Dream and Mantle arrived in a bloom of hyperbole—the new Joe DiMaggio; the next Babe Ruth. Baseball was excited by the promise of his brute power and his bursting speed, but it was his intensity that fired the imagination. His passion overflowed the white lines. He was "The Natural."

The rest of America saw that, too. After twenty years of depression and war, the country was hungry for a hero without a gun, and here was a boy with a bat and a cardboard suitcase, a nineteen-year-old from Indian Territory, son of a lead miner, an Okie, who would take New York on sheer talent and energy. Mickey Mantle was a symbol for the new era of peace and prosperity.

There was even a dark side to this mythic hero, which made him more appealing. He was physically flawed; his leg was vulnerable to injury because of osteomyelitis, a degenerative bone disease. And his psyche was wounded, too; he was driven by a desperate need to succeed, to be perfect, to prove himself to his father.

Mickey Mantle was a legend before his time, an enormous burden for even so wondrously gifted an athlete. He did not always carry the burden with grace—he didn't have DiMaggio's icy reserve or Ruth's Rabelaisian spirit. The public Mantle was rarely as attractive as the private Mantle. He had one of the sunniest smiles in all of sports, yet he usually wore it only in the locker room. It was ten years before fans gave him the credit he deserved as the dominant player of his time.

His statistics—2,401 games, 536 home runs, sixteen all-star appearances, ten seasons batting more than .300, three Most Valuable Player awards, the 1956 Triple Crown—do not suggest the breathtaking moment of Mantle at the plate, thousands frozen at the possibilities. He could, with the exquisite delicacy of a surgeon, drag a bunt, then beat it out with sprinter's speed. He could lash a line drive into the outfield, and take an extra base. He could bludgeon the ball—the baseball jumped off his bat, old-timers liked to say—farther than anyone else; the so-called tape-measure home run was a Mantle specialty.

Mantle's playing years—1951 through 1968—roughly coincided with the explosive growth of television, particularly as a vehicle for baseball, and with the childhood and adolescence of the so-called baby-boom generation. No athlete before him had ever come of age under such scrutiny. He didn't complain or explain. He did not ask for sympathy or even understanding. He was tough in old-fashioned ways, perhaps the last of

baseball's frontier personalities.

Mickey Mantle was born on October 20, 1931, in Spavinaw, Oklahoma, in a two-room shack on a tenant farm. His father, Elvin (Mutt) Mantle, was trying to support his family raising corn and wheat. But there was no market. It was the Great Depression. The same distant events that had caused Mutt to lose his job grading county roads now ruined his chance for independence as a farmer. He had two options—to join the caravan of Model Ts filing out of the Dust Bowl toward California, or to stay in Oklahoma and go down into the mines.

Mutt stayed. He moved his family into the northeastern corner of the state, near the Missouri and Kansas borders, a region of lead and zinc mines. The Mantles lived on hardscrabble patches surrounded by hills of chat—slag heaps of spent, leftover ore. Nearby were the beautiful summer homes where the well-to-do of Tulsa vacationed near their reservoirs.

Mickey Charles—he was named for the Hall of Fame catcher Mickey Cochrane and for his grandfather—was raised by his parents to escape their lives. He remembers a rural boyhood of sixteen cows to milk, a horse to ride to school, football with his brothers and sister, Saturday matinees, even a turn as an editor of the high-school newspaper, but his overriding memory is of baseball. Mutt was a local star, but Mickey's career became his passion. Still grimy from a shift in the mines, Mutt would meet little Mickey in the backyard and hand him a leftover cupcake from his lunch bucket, and a ball. Until supper, they practiced. Mutt was a natural coach, and Mickey remembers those days with pleasure. Mutt was also a visionary—he foresaw two-platoon baseball, and insisted Mickey learn to switch-hit. Mutt took Mickey to minor league games. "See that guy? He's going to be a major league star." It was Stan Musial.

By the time Mickey was in high school, Mutt's dream for his boy seemed breathtakingly possible. Baseball would set him free, set him on the same road as Musial. As Mutt advanced at the mines, he sometimes put Mickey on—Mantle credits his powerful upper body to part-time and summer jobs as a "screen ape," pounding rocks with a 16-pound sledgehammer into shards small enough to pass through a screening sieve. But the jobs were only temporary, Mutt made clear. Baseball was the ticket; the chance he didn't have would be Mickey's.

The osteomyelitis appeared during his sophomore year at Commerce High. Mickey went out for the football team despite his father's fears he would be hurt for baseball. He was a speedy halfback with sure hands. One day in practice, he was kicked in the left shin. A day later, his leg swollen, running a 104-degree temperature, he was in the local hospital,

He came out of Commerce, Oklahoma, after one minor league season, wearing a straw hat and toting a cardboard suitcase. He became pals with a street-wise San Franciscan, Billy Martin.

Courtesy Marvin Newman

Elvin "Mutt" Mantle (left), a zinc miner, taught his kid to switch-hit, ragged him to persevere when a slumping Mickey wanted to quit. Mickey brought Yankee outfielder Cliff Mapes to visit his father at the mines where the son had worked repairing pump engines.

Courtesy New York Yankees

taking sulfur and compresses. He lay there two weeks before osteomyelitis was diagnosed. The doctor predicted amputation.

His mother saved the leg. She found a local lawyer to draw up papers transferring Mickey to the charity ward of a major hospital in Oklahoma City, 175 miles away, where a new drug, penicillin, was being used. Mickey was home a few days later.

In 1948, Tom Greenwade, the famous Yankee scout, spotted Mickey as the best prospect he had ever seen. The foxy Greenwade returned in a year to tell Mutt that despite the boy's poor arm, erratic fielding, and suspect bat, he might be willing to risk his scouting career by signing him. They settled on a $1,100 bonus.

It was Greenwade who badgered the Yankees to include Mantle in the innovative instructional camp they held in Phoenix, Arizona, before spring training in 1951. The Yankee owners wanted to preen before their West Coast pals, and Manager Casey Stengel, always a teacher, wanted to work with his young players before the veterans arrived. He was eager to shape the raw clay of Mantle.

It was raw clay. After two years as a minor league shortstop, Mantle was still far from a polished performer. His throws often landed in the stands. Stengel moved him to the outfield.

In an early exhibition game, wearing his first pair of flip-down sunglasses, Mantle hustled under a high fly and lost it in the sun. While he was trying to flip down the shades, the ball bounced off his forehead for 3 bases. Humiliated, Mantle threw himself on the ground.

But his talents were obvious. He could run from home to first base in 3.1 seconds, an amazing speed, and the coaches would stop to watch him at batting practice, hammering long drives into the bleachers. He was willing to work hard to improve his outfield skills. Stengel, a former outfielder, coached him.

But there was little even Stengel could do to shield him from the problem that would dog him throughout his career—Mantle internalized pressure. If he was less than perfect, if he felt unfairly judged, he became moody, surly, he got down on himself. He felt the pressure from Mutt, from the crowd, from the Yankees.

There was controversy that first year over his draft status. Because of the osteomyelitis, he had been classified 4F. Columnists wondered in print how he could play baseball if he wasn't healthy enough to join American troops in Korea. Bleacher bums called him "draft dodger" and "coward" and "commie." The Yankees flew him back to Oklahoma for a reexamination, and he was again classified 4F. He was confused and

By 1953, prodigious homers like the one that sailed over the 55-foot wall at Griffith Stadium in Washington and came to rest in a backyard 565 feet from home plate introduced the statistic of tape-measured blasts. Another rocket at Yankee Stadium clanged against the upper facade in right field, about three feet shy of clearing the stands for the first major league fair ball out of that park. Mantle had become the leader of the Yankee band; his grand-slam homer against the Dodgers in 1953 in game five of the Series brought the entire New York crew to its feet.

Courtesy AP/Wide World

"Later in the contest, Mickey dragged a bunt that landed in front of second base and he outsped it for a single. Thus in the same afternoon . . . the young man from Commerce, Okla. fashioned one of the longest homers and the longest bunt on record."— Louis Effrat, New York Times

Until injuries weakened his legs Mantle was an adept bunter.

Courtesy Herb Scharfman, *Sports Illustrated*

hurt. Didn't people understand that he would rather go into the Army, where he would probably play ball anyway, than have osteomyelitis, which had already put him in the hospital twice and could end his career at any time?

He hit long homers when that first major league season began, but he also struck out often, and he became depressed, punching dugout walls and losing concentration in the outfield. By mid-June his average dropped to .269, and Stengel sent him to the minors to get back his confidence.

The slump continued, and so did his depression. He called his father at the mines and told him he was going to quit. Mutt hung up and drove five hours from Commerce to Kansas City, and burst into Mickey's hotel room, furious. As he tells it, Mantle said to his father, "Ah, Dad, listen, I tried as hard as I could. And what for? Where am I headed? I'm telling you it's no use and that's all there is to it. I'm not . . . ."

"Now you shut up. I don't want to hear that whining. I thought I raised a man, not a coward." Mutt began to throw Mickey's clothes into his suitcase, and the boy saw the end of the man's dreams.

"Give me another chance. I'll try, honest I will."

"What the hell. Why not?"

In the hotel coffee shop, Mutt told Mickey, "So you've had your slump. Everybody has them, even DiMaggio. Take my word. It'll come together."

Mutt went back to the mines, and Mickey traveled with the club to Toledo, where he burst out with a single, a double, a triple, and 2 homers. In the next 40 games he hit 11 homers, drove in 50 runs, and batted .361.

By August he was back with the big club, off and running. In September he was starting in right field in the opening game of the World Series.

Stengel told him to cover the entire outfield, to protect the aging DiMaggio. "Take everything you can get in center," Mantle remembers Stengel saying, "the Dago's heel is hurting pretty bad."

In the second game, that other hot rookie of 1951, Willie Mays, hit a high fly to center field. Mantle ran over from right, but when DiMaggio yelled, "I got it!" he stopped short and caught his spikes in the rubber cover of a drain hole buried in the outfield. His knee popped. He went down.

The next day, on the way to the doctor, Mickey leaned on his father for support. Mutt collapsed. They watched the Series together, in adjoining beds in a hospital room. Mutt was diagnosed as terminally ill with Hodgkin's disease, a form of cancer that had killed his brother and his father.

Courtesy Marvin Newman

Originally a shortstop, Mantle claim[ed] committed 77 errors while playing [Jo]plin. Actually, it was only 55 but th[e Yan]kees shooed him to the outfield wh[ere he] engaged in blowing bubbles, compen[sating] for lapses in technique with his great [speed.]

Courtesy UPI/Bettmann News photos

Mickey used his World Series check to buy his family a seven-room house in Commerce. For the first time, they had their own telephone. At his father's urging, he married Merlyn, a local girl he had dated. He rested his bad leg that winter, but he never did the prescribed exercises to strengthen it. He would come to regret that later. The muscles deteriorated and his knee was always weak and easily injured.

Mantle batted .311 in 1952 and hit 23 home runs, but he lost the critical figure in his life. Mutt died, at thirty-nine, without seeing Mickey out of boyhood. He was still shy and suspicious, a lumpy mixture of cynical fatalism and unsophisticated optimism.

"I got into trouble with the press early, because I was scared," says Mantle.

I was young when I came to New York, and I got misquoted, well, maybe not so much misquoted as it came out not sounding like me talking. I was scared and I didn't really know how to handle it, so if you misquoted me, I just wouldn't talk to you anymore, and if you came up in a group around my locker, I wouldn't talk to anybody, which made the whole joint mad.

Mantle was often rude to fans and abusive to journalists; this rarely came to print because the New York writers, for the sake of their careers and their relations with the Yankees, were building a superstar. They had one by 1956. That was Mantle's golden year. He led the league in average (.353), homers (52), and RBIs (130). It was the first of his three Most Valuable Player Awards. The fans and the reporters somehow thought that year was a prelude, not a peak, and the pressure increased for him to do even better. He was booed for not hitting home runs. He was criticized in print for striking out, the only category in which he would eventually set a career regular-season record (1,710), surpassed since by Reggie Jackson.

Ironically, it was not until the fans and the press came to realize that Mantle would never become the next Babe Ruth that he began to receive his due as a great player. It happened in 1961, the year that Ruth's most cherished record—60 homers in a single season—was broken by a Yankee teammate, Roger Maris, a decent man and an excellent ball player, if less than charismatic. Roger was no one's choice to be the next Babe Ruth.

"I couldn't do no wrong after Roger beat me in the home-run race in 1961," says Mantle. "Everywhere I went I got standing ovations. All I had to do was walk out on the field. Hey, what the hell. It's a lot better than having them boo you."

He shrugs, a cynical gesture. "I became the underdog, they hated him and liked me."

His contempt for the fickle fans is offhand. So is his compassion for Roger. "He was just pitched into the middle of all this publicity. We used to have more sportswriters following us that year than we had baseball players. All of a sudden it was on top of him, it was tough. That's why I think it was such a great thing he did, breaking Babe Ruth's record."

By the second week in September, Maris had 56 homers and Mantle 53, with 18 games remaining. Mantle had a bad head cold. He felt sore and stiff. He was recommended to a notorious Dr. Feelgood for an amphetamine boost. The injection caused an abscess on his hip that put him in the hospital. He managed only 1 more homer that season.

Roger Maris got an asterisk for breaking the record and Mantle got a new public image. It took another ball player, Jim Bouton, to provide a balanced picture of Mantle. In *Ball Four,* the diary he wrote with Leonard Shecter, Bouton recalled his first Yankee pitching victory, in 1962.

When the game was over I walked back into the clubhouse and there was a path of white towels from the door to my locker, and all the guys were standing there, and just as I opened the door Mickey was putting the last towel down in place. I'll never forget him for that.

And I won't forget the time—1962, I guess it was—in Kansas City. I was sitting alone in a restaurant eating, when Mickey and Whitey Ford came in and Mickey invited me to eat with them and picked up the tab and it made me feel good all over, and like a big shot besides.

On the other hand, Bouton and others remember a Mantle who sometimes pushed past kids seeking autographs, rolled shut a bus window when they came after him. When angered by reporters whom he felt misquoted him or made him look bad he would refuse interviews and cut them down with a stony glare.

Like many celebrities Mantle was uneasy when confronted by the frenzy of autograph hunters. They drove him from an amusement park where he had taken his kids for an outing; they interrupted his meals and snarled at him when he was reluctant to sign. Once a member of the autograph crowd surging onto the field after a game struck him a stunning blow in the face. Still, he must have signed his name thousands of times and with organized groups he was more forthcoming. Former Yankee executive and American League official Bob Fishel insists, "Mickey could

"You're Mickey Mantle and your l[...] wrapped up like a mummy's. Yo[...] standing at the batting cage yesterda[...] a foul ball glanced off your hand and[...] your thigh. It knocked you dow[...] trainer used medication to freeze the [...] areas. The hand was difficult to close[...] stiff. There was the imprint of base[...] the flesh of your leg. This was t[...] . . . What about your legs? What ab[...] operation. . . . The right leg, hurt wh[...] tripped in a drain chasing a ball [...] 1951 World Series, damages you[...] handed swing."—Jimmy Cannon,[...] York Post

Courtesy Marvin Newman

(Opposite) *Mantle and Maris as a[...] tandem outgunned even Ruth and [...] with Mickey clouting 54 homers, R[...] record 61. It was Mantle who coun[...] despairing Maris during the stressful [...] of the Ruth mark.*

Courtesy William La Force, *Baltimore*

be just great with kids. And he was always completely without prejudice."

Bouton wrote, "Like everybody else on the club, I ached with Mantle when he had one of his numerous and extremely painful injuries. I often wonder, though, if he might have healed quicker if he'd been at the bar less."

Mickey, who like many baseball people turns chilly at the mention of Bouton and his book on the grounds that Bouton breached confidences and privacy, in his own synopsis of those years is no more charitable to himself.

"From say '60 until I retired, Merlyn and the kids didn't come to New York with me. I stayed in a hotel. I would start drinking just from monotony, from just not having anything else to do."

In the spring of 1967, Mantle was moved to first base. His wounded legs were aching but the Yankees had placed tenth the previous season and he was their only draw. Pitchers were instructed to go for every grounder in his general direction (shades of Stengel telling the rookie Mantle to cover for DiMaggio). Mantle's last two years were not particularly eventful. He batted .245 and .237, his lowest averages, which pulled his lifetime average down to .298. But he appeared in 144 games, got more than 100 hits, and drove in more than 50 runs each season. He earned his $100,000. But he was not his image of Mickey Mantle.

In September 1968, his right leg shaky, he hit his next-to-last home run, number 535, to pass Jimmie Foxx on the all-time list. Denny McLain, en route to his 31-game winning season, was beating the Yankees 6–0 before a crowd in Detroit when, in a moment of sentiment, he told his catcher, Bill Freehan, "I'm gonna let him hit one."

Mantle, overhearing, asked Freehan, "Is he setting me up for something?"

"No, Mick. He wants you to hit one."

Mantle fouled off one fat fastball, then blasted the next into the upper deck.

The following spring training, he announced his retirement.

"I'm not going to play baseball anymore, that's all I know," he said slowly. "I can't play anymore. I don't hit the ball when I need to. I can't steal when I need to. I can't score from second when I need to."

In the years after Mantle's retirement, the youngsters he had dazzled in the fifties grew up. Some became business executives who sent him warm letters on engraved stationery or offered him business deals. They made his memorabilia, his bubble-gum cards, his record with Teresa Brewer, his magazine covers, among baseball's best-selling knickknacks.

"I always loved the game, but when ↑ weren't hurting it was a lot ea↑ love."—Mickey Mantle

Courtesy _Baltimore Sun_

(Opposite) "Mickey was a difficult ↑ his early days. He was sullen and br↑ When he struck out he was booed, ↑ would throw his cap, toss his bat s↑ kick water coolers, slam his fi↑ walls."—Phil Pepe, Winners Neve↑

"At the end of the season [1968] ↑ time average had dipped under .3↑ most disappointing thing ever. I ↑ hardly stand to think about it. Eve↑ my second year with the Yankees, wh↑ .311 and finished third behind Fer↑ of the A's and Dale Mitchell of Cle↑ even then it was almost impossible to↑ I felt I should've led the league an↑ did that once in my major league car↑ goddamn, to think you're a .300 hi↑ end up at .237 in your last season, t↑ yourself looking at a lifetime .29↑ age—it made me want to cry."—↑ Mantle, The Mick

Courtesy UPI/Bettmann News photos

A New Jersey woman engaged Mantle to attend her husband's fortieth birthday party. "When I walked in," Mantle recalls, "he broke down and cried." Mantle pauses. "I just about cried, too."

In 1974, Mantle was inducted into the Hall of Fame, with Whitey Ford. "When you were playing," said Mantle, reminiscing on their friendship, "especially if you were alone or if you struck out a couple of times, you'd say, 'What the hell's it all for anyway?' But if you hit a home run and your teammates jumped all over you, you knew what it was for."

Later, he added, "Somebody asked me how would I like to be remembered, and the first thing I thought of is that I really believe that all the players that played with me liked me.

"My only regret is that I didn't take better care of myself. People think that my legs and my injuries hampered me a lot, they did, but if I had taken better care like Willie Mays and Stan Musial and Hank Aaron, the guys that are up in the record books, Pete Rose . . ." His voice trailed off.

In 1983, when Mantle joined the public relations staff of an Atlantic City hotel and gambling casino, Commissioner Bowie Kuhn banned him from working in baseball, even as a spring training batting coach. He took it philosophically—after all, nobody in baseball was offering him $100,-000 a year to hang out and smile. His middle-age fans thought it was sad that baseball could find no place for him, and some thought there was something poignant in the golden boy of their youth scrabbling for chips. Mantle never thought so. "It's not like I'm out front telling people to come gamble," he would say. "I go to charity functions, I play golf, it's public relations and I always did that."

In 1985, the new commissioner, Peter Ueberroth, reinstated Mantle and Mays, who had been working for another casino. Mantle began broadcasting games for a pay-TV service. In 1986, he published a lively autobiography, *The Mick,* written by Herb Gluck.

He seemed mellower now, easier with strangers. He was no longer so hostile with reporters. He had a routine to charm them that included a rendition of "The Dream."

Well, first of all I take a cab to the ballpark, and I'm in my uniform and I've got a bat. And I get there and the game's going on and I hear them say, Mickey Mantle hitting, number 7, Mickey Mantle.

But I'm not in the ballpark and the gates are closed. There's a hole that I can crawl under and halfway through the hole I get stuck and I can still hear the guy saying, now batting number 7, Mickey Mantle.

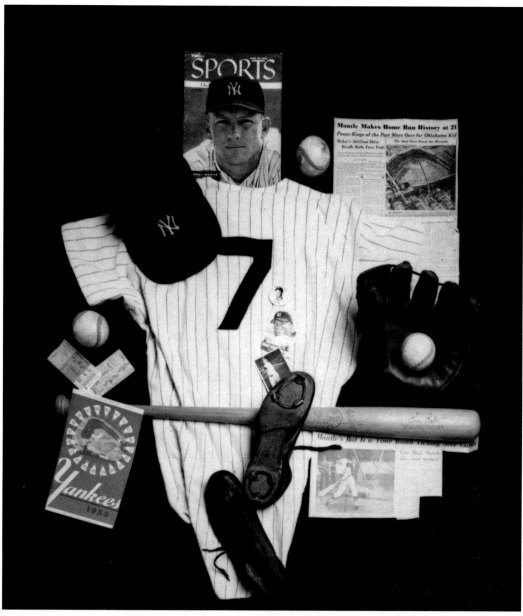

"You're Mickey Mantle and who throws harder or with more accuracy? Who runs faster? Who hits a longer ball? Who in baseball has more natural ability? Did you damage yourself beyond repair when you played lame-legged early this season? Are you Mickey Mantle who is in the records for striking out five straight times? Or are you Mickey Mantle who hit yesterday's bases-loaded home run?"—Jimmy Cannon, New York Post

Courtesy Ted Astor

And I can see Casey and Billy, Whitey, Hank Bauer, all the guys are looking around, like where's he at? And I'm stuck in the hole and they can't hear me and . . . then I wake up. And I usually can't get back to sleep.

It was disarming, "The Dream," coming from Mantle. Had he finally come to believe his press clippings after all these years?

"Sometimes," he said, "I sit in my den at home and read stories about myself. Kids used to save whole scrapbooks on me. They get tired of 'em and mail 'em to me. I must have 75 or 80. I'll go in there and read 'em, and you know what? They might as well be about Musial or DiMaggio. It's like reading about somebody else."

Enormous fan interest was generated by the Ruthian exploits of Mantle, Mays, and Snider; the influx of top black players on the heels of the still spectacular Jackie Robinson; the likes of Musial, Wynn, Spahn, Wilhelm, and assorted others; as well as the spectaculars like Dodger Al Gionfriddo's 1947 World Series catch of DiMaggio's home run bid, the Thomson homer, and Larsen's perfecto. The presentation of baseball, meanwhile, started to change along with the American scene. Happy Chandler lasted only six years as commissioner before the owners, perhaps sensing shifting currents, sought someone more heavily steeped in baseball tradition. They chose the National League chief, Ford Frick. To succeed him, the League in turn elected the successful Cincinnati Reds front-office boss, Warren Giles, ★ who would serve for eighteen seasons

The most visible sign of change mirrored the evolving demographics of the country. After many years of struggle, some cities could no longer support two major league franchises. First, the Boston Braves shifted their act to Milwaukee in 1953. A year later, Bill Veeck, who tried desperately to breathe life into the St. Louis Browns (including such resuscitative attempts as his celebrated midget pinch hitter, Eddie Gaedel, listed in *The Baseball Encyclopedia* as 3'7", 065 lbs.), surrendered his ownership to investors who moved the team to Baltimore. In 1955, with Connie Mack in retirement, the history of the Philadelphia Athletics ended; the Kansas City version opened shop.

These were relatively minor transformations. The 1958 upheaval affected the game far more significantly. Walter O'Malley, who had succeeded Branch Rickey as chief executive for the Brooklyn Dodgers, and Horace Stoneham, owner of the Giants, forsook their eastern roots and planted their franchises in Los Angeles and San Francisco. As in other cases, the proprietors could point to obsolete ballparks (Ebbets Field seated less than thirty thousand), deteriorating neighborhoods, and a drop in attendance. But the faraway new homes offered not only improvements in these areas but also vast untapped markets.

The boisterous controversy surrounding the transfers died away as both the Dodgers and Giants prospered, with attendant benefits to their colleagues. New locations changed more than uniforms and the names of clubs. As cities and their suburbs grew, they beckoned to established teams and investors anxious to wear the cloaks of sportsmen. Inevitably, major league baseball expanded from its more than fifty-year-old limit of sixteen clubs, opening stores in Minneapolis and Los Angeles (later Anaheim) for the American League in 1961, followed in 1962 by the National League entries of the Houston Colt 45s and the New York Mets.

Major league baseball was now a truly national sport; it would become international with the establishment of operations in Montreal and Toronto. In some instances, the teams hung around for only a few years before packing up for what were considered even greener pastures: The Braves forsook Milwaukee after thirteen seasons for Atlanta in 1966 and Kansas City, established in 1955, temporarily lost its team as the contentious and voluble owner, Charles O. Finley, carried the Athletics to Oakland for the 1968 season.

With the bigs now well spread across the country, TV and radio broadcasts saturated the public. A natural consequence was the decline of the lesser leagues. Many small cities could not compete with the attractions offered by nearby metropolises.

Another formidable change was the relationship of the field hands and the owners. Dissatisfaction with the standard contract and particularly the reserve clause dated back to the nineteenth century and the Brotherhood of Professional Base Ball Players revolt. Stymied by the 1922 Supreme Court ruling that the game was not an interstate activity, a few players tried unsuccessfully to obtain relief in the courts, most notably after baseball barred those who left major league ball to play in the Mexican League following World War II. Although such stalwarts as Allie Reynolds, Bob Feller, Warren Spahn, Stan Musial, and Ralph Kiner sought to organize for improved pension benefits and other improvements, they were frustrated by the unwillingness of management to concede significant changes. But the migration of franchises, the influx of tycoons of industry and commerce, and the big bucks from broadcasting stirred the juices of congressmen interested in baseball for their

Eddie Gaedel, 3'7", 65-pounder, p ting for the St. Louis Browns in on Veeck's desperate efforts to save t chise, took a high pitch.

Courtesy UPI/Bettmann News photos

Sweater: *Christy Mathewson's Giant warm-up sweater with ball he autographed and his Bible.*

Facing page: *Walter Johnson's cap and glove and his contract for 1925 and 1926. (He earned $20,000 for the two years.)*

Above: *"Stanley Musial" by John Falter, the* Saturday Evening Post *cover of May 1, 1954.*

National League: *National League uniform and cap from first All-Star game (1933) with program and ticket stub from game. (The ticket cost $1.10.)*

Following spread, left page: *Sheet music from 1935. ("I Can't Get to First Base with You" was written by Fred Fisher and Mrs. Lou Gehrig. The inscription reads: "To Judge Landis: Right off the press—with our best wishes. Eleanor and Lou Gehrig.")* Right page, clockwise from top: A Ball Players Career *by Adrian C. Anson (1900),* Boston Base Ball Club 1871–1897 *by George V. Tuohey (1897),* America's National Game *by A. G. Spalding (1911), baseball board and card game from 1889, cast iron bank from 1880s.*

Cards: *Baseball cards from different eras. (John Clarkson, Chief Bender, Yogi Berra, Lefty Gomez, and Ted Williams are all in the Hall of Fame; Heinie Wagner—as opposed to Honus Wagner—is not.)*

This Song Was Written By FRED FISHER and Mrs. LOU GEHRIG
Dedicated to LOU GEHRIG - FAMOUS FIRST BASEMAN
I CAN'T GET TO FIRST BASE
WITH YOU
Gehrig
Mrs. Lou Gehrig
Music Publishers
NEW YORK CITY

constituents or perceiving a genuine imbalance between the forces of management and labor. It would take another decade before some of the prerogatives traditionally held by the owners would crumble but the business transactions of the 1950s inevitably undermined their positions.

The newborn Braves of Milwaukee in the pennant years of 1957 and 1958 were led by Spahn and his soul mate, right-hander and occasional spitballer Lew Burdette; a heavily muscled third baseman, Eddie Mathews; and a slender outfielder with astonishing power, Henry Aaron. With Aaron and Mathews the club presented a one-two punch that rivaled Ruth–Gehrig, Mantle–Berra, Mantle–Maris. Mathews, like a solar flare in the blaze of midday sun, tended to vanish in the glare of Aaron. But he produced 512 homers for the Braves. And he brought to third base more than the traditional stalwart chest and strong arm. He ranks fourth in total chances and in assists at the post. Until Mike Schmidt of the Phillies overtook him in 1986, he was fifth in double plays involving third.

Aaron, of course, broke Ruth's career record of 714 homers with his 755, albeit spread over 12,364 at bats compared to the Babe's 8,399. (Ruth walked 2,056 times while Aaron received 1,402 passes.) Idolaters of Ruth note his .690 slugging percentage as opposed to Bad Henry's .555, and that the Babe struck a homer 8.5 percent of the time he faced a pitcher while Aaron reached the seats 6.1 percent. Ford Frick, a one-time ghostwriter for Ruth, had affixed an asterisk to Roger Maris's record of 61 homers because he played in 7 more games than Ruth but comparisons of achievements during different eras are not simply odious; they don't recognize the infinite variables—the effects of night baseball on a hitter's vision, the development of relief specialists (enabling starters to go all out for less than a full game), innovations in pitching, the changes in ballpark dimensions (by and large the old ones were smaller). Some might argue that expansion has allowed lower-quality athletes but the huge pool of black talent, untapped during Ruth's time, now sharply lifts the general level of skill. More scientific training and the actual physical changes in young men because of improvements in the standard of living have combined to produce better athletes and better performances in almost every form of sport. Arguments comparing ancients and moderns generate sound and fury, signifying nothing.

Aaron, a Mobile, Alabama, alumnus of the Negro Leagues, arrived in Milwaukee as a twenty-one-year-old stripling in 1954. He was an instant success: .280 in his rookie year; .314, 27 homers, 37 doubles in the second. But if baseball had now grudgingly accepted the presence of blacks, parts of the United States still had not. *Brown* vs. *Board of Education,* the landmark U.S. Supreme Court decision against segregated schools, came a year after Aaron's debut in the majors. As teammate Mathews recalled, ". . . with Aaron, there were times when he wasn't even allowed in the dining car of the train. We'd have to bring his meal back to him."

For several years, during spring training, Aaron and other nonwhites like outfielder Billy Bruton could not live in the same Florida motel as the Braves but stayed in rooms rented from blacks.

During his twenty-three years, Aaron topped his competition four times in homers, doubles, and RBIs. When he quit the game he held first place not only in homers but also in total bases and RBIs, with runner-up status to Cobb for runs and show money for hits, behind Pete Rose and Cobb.

Don Drysdale, ★ throwing righty and sidearm so that a ball seemed to zoom in from third base, gave Aaron enough trouble early on to nearly bench him against the big Dodger. But Aaron, a self-confessed guess hitter, forced himself to hang in against such outrageous slings. His persistence transformed him into a nemesis for Drysdale, off whom he smacked 17 of his homers, the most yielded by any pitcher to the man whom the Braves called "Supe," as in Clark Kent's alter ego.

Drysdale told George Plimpton in *Sports Illustrated:*

I always used to think that he had a lot of Stan Musial in his stance. From the pitcher's mound they both seem to coil at you. The only sensible thing—if you couldn't get the manager to let you skip a turn against him—was to mix the pitches and keep the ball low, and if you were pitching to spots it was important to miss bad. If you missed good, and the ball got in his power zone, sometimes you were

Milwaukee and Atlanta third baseman Eddie Mathews achieved the 500 homer club. His total combined with that of teammate Henry Aaron adds up to bigger numbers than those amassed by Ruth and Gehrig in their years together.

Courtesy Marvin Newman

Homer number 713, in Atlanta: "The odd thing about Aaron's attitude at the plate is that there is nothing to suggest any such intensity of purpose. . . . Aaron steps into the batter's box as if he were going to sit down in it somewhere. . . . First of all, Hank Aaron's swing is all wrong. He hits off the front foot. The great hitting textbook in the sky says you swing with weight more on your back foot to get—the irony for Aaron—more power."—George Plimpton, One for the Record

Courtesy UPI/Bettmann News photos

glad it went out of the park and was not banged up the middle.

Aaron's pursuit of Ruth's record drew a mixed but frenzied reaction. Eddie Mathews managed the Braves during that season.

Very few people could have handled the pressure as well as Hank did. I had problems with it and I was just the manager. Would you believe two or three hundred writers were traveling with us. And everyone wanted an exclusive interview. We had to change Hank's name, hide him in the hotels, hire special limousines to chauffeur him in and out and around.

Some bigots scribbled nasty notes to Aaron for challenging a white hero and idiots in the stands jeered him. Management considered holding him out of road games, preferring he surpass Ruth before a home crowd. Through it all, Aaron maintained remarkable aplomb.

As he crept within striking distance of the magic number, officials marked baseballs with special codes, preventing attempts to cash a fake for the $25,000 reward promised to the person retrieving number 715. On the great evening, April 8, 1974, in front of 53,775 paid eyewitnesses, Aaron hammered a fastball from Al Downing of the Los Angeles Dodgers in what Plimpton described as "the arc of a four-iron shot in golf." It rose over short, then soared to left center where it cleared a fence to be caught by a Braves bullpen resident, reliever Tommy House.

House trotted in to deliver the trophy to Aaron:

In that great crowd around home plate I found him looking over his mother's shoulder, hugging her to him, and suddenly I saw what many people have never been able to see in him—deep emotion. I'd never seen that before. He has such cool. He never gets excited. He's so stable. And I looked, and he had tears hanging on his lids. I could hardly believe it. "Hammer, here it is," I said. I put the ball in his hand. He said, "Thanks, kid," and touched me on the shoulder. I kept staring at him. And it was then that it was brought home to me what this home run meant, not only to him, but to all of us.

During the 1950s, the two Chicago clubs featured Hall of Fame shortstops Ernie Banks ★ of the Cubs and Luis Aparicio ★ of the White Sox. Tall and lean, Banks went directly from the Kansas City Monarchs to the Cubs in 1953. He was the first black on the team. Like Aaron, he found himself detoured to a different hotel from his white associates in cities such as St. Louis. He spent nineteen years with the forlorn Cubs who won not a single pennant during his time. Still, Banks enjoyed the game so much that on those bright sunny afternoons he would say, "Let's play two." He stands tied with Mathews in total homers, 512.

Aparicio, who spent five years with Baltimore and three with the Red Sox, played short in 2,581 games, more than any man in history. He participated in the most double plays, beating out his predecessor with the Sox, Luke Appling. (He was a .310 hitter and, like Banks, he served his twenty years in Chicago without a single World Series appearance.) Aparicio threw out far more people than any rival; in fact he accumulated 516 more assists than the runner-up, turn-of-the-century shortstop Bill Dahlen. Offensively, Aparicio averaged .262 but he led the league in stolen bases for nine straight years, starting as a rookie in 1956.

The Venezuelan-born Aparicio studied baseball at his father's knee, who was regarded as the best shortstop in baseball-rabid Venezuela. "I almost never saw him [his son]," the father once remarked. "I was always playing ball somewhere. The first time I saw him he was eight months old." But once the boy grew old enough to handle a glove, he became a star pupil. And in 1953, at Maracaibo, Luis senior fielded a ball and made his throw. Then his son trotted to short where the parent handed over his glove and embraced his child. The nineteen-year-old was now a professional.

With their all-star shortstop in position, the 1959 White Sox captured the pennant. They hooked up with the Los Angeles Dodgers in a World Series played in the Dodgers' temporary home, the Los Angeles Coliseum, an arena designed for football and a curse on pitchers with its 250-foot, left-field fence. Early Wynn split his pair of games and Aparicio hit .308 but the Dodgers triumphed 4 games to 2. The box scores listed a pair of Dodger names, Don Drysdale and Sandy Koufax, whose deeds brought National League hegemony west.

Homer number 714, in Cincinnati: of the contributions Hank Aaron ha to baseball in twenty blameless years his accomplishments as a person, no half so valuable as his achievement day. It isn't only that his 714th ho matched a record that for more th years was considered beyond human and it isn't particularly important t courteous, modest man has at last ov Babe Ruth's roistering ghost. Wha counts is that when Henry laid the v Jack Billingham's fast ball, he struck for the integrity of the game and for faith in the game.

"With one stroke he canceled sch cheapen his pursuit of the record by it a carnival attraction staged for office alone, and he rendered mo months of wrangling between the changers and the Protectors of the Fa Red Smith, New York Times

Courtesy NBL

(Opposite) Homer number 715, in A "Aaron was cool in the shadows, wh Maggio was in the glaring cynosure o Aaron is reserved like DiMaggio, to like DiMaggio, versatile like DiM But he did not play in New York l Maggio. And he is not white li Maggio."—Ira Berkow, Beyond the

Courtesy UPI/Bettmann News photos

Billye Aaron shared her husband's
with the softball-playing governor
state, Jimmy Carter.

Courtesy Donnie Johnsten

(Left) *Condemned to the shadows*
weakness of his team, cheerful Erni
sparkled at short in the afternoon
Chicago's Wrigley Field, connec
512 home runs.

Courtesy Marvin Newman

(Right) *"[Luis] Aparicio plays shor*
the Chicago White Sox with majo
passion and invention and a li
dog."—Gilbert Rogin, Sports Illu.

Courtesy Richard Meek, *Sports Illustra*

In January 1979, I was in Boston pursuing with only moderate success a story on Red Sox star Jim Rice when the opportunity presented itself to attend the annual dinner of the local chapter of the Baseball Writers Association of America. Rice had been an elusive, even reluctant interview subject, and I felt the need of a respite from the ordeal. The reassuring company in congenial circumstances of some journalistic colleagues might be just the ticket. Besides, Rice was to be honored at the dinner for being the American League's Most Valuable Player, so, in effect, I wasn't really goofing off by going. But my real reason for being there was Willie Mays.

Willie had only recently been elected to the Hall of Fame, and he was to be a special guest of the Boston writers. Although we had never been close friends, not even friends at all up to then, I felt a special kinship that night with the great center fielder. We were both San Franciscans, after all (Mays lives in suburban Atherton), and we were far from home. Maybe he was feeling as lonely as I was and might even be comforted by the sight of a familiar face from home. Mays had come west with the Giants in 1958 and had lived there ever since, though he kept temporary residences in various other places. He had played in San Francisco for fourteen years and would have finished his career there if Giants owner Horace Stoneham hadn't traded him back to New York and the Mets early in the 1972 season. He came to the Bay Area as a young player who, though a legend already, was just approaching his prime; he left a tired veteran playing out the string. At his peak—and he reached it in San Francisco—he was the greatest player in the game, perhaps the greatest player in the history of the game. I wanted to share with him, however vicariously, any rewards the evening in Boston might bring him. I was filled with civic pride when I went to that dinner. And I knew one thing for certain: No one in that banquet room had seen Willie Mays play as often as I had.

One of the speakers that evening was Dennis Eckersley, a young pitcher then who had won 20 games for the Red Sox the previous season. Eckersley, who had grown up in the Bay Area, told the writers and their guests that Willie Mays had been his childhood idol and inspiration. Whenever he could he'd get out to Candlestick Park to see Willie play. It was an honor to be in the same room with him this night. It was a nice, respectful, even touching little speech. But the next speaker, a well-known network sportscaster, seemed somehow to take exception with it. Sure, Eckersley had his memories, he seemed to be saying, but what did he know? He was still just a kid. Now, he, the broadcaster, had grown up in New York and seen the *real* Willie Mays play. His implication was clear: The Mays Eckersley and I had watched was some sort of imposter. The real Mays had ceased to exist the moment he left New York.

I was appalled by this appropriation of our hero. Was this nut actually saying that Mays's career had ended at age twenty-six, when, in fact, it had lasted another sixteen years, almost all of them in San Francisco? Was the Willie Mays who hit 49 homers and drove in 141 runs in leading the Giants to a pennant and near–World Series win in 1962 not the "real" Willie Mays? Was the man who hit 52 homers in 1965 just a pallid imitation of the genuine New York article? Utter nonsense, I muttered to myself. I knew that Mays had had his career-high seasons in homers, RBIs, and runs scored while playing for the San Francisco Giants, that he had hit his five-hundredth and six-hundredth home runs wearing that uniform. And catches? Well, even Mays himself had told me that his best might well have been in Candlestick Park in the late sixties, a beauty in which he climbed the fence in right center field, snared the ball, then collided in midair with right fielder Bobby Bonds and hit the ground, ball still held aloft, out cold. I wanted to scramble to my feet at that banquet and publicly rebuke the fatuous sportscaster for criminal parochialism. But I feared such a scene, no matter how personally satisfying. I might have sundered what was supposed to be a happy occasion. Provincial warfare would have been unseemly. And yet I was suddenly feeling even more like an alien. I kept an angry silence, mentally writing off the broadcaster as just another unregenerate New Yorker still bitter about losing the Giants and the Dodgers. These persons will, after all, surface from time to time. I can't blame them for being angry, just for not recognizing that there was baseball on this planet after 1957.

Mays's speech was unremarkable. He thanked everybody, rambled on at some length on how he hoped people still appreciated him, and then sat down. It was typical of Willie at that time, an undercurrent of whining defensiveness spilling into the mainstream of his narrative. He had been out of the game a little more than five years, and he still sounded like a frustrated player who knows he could have gone on forever if they'd only given him the chance. He was still trying to find a place for himself away from the ballpark. He was financially secure enough, thanks to the generosity of his last baseball employer, Mrs. Joan Payson, and some investments made for him in San Francisco. But he was a little lost otherwise. Here was a man accustomed to adulation. Now, except for occasions such as the Boston dinner, he was deprived of his daily dose.

This Mays, this middle-age man in the winter of his discontent, was not

"Snider, Mantle and Mays—you c[o] a fat lip in any saloon by starting a[n] ment as to which was best. One po[int] beyond argument, though. Willie wa[s] odds the most exciting."—Red Smi[th,] York Times

Courtesy UPI/Bettmann News photos

260

at all the Willie Mays the New York broadcaster had in mind. It now occurred to me that that fellow had not really been talking about a ball player so much as a personality, the adorable "Say Hey Kid" that New Yorkers had clasped to their collective bosom. And, indeed, the broadcaster was right on one score—that kid never made it to San Francisco. In fact, that kid never really existed. The "Say Hey Kid" was less an actual person than the creation of an overly protective manager and a fawning press. It was New York, after all, that never got to know the "real" Willie Mays. The one they had was an illusion.

The story by now is part of baseball lore: Black wunderkind is discovered playing Negro League ball in Alabama, is signed to major league contract, tears up minor leagues, is brought up in May 1951 season to fill desperate outfield need on faltering ball club, is initial bust, then becomes beloved star on championship team, the toast of the town. This Mays is an exuberant man-child, an innocent abroad in the Big Town who nevertheless captivates it with his falsetto giggle and playful nature. He's the grown-up who still has so much kid in him he plays stickball in the streets with urchins before or after one of his own games. His surrogate father is Leo Durocher, the Giants' crusty manager, who steadies him on the course to superstardom and shields him from wicked exploiters.

That this enchanting child could indeed perform wonders on the field fed the gathering legend. Here was a player who could outrun any ball hit into the trackless wastes of center field in the old Polo Grounds, who could catch fly balls barehanded, and whose arm was so strong and his reflexes so quick that he could, as he once did in his rookie season, catch a ball in left center field, away from his throwing arm, then spin in a whirlwind after the catch, and throw a speedy runner tagging up at third—Brooklyn's Billy Cox—out at the plate. Whitey Lockman, the cutoff man on that astonishing play, said later that Mays's throw had passed him with the velocity of a throw from the infield. Catcher Wes Westrum, who had not expected a play at the plate, didn't even remove his mask. Cox, the base runner, gasped in disbelief as the ball beat him to the plate by three feet. Charlie Dressen, the Brooklyn manager, was stunned to incoherence. "I'd like to see him do that again," he finally said.

Then, of course, there was the interborough center-fielder competition. Who was the better—Willie, Mickey, or the Duke? It was all storybook material. And these were the fifties, it should be remembered. Sportswriters then were writing paeans, not indictments.

At this considerable distance from those extraordinary times, it is also

In spite of his lustrous career, Mays failed to win unanimous election to the Hall of Fame.

"If Jesus Christ were to show up with his old baseball glove, some guys wouldn't vote for him. He dropped the cross three times, didn't he."—Dick Young, New York Daily News, *January 24, 1979.*

Courtesy UPI/Bettmann News photos

possible to detect the presence of racism in Mays's New York experience. Blacks had been in the major leagues for only four years when Willie joined the Giants. The pioneer had been Jackie Robinson, who had played for another New York team. Robinson was a man who defied the stereotypes: he was a Californian, not a Southerner; a college-educated war veteran, not a refugee from a sharecropper's cabin; and a fiery freethinker, not an acquiescent shuffler. Robinson wasn't even a kid; he was twenty-eight when he joined the Dodgers as a rookie in 1947. He was a brilliant and exciting player and courageous beyond recounting, but he was hardly the sort of black man a white fan could take to heart in the decade after World War II. Mays was even more gifted, and his surface appeal was more to the stereotype. He was just right. Even the name, "Willie," fit the bill.

The Giants had four blacks on the major league roster—third baseman Henry Thompson, outfielder Monte Irvin, infielder Artie Wilson, and catcher Rafael Noble—before Mays was brought up in May 1951. Durocher argued persistently that if the team was to be a contender he needed the twenty-year-old center fielder immediately. Owner Stoneham was reluctant. Mays had only one season in the minor leagues. Besides, with the four blacks the team already had, the Giants could be the first big-league team to field a predominantly black lineup, a civil rights gesture Stoneham was then loath to make. But Durocher, no enlightened advocate of racial equality but a sound baseball man, prevailed. Mays was called up on May 24 and given uniform number 24. The team was 6 and 20 at the time, but the Miracle of Coogan's Bluff was only a few months distant. To make room for the young savior, Artie Wilson, age thirty, was sent to the minors, never to return. Wilson had played with Mays on the Birmingham Black Barons in the Negro League, had been, with Piper Davis, his mentor and protector and, in a sense, his discoverer, since it was he who first urged the Giants to sign him. It's a tough business.

The Mays personality, or rather the personality chosen for him, seemed frozen in place during those New York years. Never as endearingly childish off the field as he was made to appear, his zestful play on it tended to reinforce the image. A different sort of Mays began to appear, however, in 1956, the year Durocher left the team. The Lip's successor, Bill Rigney, was only thirty-seven, hardly a father figure. Far closer to the rest of the team than his predecessor had been, Rigney quickly realized that in coddling the star Durocher had succeeded in alienating many of the other players, particularly the veterans. Willie, therefore, stopped getting the Durocher treatment, and, as with any spoiled child, he reacted queru-

When Mays first came to New York he with a family in the Harlem ghetto, stickball was the indigenous sport. much he actually played the game is tionable, although in an autobiograp credits stickball as an "eye-sharpener

Courtesy UPI/Bettmann News photos

The catch: "[Vic] Wertz hit the ball a ___
way. But it was to straight center in the ___
Grounds, and you could hit 'em a lon___
to straight center at the Polo Grou___
turned my back and ran, looked ov___
shoulder once to gauge the flight of the ___
then kept running. I caught it the ___
football end catches a long leading ___
Then I spun and threw . . . my ca___
off."—Willie Mays

"But the throw! What an aston___
throw, to make all other throws ever ___
it, even those four Mays himself had ___
during fielding practice, appear the fli___
teenage girls. This was the throw of a ___
the throw of a howitzer made huma___
Arnold Hano, A Day in the Bleache___

Courtesy AP/Wide World

lously to the slight. Still, he remained an innocent in the eyes of the public. But Rigney felt the resentment.

When Mays, Rigney, and the Giants moved West in 1958, there was no need to maintain pretense. The man-child didn't disappear; he just started to grow up. Far too much has been written about San Francisco's supposed rejection of Mays. It has been said that Willie wasn't welcome because he somehow violated the memory of the town's one true center fielder, Joe DiMaggio. An interesting enough analysis, but it had been twenty-three years since DiMaggio had played in a San Francisco uniform. An entire generation had grown to maturity remembering him as a Yankee and a husband of Marilyn Monroe. DiMaggio, the local boy who made good, will forever remain in the San Francisco sporting pantheon, but he was scarcely a rival for Mays in 1958. The town was ready for a new star.

What is true is that there was a certain resentment among the city's fans in having a ready-made star force-fed to them. They were being told, mostly by New Yorkers, that if they didn't revere this baseball colossus, they were no fans at all. The question seemed to be, "Does San Francisco really deserve Willie Mays?" The answer was, "Let's have a look at him first." Mays had to live up to his own reputation, to demonstrate that he was worthy of the adulation demanded of him.

In truth, there were skeptics that first season. Mays was getting his hits, but too many of them seemed to be infield bleeders, not heroic drives. He was the holdover celebrity on a team with a number of exciting new players—Orlando Cepeda, Jimmy Davenport, Felipe Alou, Willie Kirkland, Bob Schmidt—who were building their own fresher reputations. The fans warmed to these young Giants, and they responded with a surprising third-place finish. Mays hit .347, the highest average of his career, and led the league with 121 runs scored and 31 stolen bases. But he hit *only* 29 homers and drove in *only* 96 runs, figures actually comparable to his final season in the Polo Grounds—35 and 97. It was, nevertheless, an excellent season for him, even if it didn't measure up to his advance buildup. No player, not even Mays, could have been as good as the Giants had said he was before the season. Because they had no way of forecasting the success of the rookies, Mays was the only product the team's publicists had to sell, and they sold him hard. Maybe a little too hard. San Franciscans are unusually proud of their sophistication, and they don't like to be taken for bumpkins.

From this rather guarded response to him in the first season, and from the team's late-season fade in 1959 and a fifth-place finish in 1960, word

"Willie Mays combined the skills of fielding, throwing, bunting, hitting for distance and hitting for average better than anyone else in baseball history. For my money, he was the best. . . . And he had the other magic ingredient that turns a superstar into a super superstar. He lit up the room when he came in. He was a joy to be around."—Leo Durocher

Courtesy UPI/Bettmann News photos

spread that San Francisco fans were blind to Mays's greatness. During Nikita Khrushchev's visit to the city in the summer of 1959, Frank Coniff, then national editor of the Hearst papers, was impelled to comment, "What a city! They cheer Khrushchev and boo Willie Mays." Willie should've never left New York, New Yorkers were saying. The truth is, of course, that all ball players, even demigods, get booed. DiMaggio was booed in Yankee Stadium, Williams in Fenway Park. Had Mays remained in the Polo Grounds he would have been booed there. It may have taken Willie somewhat longer to catch on in his new home than expected, but that can be blamed on a big buildup and a show-me attitude. Still, it didn't take long for the fans and the star to hit it off as they were intended to do. And when he carried the team to the brink of a Series win in 1962—his ninth-inning double in the seventh game might have scored the tying run—Willie Mays became a true San Francisco hero. There would always be many more cheers than boos for him in Candlestick Park.

Where image and reality were least compatible was with the Mays persona. San Franciscans had been led to believe they were getting some kind of black Tom Sawyer. They got someone quite different. Mays was never, even as a twenty-year-old rookie, a true naif. He was as uncomfortable as most rookies are, but he was buoyed by a supreme confidence, and he was never terrified. He was the oldest child in a family of twelve, and he was always the best athlete in any sport in his hometown of Fairfield, Alabama, a mill town outside Birmingham. Mays told me several years ago that the only time he was ever genuinely scared—"scared to death"— was when he left home for the first time at sixteen to play for the Chattanooga Black Lookouts. But at seventeen he was a star with the Birmingham Black Barons, earning $600 a month before he graduated from high school. "You know," he said, "the crowds never bothered me when I went up to the big leagues. At Birmingham we were drawing eighteen thousand, nineteen thousand a game. I had no problems with crowds."

San Francisco is an extraordinarily compact city, crammed as it is on a peninsula. It is tightknit. A person can't get lost there as one can in New York. Mays quickly passed under the magnifying glass, and there was no Durocher to shield him. It was obvious from the first that he was no kid. He got divorced in San Francisco from his first wife, Marghuerite. He got into some financial difficulties, partly as a result of the divorce, and had to be bailed out by a local banker. His stickball days were clearly behind him. In fact, he became one of the team's toughest autographs, liable as

"I can remember one ball I caught never hoped to catch. Ed Bouchee Cubs . . . hit a sharp liner, good de[ ] right center. I ran to cut it off . . . and past me, not only past me, but bendin[ ] farther away from me in the wind. At t[ ] minute I literally stuck out the glo[ ] snatched it out of the air when it wa[ ] me. . . . Charley Doherty, the San Fra[ ] Examiner *photographer, has a pict[ ] that catch."—Willie Mays*

Courtesy *San Francisco Examiner*

not to bust through a crowd of well-wishers as stay behind and mingle. He was occasionally abrupt with the press. He was late for appointments or he didn't show at all. He sometimes seemed cavalier about his obligations to the public. He openly resented the fact, he said later, that fans seemed to think "they owned you." On the field, he pretty much went his own way, and he could make life difficult for any manager, Clyde King notably, who didn't recognize his independence. He was happiest playing for Herman Franks, an old Durocher man who let him put himself in and take himself out of the lineup when he felt like it. He was very much like the rest of us—far from perfect.

But he could always play. It is debatable if there ever has been a player with Mays's baseball instincts or, yes, intellect. The exquisite subtleties of his play eventually became apparent to the fans. He would glide on the bases, cruising at half-speed, watching the opposing outfielder for the slightest hesitation, then, with a burst, take the extra base. Or, for that matter, he would purposely not take the extra base so as to preserve a meaningful time-at-bat for his cleanup hitter, Willie McCovey. Why stretch a single into a double if that would leave first base open and invite an intentional walk to McCovey and nullify his home run bat? Mays would even on occasion deliberately swing and miss at a pitch early in a game because he would want to see that pitch again later when he could drive it for perhaps the winning run.

And oh how he could catch the ball, racing under long drives with that effortless glide, tapping his glove, cap flying behind him. It was, he has said, the favorite part of the game for him—"I loved running that ball down." The catch he made off Vic Wertz in center field at the Polo Grounds in the 1954 World Series is his most celebrated, but, according to him, "I made a lot of catches better than that." And, as with the play on Cox, he always knew what to do with the ball after he caught it. Charles Einstein, a Mays biographer, has told of a play Willie once made on Hank Aaron when both were at the top of their games. With Aaron on first, Mays caught a line drive in right center field with his back to the infield. Aaron had been running with the pitch and was past second base when the catch was made. In trouble now, he quickly hurried back to first, fully expecting a Mays throw there. That would have been the expected play. But Mays threw instead to second. This confused even second baseman Tito Fuentes. Then he saw Mays urging him to touch the base. Fuentes, still confused, did, and Aaron was called out. In retreating to first, Aaron had missed second base. But how did Mays know this? His back was turned when Aaron was at second. Simple. He told Einstein that he

noticed Aaron reproaching himself with a downward thrust of the head and a little punch in the air and figured that he hadn't touched the bag. That's beyond heads-up baseball. That's closer to mind reading.

Mays was deeply disappointed when Stoneham traded him to the Mets in 1972, because he had hoped to finish his career that year with the Giants. But, predictably, he got a hero's welcome in New York, and with Mrs. Payson's prodding, agreed to play one more season. He should not have. When he returned to the Bay Area for the 1973 World Series, his decline seemed complete. In the ninth inning of game two against the Athletics at the Oakland Coliseum, he set off in pursuit of a line drive by Deron Johnson, the sort of ball he would have routinely caught only a few years earlier, and fell flat on his face. Flat on his face before fifty thousand fans and a national television audience. "Willie would've had it," a reporter in the press box remarked more in sadness than jest.

The Say Hey Kid had become, in baseball time, an old man. His supremacy is now etched in his remarkable statistics. "I don't have any records," he said not long ago, "but whatever records there are, I'm there in the top ten. That's the kind of player I wanted to be—an across-the-board kind." And so he was, as career totals of 3,283 hits, 660 home runs, 2,062 runs, 1,903 RBIs, and 338 stolen bases strongly attest. But these are merely numbers. They cannot show the flying cap, the basket catch, the quick feet, the whirl, and throw that are etched not in record books but in precious memory.

The Mets kept Willie on for a time as a coach of sorts, but he found he couldn't watch a game he wasn't playing in, so he moved on. In 1980, after he had accepted a job with the Bally's casino in Atlantic City as a promotion man, Commissioner Bowie Kuhn banned him from holding any salaried job in the game. In 1985, one of Commissioner Peter Ueberroth's first and most popular acts was to reinstate him, along with another casino employee, Mickey Mantle. The Giants, whose president, Al Rosen, once worked for a casino himself, brought him back to Candlestick in 1986 as, Mays's business card informs, a "Special Assistant to the President and General Manager." He was a familiar, if slightly chunkier, figure in the Candlestick clubhouse all year, bantering easily with players he mistakenly feared would not warm to him. His old teammate, McCovey, joined him in this role, and together they brought a sense of history to a young team, as well as, according to Manager Roger Craig, "a sense of what it's like to be a winner."

Willie Mays is still a legend. It surprises him and pleases him that he is so fondly remembered. He's prospering in a variety of business enter-

(Opposite, top) *In 1955, Mays (far left) roamed the outfield for the Santurce Crabs of Puerto Rico. His colleagues included (from left to right) a Pittsburgh prospect named Roberto Clemente; James Clarkson, who never reached the bigs; Bob Thurman, a Cincinnati hopeful; and George Crowe, who lasted nine seasons in the majors.*

Courtesy NBL

(Opposite, bottom) *"I'm foolish about Willie Mays. He is just full of intellectual energy. He kind of lets everything go for the end in view. Quite scientific and he certainly gets around the bases."—Marianne Moore*

Courtesy NBL

(Following pages) *Reduced to a bit player in his final season with the New York Mets, Willie even lost a debate with umpire Augie Donatelli during the World Series at Oakland. "[Mays] was the ultimate combination of the professional full of talent and the amateur, a word that traces to the Latin 'amator' and suggests one who brings a passion to what he does."—Roger Kahn*

Courtesy Oakland Tribune

(Left) *Jackie Robinson congratulated*
after the Giants clinched the 1954 pe
against the Dodgers.

Courtesy UPI/Bettmann News photos

prises, and he's back, at least on a part-time basis, in his game. But it's
"the big world" that involves him now. He has a sense of himself, of the
significance of his actions, that he admits he never had before. The young
Mays, abrupt, sometimes inconsiderate, is gone with the image that protected him. He can still smile when he doesn't mean it, but he now means
it more often than not. DiMaggio, never a rival but a good friend, and
he were in the first class of enshrinees—along with Hank Luisetti and Bill
Russell in basketball and Ernie Nevers in football—in the Bay Area
Sports Hall of Fame. Mays's acceptance speech that night was stunning
in its graciousness, since he spent far more time talking about DiMaggio,
"my idol," than about himself. And he was on hand again at Candlestick
Park late in the 1986 season for a day honoring McCovey's induction into
the Baseball Hall of Fame. The convertible carrying him to the reviewing
stand had scarcely passed the outfield gate when a tremendous roar issued
from the stands. For five minutes, the fans, there ostensibly to honor
McCovey, stood and cheered for Willie Mays. And when it was McCovey's
turn to speak, he said, eloquently, "Willie Mays, it was an honor to wear
the same uniform you wore." Mays lowered his head in respect.

   Image and reality. In the beginning, they weren't very close for Willie
Mays. The Say Hey Kid was only an image. The odd thing is that now,
in his middle years, he's actually closing the gap. His career is only a
shining memory, but the man achieves new stature every day. He may
not be the Say Hey Kid; he probably never was. But he's much more than
that now. He's a good man.

John F. Kennedy, elected president in 1960, spoke of "the new frontier" and the "passing of the torch," as he sounded his trumpet for bold initiative and "viggah." For organized baseball, too, the decade began with a harbinger of change. After nineteen years of active service, sandwiching two Marine tours, Ted Williams retired in 1960. He had logged 521 home runs, compiled a lifetime .344 average, the best by far of any man in baseball since Rogers Hornsby laid down his club. In Williams's final game, he fulfilled great expectations with a huge home run to center field. His farewell dramaturgy fittingly produced a pair of highly praised essays, "The Kid's Last Game" by Ed Linn in *Sport* and John Updike's "Hub Fans Bid Kid Adieu" in the *New Yorker*. Linn accurately delineated Williams's curmudgeonesque attitude toward the press, his intensive concentration on his craft, and his unbending honesty, and summed him up as "sometimes unbearable but never dull." Updike captured the essence of Williams the demigod—"he knew how to do . . . the hardest thing. Quit." As a rookie, Ted confided: "All I want out of life is that when I walk down the street folks will say, 'There goes the greatest hitter who ever lived.' " Few have come closer to their deepest wish.

With clubs added in Los Angeles and Minneapolis, the American League in 1961 enlarged to ten teams, breaking the limitations of eight to each major league set at the 1903 peace treaty. The next year the National League followed suit, opening operations in Houston and New York. The newborn Mets became a symbol of expansion futility, but with Casey Stengel as chief nanny, the infant became the darling of those disaffected by the flight of the Giants and Dodgers. Baseball planted major league flags in four more cities in 1969: Montreal, Seattle, San Diego, and Kansas City (the previous tennants having trekked to Oakland a year earlier). The Washington Senators fled to Arlington, Texas, to be resurrected as the Texas Rangers in 1972. The American League, five years later, added Toronto and Seattle (the earlier incarnation had decamped to Milwaukee, replacing the National League Braves who had migrated to Atlanta). The result was fourteen American League and twelve National League entries.

Still, even as the Splendid Splinter removed himself from the scene and baseball redrew its map, there was a sense of order in the world. In the American League, the Yankee colossus bestrode the heap, with Casey Stengel in charge for 1960, Ralph Houk for the next three World Series years, and Yogi Berra for 1964.

Chairman of the Board Whitey Ford recorded his two most profitable years, 25–4 in 1961 and 24–7 in 1963. The five pennants from 1960 to 1964 enabled the debonair left-hander to set the highest marks for World Series participation: 10 wins, 8 losses, 22 games started, 146 total innings, 94 strikeouts, 34 bases on balls. His effectiveness also attracted allegations that his technique included illegal spitters and various forms of ball defacement. Twenty years after he retired, Ford, also known as "Slick," confessed that in his final two seasons he occasionally threw a mudball or cut the cover with a specially manufactured ring. But his glory years occurred well before that time; his impressive string of firsts in World Series, wins, losses, innings pitched, and strikeouts all predate his illegalities.

Ford's exploits were aided and abetted by a number of sources. Yogi Berra, now a baseball senior citizen, while hitting a few points below his final lifetime figure of .285, homered 55 times over the four seasons. The club's first black regular, Elston Howard, caught more and more games. Mickey Mantle walloped 40 homers in 1960 and improved to 54 the following year, in which he and Roger Maris vied for a challenge to Ruth, until Roger pulled away in the last month when Mickey missed several games because of injuries. Like Ford, Mantle's participation in so many championships enabled him to pocket some top World Series honors: first in home runs (18), runs (42), RBIs (40), walks (43), and the dubious distinction, strikeouts (54).

But while the Yanks dominated their league during these five years, they were less successful against their National League adversaries. In 1960, the Pittsburgh Pirates offered a neatly balanced presentation, no regular below .260 and a pair of .300 hitters, five pitchers in double figures, and great strength up the middle, starting with catcher Smoky Burgess and moving out to shortstop Dick Groat, second baseman Bill Mazeroski,

Chairman of the Board, Whitey Fo *himself in the World Series record boo. his performances of the 1950s and . "I don't care what the situation wa high the stakes were—the bases co loaded and the pennant riding on pitch, it never bothered Whitey. He [his game. Cool. Crafty. Nerves of . . . While Casey managed us he woul. use Whitey in rotation. He saved him stronger clubs and held him out agai weaker ones. . . . When Ralph Hou over, Whitey really came on, racking wins in 1961, then winning 24 in 1 lead the league in wins and percentag years."—Mickey Mantle*, The Mick

Courtesy AP/Wide World

President John F. Kennedy who spoke of "the new frontier" threw out the first ball in 1961 as baseball sailed onto the choppy, unchartered seas of new franchises, new cities, playoffs, and unions. Some old faces hovered around Kennedy. Behind his throwing hand is Democratic Senator Hubert Humphrey and to the President's right, Vice-President Lyndon B. Johnson. Directly behind Kennedy is the Senate Republican chief, Everett McKinley Dirksen and to his left, Senator Mike Mansfield. Behind Dirksen, Baseball Commissioner Ford Frick observes the presidential pitching form. In the baseball suits are White Sox manager Al Lopez and Senator straw boss Mickey Vernon.

Courtesy *Washington Post*

(Left) *Put out to pasture by the New York Yankees, Casey Stengel was hired by General Manager George Weiss to parade the Mets through the hearts of the hometown rooters.*

Courtesy NBL

(Following pages) *A remarkable photograph tells the story of the seventh and deciding game of the 1960 World Series between the Yankees and the Pirates. The Forbes Field scoreboard shows a 9–9 tie in the last of the ninth. Bill Mazeroski of Pittsburgh has just hit a high drive, the ball above and to the right of the clock clears the fence to bring the championship to the Pirates.*

Courtesy Marvin Newman

and a fine center fielder, Bill Virdon.

Ford threw two shutouts and the Yankees outscored their opponents 55 runs to 27. They outhit them .338 to .256, and with Mantle notching a trio and Maris a pair, they smacked 10 homers to the Pirates' measly 4. But Pittsburgh prevailed through the ultimate blow. Deadlocked at 3 games each, the teams met for the finale at Forbes Field. New York gained a 7–4 lead going into the bottom of the eighth, but after a simple grounder caromed off a pebble and struck shortstop Tony Kubek in the throat, the Pirates rallied for 5 runs. Still, the American Leaguers tied the affair with 2 in the top of the ninth. The first of the Pirates to face Yankee Ralph Terry (also known as Tom Edison for a penchant to experiment) in the home half was Bill Mazeroski. He belted a ball over the center-field scoreboard to give the Pirates a 10–9 win and the championship.

Although he engaged in no celebrated heroics during the Series, the most distinguished member of the victorious team had come off the first of eight consecutive .300- or-better seasons, to be followed by four out of five in his last years. Roberto Clemente, a native of San Juan, Puerto Rico, was working his way through the Dodger chain when the Pirates acquired his contract. The best explanation for the lapse in Dodger judgment is that early in his career Clemente was something of an enigma. He labored nine professional seasons before he achieved .300 (in his second major league season). He fooled the most expert witnesses. Said Robin Roberts:

> . . . he was the most unorthodox good ballplayer I ever saw. Most good ballplayers are smooth. They do things with rhythm. Well, Roberto had his own rhythm. He looked like he was falling apart when he ran. Looked like he was coming apart when he threw. His stance at the plate was ridiculous. When he swung he'd lunge and hit bad balls. There was no way he could hit the ball like that. But no one told Roberto that. . . . He really looked less like a ballplayer than anyone I've ever seen. It was a crazy thing. The only thing that made him look sensational was the results.

It was not just the crackle of base hits that distinguished Clemente; he ran the bases and pursued even the most distant fly balls with fury. Wrote Roger Angell after Clemente batted .414 in the 1971 World Series: "[He played] a kind of baseball that none of us had ever seen before—throwing and running and hitting at something close to the level of absolute perfection, playing to win but also playing the game almost as if it were a form of punishment for everyone else on the field." When he died in a plane crash while bringing relief supplies to victims of a Nicaraguan earthquake, he was thirty-eight years old, still clubbing the ball at well over .300.

Cincinnati faced the Yankees in 1961, and while the Reds lost the Series, the lineup was graced by another ball crusher, Frank Robinson. Physically closer to the Aaron mold, Robinson mirrored the ferocity of Clemente. Angell described him as a slugger of fearsome power (fourth in home runs behind Aaron, Ruth, and Mays) "whose customary stance at the plate was that of an impatient subway traveler leaning over the edge of the platform and peering down the tracks for the D train." Others spoke of a pronounced tendency to hang his head in "concussion alley." He topped all comers in six of his ten National League seasons for the dubious honor of most times hit by a pitch. On four occasions a bean ball felled him.

Forceful assertion marked his efforts all over the field. In his rookie year he charged into the outfield fences five times. He was lethal to himself and others on the base paths. During an attempt to steal home against the Pirates, the catcher stepped on his left arm. Ron Hunt of the Mets leaped to avoid a Robinson slide and when he landed, his spikes cut deep into Frank's biceps. Sliding into third against the Braves, Robinson held his hands over his face. Still, the tag by Eddie Mathews swiped his nose bloody. As he rose to walk off, he removed his helmet and Mathews took that gesture as a challenge to fight. Along with his battered nose, Robinson carried off a contused cheekbone, cut lower lip, bruised thumb, and swollen eye. He played the second game of the doubleheader, although while at bat he was obliged to call time in order to pack gauze in his oozing nose wound. During his stint with the Orioles, he tried to break up a double play with a slide into Chicago second baseman Al Weis, whose knee slammed into his head. Robinson lay unconscious for five minutes

"The Yankee staff would hold a[...]every week and talk about the ball c[...]every week they'd ask me, 'You gon[...]a catcher out of Berra?' And I kept[...]them off because I hadn't seen en[...]him. Finally I gave them their an[...]think he ought to make a pret[...]catcher.' . . . He became one of t[...]all-time great catchers of baseb[...]tory."—Bill Dickey

"Stengel . . . has a deep admire[...]the man who 'feels' the game, whose[...]and reflexes are perfectly geared to[...]ronment of 98-mph pitches, 200-po[...]runners with spikes high, sudden v[...]in the age-old theme of bat, ball ar[...]No one feels baseball better than Yo[...]no one relishes the excitement of its[...]tion more, no one reacts more quic[...]constant challenge. He is a masterp[...]ballplayer.—Robert Creamer, Spo[...]trated

Courtesy UPI/Bettmann News photos[...]

but finally rose and walked off, albeit troubled by double vision. Weis needed knee surgery to repair his damage.

After ten years Cincinnati traded him to Baltimore. Redleg executive Bill DeWitt explained, "Robinson is not a young 30 years of age." Robinson demonstrated the acuity of DeWitt's perception with a Triple Crown* in his first Oriole year, earning the MVP award to make him the only man ever to be so honored in both leagues (1961 with the Reds). He continued his exploits in the Series, carrying off MVP for the world championships.

During his six years with Baltimore he averaged .300 and was an integral figure on four World Series clubs. Among other attributes Robinson possessed inspirational qualities. Averages and power of other Birds ascended when he came to the Orioles while the fellows he left behind fell into a steep decline. In his first month in Baltimore he launched a Luis Tiant low-and-inside pitch 451 feet on the fly, the first ball ever knocked out of the cavernous Memorial Stadium. If that failed to bring a *presto* beat in the breasts of his associates, there was a play against New York at Yankee Stadium. The Orioles led in the bottom of the ninth, 7–5, but two Yanks were on base when Roy White lined one toward the lower right-field seats, the resting place for so many homers by the likes of Ruth, Gehrig, Mantle, and Maris. Robinson backed up, then leaped at the ultimate microsecond. His body rose high above the low wall and then toppled backward into the seats. Umpire Hank Soar ran over to discover Robinson emerging, ball in glove, and thumbed White out. Robinson's intelligence and his gift for dealing with men earned him the role of the first black to manage a major league club, as well as the unhappy distinction of being the first to be canned from such a post after he served with Cleveland and then San Francisco.

The 1962 show introduced San Francisco to the World Series. The Bay Area fans saw the prime of Willie Mays—49 home runs, 141 RBIs for the season. But the play of two younger Giants clamored for notice. The second Willie, McCovey, ★ surfaced in 1959 as

a first baseman. At 6'4", "Stretch" composed a great target for infielders, but to accommodate Orlando Cepeda, management exiled McCovey to the outfield for three years. Less than an instant success in his new position, McCovey heard the yawps of boo birds. San Franciscans could also complain that he made the last out in a 1–0 game with a pair of Giants on base, ending the 1962 World Series to the Yankees with a blistering line drive into Bobby Richardson's glove. (Pitching for the Yanks was the same Ralph Terry who gave up Mazeroski's homer a year earlier.)

But McCovey persevered to become a passable outfielder and his bat, a whippy 34-ounce model he adopted on the advice of Ted Williams, made him a crowd favorite. His 521 homers is the highest mark for a National League lefty. He tops everyone in his league for bases-loaded home runs (18). (Gehrig's 23 beats all.) Three times McCovey posted the best slugging percentage. Three times he blasted a trio of homers in a single game.

Also starring for the 1962 Giants was a Dominican Republic native, Juan Marichal, ★ whose extravagantly high kick with his left leg not only added leverage but also hid the ball a tick longer. Ancients compared him to Dazzy Vance. Marichal worked a typewriter keyboard to keep his fingers nimble, squeezed a rubber ball very fast for finger strength, and fussed over the length of his fingernails because too short or too long meant a loss of ball feel.

Said Henry Aaron:

The foot's up in your face, and that's bad. Then he comes through like a fullback charging. He lunges off the hill. Sometimes he even stumbles from the force of his delivery. With all that confusion of motion it's a problem seeing the ball. But his control is a bigger thing. He can throw all day within a two-inch space, in, out, up or down. I've never seen anyone as good as that.

In his third season, Marichal won 18 games, although he pitched only 4 innings in the Series before retiring with an injury. He improved to a better-than-20-game winner in

The only fellow ever to receive the Most Valuable Player Award in both leagues, Frank Robinson did not fear pitchers, outfield walls, or bigots.

Courtesy Paul Tepley

"He just doesn't get intimidated by beanballs or brushback pitches. He [Robinson] merely picks himself out of the dirt, dusts himself off, digs in deeper and becomes more formidable than ever."—Arthur Daley, New York Times

Courtesy AP/Wide World

---

*The Triple Crown, top average, most homers, most RBIs in a league, has been attained only sixteen times, with two players, Rogers Hornsby (1922, 1925) and Ted Williams (1942, 1947), double winners. Others, aside from Robinson, are: Paul Hines (1878), Hugh Duffy (1894), Nap Lajoie (1901), Ty Cobb (1909), Heinie Zimmerman (1912), Chuck Klein (1933), Jimmie Foxx (1933), Lou Gehrig (1934), Joe Medwick (1937), Mickey Mantle (1956), and Carl Yastrzemski (1967).

Robinson toppled into the stands with *kee Roy White's homer bid in 1966 as* *the Orioles to a pennant.*

Courtesy AP/Wide World

six of the next seven years, striking out more than two hundred in each of those stellar seasons.

In 1963, he and Warren Spahn engaged in an atavistic duel—something from the sports pages of forty or fifty years earlier. For 16 innings, Marichal, on 227 pitches, shut out the Braves. Spahn, even more efficient, used only 200 to reach the bottom of the sixteenth before, with one away, Willie Mays pounded a homer for a 1–0 win. That same season Marichal no-hit Houston.

In 1965, an ugly incident stained the glory of Marichal's earlier achievements. As usual, the two West Coast teams, the Dodgers and Giants, were contending for the pennant. Ill will, the result of disputed decisions, tight pitches, and vague threats, permeated the batter's box as Marichal stepped in for his cuts. When catcher John Roseboro fired the ball to pitcher Sandy Koufax, via Marichal's ear, Juan claimed he whirled and asked for an explanation. Roseboro took off his mask and advanced on Marichal. The Giant pitcher said: "When I saw him come after me with the chest protector and mask, I hit him with the bat. I'm glad I don't get hurt. I feel sorry to use the bat because that's the only thing I do wrong."

Blood streaming from his head, Roseboro charged Marichal. Players from both squads joined in the melee. Principal peace maker was Willie Mays who emerged with his uniform smeared by the residue of Roseboro's wound. Umpire Shag Crawford ejected Marichal and National League President Warren Giles subsequently suspended him for eight days, fining him $1,750. Since San Francisco lost the pennant race by 2 games and Marichal missed a pair of opportunities to start, the affair may have been critical. Costly as it may have been for the club, the price to Marichal was enormous. It would be years before his continued mastery on the mount—138 of his total 243 victories came in succeeding seasons—eradicated the blotch on his reputation.

The Yankees' foes in 1963 were the Los Angeles Dodgers. Yogi Berra was in his first year of managing the Yankees and in spite of a pennant and his long, meritorious career with the club he was dumped after the Series. Walter Alston, ★ the Dodger skipper who owns only one line in *The Baseball Encyclopedia* section on players, was in his tenth

year as Dodger boss. This was the fourth of seven pennant-flying clubs he would guide. The Californians offered their traditional modest offense; six National League contenders hit more homers, three had higher team averages, five scored more runs. But the Dodgers, in what has become their trademark, dominated pitching, thanks probably to the finest starting tandem ever, Sandy Koufax and Don Drysdale, plus the year's best reliever in Ron Perranoski (21 saves, a 1.67 ERA). In the 1963 Series, Los Angeles muffled the American Leaguers' big hitters, allowing them only 4 earned runs in the 4-game set. Koufax won a pair; Drysdale and veteran Johnny Podres, who pitched only a couple of innings during the season, each took a game.

Koufax in his tenth year finally surpassed the great expectations for him. Taken off the University of Cincinnati campus as a bonus boy by Brooklyn in 1955, he came under a short-lived rule that forced clubs to keep such high-priced specimens with the parent club. And for three years, Sandy learned on the major league job instead of studying his art full-time in the minors. As late as 1960 he was operating from a deficit (36–40), hanging on in spite of walking myriads of hitters only because he fanned so many more.

In his final four seasons, beginning with 1963, Koufax won 97 games while dropping only 27. He threw 4 no-hitters and three times whiffed well over three hundred batsmen. Declared Musial: "By the time I hung up my spikes, he was the best pitcher in baseball."

Don Drysdale, the 6′5″ right-handed half of the combination, buttoned on a Dodger shirt the year after Koufax. He was nineteen years old when he squelched the Phillies 6–1, setting down nine on strikeouts. Unlike Koufax, however, Drysdale benefited from a crash course in the minors, spending the summer of 1954 with Bakersfield and all of 1955 with Montreal for a total of 44 starts in organized ball. Dodger pitching coach Joe Becker convinced Drysdale to throw three-quarters rather than full sidearm with his curve in order to add a vertical break to the horizontal deflection. Still, it was the route via third base that bedeviled many opponents, the more so since Drysdale, unlike sidearmer Walter Johnson, was not solici-

They called him "Stretch" and Willie McCovey extended himself into a passable outfielder when obligated to surrender his natural post at first. He finished with 521 homers.

Courtesy AP/Wide World

Quiet man Walter Alston guided the Dodgers for twenty-three years, leading them to their first championship while in Brooklyn and five pennants, two Series titles in Los Angeles.

Courtesy AP/Wide World

tous of enemies' physical well-being. During his career he was often accused of intent to commit bodily harm, and he led pitchers in the hitting of batsmen five of his fourteen seasons. When he clipped Frank Robinson on the wrist after having been warned by an umpire for his brushbacks, he was ejected from a game. However, according to the charts, Drysdale's best (or worst) record of twenty victims falls far short of the forty-one notched by Joe McGinnity while with Brooklyn in 1901.

Drysdale argued that the wounds were not deliberately inflicted but the result of failing to respect his territorial imperative, to wit:

When the ball is over the middle of the plate, the batter is hitting it with the sweet part of the bat. When it's inside, he's hitting it with the part of the bat from the handle to the trademark; when it's outside, he's hitting it with the end of the bat. You've got to keep the ball away from the sweet part of the bat. To do that the pitcher has to move the hitter off the plate.

He was tutored in the lore of knockdowns by Sal Maglie who practiced his preachments for both the New York Giants and the Dodgers. Maglie, according to Drysdale, theorized: "It's not the first one, it's the second one. The second one makes the hitter know you meant the first one."

He confessed to enlarging upon the biblical eye for an eye: "My own little rule was two for one—if one of my teammates got knocked down, then I knocked down two on the other team."

Drysdale set major league records for consecutive shutouts (6) in 1968 and during his string established a mark of 58 straight innings without a tally. He posted six seasons of more than 200 strikeouts. Drysdale wound down his career with a total of 209 victories.

In 1964, in their final World Series appearance of the decade, the Yankees succumbed to the St. Louis Cardinals. Three homers by Mantle and strong pitching from rookie Mel Stottlemyre and Jim Bouton (who would be remembered more for his book than for his hurling) could not overcome the Redbirds, who captured a 7-game Series.

On June 15, 1964, the Cardinals had swapped field hands with the Chicago Cubs. The Cards obtained a seemingly unspectacu-

lar outfielder whose best major league effort during his two-and-a-half-year career was .263. When he joined St. Louis, Lou Brock lay becalmed at .251 but the change of venue wrought miraculous improvement. During his 103 games for his new club, Brock batted .348 and he gave the team a base stealer whose eventual total of 938 stolen bases bumped Ty Cobb with his 892 out of first place. Eight separate seasons the speedy Brock outburglarized everyone and his high of 118 thefts is surpassed only by Rickey Henderson's 130 in 1982. His batting average hovered around the .300 mark for the remainder of his nineteen years with the exception of a .221 in 1978. Unwilling to retire on such a base note, Brock at age forty played one more year, toting up a .304 mark and his 3,023rd hit. Brock needed to be a high-average hitter in order to become a great base stealer, because as a free swinger he went down on strikes often, placing a surprising fifth on the all-time list. But his approach with the bat as on the bases was pure aggression.

When Brock committed his 118 robberies, he was already thirty-five years old and a step slower than ten years earlier, he said. But he studied pitchers as if they were textbook problems. He clocked their movements with a stopwatch, timed catchers' throws, noted first sackers' patterns for holding runners. During spring training, he filmed the motions of men like Drysdale and then pored over the pictures, almost frame by frame.

Along with his science, Brock brought "arrogance"—his word. "You know you're always on the verge of disaster as a base stealer. If you're thrown out, you could be wiping out a potential rally. But you have to have utter confidence. You've got to figure that you'll steal four out of five times. And if they catch you, well then they owe you four."

He paid a price. "You brace your slide—if you slide feet first—with your hand. Pretty soon, the pain is terrible. At one point in 1974, I could hardly hold a glass of water."

Tom Seaver, with twenty major league seasons in his right arm, said: "Lou Brock, along with Maury Wills, are probably the two players most responsible for the biggest change in the game over the last 15 years—the stolen base."

(Opposite, top and bottom) *Juan Marichal of San Francisco kicked high, leg and shoe distracting and obscuring hitters' views, sufficient for six 20-game winning years, a no-hitter, and nomination to ten all-star squads.*

Courtesy AP/Wide World

(Following page) *Don Drysdale of the Los Angeles Dodgers in 1968 fired 58⅔ consecutive scoreless innings to surpass both the National League record of 46⅓ set by Carl Hubbell (1933) and the previous all-time figure of 56 run up by Walter Johnson (1913). The streak included 6 straight shutouts, wiping out a mark made by Guy Harris in 1904.*

"Home plate is 17 inches wide. But to Don Drysdale it is divided into three parts— the inside four inches, the middle nine inches and the outside four inches. To him only the middle part belongs to the hitter; the inside and outside parts belong to the pitcher."—Dave Anderson, New York Times

Courtesy UPI/Bettmann News photos

Statistics support Seaver's contention. During the early 1920s, the league figures for steals fluctuated between nearly 700 and 1,000. But after 1925 they dipped downward; even more significantly, the pennant winners increasingly eschewed theft. Why should the Yanks or Cardinals or Athletics gamble on a rally snuffing out the potential for the 2- or 3-run homer?

The steal steadily declined in attractiveness until men like Luis Aparicio, the Dodgers' Maury Wills, and Lou Brock revived it as a weapon, beginning in the late 1950s. To be sure, Jackie Robinson won acclaim for his steals but his best was 37 and Mays actually led the league four times, with totals of 40, 38, 31, and 27. Until the age of Aparicio, Wills, and Brock, league totals languished between 300 and 450 thefts per season. By the 1980s, the overall figures approximated those of sixty years earlier.

Brock was credited as the catalyst in the Cardinal mix of talent but no one came to the park with a more feral yearning to win than Bob Gibson, ★ the right-hander good for 251 victories over a seventeen-year span. His 7 Series wins are second only to Whitey Ford's 10.

Gibson's introduction to his profession was dismal. Instructed by club officials in 1958 to report to the Florida spring training hotel, Gibson, a Nebraska native, found himself dispatched by the desk clerk to a private house in the black ghetto. "It was a terrible shame and disappointment," said Gibson, who quickly became known as a fellow unwilling to tailor his pride to fit circumstances. And by 1962 pressure from Gibson, along with Bill White and Curt Flood, opened up the Cardinal hotels in Florida to black ball players.

That year also marked the first glow of his nova as he struck out 208 hitters, winning 15 games for the sixth-place Cardinals. He whiffed 200 or better eight additional seasons. Gibson threw a fastball that sailed away from righties and in on their opposite numbers. In velocity it compared with that of Sandy Koufax. The movement he imparted by cutting the ball—his forefinger and middle finger flicked downward on release—resembled a slider but that pitch, also in his repertoire, sashayed at a more deliberate pace. He varied his fastball on occasion,

changing the grip to produce a heater that broke down. Gibson created awesome power by synchronizing his swift, slinglike arm motion to a sustained forward thrust of his long legs, climaxed by a touchdown to earth of the front foot, with his entire body packed into the ultimate movement.

In July 1967, Roberto Clemente whacked a line drive that smashed Gibson just above his right ankle. The trainer sprayed the injury with a painkiller. Gibson went back to work, walked one hitter, induced Mazeroski to pop up, and then bore down for a 3-and-2 pitch to Donn Clendennon. This time when his right foot hammered the ground, the cracked bone in his leg snapped. He recovered to perform sensationally in the World Series, going on in 1968 to finish 22–9 with an ERA of 1.12, the lowest since Walter Johnson's 1.09 in 1913.

Bob Gibson brought to bear the same kind of intimidating demeanor that marked Early Wynn, and he was at least as compulsive about his turf, the outside part of the plate. Bill White, while with the Cardinals, was a friend but Gibson told Roger Angell that after White was traded, he hit him with a pitch:

Even before Bill was traded I used to tell him that if he ever dived across the plate to swing at an outside pitch, the way he liked to, I'd have to hit him. And then, the very first time, he went for a pitch that was *this* far outside and swung at it, and so I hit him on the elbow with the next pitch. Bill saw it coming, and he yelled, "Yaah!" even before it got him. And I yelled over to him, "You son of a bitch, you went for that outside ball! That pitch, that part of the plate, belongs to *me!* If I ever make a mistake inside, all right, but the outside is mine and don't you forget it." He said, "You're crazy" but he understood me.

Billy Williams, ★ the quiet Cub outfielder whose 426 homers speak clearly for his credentials, said: "Bob Gibson always got *on* with it. . . . You always got the same message from him. 'Look, I'm goin' to throw this pitch and either you hit it or I get your ass out.' You like a guy like that. The infielders are never on their heels out there behind him."

Tim McCarver, who caught Gibson, told Angell: "He was an intimidating, arrogant-

"Base-running arrogance is just like pitching arrogance or hitting arrogance. You are a force and you have to instill that you are a force to the opposition."—Lou Brock

Courtesy AP/Wide World

When required, Brock could apply his larcenous quickness and speed to his outfield job, as in the theft of an extra base hit from the Mets' Dave Kingman.

Courtesy AP/Wide World

looking athlete. The arrogance he projected toward batters was fearsome. There was no guile to his pitching, just him glaring down at that batter. He wanted the game played on his own terms."

His terms accounted for 2 of the Cardinals' wins in the 1964 Series including the final game; he improved to 3 victories against the Red Sox in 1967, including a 1.00 ERA, and 2 out of 3 against the Tigers a year later. In game one against Detroit he whiffed a record seventeen hitters.

Gibson, along with others, proved so effective during 1968 that the combined league batting averages depressed to a low of .237 and more than one-fifth of the games played featured shutouts. The rule makers, fearful that all pitch and no hit makes baseball a dull game, then reduced the height of the mound by one-third, to 10 inches, and drew a more restrictive strike zone.

The Los Angeles Dodgers commandeered control of the National League for 1965, boosted by Koufax (26–8) and Drysdale (23–12). Having cooked such an elegant feast for Dodger interests by winning more than half of the club's total victories. Koufax and Drysdale then stirred the pot with a brand-new ingredient in salary negotiations. They presented themselves in 1966 as an entry, asking for a total of $1 million over a three-year period to secure the services of both men. Furthermore, they hired a Hollywood agent, J. Williams Hayes, to forward their case. Ty Cobb and some colleagues tried to band together before World War I and Joe DiMaggio sought to interpose a third party to his salary bargaining but neither of these efforts succeeded.

The Koufax–Drysdale initiative was not welcomed. Dodger chief Walter O'Malley growled, "I have never discussed a player contract with an agent, and I like to think I never will." The pitchers talked of a film offer, even signed their names to the voluntary retired list. Management finally offered substantial salaries for a single year. Koufax got $130,000 and Drysdale $115,000.

Koufax produced a close facsimile of the previous season with a 27–9 record. Drysdale slumped to 13–16 but Claude Osteen picked up the slack with a 17–14 record as Los Angeles won its second consecutive pennant. However, a new power, the Baltimore Orioles, established themselves with a 4-game sweep of the Dodgers. Two homers from Frank Robinson, 1 from Brooks Robinson, ★ and 3 shutouts destroyed Los Angeles.

The 1965 World Series had pitted the Dodgers against the Minnesota Twins, like the Orioles, first-timers in a championship. It went 7 games but 2 victories for Koufax and 1 each for Drysdale and Osteen gave the title to Los Angeles. The games were noteworthy as the only World Series for a good-natured refugee from the old Washington Senators, Harmon Killebrew. ★

Killebrew had the distinction of having been scouted by a United States Senator; Herman Welker of Idaho cajoled Clark Griffith of the baseball Senators to give his constituent a tryout. Scout Ossie Bluege journeyed to Payette, Idaho, for the Senators and saw the seventeen-year-old "hit the ball a country mile over the left field fence." Unwilling to accept local assurances that the distance was more than 400 feet, Bluege persuaded the club to leave the lights on so that he could measure how far the ball traveled before it came to rest in a beet field. When the tape confirmed the distance at something in the neighborhood of 435 feet, the Senators hired Killebrew. Oddly, Killebrew had never driven a ball over the Payette fence, even during batting practice, before Bluege came to inspect him.

In 1954, at age eighteen, the future "Killer" entered the majors. For five years he stuck with the club as a utility infielder and pinch hitter. In 1959, his first full season of play, he smacked 42 homers to lead the league, as he would five more times. In the field he began at third, shifted to the outfield, and concluded at first base. Never much for average (lifetime .256), Killebrew in twenty-two years banged the fifth highest total of four-basers. Just as telling, he placed third in the frequency of homers per at bats, behind Ruth and Kiner.

The Drysdale–Koufax ploy prior to the 1966 season had bruised a few egos but changed nothing in the basic relationship of management and labor. While attention focused on that ruckus, a greater threat to the old way of doing business stalked spring training. After years of dickering for changes in the standard contract, the players had succeeded only in some improvements in the pension system. They now began to search

Courtesy Walter Iooss

"[Bob] Gibson stretched and threw *and Horton, a righty batter, flinche* *from the pitch, which seemed headed* *rib cage, but the ball, another slide* *abruptly away under his fists and ca* *inside corner of the plate. Tom Gorr* *home-plate umpire, threw up his rigl* *and the game was over. . . . Gibson's* *was Tim McCarver and 12 years* *said, 'I can still see that last pitch,* *bet Willie Horton thinks to this day* *ball hit him—that's how much it* *Talk about a batter* shuddering!' "- *Angell,* Late Innings

". . . the key to his overpowerin *and stuff was not the strength of his* *arm—it was the powerful, driving* *his legs, culminating in that final ex* *which brought his right foot clampi* *on the sloping, left-hand side of the* *with the full weight of his body sl* *and twisting behind it. . . . All in* *pitch and its extended amplificatio* *it look as if Gibson were leaping at t* *with hostile intent. He always look* *closer to the plate at the end than a* *pitcher; he made pitching seem un* Roger Angell, Late Innings

(Opposite) Courtesy Marvin Newman

The forearms and wrists of Chicago C[...]
fielder Billy Williams lashed balls [...]
the ivy-covered bricks of Wrigley Fi[...]

Courtesy UPI/Bettmann News photos

Courtesy AP/Wide World

for a person to push their interests with management. Committee member Robin Roberts contacted Professor George William Taylor of the University of Pennsylvania Wharton School of Finance for advice. Taylor recommended a steel union executive, Marvin Miller. He agreed to assume the job of director of the Players Association, contingent on the approval of the membership. Thus, in the spring of 1966, the soft-spoken, slightly built Miller journeyed south and southwest in search of support. Accepted by almost all of the players, Miller and the Players Association confronted the owners. Collective bargaining had come to organized baseball and in its wake would come huge increases in pensions, strikes, lockouts, soaring salaries, and significant changes in working conditions.

Miller, however, had only begun to make his case as the Dodgers came a cropper in 1966. Baltimore whipped them in 4 games. This was the Orioles' (the transplanted St. Louis Browns) first Series and in addition to the new recruit, Frank Robinson, they had a slightly older Robinson—Brooks—who entered the majors a year before Frank, at third base. Brooks clearly and early established third base as his preserve. He survived twenty-three years fending off chest busters, diving into the hole, turning down-the-line doubles into outs. His closest rivals for chances handled at the position are more than two thousand behind, more than one thousand to the rear in assists. He also heads the list for fielding percentage and, of course, games at third. Until Brooks came along, an adequate glove was considered a bonus to the real prerequisite for a third baseman, a loud bat. His respectable .267 is the lowest

of the seven major-league third sackers in the Hall of Fame. He collected sixteen Gold Gloves for his trophy room but he told William Curran, author of *Mitts,* that in all his years of negotiation for salary, not once did a general manager ever ask: "Brooks, how many runs did you cut off?" Instead the bottom line focused on offense.

While Bob Gibson, coming off his wondrous league season, won 2 games in the 1968 World Series, the Cardinals lost to Detroit. Mickey Lolich, a pitcher who gave every size-portly something to cheer for, allowed a total of 5 runs over his 3 winning games. Even better for the devout Motor City fan was the first Series opportunity for their graying whiz kid, right fielder Al Kaline. ★

A bonus baby out of high school in 1953, it was only two years later that Al Kaline led the league at .340 and gathered 200 hits including 27 homers. Consistency over a twenty-two-year span resulted in 3,007 hits, a lifetime average of .297, and 399 homers. Among Hall of Fame right fielders, Kaline ranks third in slugging average, behind Ruth and Billy Williams.

Doomed to the shadows by the bright lights cast by Mantle and Mays, Kaline at least saw service in one World Series. Ernie Banks put in nineteen years with the Cubs without ever having a chance to display his wares in a championship. His teammate Billy Williams came to Chicago in 1959 and shared the same futility with Banks. As a schoolboy prodigy from Whistler, Alabama (Cub colleagues sometimes called him "Whistler"), Williams met Henry Aaron, who "helped me no end, just by talking baseball with me, telling me about hitting, what to look for, what to expect." Williams per-

(Left) *"[Al] Kaline runs to first and circles the bases with a soft, deerlike grace, barely disturbing the soil underfoot."—Ira Berkow,* Beyond the Dream

And when required to sprint for the catch, the Detroit hero was none-too-slow either.

Courtesy Herb Scharfman, *Sports Illustrated*

Teenage Harmon Killebrew signed with the Washington Senators and aged as a Minnesota Twin where he finished up with 573 round-trippers. He threatened pitchers enough to draw more than 100 walks a season a total of seven times.

Courtesy NBL

fected one of the shortest swings in the game and as a Chicago prospect he also received coaching from Rogers Hornsby. The master knew better than to tinker with a stroke Willie Stargell ★ of the Pirates later described as "poetry in motion." Instead, Hornsby taught Williams to confine his swing to the strike zone.

Talent, instruction, and ambition molded Williams into a near-.300 hitter with 392 National League homers. From 1967 to 1973, toiling for the hapless Cubs, Williams produced more runs, more doubles, more triples, and more total bases than anyone in the game. The American League's Designated Hitter rule, installed in 1973, gave him an extra two years to swing the bat for Oakland and to reach his grand total of 426 homers.

Ed Linn on
SANDY KOUFAX

In the seventh game of the 1965 World Series, you could see that Sandy Koufax had almost nothing. You could see that his curve was hanging high in the early innings and, as the game went on, you could see that he had pretty much tucked the curveball away and was sticking to the fastball. And yet, you also knew that he was going to win. Koufax stood there on the mound looking ten feet tall, and you knew that he was in complete command. In the fourth inning, Dodger outfielder Lou Johnson hit a home run off the left-field foul pole, and up in the press box half-a-dozen writers said, in unison, "The ball game is over." It was hard to escape the feeling that down in the Minnesota dugout, the Twins knew that it was over too.

"When you had a game that you absolutely had to win," says Joe Black, the former Dodger pitcher who became an executive with Greyhound, "Koufax was untouchable." To illustrate the persona Koufax was able to establish, Joe Black recalls a game against Milwaukee in which Hank Aaron, always the toughest hitter for Koufax to handle, had fouled off a dozen straight 3–2 pitches. "Koufax came down off the mound rubbing the ball and said, 'Hank, it's me and you now. I'm going to throw my best fastball right down the middle and you're going to either hit it out of the park or not hit it out of the park. But there will be no more foul balls.'"

Popped him up.

Off the field, Koufax was an entirely different person. What was Sandy Koufax really like? "A wall of amiability." That's what I think of when I think of Sandy Koufax. A wall of amiability. He was always pleasant and he laughed easily. He was unfailingly courteous. And yet, there was always the sense of something being held back. Some private person in there whom you were never going to get at. The best way to put it, perhaps, would be to say that while he would not go out of his way to ingratiate himself with anybody, he was not looking to make any enemies either. One of his proudest boasts at the end of his career was that he was leaving baseball with a good reputation.

If you really want to get philosophical about it, you could make a case that this part of his personality was reflected in his pitching too. Sandy would come at you like a howitzer, straight overhand. The batter had no trouble picking up the ball as it left his hand and following it all the way in. Nor did he have to worry about being thrown at. Sandy never threw at a batter in his life. "Sandy Koufax pitches in a different league," the opposing players would say. But they'd also say that they didn't mind hitting against him. "He'll strike you out," they'd say to a man. "But he won't embarrass you."

"Kicking swiftly, hiding the ball un[til the] last instant, Koufax throws in a blur [of mo]tion, coming over the top and the fast[ball] appearing suddenly in the zone, some[times] jumps up so immoderately that his c[atcher] has to take it with his glove shootin[g up]ward, like an infielder stabbing a b[ad] grounder. I remember some batter tak[ing a] strike like that and then stepping out [of the] box and staring back at the pitcher [with a] look of utter incredulity—as if Kouf[ax had] just thrown an Easter egg past hi[m."] Donald Hall, Fathers Playing Catch [with] Their Sons

Courtesy Walter Iooss

Even the left-handers didn't mind batting against him. During Sandy's early years, in fact, left-handers hit him far better than right-handers. And not without reason. Sandy didn't pitch in and out; he pitched up and down. His fastball, as it rose, tended to tail away from a right-hander and *into* a left-hander. The "curveball" about which so much has been written wasn't a curve at all by normal standards, it was a sinker. It broke straight down. OK, by moving his fingers slightly on the ball, he was eventually able to exploit his natural advantage by throwing a breaking ball which moved slightly away from the left-handed hitters, as it was going down, but even then it was hardly enough to make the guy go fishing after it.

The only time anybody can remember where he directed his anger at anybody except himself came in Chicago, in 1963, at a time when he was just beginning to establish himself as the premier pitcher in the game. Sandy was facing Dick Ellsworth in what had developed into a highly publicized pitching duel since they were sharing the National League pitching lead with records of 8–3. Sandy was leading, 4–1, in the fifth inning when Ernie Banks and Ron Santo hit home runs to knock in 5 runs, and to make it doubly aggravating, the Santo home run, which knocked him out of the box, was a high fly that kept carrying and carrying until it carried right out of Wrigley Field.

At any rate, the Chicago fans were giving it to Sandy pretty good as he was departing the scene, and as he got to the lip of the dugout he turned around, tipped his cap, and bowed deeply from the waist.

Sandy being Sandy, he regretted what he had done as soon as he got into the clubhouse and began to cool off, especially since the radio was informing him that the Dodgers were battering Ellsworth for 4 quick runs.

"It was a real hot day," Sandy explained, afterward. "I think I might have gotten sunstroke or something."

For the most part, he would vent his anger in the traditional way by kicking the water cooler on his return to the dugout. The bottom of the water cooler was constructed of sheet metal in those days, which made it a wonderfully inviting target. "It makes more noise than anything you can kick," Sandy would say with satisfaction. "And it won't hurt your foot. Oh, I've seen water coolers take some awful punishment in my time."

When things were going badly for him—a rare enough occurrence in those latter years—a pained expression would come over his face as if he couldn't quite believe what was happening. He would grimace, he would

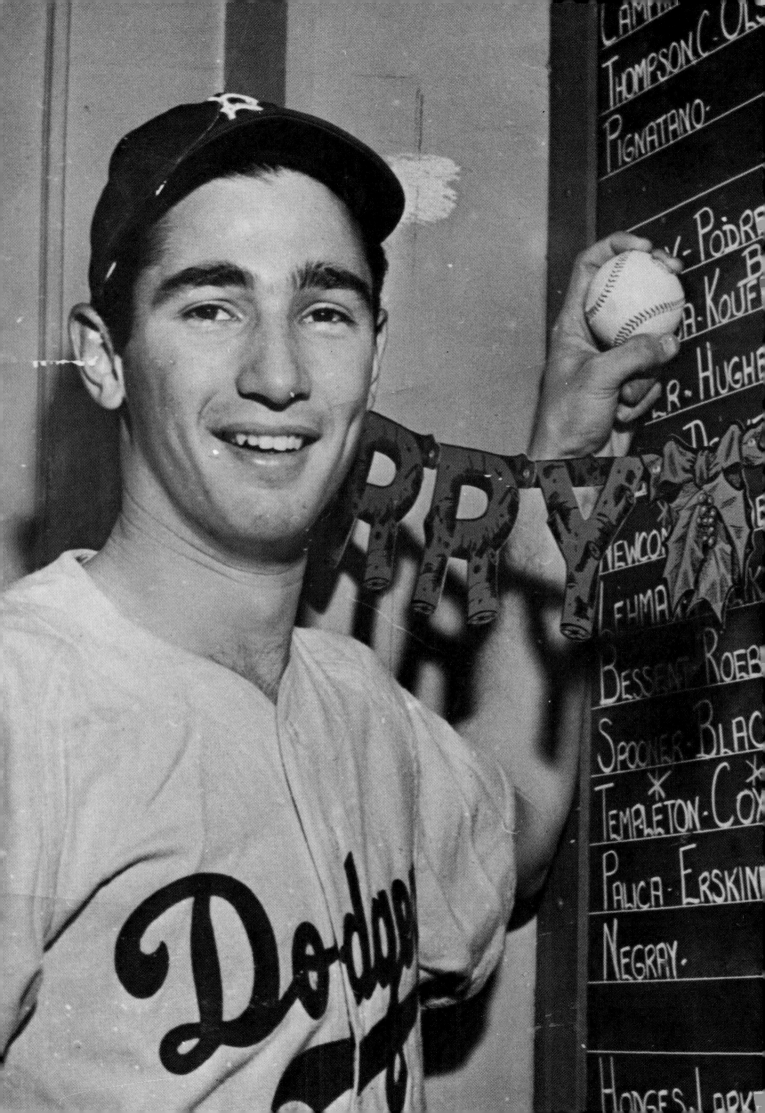

scuff at the mound; he would take his cap off and rub his hand along the side of his black, sweaty hair. When he walked a batter—particularly if there was a man or two on base—he would kick the mound in disgust, in a sort of high-flying finish to his follow-through.

On the other hand, he almost never argued with the umpire. The one time he did have a thing or two to say came late in his final year while he was pitching against the hapless Mets at Dodger Stadium. It was, as it happens, a performance that is also worth looking at from the perspective of Koufax as a craftsman. He had nothing at the start of the game, nothing in the middle, and nothing at the end. No fastball, not much of a curve, and only sporadic control. All in all, he threw a hellacious 178 pitches and walked five men (the most he had walked since the opening game of the previous season). He allowed 8 hits, and his teammates chipped in with 3 errors. And still, Koufax won the game, 6–2, with the second run coming in the ninth inning as the result of two throwing errors on the same topped ball.

But, as we say, Sandy had gone so far as to come off the mound to complain about some of the calls, something so unusual as to cause comment. After the game when he was asked how it felt to struggle through a game like the common folk, he said, "Well, you try a little of this and a little of that, and try to survive." And then, smiling rather ruefully at the memory of all that griping, he added, ". . . and you beg a little."

In truth, he took more pride in winning without his good stuff. "You're supposed to win when you have all your pitches going for you," he felt. "You haven't become a good pitcher until you can win when you don't have anything."

To say that Sandy Koufax was a private person doesn't mean very much in a day when every actor and actress promoting his or her latest epic rushes onto the Johnny Carson show to tell the whole world how private they are. With Koufax, however, it was the other way around. Koufax wanted nothing from the whole world except to be left alone.

I have a story to tell in that regard. Shortly after the end of the 1965 World Series, I signed to write Sandy's autobiography with him. The original plan called for me to meet him on one of the small Hawaiian islands, off the tourist beat, where we would be able to lie on a lonely expanse of beach with a tape recorder. On the day before I was leaving he called to tell me that the hurricane season had set in, and he had been unable to get out of Honolulu.

In 1955, as an eighteen-year-old bonus baby from the University of Cincinnati who fanned thirty-four hitters in a pair of games, he reported to a club whose roster included the likes of Roy Campanella, Johnny Podres, Joe Black, Carl Erskine, and Gil Hodges. He won 2 shutouts, lost 2 games.

Courtesy AP/Wide World

◀ 293 ▶

The day after I arrived in Honolulu, I received a telephone call. "I hope you have a pencil handy," the caller said, "because I'm going to have to give you some directions." Sandy was staying at the beach house of a deserted golf course that was about to be converted into a housing development by the richest man on the Islands, a Chinese entrepreneur whom Sandy had met at a private gathering the previous evening.

The golf course was fifty miles out of the city. There was no way to get there, I was told, without following the directions exactly, and no way to ask for directions if I went wrong. I had to find the right town and the right traffic light and the right little grocery store; I then had to turn up a small dirt road (not the one behind the store, the one in front of it), and take the correct turn at two different forks. If I did everything right I would eventually come upon a heavy wire fence at the dead end of the road. "Leave your car there," I was told. The gate was supposed to be left open for me. If it wasn't . . . well, it might not be a bad idea to bring along a pair of pants suitable for climbing. The beach house would be around there somewhere. "Good luck."

I don't know what I expected—a golf course along the ocean, I suppose—but when I did get to the sure-enough gate at the sure-enough dead end, there was nothing in front of me except the rolling hills of an empty golf course. The only building in sight was a small brick structure at the highest point of land, which was evidently either a pro shop or—since there were four or five workers on the other side of the gate taking their lunch break—a foreman's shop or tool shed.

I asked them if they had any idea where I could find Sandy Koufax, and they didn't have the slightest idea what I was talking about. "The pitcher, Sandy Koufax?" one of them finally smirked. "He's about twenty-five hundred miles that way." Just then, I looked up and saw Sandy Koufax up above us in bathing trunks strolling from the building toward what turned out to be a swimming pool. "No," I said, in one of those golden moments life occasionally visits upon us, "he's about sixty paces that way."

They gaped at him. "You mean the young guy who's been hanging around there? I thought you were asking about Sandy Koufax, the pitcher. *That* Sandy Koufax."

The small brick structure was, it seemed, the beach house. And that was it. The little house, the pool, and the green rolling hillocks. In the time of his greatest triumph, he had taken himself away from everybody and everything.

One thing very quickly became clear to me. Sandy Koufax was a man who was not only comfortable in his own company, he was a man who enjoyed his solitude. "I think," he said, "that you have to stop now and then and take a little inventory. I think everyone has a need at times to relax with his eyes wide open and, you know, think things out." If he were to stay at the hotel and insist on having his privacy respected, he added, he would have to be either a fool or a fraud.

To get right down to it, though, Koufax always had a lot of hermit in him. His home in Studio City, a suburb of Los Angeles, was on the sharply ascending curve of a narrow side street and—as if that wasn't cover enough—set back behind a high retaining wall and a heavy growth of landscaping. If you didn't know what you were looking for, you could not possibly have found it. Across the street from him, there was nothing except a long row of mountain ranges off in the far horizon behind the morning mist.

The telephone in his home didn't ring. It had a little red lamp on it that flashed. What that meant was that if Sandy didn't happen to be in the room, he wouldn't know that anybody was calling. The Dodger officials didn't even try. When the Dodgers wanted to talk to him during the height of his career they would send a telegram to his home asking him to please get in touch with them.

By Cooperstown standards, the career of Sanford Koufax was short and—how to say it?—not always sweet. Six years of frustration, followed by a transition season in 1961, and then the five overpowering years on which his reputation rests.

He had come to the Dodgers as a bonus boy at the age of nineteen, after pitching no more than a dozen games in his life. He departed at the age of thirty, at the very apex of his career, following his second straight Cy Young Award as the most outstanding pitcher in the major leagues.

Since nobody had ever come to the majors with less experience than Sandy, his first six years were spent trying to prove that he could pitch. And, worse yet, trying to prove it to a manager, Walter Alston, who had viewed him originally as little better than an empty locker and had then come to believe that he didn't have any guts—an opinion that Alston may well have reflected back on in those later years when he would call on Koufax to pitch the final game of the season on two days' rest.

The years of frustration helped him in the end; not so much in the development of technical skills as in attitude. Having been taken out of so many games in the middle innings, after the first runner got on base, he was determined almost to the point of fanaticism to finish every game.

Still uncertain of his trade, Sandy enrolled briefly at Columbia University as a student of architecture.

Courtesy Columbia University News Office

The biography of any Hall of Fame player can be turned into a Child's Garden of statistics. That almost goes without saying. With Koufax, however, the statistics serve an additional purpose, in that they demonstrate how he thrived on adversity.

A month into the 1962 season, he tied a single-game record by striking out eighteen batters in Chicago. A week later, a numbness developed in the index finger of his pitching hand, then the index finger turned white and lifeless and, in the final stages, took on a deep–reddish blue hue and—just before gangrene was ready to set in—swelled up like a grape.

In the 8 games he pitched with his finger rotting under him, he allowed 4 earned runs in 67⅓ innings for an ERA of 0.53, struck out seventy-seven, and walked twenty.

But that's only the half of it. After the finger had gone dead, he had the most remarkable run of firsts in his career. He began by hitting the first home run of his life—off Warren Spahn yet—in what turned out to be a 2–1 victory. In his next start, he not only beat Bob Gibson, 1–0, but pitched his first complete game without giving up a base on balls. From there, he went into New York and pitched his first no-hitter, striking out thirteen. And then, with the finger taking on its ghastly color scheme, he beat the Phillies, 16–1, to put the Dodgers in first place, then went into San Francisco to face the team that was challenging the Dodgers for the pennant and pitched what may have been the most extraordinary game of all. When he took the mound he found that the formerly lifeless finger had become so sensitive that when he tried to rest the ball against it, in order to throw his curve, it felt as if a knife were cutting into it. With the Giants fully aware that he couldn't throw anything except fastballs he had a no-hitter until the seventh inning. He still had a 3-hit shutout in the ninth inning when the whole hand went so numb that he could no longer hold the ball.

Four days later in New York, he had a 3-hit shutout through 7 innings before he lost all feel on the ball again and had to come out of the game. And still he insisted on taking his turn. He was warming up in Cincinnati when Carl Erskine came over, took one look at the bloated finger, and said, "Don't even try it, Sandy. Do you think anybody around here is going to thank you?"

Before the first inning was over, the finger split wide open. No blood. Just a deep cleave in the dead meat. Finally, he was sent back to Los Angeles. Another day or two, and the finger would have been lost.

In 1964, after an indifferent start, he won 15 out of 16 games, and had been leading in number 16, 2–1, when the Giants scored 4 unearned runs in the ninth. The last two of those runs are particularly instructive. Sandy had bruised his elbow diving back to second base, but had gone on to win his eighteenth and nineteenth games of the season, 4–1 and 3–0, striking out ten and thirteen in the process. The morning after the shutout he awoke to find that his arm was swollen from the shoulder down to the wrist; and that his elbow, which was every bit as thick as his knee, was locked into a hooked position.

The season was over for him. And when it happened to him again the following year, a week before the end of spring training, it looked as if his career might well be over, too.

Sandy had traumatic arthritis, a degenerative condition. Put simply, the joint of the elbow had developed a series of spurs and irregularities over the years for the purpose of protecting the constantly inflamed elbow by immobilizing it.

Dr. Robert Hyland, the man who practically invented sports medicine, informed him that pitch or no, the condition would grow progressively worse. He also told him that every time he threw the ball he would be accelerating the process. If, in the face of that warning, Sandy insisted on going on, Dr. Hyland could only suggest that he try to limit the damage by going on a five-day or even six-day rotation.

Fat chance. Koufax remained adamant about holding to his regular rotation for as long as he could. And hold it he did. Through the year, he took anti-inflammation pills and diathermy treatments. Before every game, he would apply massive heat to ease the arthritis. After the game he would soak the elbow in a bucket of ice to hold the swelling down.

Not only didn't he miss a turn, he pitched both the pennant-clinching game and the seventh game of the World Series on two days' rest. Down the stretch, under the heaviest of pressure, the scores were 1–0 (a perfect game no less), 1–2, 1–0, 2–0, 5–0, 3–1.

"Oh sure," said Manager Dick Sisler of the Phillies, "he has a sore arm except when he's pitching." And, as it happened, Sisler was righter than he thought. The arm hurt like hell all through the year—except when the act of pitching got the natural lubrication flowing into the elbow.

Sore arm and all, he pitched 336 innings, more than any left-hander since 1906, won the most games (26), tying the record for most wins by a left-hander, had the best winning percentage (for the second straight year), and the best ERA (for the fourth straight). Of his 26 wins, 25 came on complete games, and in the only winning game he did not complete, he was tied 1–1 after 10 innings.

While he was about it, he set an all-time major-league record by

An exultant Koufax leaps off the mound after closing out the Yankees 2–1 in the fourth game of the 1963 World Series. Koufax pitched 2 victories in the rout of New York. "You're talking about the greatest pitcher alive. And maybe dead. I would say the only thing I can do better than Sandy Koufax is sing and dance. If it's pitching you want, I'll wait till he's through."—Jim "Mudcat" Grant

Courtesy AP/Wide World

striking out 382 batters. Most major league pitchers will strike out ten batters on the best day they ever have. Koufax struck out ten or more batters twenty-one different times during the season, and twice more in the World Series.

But don't worry. The next year, he did better.

In 1966, his final year, he won more games (27), pitched more complete games (27), finished with his best ERA (1.73), and became the first pitcher to strike out three hundred batters in three different seasons. Down the stretch, he was as impregnable as ever. In his last 6 starts, Sandy won 4–0, 5–1, 11–1, lost 2–1 (when a single was played into a triple and a fly ball was dropped), then pitched the last 2 games the Dodgers won all year, 2–1 and 6–3, to clinch the pennant. And did it with an arm that had become so painful that in addition to the pills, the icings, and the rest of it, he was laying in a shot of cortisone before every game.

"A few too many shots, a few too many pills," he explained, when he sent shock waves through the baseball world by announcing his retirement. But that was all. It was hardly Sandy Koufax's style to rail against the unkind fate that was bringing his career to an end. On the contrary. At the beginning of what he knew was probably going to be his last season, he could point out that the weakness in his elbow had come out of the same overall construction that had given him the ability to throw the ball so hard: "I have unusually long arms, large hands and long fingers. The long arms give me the leverage, the long fingers put an extra spin on the fast ball and the curve." As for the elbow . . . well, if the arm functioned as a catapult it was a catapult with a hinge. "Pitching, which is an unnatural act, puts the hinge under enormous pressure. Since I have accepted all the advantages of the way I am built, I don't see how I can complain about the disadvantages."

You couldn't even get him to say that he had been operating at any disadvantage by pitching for as weak-hitting a team as the Los Angeles Dodgers of that era. "There may even be an advantage to pitching for a team that doesn't score many runs." With a big lead, the pitcher was inclined to get lazy, he said, and lose his concentration. "Before you know it, a couple of runs are in, and you're probably going to be gone before you have a chance to get your concentration back. No, it doesn't harm you a bit to become conditioned to the idea that you do not have the luxury of ever throwing a thoughtless or careless pitch."

Courtesy UPI/Bettmann News photos

It would be nice though, he could not help but muse, if just for once the pennant race didn't go down to the final game.

*Koufax fires the final pitch of the first
four no-hitters, this one against the M
1962.*

*"If such a word is possible in wh
after all, just a game, I would have
Sandy Koufax is a 'genius' at pitch
think he rolled out of bed one mornin,
his fast ball, just the way Sam Sne
with his golf swing. You can't teach
a fast ball. If he's not born with it,
to learn a knuckle-ball or a spitter—c
up parcheesi. . . .*

*"What makes Sandy Koufax great
same thing that made Walter Johnson
The team behind him is the ghastlies
ing team in history. They pile up runs
rate of one every nine innings. This is
like making Rembrandt paint on the t
cigar boxes, giving Paderewski a pian
only two octaves, Caruso singing with
school chorus. With the Babe Ruth Yo
Sandy Koufax would probably have be
first undefeated pitcher in history.'
Murray, Los Angeles Times*

Courtesy UPI/Bettmann News photos

He would not have been taking all those cortisone shots at the end if he hadn't already come to the decision that it was going to be his last year. The left arm had begun to turn inward, and while the crook was barely perceptible to the naked eye, it had already deteriorated to the point where he'd had to have the left sleeves on all his coats shortened.

He didn't want to go through the rest of his life crippled, and so he wasn't going to risk a permanent, disabling injury. It was as simple as that. Twelve years later, he returned to the Dodger organization as an all-purpose pitching coach. Not because he was no longer able to resist the call of the diamond but because the raging inflation of the time had played havoc with his finances. He goes to spring training to lend his expertise to the pitching staff, and he tours the minor leagues to help out wherever he is needed.

When he throws batting practice during spring training, he looks as stylish as ever, and—as incredible as it may sound—his fastball has been timed in the high eighties. So what about it? Does Sandy Koufax wonder from time to time whether he might have retired a year or two too soon?

"How can you ever know?" he shrugs. His reasons for quitting were good and sufficient unto the time. Regrets, he has none.

The arm still has that slight crook in it, but it doesn't seem to have gotten any worse. Or has it?

"It hasn't got[ten] any better," he says. And then, Sandy Koufax, amiable as ever, begins to laugh that pleasant, self-deprecatory laugh of his. "What do you want, it's an old arm. For a fifty-year-old arm, it's doing just fine."

Roberto Clemente was always a bit . . . much. And I don't mean Latin. "Even the way he died," a Puerto Rican scout once told me, shaking his head. "He was a hero, sure. But Clemente was the *chairman* of the relief, he didn't have to fly on the plane. And on New Year's Eve! In Puerto Rico, New Year's, for everybody—it's such a *holiday.* Clemente, in things he did, he always went so *far.*"

But the earthquake victims in Managua weren't celebrating; they were desperate for the supplies Clemente's plane was carrying when it crashed on December 31, 1972. Did Clemente actually need to accompany the supplies himself? Well, if you look at Managua today, you still see the destruction. Funds for rebuilding were pocketed by bigwigs of the Somoza regime. Accountability—as we have seen recently—can be very tricky where Nicaragua is concerned. Clemente paid closer attention than our National Security Council.

He took things so personally, and in such uncommon ways, that people who thought in categories (a category that includes nearly everyone) found him awkward to deal with. A furniture store owner in New York tried to steer him to the cheap stuff, until Clemente pulled out $5,000 in cash and someone, not Clemente, took the guy aside.

"Why didn't you tell me who you were?" the guy asked.

"I shouldn't have to tell you," Clemente said. "Everyone is the same. We are all as good as each other." Well, sure, but . . .

Baseball writers, Clemente said, regarded Latins and even black Americans as foreigners. "Look when Martin Luther King died. They come and ask the Negro players if we should play. When they ask me I say, 'If you have to ask Negro players, then we do not have a great country.'" Hey, lighten up, Roberto.

I might mention that Clemente is the only member of the Hall of Fame who ever told a photographer he was going to kill me. Figure of speech, no doubt, and today I am honored by the recognition. But at the time I was dismayed. All I had done was write, in *Sports Illustrated* in August 1970, as follows:

For the occasion [Roberto Clemente Night] Clemente made a great sitting-down catch to go with a great skidding-on-his-knees catch, and ex–Pirate Manager Harry Walker said, "I have never seen a greater player than Roberto Clemente." Which isn't news. News would be Harry Walker saying, "I have seen a greater player than Roberto Clemente," or Roberto Clemente saying, "I have never seen a greater player than Harry Walker." The public at large has gotten used to Clemente. He is hitting .356 and fielding and

"[Clemente played] a kind of baseball that none of us had ever seen before—throwing and running and hitting at something close to the level of absolute perfection, playing to win but also playing the game almost as if it were a form of punishment for everyone else on the field."—Roger Angell, The New Yorker

Courtesy NBL.

throwing as well as he ever has, which is to say about as well as anyone ever has. But, then, that is the same old story, too.

So are Clemente's injuries. Having got 'em, he flaunts 'em—until, of course, somebody accuses him of being a hypochondriac. He has a favorite St. Louis chiropractic clinic now and carries a chart showing where chiropractors trained by that clinic can be found all over the country. Also, he has an interesting new circulatory theory. Clemente has been out of action lately as result of a pitch that hit his wrist, and last Saturday he was telling Tony Bartirome, the team trainer, that the bad blood seemed at last to have left the painfully bruised and swollen area: "I felt a pain in my stomach, like poison there, you know? I think that was the blood running down out of my wrist."

In retrospect, I can see why that set him off. My story had dwelt with more delight upon more comfortably interviewable Pirates: Dock Ellis, Manny Sanguillen, Steve Blass, Orlando Pena, Willie Stargell. None of these, not even Stargell, was nearly so exciting a performer as Clemente, whose brilliance I had taken for granted, whose ailments I had taken lightly. The more galling because that was pretty much the way most people wrote about Clemente, until his great World Series of 1971 and his death on a charity mission.

I wrote about Clemente several times (once, I would like to take this opportunity to state for the record, in a *New York Times Magazine* cover story under the byline C. R. Ways, because I was on the staff of *Sports Illustrated* at the time and wasn't supposed to write about sports for other publications), but always somehow from a distance. Whenever I saw him he had a somber, aggrieved air, which seemed to say, *"Why aren't you going to recognize my greatness? Why is it up to me?"* And when asked how he felt—a question that always seemed in order—he would respond not like a hero, and not whiningly either, but ingenuously: earnestly expressing a natural resentment against having to suffer.

"It hurts sooo *bad,*" he would say. Clemente grew up as the youngest child in a large, happy, hard-working but comfortable family, his father the foreman on a sugar-cane plantation, and he often gave heartfelt thanks to his parents for taking such good care of him. He talked about his hurts as a favorite son might in all honorable candor to his mother.

This did not always look good in print, especially to Clemente, who was not only very sensitive to his body's signals but also very proud. Sometimes innocently proud, as when he said, "If I am going good I don't need batting practice, but sometimes I take it so the other players can see me hit." Sometimes he was proud in self-defense.

(Opposite, top and bottom) Clemenches a double in his final game. sneered at his seemingly clumsy, swing but somehow the mechan meshed when bat met ball. After e years he compiled a .317 lifetime average with an even 3,000 hits at t of his death.

Courtesy AP/Wide World

302

"Lots of times I have the feeling people want to take advantage of me, especially writers," he said. "They talk to me, but maybe they don't like me, so they write about me the way they want to write."

Maybe he was spoiled by the adulation he got in the off-season in Puerto Rico, where he lived palatially in the hills outside San Juan with his beautiful wife (whom he met in a drugstore while buying medication for a bad leg) and children. In Puerto Rico he constantly gave talks and appeared at ceremonies. He was named an honorary doctor of education by the Catholic University of Puerto Rico. "When he die," Sanguillen said, "it was so big in Puerto Rico people stop everything. Nobody have any more parties for New Year's. Everybody go to the beach to try to find him. Try to find the body or at least something. You know how great he was in the outfield. And he gives his life for somebody he don't know."

Or maybe Clemente wanted to be accorded the simple gee-whiz deference that his contemporary great outfielders Willie Mays and Henry Aaron received. But Clemente was not like other great players. He had more to say. Mays and Aaron did not go around protesting baseball's reserve clause, which, before it was tossed out by the courts, kept players from changing jobs on their own accord and therefore, as Clemente pointed out, deprived them of one of the freedoms of a plumber. Long before it was accepted practice to speak out about the paucity of product-endorsement offers for black and Latin players, Clemente was already tired of protesting. "I've had a couple of endorsements," Clemente said toward the end of his career, "but they never came to nothing. I don't want to make any. I don't need them. If the people who give them out don't think Latins are good enough, I don't think *they* are good enough. The hell with them. I make endorsements in Spanish countries, and give the money to charity."

On the other hand, when it came time for formal gratitude, Mays and Aaron did not speak so feelingly as Clemente did when presented his trophy as the most valuable player of the 1971 World Series: "I respect people. I respect my mother and father. This has given me the opportunity to know people, to hurt people once in a while, but mostly to love people."

Nor did either Mays or Aaron ever tell so strange a story as Clemente told suddenly in August 1970, when he revealed that one night during the previous season, as he was walking back to the Pirates' hotel in San Diego with a bag of fried chicken, he was kidnapped at gunpoint by four men and driven into the hills. There, he said, his abductors forced him to strip and took his wallet, his All-Star ring, and $250, and were all set to shoot him—"They already had the pistol in my mouth"—when he managed belatedly to convince them of his identity. Whereupon they gave him back his clothes, wallet, and ring and drove off. Then he heard them drive up again behind him.

"I started looking around for a rock," he said, "but I couldn't find one."

They rolled down the window of the car, said, "Here," handed him back his fried chicken, and drove off again.

Hard to know what to say, exactly, about a story like that. Even Clemente didn't tell it, except to his general manager and his batting coach, for over a year. "I forgot about the whole thing until somebody brought it up. Then I figure I better tell the story so it be printed right."

It may be that nothing about Clemente was ever printed quite right. Hard to do justice, in writing or at any rate in English, to his fielding, for instance. In July 1971, just before his thirty-eighth birthday, he made what may have been the most spectacular catch in the history of right field. In the eighth inning, with the Pirates ahead 1–0 in a crucial game, two out and a man on base, Houston's Bob Watson, a right-handed hitter, sliced a vicious shot into the corner. Clemente ate up a great stretch of turf with his back to the ball, leapt with a half-twist in full flight, made a one-hand catch above the Astrodome's yellow home-run line, and in fully extended, leaping-stab posture hit the wall wide open. He didn't climb the wall, he didn't feel for the wall, he ignored the wall, and *WHAM.* When he got up, the left or glove side of his body was swelling, bleeding, and bruised at, respectively, the elbow, knee, and ankle; and the game was saved.

That's one reason Clemente was always hurting: he was always so brave in the field. Men in their late thirties just don't make sliding-on-the-stomach catches, skidding-on-one-hip catches, on a regular basis.

"Somebody would hit the ball against us," Sanguillen recalled the spring after Clemente's death, "and we all say, 'It's gone.' We don't even know Clemente is running. And then he go 'poom' against the fence and catch the ball—oh, I don't know how he do it."

Once Clemente fielded a *bunt.* There were runners on first and second, and the Pirate shortstop was covering third. The ball was bunted to where the shortstop would have been. Clemente, playing in right, the position farthest from shortstop, came running up, grabbed the ball on the ground, and threw the runner coming from first out at third.

He had to go to great lengths to use his arm, which was so good that runners seldom tested it, even when he fumbled the ball a bit on purpose, tempting them. "Sometime this year," said Blass before his first season

As a young center fielder, Clemente [...] snare a ball hit by Pee Wee Reese. [...] veteran right fielder, Roberto steals o[...] Duke Snider. An awkward leap robs [...] Mays of a two-bagger. Mays loses a [...] to the thieving Pirate outfielder.

Courtesy AP/Wide World

without Clemente, "somebody is going to go from first to third against us on a single to right. And I'm going to be shocked. It's never happened before, in all the time I've been in the big leagues, because Clemente has always been there. I'll find myself backing up first base on the play, because Clemente knew the lead runner wasn't going to try anything against him, so he'd try to pick off the hitter taking too big a turn." By hook and crook, he managed to lead the league in outfield assists five times, a major league record. Nobody quite combined a running catch, a whirl, and a throw the way Clemente did—so that he was occasionally photographed suspended in air, four feet above the ground and horizontal to it, releasing a lightning bolt.

Clemente's batting stroke—with which he led the league in batting four times and hit .317 over his eighteen-year career—was also a miracle of torsion. The good big-league hitter holds back late, to see how the pitch is going to behave, and then somehow obtains enough sudden leverage— enough elbow room to get around on the ball—to avoid being jammed when it is full upon him. Aaron managed this with fabled wrists, Stargell with sheer trunk-and-arm strength. Mays would bail out, pulling away from the plate with his front foot so that he could pull the ball to left field, while keeping his hands back so he wasn't overcommitted. Clemente's maneuver was almost the opposite of Mays's. He stood far back from the plate, waited very late, and then, with his two-of-a-kind hands close in to his chest, typically shrugged the front of his body in on the ball so that he could reach way back and swipe it out of the catcher's mitt, virtually, and "inside out," as they say, into right field. The tensile stress involved was enough to make anybody's body develop kinks. Clemente said one of his chiropractors told him "that what I have wouldn't bother most men so much. But I am so strong, I strain my back so."

Sometimes when he swung and missed the back hurt him so much he would wince, flinch, drop the bat, and, grimacing, bend slowly, gingerly over and pick it back up. Every morning he would have to "boop" his back into place. He was forever rotating his neck on the field, trying to get it adjusted. He'd go out into the bullpen during a game so relief pitcher Al McBean could give him a massage.

"When my back hurt me in 1957," he complained once, "all the doctors said there was nothing wrong with me. They said my shirt was too tight. Another said I had to have my tonsils out, so he pulled them."

"My back hurts me when I sit down," he said another time. "It hurts me when I stand up. It hurts me even when I breathe sometime. I have to breathe through my nose. When I breathe through my mouth something hurt real bad in the back."

The back was only part of it. In his time Clemente was bothered not only by the usual pulled muscles but also by tension headaches, nervous stomach, a tendon rubbing against the bone in his heel, malaria, a strained instep, bone chips in his elbow (which were there in the X-rays but somehow weren't when the surgeon cut in), a curved spine, one leg heavier than the other (according to a chiropractor), hematoma of the thigh incurred in a lawn-mowing accident, wayward disks in neck and back, a systemic paratyphoid infection from the hogs on his farm, severe food poisoning, and insomnia. He couldn't stand to have a roommate because the least sound of coat hangers would wake him up. "I hear a plane go over the ballpark and it hurts my ears. I go to the doctor and he says I have bad sinuses. There is all poison in my body."

Poison and electricity, which he didn't talk about. Why should he have to? It was there on the field to see. The stats he left behind don't do him justice. He got exactly 3,000 hits, his batting average was consistently high, but his lifetime home-run total was only 240. He hit some balls as far as Mays ever did and farther than the exquisitely economical Aaron, but nobody ever hit many home runs in cavernous Forbes Field, Clemente's home park for all but two and a half seasons. Furthermore, Clemente's wasn't a patented home-run stroke, it was a *Latin* stroke: go after a pitch that looks sweet and challenging—even if it's about to hit you in the ear, even if you have to leave the ground to reach it—and line it in some direction.

Am I being ethnocentric? ("You have to be American," Clemente said, "or you can't be 'my sweetheart next door.'") Yogi Berra also hit pitches that were way out of the strike zone. But not in the Spanish manner. Once I asked Sanguillen why he kept on swinging at the first pitch, even though he knew it was imprudent. "Because it make me feel good!" he said happily. Clemente was more calculating than that, and it may be that *nothing* made him feel good, but when he swung the bat he went with his viscera, not the percentages.

He scored as many as 100 runs in only three seasons and he drove in that many only twice. With his injuries, he tended to be in and out of the lineup. In his early years he was not popular with his fellow Pirates. There were managers who accused him of not being a team player. This more than anything probably accounted for the hurt-dignity look that almost always showed up in photographs that included Clemente's eyes.

It was not until the 1971 Series that he established himself as a kingpin, a *macher*, a man who made the difference. When the Pirates upset the Orioles 4 games to 3, Clemente batted .414, hit 2 home runs and missed another by three inches, made two notable running catches, intimidated runners with his throws, and was named Series MVP.

That would have been a fine consummation of anyone's seventeenth season in the majors, but in the case of Clemente it was especially right and timely. Clemente was due to lead a team to glory. The man who makes the difference is the team leader, the man who plays hurt, makes no excuses, and comes up with the big play when it counts the most. Mays and Aaron and Stargell were prime examples. Clemente was always a special case.

In 1960, when the Pirates were world champions, Clemente hit safely in every Series game for a .312 average, but he came up with no heroics and was virtually ignored in post-Series coverage—until it transpired that he had rushed away from the dressing room and back toward Puerto Rico after the final game, before the team's beer-sloshing celebration began. Then, when word came that teammates Dick Groat and Don Hoak had finished first and second in the voting for Most Valuable Player in the National League and Clemente had come in eighth, Clemente sent up a cry of outrage.

This was embarrassing. It inhibited the development of a proper make-the-difference mystique for Clemente. In the 1961 All-Star game in Candlestick Park, Clemente tripled, drove in a run with a sacrifice fly, and knocked in the winning run in the tenth. The papers gave more space to the wind that blew pitcher Stu Miller off the mound.

Then, in 1966, when Clemente was the league MVP, the Pirates failed to win the pennant. In 1970, when they finished first in their division, Clemente hit .352, but played in only 108 of 162 games. In 1971 he hit .341 for the regular season, but he missed 30 games, and the big man in the order was the prepotent Stargell, whose number was written on his bats and shower shoes in Roman numerals and whose home runs, big-brotherish presence, and run production, all achieved in spite of agonized knees, overshadowed Clemente's contribution.

But in that Series, Stargell didn't hit. Clemente did. He hit and hit and hit, as TV looked on intimately, in close-up from several angles. He got at least one hit in every game (so that he never went hitless in a Series game, a nice item for myth-making), he produced runs, and his second home run put the Pirates ahead to stay in the final game. You could feel throughout the media a great rush of relieved commemoration. Clemente, the great strange talent, was finally a certifiable winner, a heavy dude.

All of which should be rethought. It is Casey-at-the-Bat thinking, which ignores the true distinction of Clemente. Plenty of ball players have starred in World Series, but only Clemente ever said, "When I wake up in the morning, I pray I am still asleep." Only Clemente ever explained that he scored all the way from first on a single to beat the Dodgers because "I had a sore foot. I wanted to rest it." Only Clemente could arrive for the first day of spring training in his long-collar-tab shirt and brilliant slacks, as vivid a major leaguer as anyone could ask for, with features that might be carved in ebony and teeth that might be painted on black velvet, signing autographs with dignity and a few gracious words for clusters of fluttering elderly ladies; and then go into the dressing room and pull on the knit uniform that did not flatter a fat or an irregularly conformed man but made Clemente look even trimmer and stronger limbed; and then run hard and throw hard and hit hard as ever; and then come back to the bench where his teammates were horsing and whooping around as only the loosey-goosey Pirates of the 1970s could; and then wince and sigh and say, "Oh, I am as tired now . . . as I was at the end of last year. They took X-rays of my stomach and found nothing but spasms."

That's the way he was the last time I saw him in person, in his last spring. By then his teammates loved him. It's true that when pitcher Dave Giusti crept up behind him after the Series triumph with fizzling champagne Clemente cried, "Don't spray me! I got a bad eye!" But in his acknowledged greatness Clemente could finally be kidded.

Dock Ellis was singing to loud music in the clubhouse. Clemente turned it down. Ellis turned around, demanding, "Whose idea was that?" Someone pointed to Clemente. There was a pause. "Did you notice how the room went silent?" whooped Ellis. And he broke into his Clemente imitation. Hobbling, twitching his neck, and saying in a Latin accent, "Oh, I not like I used to be. I a little bit of a old man now."

"Did you see the way Clemente slide?" yelled Sanguillen, flying halfway across the room and then freezing on the floor. "I want to go help him up, the old man!"

Less than a year later he was dead and in the Hall of Fame. "The first Pirate I met when they were trying to sign me was Clemente," said pitcher John Candelaria. "Clemente was supposed to be arguing for the front office. But while they tried to talk me into signing, Clemente kept telling me in Spanish, 'You can get more money.' "

"This was a man who looked at the television pictures coming back from the moon and saw the world. No man is alone on earth, though one will be remembered forever as the first of the human race to stand on the moon. But Clemente thought of all the people who came together to get that guy there. He conceived of them as a brotherhood. 'That is the way the world should be,' said Roberto Clemente, a ballplayer, who was accepting an award for playing baseball, which is manual labor. He talked about Puerto Rico, and he was glad he was from there and happy the island was part of the United States."—Jimmy Cannon, New York Post

He died the year Cannon wrote the piece, while on a mercy flight to help earthquake victims. The following August, Roberto Clemente was posthumously inducted into the Hall of Fame. Celebrating with his widow, Vera are (left to right), other titans elected with Clemente: pitcher Warren Spahn; Giant outfielder and a Negro League gem, Monte Irvin; a Giant of another era, first baseman George Kelly; and William Evans, representing his deceased father, umpire Billy Evans. Presiding over the ceremonies was Commissioner Bowie Kuhn.

Courtesy UPI/Bettmann News photos

Only the pilot's body was found. The only things of Clemente's that washed up on the beach in Puerto Rico were his black briefcase, empty and tattered, and a brown sock. His wife found them. " 'Was he wearing this sock?' I asked myself, or did it fall out of his suitcase?" she said. "I hoped it might have come from his suitcase."

"There was that one area out there at the knees off the outside corner," said Tom Seaver after Clemente's death. "If you hit that spot with a pitch, he'd look and walk away. If you missed it, he'd hit the ball very hard."

Jim Russo, the Orioles' chief scout, agreed. "His weakness was so close to his strength that you were always in danger."

The burgeoning number of teams opened the way for a significant addition to the traditional postseason show, the playoff between top clubs from East and West in each league for the right to meet in the World Series. (Playoffs had been staples of the diets in other pro sports and on the menu in the baseball minors since 1933.) The inauguration of major league baseball's version in 1969 fittingly witnessed the first genuine expansion team, the implausible, once totally hapless, New York Mets, eliminate Atlanta (from the West in the bizarre geography of baseball). The Mets then conquered the American League champs, Baltimore.

The Mets vanquished the Braves with major contributions from two young right-handers, Tom Seaver and Nolan Ryan, in spite of 3 homers from Hank Aaron. Over the succeeding years Seaver and Ryan struck out thousands and Seaver has won more than 300 games. Seaver pulled in the Cy Young Award three times in his career. Game one's starter and loser for Atlanta was a thirty-year-old who was still pitching eighteen years later; Phil Niekro befuddled hitters not with the intense packages of heat furnished by Ryan and Seaver but with the knuckler taught to him and his brother Joe as boys by their father. Phil Niekro also would join the exclusive 300-win club.

In the American League, Baltimore whipped Minnesota with heavy lumber work from the Robinsons—Brooks (.500) and Frank (.333) plus the young right arm of Jim Palmer, who later added a new dimension to off-diamond income by posing for skivvies ads. This was the second year of the reign of Earl Weaver, who never had a lick of major league playing experience. Yet the bumptious Weaver rates among the winningest managers in the game, with seven pennants in fifteen years for the Orioles. Weaver also has the distinction of being the most frequently declared persona non grata by umpires. In the losing cause Jim Perry labored for the Twins; his 215 wins, added to those of his even more effective brother Gaylord, totaled 529 victories, the best ever by siblings until the Niekros overtook them in 1987.

The neophyte Mets subdued Baltimore in a 5-game World Series, making them the first expansion club (a club created from scratch rather than an emigrant franchise) to become world champions. The final game provoked such a frenzied outpouring of joy by Met fans, including those in the Manhattan towers of finance, that thieves, seizing the confusion of the celebration, were able to remove $13.6 million in securities from the offices of Morgan Guaranty Trust for what was then a world's record.

The following year, Cincinnati, which became known as "the Big Red Machine," squeaked by a muscular Pittsburgh club for the National League title. Pete Rose in the outfield, Tony Perez at third and first, and Johnny Bench behind the plate were the nucleus of the juggernaut. The losing Pirates mustered Willie Stargell, a left-handed behemoth who amassed 475 homers, along with Clemente and Al Oliver, an unsung star good for a .303 lifetime batting average. "Pops" Stargell gave the Pirate pennanteers of 1971 and 1979 not only his weighty bat but also a spirit that turned the club into a kind of family. His 1,540 RBIs of course helped.

Returning to the World Series in 1970 for the American League was Baltimore, which again had frustrated Minnesota in 3 games. The Birds rallied from behind three times to down the Reds.

While the American League had played its rivals equally in World Series play for a decade, the National League had dominated All-Star competition, starting with a pair of wins in 1960* and unbeaten, except for 1962, through 1970. The American League famine ended in 1971 with a trio of 2-run homers by Frank Robinson, Harmon Killebrew, and Oakland Athletics slugger Reggie Jackson, whose clout jarred a light tower in Detroit. Jackson's more than 550 career home runs and his freely offered opinions rattled pitchers, teammates, managers, and owners.

As baseball entered the 1970s, more than the season format and city alignments were in transition. The entire country rocked, rolled, shook, and quaked with strident voices, marching feet, and the violence of those who no longer accepted the margin of compromise. There was an ugly war killing Americans and Asians twelve thousand miles away. Great numbers of people took

Courtesy UPI/Bettmann News photos

Tom Seaver began life as a Met in served a few years in Cincinnati, Cl and finally achieved win 300 with tl ton Red Sox.

Courtesy UPI/Bettmann News photos

---

*For four years, from 1959 to 1962, baseball showcased a pair of All-Star games.

to the streets and lobbied legislators, first over the denial of civil rights to nonwhites, then the Vietnam War, the status of women, and finally the standing of the gay community. There were confrontations with the cops, campus upheavals, sit-ins, explosions, National Guard mobilizations, shootings, and deaths.

Baseball was largely isolated from the tumult; no one burned lineup cards or refused to play because of a larger agenda. But the sense that the old order no longer ruled permeated even the most sealed-off bunkers of baseball management. And, already uneasy with the militance of the Players Association, the proprietors wrestled with the stiffest challenge yet when Cardinal outfielder Curt Flood sought by a lawsuit to free himself after St. Louis traded him to Philadelphia. He thus challenged the reserve clause, the heart of the standard contract.

The 1972 U.S. Supreme Court decision on Flood refused to overturn the findings of 1922, which had immunized the sport against federal antitrust statutes. That may have seemed a total victory for the management but the Court also was aware that fifty years had passed. In its opinion it remarked on the peculiarities of baseball's exemption and recommended that Congress deal with the issue. Indeed, the great Constitutional scholar, Senator Sam Ervin of North Carolina, had begun to examine the legal structure of all professional sports. It was unlikely that another Casey Stengel could be produced for a Congressional hearing to so amuse the audience that the legislators would forget their purposes.

Meanwhile, the spring of 1972 saw the first industrywide strike in baseball as the Players Association and the owners could not agree on terms for the standard contract. The two sides settled but not before the cancellation of 86 games over the first thirteen days of the season.

The biggest losers in the settlement were the Boston Red Sox. The condensed schedule permitted them only 155 games while Detroit squeezed in 156 and took the Eastern Division by the margin of a single game in the win column. The pact brought no change in the reserve restriction but the players won the right to arbitration in cases where management and labor could not agree on a salary. Anyone with ten years of major league experi-

ence and the last five with a single club could no longer be traded without his consent. What Curt Flood lost in court, the Players Association won in negotiations.

The reserve clause, the cornerstone of labor–management relations so skillfully constructed by A. G. Spalding and his associates in the nineteenth century, finally crumbled three years later. In 1975, two pitchers, Dave McNally of Montreal and Andy Messersmith of the Dodgers, having played a full season without signing a contract, argued that the renewal feature, the mechanical means that perpetuated the reserve clause, no longer applied. They declared themselves free agents. Baseball demurred and the dispute became the province of arbitrator Peter Seitz. He ruled in favor of McNally and Messersmith. The reserve clause seemed about to die. Subsequently, however, the Players Association agreed to a modified system of reserve covering a man's first few major league years.

The decline of the reserve clause coincided with the steep ascent in baseball revenues. In 1955, with sixteen teams, the two leagues drew just shy of 17 million. Ten years later the total had risen to 22 million and in 1975, when Seitz issued his decision, 30 million folks paid to see major league ball. By 1986, the figure was up to 47.5 million and at prices well above those charged ten years earlier. In addition, TV income had increased precipitously with the introduction of network broadcasts, bidding among cable and regular local channels, and with the attention focused on playoffs as well as the World Series.

Compared to Fortune 500 companies baseball was still small business, but big bucks had become available to invest. Furthermore, whereas franchises once belonged to a clique of men whose only interest was baseball and who had grown accustomed to dictating terms, ownership increasingly was vested in captains of commerce, individuals acquainted well with strong unions or hard bargaining from powerful suppliers. The new breed—men like Ray Kroc in San Diego, Gene Autry in Anaheim, Ted Turner in Atlanta, George Steinbrenner in New York—were high rollers when they saw an opportunity to turn their operations into winners.

During the 1960s, however, there were

Gaylord Perry toiled for six different clubs, and he and brother Jim rank second in victories by siblings to Phil and Joe Niekro.

Courtesy UPI/Bettmann News photos

still a few owners with baseball as their only interest. Among them was Calvin Griffith, nephew of Clark, the former pitcher and proprietor when the franchise was in Washington, D.C. Seemingly always strapped for cash, Griffith nevertheless constantly fielded quality players, like Harmon Killebrew, Tony Oliva, and then the remarkable Rod Carew, whose .328 lifetime average is the highest of anyone who began his career after World War II. It was Carew's fate over nineteen years never to reach a World Series, although he appeared in the very first Championship Playoff Series in 1969 when the Twins lost to Baltimore. Unable to pay the worth of Carew, the Twins traded him to the more affluent California Angels of Autry in 1979.

The first sign of the effects of a free market appeared a year before Peter Seitz decided the McNally–Messersmith case. Jim "Catfish" Hunter, ★ a moustachioed part-time North Carolina farmer and winner of 161 games pitching for the Kansas City and Oakland Athletics, declared himself no longer bound to Oakland. Hunter claimed his contract with Oakland void after the failure of the rambunctious owner, insurance magnate Charles O. Finley, to pay a stipulated bonus. Seitz heard the arguments from both sides and declared Hunter a free man. George Steinbrenner, the ship builder and controlling power at the Yankees, panting to reverse the course of the club that had won its last pennant eleven years earlier, posted a winning $3.25-million bid for Hunter.

The Yankees bought a fellow who had never spent a day in the minors. Scouts had picked up on the precocious farm boy who switched from sidearm to overhand as a high-school senior and who won 23 while dropping only 2 in his final years. Charlie Finley offered a $60,000 bonus contract. But an accident during a rabbit hunt nearly prevented him from a single professional pitch.

> My brother Pete was a game warden and he was carrying this 12 gauge magnum shotgun. The safety was off and it kind of went off and put a few holes in me. Didn't know it at the time. I said, "Damn, you almost blew my foot off." Then I saw the blood and he fainted.

Surgeons removed the little toe of the right foot, a chunk of bone, and some pellets and left fifteen or so pieces of shot embedded in the flesh. During 1964, the Athletics carried him on the disabled list. To protect him in the player draft in 1965, he remained on the roster. Injuries to the regular starters gave Hunter a chance to show his stuff. By the time he had matured to a 21-game winner in 1971, Oakland had built an outfit that would win 3 straight World Series from 1972 to 1974, with Hunter accounting for 3 victories, 1 loss.

Not an overpowering type, Hunter nevertheless had just come off a Cy Young Award 25–12 season in 1974 and in each of the three preceding years had won 21 games. He had even thrown that rare gem, a perfect game, against Minnesota in 1968. His first year for New York, Hunter performed brilliantly, 23–14 with a 2.58 ERA. With the Catfish boated, the Yankees reached Steinbrenner's objective between 1976 and 1978.

Under the command of Steinbrenner the Yankees staffed their regiments with crack soldiers of fortune, and during the early campaigns they swept to a number of victories. But other potentates who emulated the New York strategy discovered at painful cost that they were fighting new wars with the weapons and tactics of the previous ones. Some, like the Los Angeles Dodgers, refused to bid for free agents and instead sufficiently rewarded local boys to remain contenders.

Catfish Hunter was the first of modern stars to peddle himself to the highest bidder. Until the lifelong bonds of the reserve clause were cut, players had changed their place of business only at the discretion of their employers. For the most part, superstars—Ty Cobb, Walter Johnson, Honus Wagner, Lou Gehrig, Joe DiMaggio, Ted Williams, Jackie Robinson—were recognized by management as "franchise" players; to trade or sell them not only would weaken the club but also would antagonize the home fans. To be sure, some outstanding figures did pack their duds and move—Babe Ruth, Lefty Grove, Jimmie Foxx, Rogers Hornsby, Dizzy Dean—but they were transported solely because of a management decision. After the Seitz decision, however, qualified players could auction themselves off as free agents. In the great tradition of free enterprise, competition for valuable services drove salaries beyond any contemplated limits. The consequences of baseball's new economics and its

Owner Charles O. Finley of the O Athletics hung the "Catfish" moni Jim Hunter, who prospered mightil the new contract rules.

Courtesy UPI/Bettmann News photos

revised labor–management agreements have radically influenced the fortunes of players and teams.

Several of Hunter's more illustrious colleagues on the 1974 Oakland team, which beat the Dodgers in the Series, went the free-agent route in 1976—outfielder Joe Rudi, third baseman Sal Bando, reliever Rollie Fingers, and the self-assured blaster, Reggie Jackson. Fingers, with his Daliesque moustache, displaced Hoyt Wilhelm for first in saves and wins for a reliever. Harking to the cry of the highest bidder, Fingers left Oakland for San Diego and then through a trade took up station in Milwaukee. During his prime, Fingers' closest rival for soothing pitching *agita* was Sparky Lyle, who applied his balm principally to the Yankees but also dispensed for Boston, Texas, and Philadelphia. Lyle, too, moved both as a free agent and subject of trades. While with New York he had 11 consecutive saves, a record eclipsed by Steve Bedrosian of the Phillies in 1987.

Reggie Jackson, with his penchant for egocentric quotes—"I'm the straw that stirs the drink"—stayed a season with Baltimore and then did a noisy five-year stretch with the Yankees where he produced 144 homers. He silenced even his most vociferous critics with a 5 home-run burst in the 1977 World Series against Los Angeles. He destroyed the Dodgers in the sixth and final game with 3 successive drives to the seats, each on the first pitch, each from a different pitcher. He passed Mantle's 536 total homers in 1986 while with the California Angels (as well as the less-glorious record for most Ks), and then returned in 1987 to Oakland as a premier beneficiary of the designated hitter rule.

An increasingly rare phenomenon, the trade of the superstar, affected Tom Seaver. Dubbed a cartoon hero, "Tom Terrific" as a Met pitched brilliantly for ten-and-a-half years, starting in the dim cellar-dwelling days of 1967. Never a loser during his New York seasons, with only one .500 season, Seaver won 25 in the 1969 pennant year and was a 189-game victor when the Mets traded him to Cincinnati. He returned to New York briefly, then was swapped to the White Sox and ultimately to the Boston Red Sox, as he toted up 311 wins. His classmate on the 1969 champion Mets, Nolan Ryan, in the

days before free agentry, was dealt off to the California Angels in the Mets' perennial quest for a third baseman, in this instance Jim Fregosi. By 1979, however, after leading the league in strikeouts for seven out of eight years, including the all-time high of 383 in 1973, Ryan auctioned himself off to Houston where he continued to whiff close to 200 a season.

The 1970s saw the struggle for baseball supremacy batted and pitched around by a handful of cities, the migration of top players notwithstanding. Four times the Cincinnati Reds appeared in the World Series and the Los Angeles Dodgers showed up on three occasions. Baltimore, Oakland, and New York each represented the American League thrice. Among the most exalted of Series was that of 1975. The Big Red Machine out of Cincinnati rolled over its Western opponents for a 20-game margin and crunched Eastern Division title-holder Pittsburgh in 3 games. At the altar for the American League were the perennial bridesmaids, the Boston Red Sox, who finished a comfortable 4½ to the fore in the East before knocking off Oakland.

In the opening game at Fenway Park, Luis Tiant, perhaps thirty-five years old, a native of Cuba with a fondness for long black cigars, shut down the Reds 6–0. Tiant wore a major league uniform for nineteen years. He won 229 games with a unique style in which he seemed to start his motion while gazing at the left fielder before whirling in a singularly jerky motion to face his opponent.

Cincinnati tied affairs in game two with a timely double by its standout catcher, Johnny Bench, who only three years earlier was relieved of a lung lesion by a surgeon. His 389 homers for his career overtook the previous best by a receiver, Yogi Berra's 358.

Bench never left Cincinnati, but Joe Morgan, the second baseman on the club, packed his bags often, adding San Francisco, Philadelphia, and Oakland to his working addresses. A Texan, he started with Houston and after a nine-year tour with a second-division club was traded to Cincinnati in 1972. He became a crucial flywheel for the Big Red Machine. A rare specimen, the second sacker with power (268 homers), Morgan also offered speed (689 stolen bases) and consistency (.271 lifetime average). Only

Reginald Martinez Jackson swung a mighty bat and stirred a potent straw.

". . . ever since the Yankees went to training camp last March, Jackson has lived in the eye of the hurricane. All summer long as the spike-shod capitalists bickered and quarreled, contending with their manager, defying their owner, Reggie was the most controversial, the most articulate, the most flamboyant.

Part philosopher, part preacher, and part outfielder, he carried the rancorous company with his bat in the season's last fifty games, leading them to the East Championship in the American League and into the World Series . . ."—Red Smith, New York Times, October 19, 1977.

Courtesy UPI/Bettmann News photos

5'7", 150 pounds, he personified the word "aggressive"—attacking on the bases, at the plate, and with his glove.

Game three of that 1975 Series went to the bottom of the tenth inning. A dispute erupted over possible interference on a bunt but the Sox lost the argument and Joe Morgan cashed in with a game-winning single. The following evening, Luis Tiant staggered, struggled, and persisted until his 163rd pitch induced Morgan to pop up, giving Boston a 5–4 victory.

During game five, Morgan's antics on base drew 16 attempted pickoff throws. A final feint to steal opened a hole on the right side and Bench rammed through a single. The maneuvers disturbed pitcher Reggie Cleveland enough for him to groove a pitch to Tony Perez for a homer that put the game in the Redleg bag.

Game six stretched for 12 suspenseful innings after Red Sox pinch hitter Bernie Carbo socked a 3-run blast in the bottom of the eighth to tie the game. Both teams teetered on the edge of victory over the next 3 innings before Boston catcher Carlton Fisk lofted a ball over the Green Monster. But in the decisive last game, Morgan's single in the ninth inning brought the Redlegs the championship.

The leading hitter among the 7-game players was the spiritual descendant of Enos Slaughter, third baseman Pete Rose. His Series average of .370 included getting on base eleven of his last fifteen times in the batter's box. Rose was called "Charlie Hustle," at first mocking his dash to first base even on a walk but later in admiration for his all-out pursuit of balls, bases, and base hits. He brought to the game both that small-boy enthusiasm Roy Campanella regarded as the essence of a ball player and Ernie Banks's "Let's play two" joy. Said Rose, "I'd walk through hell in a gasoline suit to keep playing baseball." As the teams scratched and clawed at one another in the 12-inning contest, Rose turned to the Red Sox's carbon of Johnny Bench, Carlton Fisk, and marveled, "Can you believe this game!"

Home-run hitters allegedly drove Cadillacs, while singles men afforded only compact cars. However, Charlie Hustle's garage housed a Rolls and a pair of fire-engine red, Mario Andretti–specialized Porsche rockets.

Rose reached the million per annum salary without impressive long-ball stats during his twenty-four years. But Rose was amazingly consistent, surpassing even Ty Cobb's 4,191 hits in 1985, coming up second in doubles after Speaker (746 vs 793), and with the most games and most at bats of any player. By 1987, he occupied third place in career total bases, behind Stan Musial and the leader Hank Aaron.

On duty for the Red Sox during this epic encounter was the legitimate heir of Ted Williams, Carl Yastrzemski. Growing up in eastern Long Island, New York, Yaz started out as an infielder with the semipro Bridgehampton White Eagles and then the Lake Ronkonkoma Cardinals. The third baseman was his father, who at age forty-one hit .410 to his son's measly .375. Yaz passed up a $45,000 offer from the Yankees and entered Notre Dame. Other teams boosted the figure until the Red Sox bid a bit over $100,000. After two minor league seasons, he filled the gap in left field occasioned by Williams's retirement. No one ever handled the caroms off the Green Monster better than he. From 1961 to his final days as a first baseman and designated hitter in 1983, Yaz hammered a total of 3,419 hits, 452 homers, and a lifetime .285.

The Reds repeated in 1976 as champions, knocking off the Yanks in 4 straight for a second championship. But the ancient rivalry of Dodgers and Yanks held center stage for 1977 and 1978. Los Angeles, eschewing free-agent recruits, relied on home-grown talents like pitcher Don Sutton, eventually another 300-gamer, and Steve Garvey, the first baseman whose antecedents dated to a father who drove the Dodger bus and a teenage job as batboy. Most of the other Dodgers also came up through the farm system. To be sure, another durable piece of pitching goods, Tommy John, was on hand but he came via the trade route. By contrast, Yank principals Reggie Jackson, Catfish Hunter, and relief flinger Goose Gossage decamped from their former hideouts in return for Steinbrenner's gold. Center fielder Mickey Rivers, pitcher Mike Torrez, who won 2 Series games, third baseman Graig Nettles, and shortstop Bucky Dent arrived through trades. Increasingly, the swaps of players were derived from an unwilling-

(Opposite, top) *The Cincinnati Reds cheer themselves after winning the seventh game of the 1975 World Series against the Boston Red Sox. But the sixth game heroics, climaxed by Carlton Fisk's game-breaker home run in the 12th inning for the Sox, provoked the most comment.*

". . . there are undoubtedly dozens and hundreds and thousands of baseball games staged from Old Orchard Beach to Los Angeles that one would have to say had more technical brilliance. But this one had captured all that baseball could be. Fisk's home run had virtually altered the autumnal equinox. . . . Baseball had seized the imagination of the entire country; the excitement and color of that World Series marked it immediately as one of the greatest ever."—Peter Gammons, Beyond the Sixth Game

Courtesy UPI/Bettmann News photos

Courtesy AP/Wide World

Pete Rose broke Ty Cobb's record for total base hits, ending up with 4,256 (below) and his head-first style contributed to his second-place finish in doubles (left).

(Opposite, bottom) Courtesy UPI/Bettmann News photos

of a club to meet the salary demands of premium performers.

For these two Series, wheeling and dealing produced the better results as the Yankees captured both championships in 6 games. In the first of the two Series, Reggie Jackson contributed his 5-homer barrage. In the second Series, the glove of Yankee third baseman Graig Nettles stifled the Dodgers in the critical third game as he turned in four spectacular plays. The left-handed–hitting Nettles, basically a .250 hitter, also gave the Yankees home-run power; the only third sackers with more four-baggers were Mike Schmidt and Eddie Mathews.

The 1980 Series, with the Phillies against the Kansas City Royals, brought out new and aging faces. Through free agentry, no less a hero than Pete Rose had quit his hometown of Cincinnati to join Philadelphia. He put on a .400 performance during the Series. Among his teammates was a reclusive lefty, Steve Carlton. In twenty-three seasons Carlton was surpassed in strikeouts only by Nolan Ryan, and he went well beyond 300 wins. The Cardinals had traded him in 1972 to the Phillies, and in the 1980 Series, Carlton stymied the American Leaguers twice. After fourteen years in Philadelphia, when age appeared to have slowed his fastball and straightened his curve, Carlton sold himself to San Francisco and followed up with stints in Cleveland and Minnesota.

Muscle in the 1980 Series came from third sacker Mike Schmidt, a more-than-500-homer type who obliged with a pair and 7 RBIs in the championship. Chief actor among the losing Kansas City performers was another third baseman, George Brett. His .390 average was the highest in season play since Williams struck .406 almost forty years before. He had clobbered the Yankees in the last game of the playoffs with a 3-run homer to the upper deck on the very first pitch from reliever Goose Gossage. But not even his .375 in the Series and the robust hitting of teammates Amos Otis, Willie Aikins, and Hal McRae could overcome the Phillies.

The 1981 strike, which split the season into a pair of separate races, required double playoffs, an exciting but messy climax to a turbulent year. In the National League, Montreal eliminated Philadelphia while Los Angeles beat Houston. The Dodgers then

bested the Expos. In the other circuit, New York first whipped Milwaukee before defeating Oakland, which had downed Kansas City. In the championship, Los Angeles achieved a measure of revenge for the 2 defeats by the Yankees in the late seventies. That was particularly sweet for the man who had succeeded Walter Alston, Tom Lasorda, whose major league playing credentials were only slightly more extensive than Alston's. As a pitcher, he worked 13 innings in two years for the Dodgers of 1954–1955 without a decision and then lost 4 and won zero for Kansas City in 1956. With a fondness for the show-biz fans of Hollywood and a gargantuan appetite, Lasorda drove his troops to three pennants and 1 divisional win in his first nine years.

Milwaukee finally made it to the World Series in 1982. A losing role in the drama belonged to veteran pitcher Don Sutton. Then in the seventeenth year of a career stretching nearly a quarter of a century and more than 300 victories, which had placed him among the top ten for career strikeouts, Sutton started 2 games. He left the first with the score tied and lost his second. Tucked away in the victorious Cardinals' section of the box score were 2.1 innings for Jim Kaat, whose career stretched over four decades; he began with Washington in 1959 and six teams and twenty-five years later finished with a total of 283 wins.

Baseball celebrated the 50th anniversary of the All-Star game in 1983 at Comiskey Park in Chicago, the site of the original gala. The American Leaguers won, just as they had in 1933, but that victory came after 11 straight defeats by the National League. Remnants of Cincinnati's Big Red Machine (Rose, Morgan, and Tony Perez) held a reunion as Phillies this year but they were no match for Earl Weaver's Baltimore Orioles who conquered them in 5 games.

The San Diego Padres appeared in their first Series as the foes of Detroit in 1984. Neither Steve Garvey nor Graig Nettles, with all of their previous championship experience, could help the National League entry to overcome the stalwart arm of pitcher Jack Morris and the batting feats of shortstop Alan Trammell and outfielder Kirk Gibson.

It was the Cardinals against Kansas City the following year. The Cardinals, ahead 3 games to 2, went to the bottom of the ninth

The 1986 Playoffs and World Series : an endless series of "gee whizzes" c can't believe its." New York Met c Gary Carter held off Astro Billy Hat the National League title bout.

Courtesy UPI/Bettmann News photos

(Left) *"During a game [Mike] Schmidt brings such formidable attention and intelligence to bear on the enemy pitcher that one senses that the odds have almost been reversed out there; it is the man on the mound, not the one up at the plate, who is in worse trouble from the start."—Roger Angell,* The New Yorker

Courtesy UPI/Bettmann News photos

(Right) *George Brett supplied the premier Kansas City beef during the 1970s and 1980s.*

Courtesy UPI/Bettmann News photos

inning of game six with a 1–0 lead. Jorge Orta of the Royals nubbed a grounder toward first. Jack Clark fielded the ball, tossed it to pitcher Todd Worrell covering. Umpire Don Denkinger called Orta safe, despite vigorous Cardinal protests and a TV replay that indicated Denkinger erred. Kansas City then eked out a pair of runs to tie the Series and in game seven blasted the best of St. Louis pitching for an 11–0 victory. While the Cardinals twittered that Denkinger had robbed them of their just rewards, the Kansas City win was generally acclaimed. Manager Dick Howser, a deservedly popular fellow cursed with losing the big ones, had finally cashed in. Sadly, he died less than two years later from a brain tumor.

For honors in 1986, the Mets battled Houston in the National League playoffs while the Red Sox took on California. Both matchups, in what was now a best of seven-games tournament, grabbed attention ordinarily reserved for the Series itself.

The Mets' sterling pitching staff included Dwight Gooden, Rookie of the Year in 1985 after winning 24 games, Ron Darling, Sid Fernandez, and Bob Ojeda, as well as relievers Roger McDowell and Jesse Orosco. Houston countered with a one-two punch of an aging but still effective Nolan Ryan and a new sensation, Mike Scott. The Mets mauled Ryan, but Scott, who spent eight years without notable success, had suddenly become astonishingly effective. He throttled the New Yorkers twice before the Mets wrapped up the playoffs after a 12-inning fifth game and a 16-inning sixth game.

For the Red Sox, the playoffs were even more desperate. Trailing 3–1 in games, with the Angels on the verge of closing them out in game five, the Bostonians tied the score on a ninth-inning homer by a recent addition, Dave Henderson. He had been about to be fitted with the goat's horns after his glove knocked an Angels' fly ball over the fence. Then, in the tenth inning, Henderson delivered a sacrifice fly for the win. The Sox vanquished California in the final 2 games.

In the World Series the melodrama lingered on; the play was not pretty, with errors, wild pitches, and managerial strategies that misfired, but the suspense and outcome glued viewers to their seats. Boston led 3–2 in games and 5–3 in the tenth inning of game six, thanks to another timely homer in the top of the inning from Henderson. An insurance run came from a double by third sacker Wade Boggs, whose batwork in his first years marked him as a prime candidate to be the first .400 hitter since Ted Williams. Indeed, the Mets were down to their last out. But catcher Gary Carter, a 300-homer type bartered from Montreal, singled. Pinch hitter Kevin Mitchell followed with a bloop to center. Then third baseman Ray Knight smacked a hit to center, scoring Carter and sending Mitchell to third.

Bob Stanley relieved reliever Calvin Schiraldi for Boston. He faced Mookie Wilson, a notorious free swinger. With the count 2–2, Stanley offered one that Wilson could not help but refuse. It almost hit him, and as he artfully dodged, he blocked catcher Rich Gedman's vision. The ball rolled away and Mitchell scored on the wild pitch to tie the game. Still, the Sox seemed relatively safe as Wilson grounded down the first baseline. But Billy Buckner, playing hurt to the point of limping, saw the ball slip between his legs and the winning run scored. Given life, the Mets overcame Boston in the final game as Ray Knight walloped a decisive homer.

As the Baltimore Oriole team bus rolled through Harlem long after midnight, Brooks Robinson tucked one foot under himself, propped his chin on his raised knee, leaned his forehead against the bus window, and looked into the steamy summer darkness. "Been coming this way for twenty-three years," said Robinson, who was then in his final season. A little of the syntax and twang of the son of a Little Rock, Arkansas, fireman still clung to his soft, rolling voice. "It never changes," he murmured, nodding toward a crap game going on in the crevice between two tenements. "That's an awful life to get born into and never get out of. Shows us how lucky we are. How grateful we should be."

The sentiment Robinson expressed that night was commonplace enough—simple empathy for the poor. What was striking was his lack of self-pity in considering himself lucky by comparison. That was hardly the most fortunate section of a blessed life. Just two years before, Robinson had been on the edge of financial ruin. Not only was he broke but he was also in debt, because of naive business decisions. Others had made the money mistakes, dragging Robinson down with them. At every turn, Robinson's flaw had been an excess of generosity. How could he send a sporting goods bill to a Little League team that was long overdue in paying for its gloves? He'd keep anybody on the cuff forever. Said Robinson's old friend Ron Hansen, "He just couldn't say 'No.'"

As creditors dunned him and massive publicity exposed his plight, Robinson answered every question, took all of the blame (including plenty that wasn't his), and refused to declare bankruptcy. He was determined to pay back every cent. With great embarrassment, he also returned tens of thousands of dollars that fans spontaneously sent him in the mail to soften his fall.

Just as twenty years of hard-earned baseball dollars trickled through his hands like a ground ball between the legs, Robinson's athletic skills also left him—suddenly and harshly. First, his power, which led him to 268 home runs, disappeared. He couldn't even get his home-run total into double figures. Next, his average dropped through the floor. He batted .201 in 1975 and .211 in 1976. Though his marvelous soft hands and reflexes never really tarnished—even at the end he was a study at third base—his range diminished radically. He couldn't hold a job with his glove alone.

Finally, by his last season (1977), he was dead weight, a charity case of sorts. Robby had to approach the Orioles on a hat-in-hand, any-way-you-want-me basis as a player-coach just so he could stay solvent and try

(Opposite) Courtesy NBL

to start over. The free-agent era was only months old; the boom days ahead—million-dollar contracts for utility men and $2-million-plus-per-year for a future Hall of Famer type—no one could have guessed. Back then, a Brooks Robinson only made about twice the current rookie minimum of $65,000. One bad judgment—a failed sporting goods store—could take it all. That night in Harlem, the guy in the alley winning the crap game might have been in better shape than Brooks Robinson, a man who had never loved anything except baseball and had no solid future plans.

When the Orioles bus rolled to a stop in front of the Statler Hilton, it was the last time Robinson would return from Yankee Stadium as a player. Everyone piled off, Robinson carrying a case in his hand. "Here," he said to a reporter. "You left your typewriter under your seat."

Robinson left the game the way he played it—uncomplaining, smiling, teasing and being teased, pitching batting practice, and picking up a typewriter for a reporter or a dirty towel for a bat boy. Of all the game's greats, perhaps Robinson was least cursed by his own fame. He had great talent and never abused it. He received adulation and reciprocated with common decency. While other players dressed like kings and acted like royalty, Robinson arrived at the park dressed like a cab driver. Other stars had fans. Robinson made friends.

In the long run, that saved him. Though many were sad for Robinson back in 1977, few seemed as worried as might be expected. "Brooks and [wife] Connie haven't changed their living style since the days we were making $6,000 a year in the minors," said Hansen. "His friends aren't millionaires and politicians, just average guys like me. People still love him just like they always have. He doesn't scare anybody. He's never snubbed anybody. For twenty years he has always had empathy for other people's feelings and now they are going to have empathy for his. Nothing really bad will ever happen to Brooks. Those who know him wouldn't allow it."

Other stars might be carried through hard times by their towns or former teams. That wasn't what Hansen meant. With Robinson, it went deeper. If Brooks's life could, in the broadest sense, go bad, then wouldn't our most basic verities, like casting bread on the waters, seem endangered?

The day Robinson retired, he was still at sea financially and personally. Yet the celebration for him in Memorial Stadium could not have been more joyful or devoid of any shadow. The biggest crowd ever to attend an Oriole regular-season game (51,798) stood and cheered in bright sun

In the 1970 World Series against Ci nati, Robinson hit .429 with a pair of runs, plus fielding spectaculars like thi ing snatch of a Johnny Bench liner.

Courtesy UPI/Bettmann News photos

for a quarter of an hour as Robinson circled the field, standing like a ticker-tape-parade hero in the back of a Cadillac convertible, 1955 vintage, his rookie year. "Brooks, not retired, just called up to Cooperstown," said one bed-sheet sign.

"Spent an hour combing my bald spot, so I could leave my toupee home," said Robinson, standing in the Orioles dugout as the microphone behind second base awaited him. "Now, I think I'll just keep my hat on. . . .

"Never in my wildest dreams did I think I would be standing here twenty-three years later saying goodbye to so many people," said Robinson when he took the stage. "For a guy who never wanted to do anything but put on a major league uniform, that goodbye comes tough. . . . I would never want to change one day of my years here. It's been fantastic."

So, Robinson quit, with barely a dollar to call his own and debts up to his neck, without even the sophistication or cunning to become a manager. And all the Orioles knew it. Robinson had given as much to baseball as a player could and was literally leaving it with nothing.

As a kind of compensation, it seemed everyone decided to leave him with their affection. "Around here people don't name candy bars after Brooks Robinson," said the Day's master of ceremonies, Gordon Beard, "they name their children after him."

Even Weaver, the toughest of cusses, broke down in public for the only time in recorded baseball history. He told the crowd about Robinson's generosity toward a nobody manager who was a career bush leaguer. He talked about how he wondered, the first time he gave the "take" sign to Robinson, if he would obey. "And I've wondered every time since." He thanked Robinson for saving his job "several times over the years." Finally, Weaver blurted out, "Thank you, Brooks. Thank you one million times."

To say that nobody knew how to react would be an understatement. "I thought of so many things while Brooks was riding around the stadium," explained Weaver later. "What I had planned to say didn't seem like nothin' to me. It wasn't true and honest feeling. So I just did it impromptu. . . . I'd like to be like Brooks. The guys who never said no to nobody, the ones that everybody loves because they deserve to be loved . . . those are my heroes."

Somehow, Robinson always elicited "true and honest feeling" from the people around him, even those never previously known to possess such things. Perhaps that was his gift. In a sense, his play was the least of him. That merely brought him to our attention so we could get to know the rest

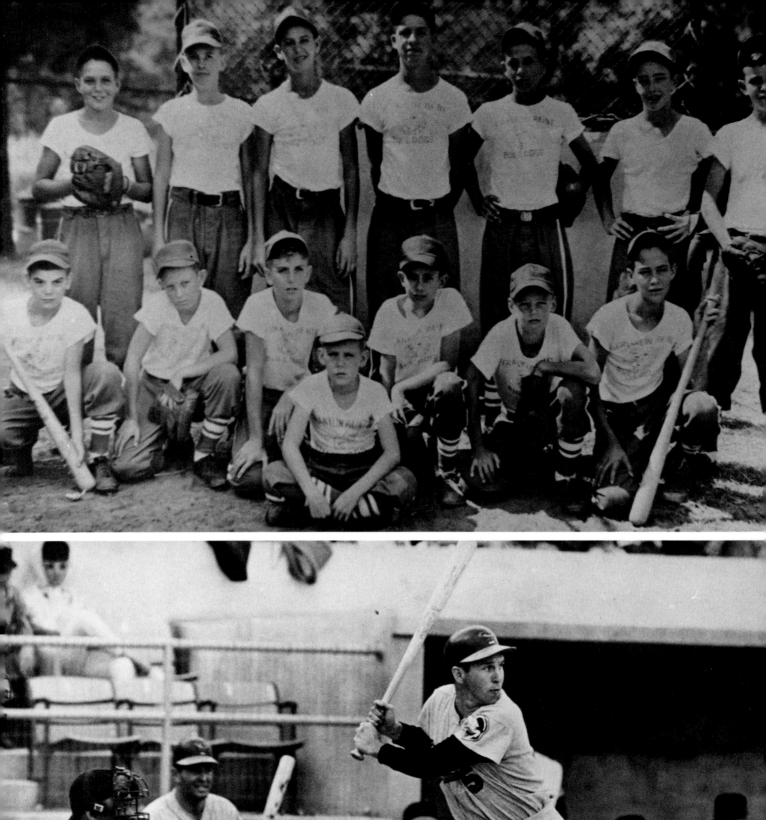

of him.

From 1964, when he was the American League's Most Valuable Player, until 1970, when he was MVP of the World Series, Robinson was a living legend. Yet when, someday in a different century, an old man tries to explain to a small boy the power of Robinson's lasting fame, he may have a hard time translating the hero's statistics into a portrait of the man that seems consonant with his oversize myth.

Few players get to hear the words "the greatest at his position in the history of the game" while they are still in their prime. Robinson heard it routinely. Hyperbole and praise followed him around like spotted pups. Cincinnati manager Sparky Anderson said during the 1970 Series, "I'm beginning to see Brooks in my sleep. If I dropped this paper plate, he'd pick it up on one hop and throw me out at first."

For his first twenty-one professional seasons, Robinson got to show his skill. If his feet were slow, his reflexes were the fastest. If his arm was average, his accuracy and quick release were the best. Somehow, he always seemed languid, especially as he threw overhand toward first; yet the fastest runners were out by larger margins when Robinson made his syrupy perfectos than when the most kinetic jack-in-the-box third basemen made similar plays as frantically as though they'd just sat on a cattle prod.

If Brooks's bat was merely good most of the time, it was at its best in the clutch. He drove in 75 runs ten times, hit .280 seven times, and had 20 homers six times. His 268 homers and .267 career average are a fair measure of his bat: useful, occasionally powerful, but not cause to lose your place in the hot dog line.

Above all, his glove was purple, like a standing invitation to a theme contest. On teams that had slick fielders like Luis Aparicio, Mark Belanger, Paul Blair, Bobby Grich, and Dave Johnson, you couldn't take your eye off Robinson. He overshadowed them all and sometimes forced you to watch the entire game through him. Others made difficult or acrobatic plays, even—a favorite baseball non sequitur—"impossible plays." Robinson made unthinkable plays. Shortstops steal singles. It seemed Robinson robbed a thousand doubles. Brooks Robby, indeed. Memory swears that he made a "Brooks Play" at least once every other game. That is, when there weren't two in 1 game. Not semitough plays, mind you. An accidental swinging bunt, an almost sure scratch hit? As soon as you realized Brooks was at third, you barely bothered to watch. He went months at a time without having to stuff a dribbler in his hip pocket. No, we are talking here about discussion plays. Plays that demand

At age twelve, Brooks (back row, first from left) *savored the championship of his hometown.*

Courtesy NBL

His wide-legged stance produced 268 homers, a lifetime batting average of .267. "I could field as long as I can remember, but hitting has been a struggle all my life."— Brooks Robinson

Courtesy Charles Segar

comparison.

Thank heaven for replays. In Memorial Stadium, to this day, his Brooksobatics are still on display every night on TV sets above the concession stands as part of a half-hour recapitulation of Oriole history; and each night it is invariably Robinson's plays that bring audible gasps of surprise. They remain incomprehensible. You don't catch hard line drives in foul territory. You don't throw out runners with your feet in the coach's box. But it's on film. A perfectionist's archive. When the Hall of Fame asked for his glove after the 1970 Series, Brooks said, "Wait a year. It'll take me that long to get a new one broken in just right."

Despite all this, none of Robinson's plays seem to stand as sharp in retrospect as the person himself. After all, since Robinson's retirement, Mike Schmidt has built a record demanding that he, not Brooks, play for the celestial varsity. Mention Robinson in baseball circles and stories about his play almost never surface. Instead, there is always some anecdote about his nature.

"It's rough to try to replace an immortal, but Brooks did everything to make it smoother for me," recalls Doug DeCinces who, on Brooks Day, tore third base out of the ground and presented it to Robinson.

"Every player I've ever managed blamed me at the end, not himself," Weaver once said. "They all ripped me and said they weren't washed up. All except Brooks. He never said one word and he had more clout in Baltimore than all of them. He never did anything except with class. He made the end easier for everybody."

Perhaps that's what amazes pro athletes more than anything: Robinson's ability to leave the stage as though it cost him nothing. In fact, it probably did cost him much less than many lesser players. Players with half Robinson's credentials had to swallow their bombast overnight. Brooksie—"Mr. Bad Body"—had always enjoyed pitching batting practice with his hat off to get a tan on his bald spot.

Gradually, in the early years of his retirement, Robinson's bleak money days became a thing of the past. To his own surprise, Robinson became a far more successful local baseball telecaster than he ever dreamed. A few guest shots turned into a regular job that kept him in the ballpark fifty times a year. His homespun tales were never the sort to attract the eye of network TV, but Robinson didn't care; and Baltimore found him as comfortable as one of his perfectly broken-in gloves. His analysis was perceptive and candid, sometimes even critical; but, as always with Robinson, his total absence of mean-spiritedness or any hint of ulterior motive protected him. "Brooks is entitled to his opinion," a chastised player would say. As likely as not, Robinson had been giving him batting tips before the game.

It is rare to find an announcer without ambition, without a need to fill air time and with no axes to grind. That's Robinson, who wouldn't take the managing job if offered and has no knack for grudges. He tells it as straight as he can, as long as he doesn't really have to hurt anybody's feelings. No job would be worth that to Robinson.

"You know, Chuck," Brooks will say to partner Chuck Thompson after a loud foul ball, "as an announcer I swore I'd never say, 'And there's the lucky fan who caught that one.' Ball comin' in there about two hun'ert mile an hour."

Later he'll say in an on-air aside, "Charlie [i.e., Thompson], been a couple of innings since we had any nachos in this booth. Think I'll go get us some."

Robinson also moved into an executive position with a petroleum company and joined a business management firm that specializes in helping pro athletes avoid exactly the sort of problems that had ravaged Robinson. Don't do as I did, do as I say.

If any baseball fairy tale ever had a perfect happy ending, it came on the last day of July 1983 when Robinson was inducted into the Hall of Fame. All weekend the interstate highways from York to Harrisburg to Scranton to Binghamton to Oneonta were littered with cars, vans, and buses loaded with orange-and-black-clad devotees making the pilgrimage to Cooperstown. In a normal summer, the Hall induction draws a crowd of perhaps five thousand with Mickey Mantle long holding the record of nearly ten thousand. That's a big mob to draw to a tiny town of twenty-five hundred that's literally a hundred miles from nowhere in the middle of Leatherstocking land. For Robinson, the caravan included forty-two charter buses, twelve airplanes, and enough private cars to equal Mantle's crowd.

Before ceremonies could begin, the crowd—which swept over knolls, spread itself under maple trees, and stretched almost out of sight of the review stand—had conducted its own singing of the national anthem, complete with an ear-splitting "O" for Orioles at the appropriate "O, say can you see" juncture. The gleeful mob, fresh from a morning of lay services at the Bold Dragoon Saloon, followed unofficial team mascot Wild Bill Hagy in spelling B-R-O-O-K-S and passing the cold beer on a hot afternoon. Bed-sheet signs and placards dotted the sea of orange humanity, their slogans perhaps more heartfelt than literary.

"You really know how to make it tough on a guy," the choked-up

Nobody played more third base than Br[ooks]
Robinson's 2,870 games or put out as m[any]
as his 2,697, assisted as often as on[his]
6,205 occasions or accepted near his 9[ ]
shots, or participated close to his 618 do[uble]
plays.

Courtesy Herb Scharfman, *Sports Illustrat[ed]*

Robinson ad-libbed as the crowd refused to end its ovation as he was introduced. "I realize I must be the luckiest man in the world. . . . I've been given more than any human being could ever ask for."

In his closing remarks, Robinson seemed to be trying to say, in an oblique way, why his life had been so exemplary, so patient, so seemingly guided by a stronger principle than merely winning ball games. "From the beginning, I was committed to the goodness of this game. . . . I think my love for baseball has been the biggest thing in my life. . . . This is the day for giving thanks. This is a life from which I want to give back."

Afterward, Robinson stood in the streets of Cooperstown in a bright pink jacket, surrounded by people with block-lettered Number 5s on their chests. "The last five years have been as happy as the other twenty-three," said Robinson. "Everybody dreads retiring, but I'm having as much fun now as I was when I was playing. I can't believe it, to tell the truth."

That afternoon, Brooks Robinson seemed ideally of a piece with Fenimore Cooper Country—home of Natty Bumppo's Cave, Blackbird Bay, Mohican Canyon, Glimmerglen Cove, and Leatherstocking Falls. Mark Twain loathed Cooper's saga of noble savages and true-blue woodsmen from the bottom of his wise, mocking, and bitter heart; Twain was a harbinger of a century that would find the word "virtue" almost impossible to pronounce without a knowing cough.

Brooks Robinson is a man who would be unpalatable, perhaps unbelievable, in fiction. Only reality, which refuses to play by any rules, has a place for him. In a fantasy creation, virtue of the sort attributed to Cooper characters is deeply suspect since it's an unprovable author's contrivance. "One of nature's noblemen," Cooper liked to say of his favorite heroes. These days, that phrase has become a trendy sneer for cynics. We know, of course, that nature has no noblemen and could not create one if she chose, not even to play third base.

The ability of one or two clubs to dominate play seems to have vanished. Whether the phenomenon stems from expansion of clubs, extension of the season, more movement of players among teams, or higher levels of athletic skills, teams rarely repeat. By early 1987, both the Mets and Red Sox found themselves struggling to emerge from the ruck of the pennant race, and only the Mets managed to come close to the division title. When the dust of 1987 settled, it was the unheralded Minnesota Twins who overcame the St. Louis Cardinals in the World Series. Change now dominates baseball, almost contradicting the nature of sports, with its highly structured play and organization. But then that also holds for the larger United States.

French-born philosopher Jacques Barzun, as baseball jingoists iterate and reiterate, said: "Whoever wants to know the heart and mind of America had better learn baseball, the rules and realities of the game."

It would be presumptuous to say baseball is America. But baseball lives within America. Just as in the nineteenth century under the doctrine of Manifest Destiny Americans sought to expand the nation to its natural geographical boundaries, so did pioneers like Alexander Cartwright, A. G. Spalding, and Henry Chadwick seek to spread baseball through the land. And as the evangelical, imperialist, empire-building urge seized Americans, Spalding, Comiskey, and others carried the flag beyond the borders. Thus the game flourishes in parts of Latin America, Japan, and of course Canada.

From a land peopled first by indigenous Indians, dissenters, fortune hunters, black slaves, and later refugees from poverty and oppression came a documented organized society. So, too, did the once unstructured game become organized. Baseball, like the larger society, has its magisterial personages, commissioners, league officials, and cops like Tom Connolly and Jocko Conlan. In the grand old democratic style, while some from what Donald Hall calls "the country of baseball" docilely accept all decisions, others bend and test the rules and loudly protest the ukases of authority. Baseball includes a common acceptance of the way things should work as well as space for challenges, for disagreement on the field and among the spectators.

In line with the American temper, it is a game that accommodates the rampantly aggressive—John McGraw, Ty Cobb, and Early Wynn—as well as the divinely self-assertive—Honus Wagner, Rogers Hornsby, Willie Mays. It is a game that, like the United States, serves the individual and the group. Ted Lyons could win 260 games, twice lead the league in victories for the season, and never see a pennant snapping in the wind over his home park. Billy Williams, with 426 homers and a lifetime .290, was similarly denied. Nap Lajoie fielded brilliantly for twenty-one years and hit for Hall-of-Fame quality but never played in a World Series. Countless less-talented men, privileged to be part of well-balanced squads with maybe one genuine headliner, however, prospered from the combined team effort and participated in championships.

Captains of industry molded the dynamic American economy. Potentates of baseball, starting with Spalding, Comiskey, and later the likes of Ed Barrow, Larry McPhail, Branch Rickey, George Weiss, and Warren Giles, followed the models of modern corporations to transform the game into a profitable business. They began with rickety wooden pavilions and then adopted the latest forms of construction.

Architectural landmarks like Boston's green-monstered Fenway Park, Chicago's brick-walled Wrigley Field, and the Camelot-evoking Yankee Stadium of King Babe Ruth, Sir Joe DiMaggio, and Prince Mickey Mantle survive even while all-purpose, doughnut-shaped anonymities have replaced the legendary Baker Bowl, Ebbets Field, and Crosley Field. The spacious game that recalls a greener America has even moved indoors, as modern technology constructed the "eighth wonder of the world," the Houston Astrodome, and other enclosed stadiums.

Once a game reserved for the more affluent, baseball became the common man's sport, consuming ever more attention as the dynamic economy opened up unprecedented leisure time. The game, however, was never immune to the prejudices that roil the melting pot. The dominant organized form of the sport, like the mainstream of the country, for far too long was closed to nonwhites. Indeed, an offhand remark by a Dodger official during a 1987 TV celebration of the 40th anniversary of Jackie Robinson's debut revealed the disease still infects the command centers of baseball. Baseball is not singularly afflicted; the condition holds for much of the country's business, political, academic, show business, and sports apparatus.

Baseball has not escaped other problems of the twentieth century. Management and labor maintain a basically adversarial relationship after long disputation. The antagonisms hinder control of baseball's portion of a national problem, the epidemic of substance abuse. Media attention has made the use of unlawful drugs the subject of rules and programs but alcoholism, a legal drug that has destroyed so many athletes past and present, is barely considered.

Rowdiness in the stands, partly a consequence of beer guzzling, also mirror another unfortunate aspect of contemporary society. As legislators move to modify behavior through laws, owners are now being forced to sacrifice potential revenues (concession sales on beer provide a healthy chunk of income) and beef up security forces.

On the positive side, as baseball heads toward the twenty-first century and some new anniversaries—50 years of the Hall of Fame in 1989, 150 years (1995) since Alex Cartwright brought his sketch of how the game should be played—baseball, like the post–World War II economy, has expanded. There are more major league cities, more spectators, and enhanced performances in many aspects. The prices of franchises have soared. Joan Payson had put up between $3 million and $4 million to create the New York Mets. In 1980, Doubleday Publishing paid her estate $21.1 million; six years later Nelson Doubleday and partner Fred Wilpon bought out the publishing company's interest for $50 million. A few years earlier, pizza tycoon Tom Monaghan, a self-made multimillionaire, claimed the Detroit Tigers for a similar price.

As 1990 hovers on the calendar, cities with the proper demographic makeup to house franchises clamor for admission. Whatever the economic gains through opening up more outlets, the owners must ponder the possible effects on levels of the game. Like any other art form, baseball might be debased without proper quality control, a pool of sufficiently talented players, coaches, managers, and entrepreneurs.

Meanwhile, its achievements continue to amaze and proclaim the game's health. And not the least of the glorious parade has been the growth of Cooperstown treasures, some old, some new, some minor memorabilia, others significant artifacts. Season passes from 1914 and 1917, an 1887 schedule of the St. Louis Browns, a Kansas City World Series ring from 1985, and the oversize 1931 shoes of Ernie Lombardi recently joined the upstate New York collection. Rickey Henderson, perhaps destined to be the grandest base thief in history, shipped to Cooperstown a pair of shoes that bore him to his record 130 mark. His colleague on the Yankees, Dave Winfield, with legs that seem to stretch to his armpits, was a good bet to overtake the 400-home-run mark. No one suggested the pigeon he dropped with a throw in Toronto be stuffed and mailed to the Hall of Fame, but a ticket from the game in which he struck homer 300 now resides in Cooperstown.

Wade Boggs of the Red Sox, winner of four out of five American League batting championships from 1983 to 1987, shipped some of his lumber. Kirby Puckett, the muscular, roly-poly center fielder who helped drive Minnesota to a win in the 1987 Series, gave the weapon that enabled him to tie the mark of 10 straight hits. From Toronto arrived a pair of weapons used by Ernie Whitt and Fred McGriff for homers 9 and 10 in the memorable Blue Jays barrage that established a new high. Bob Horner of the Atlanta Braves shipped out to Japan to embrace his yen for more bucks than the Braves would offer; he dispatched the wood with which he joined the exclusive club of 4 four-baggers in a single game. From his erstwhile teammate Dale Murphy, one of the homer artists of the National League, came a full uniform. Other suits to grace the Hall were donated by Tom Seaver during his White Sox incarnation, Steve Carlton's 4,000th career strikeout made while at San Francisco, and Fernando Valenzuela's 1986 Dodger dress blues as well. Another recent addition is the cap of Houston Astros pitching marvel Mike Scott, holder of the record for most unproven suspicions for sculpting the ball, and the 1986 Cy Young victor in the National League. Phenom Roger Clemens of the Boston Red Sox, who set a new 9-inning record of 20 strikeouts, forwarded a uniform to the Museum. After Dave Righetti, a no-hit thrower

The Astrodome in Houston, the "eighth wonder of the world." Indoor baseball was rep-
licated in Seattle, Minneapolis, Montreal,
and Toronto.

Courtesy Marvin Newman

while a starter, punched in with the major
league high of 46 saves in 1986, he sent a
cap, as did reliever Kent Tekulve of the Phillies, after his record 847th appearance.

In 1986, twenty-five special baseballs arrived in Cooperstown, including one from
Steve Carlton's record 666th start, a well-
scuffed U.S. Army ball from the American
Expeditionary Force in France circa 1917,
and the one used by Bert Blyleven to knock
off his 3,000th strikeout. To be sorted was a
box of autographed specimens from the collection of the late Joe Cronin. And Ray
Knight forwarded the batting helmet he
wore when he ended the 1986 Red Sox
hopes with a homer. The following year
Henry Aaron shipped to the Hall the uniform for his 715th homer; his Gold Glove
Awards for 1958, 1959, and 1960, and the

bat for home runs 716 and 717. Another
valuable collected in 1987 was a baseball
from the 1926 Series autographed by Grover
Cleveland Alexander.

To those who rashly dismiss the validity of
Jacques Barzun's remark, the materials enshrined in Cooperstown are the inconsequen-
tial relics of a trivial pursuit. But anyone
with a genuine sense of history must recognize that the fading photographs, the glisten-
ing bats, faded ink signatures, flashes of uniform color, insignia of long-vanished clubs,
the smudged and pristine white balls, the
gloves, masks, pads, the gee gaws, and remnants are all the physical stuff that bedrocks
tradition. This is living history, for the Cooperstown collection continues to grow, ever
adding to the memory of the game and the
people whom the Hall celebrates.

MICKEY CHARLES MANTLE
NEW YORK A.L. 1951-1968
HIT 536 HOME RUNS. WON LEAGUE HOMER TITLE
AND SLUGGING CROWN FOUR TIMES. MADE
2415 HITS. BATTED .300 OR OVER IN EACH
OF TEN YEARS WITH TOP OF .365 IN 1957.
TOPPED A.L. IN WALKS FIVE YEARS AND
IN RUNS SCORED SIX SEASONS. VOTED
MOST VALUABLE PLAYER 1956-57-62. NAMED
ON 20 A.L. ALL-STAR TEAMS. SET WORLD
SERIES RECORDS FOR HOMERS, 18; RUNS, 42;
RUNS BATTED IN, 40; TOTAL BASES, 123;
AND BASES ON BALLS, 43.

(Left) *The Hall exhibits the strike zone* ▮
its batting average potentials according ▮
Ted Williams construction.

Courtesy Ted Astor

"*The artifacts and exhibits in the Ha*▮
mind us, vividly and with feeling, of ▮
hopes for bygone seasons and teams ▮
players. Memories are jogged, even jo▮
colors become brighter and we laugh or ▮
remembering good times gone by. Bu▮
Hall of Famers themselves with their pla▮
and pictures and citations are the hea▮
something larger, for they tell us that ▮
exists a handful of baseball players . . . ▮
really did come close to our expectat▮
They played so well and so long, succee▮
eventually at this almost impossible g▮
that we can think of them as something ▮
useful than gods or heroes. We know the▮
there, tucked away up-country and ir▮
back of our minds: old men, and you▮
ones on the way, who prove and sustai▮
elegance of our baseball dreams."—▮
Angell, The New Yorker

Courtesy Ted Astor

(Opposite, top and bottom) Courtesy Ted
Astor

(Following page) Courtesy Ted Astor

Founding Fathers (pages 1–15)

(1) The description of the ball comes from *History of Baseball,* by Seymour Church, 1902.

(1) "Well do I remember . . ." Duncan Curry issued this statement in 1879. There is a copy at the National Baseball Hall of Fame Library (NBL).

(1) "Three balls being struck . . ." Rules of baseball published by the Knickerbocker, Club, New York (*Honolulu Advertiser,* June 5, 1910).

(1–2) "At that time . . ." Duncan Curry statement from 1879.

(7) "In the summer of . . ." Statement by Candy Cummings issued in 1908 and reprinted in the *Baseball Hall of Fame Newsletter* (July, 1986).

(7) "I became fully convinced . . ." Reprinted in the *Baseball Hall of Fame Newsletter* (July, 1986).

(7) "I said not a word . . ." Reprinted in the *Baseball Hall of Fame Newsletter* (July, 1986).

(9) "The first glove . . ." From *America's National Game* by A. G. Spalding (American Sports Publishing Co., 1911).

(9) "A young man . . ." From A. G. Spalding (1911).

(9–10) "The only bright skies . . ." From *A. G. Spalding and the Rise of Baseball* by Peter Levine (Oxford University Press, 1985).

(10) "Impulsively I sprang . . ." From A. G. Spalding (1911).

(10) "I had determined . . ." From A. G. Spalding (1911).

(10) "Boston is in mourning . . ." From the *Worcester Spy,* Peter Levine (1985).

(12) "As though wings . . ." Peter Levine (1985).

(12–13) "He was a creator . . ." From an interview with Fred Pfeiffer in the *Chicago Inter-Ocean* (1894).

(13) ". . . the Chicago Whites . . ." From an interview with Joe Quinn in the *Washington Star* (November 7, 1907).

(13) "He would jump . . ." From an interview with Joe Quinn in the *Washington Star* (1907).

(13) "The greatest play . . ." Interview with John J. McGraw, in an undated, unidentified newspaper clipping (NBL).

(15) "An old Irishman . . ." From an unidentified newspaper clipping circa 1888.

(15) "The effect Kelly's . . ." Taken from an article in *Sporting Life* by Mugwump (February 23, 1887).

(15) ". . . interviews which have been . . ." From *Sporting Life* (February 23, 1887).

(15) "Aw, I want the ten thousand . . ." From A. G. Spalding (1911).

First Sons, Growing Pains (pages 26–30)

(26) "Whenever he would . . ." From an unidentified, undated newspaper clipping (NBL).

(26) ". . . erratic, ill-tempered . . ." From an unidentified, undated newspaper clipping (NBL).

(27) ". . . as a token . . ." From Peter Levine (1985).

(27) ". . . we have always been . . ." From the *1919 Reach Baseball Guide.*

(27) "As a thrower . . ." From the *1919 Reach Baseball Guide.*

(29) "We don't intend . . ." From Peter Levine (1985).

(29) ". . . responsible for making . . ." From Peter Levine (1985).

(29) "They take all the risks . . ." From *Spalding Official Baseball Guide* (1890).

Two Leagues (pages 31–44)

(31) "Who wants to . . ." From an article by Sam Crane in an undated issue of the *New York Evening Journal* (NBL).

(31) ". . . splurgy long hit . . ." From *100 Years of Baseball* by Lee Allen (Bartholomew House, 1950).

(31–32) "Do not pitch . . ." From *Sphere and Ash,* by Jacob Morse (J. H. Spofford, 1888).

(32) ". . . drunkards, deadbeats . . ." From *American Baseball,* by David Quentin Voigt (University of Oklahoma Press, 1976).

(32) "The Cardinals were outbatted . . ." From A. G. Spalding (1911).

(32) "To come down . . ." From the *New York American* (June 13, 1908), quoted in *The Unforgettable Season,* by G. H. Fleming (Holt, Rinehart & Winston, 1981).

(32) "In the sixth . . ." From an undated article in the *New York Evening Journal.*

(32) "There was a noise . . ." From an article by C. B. Power in the *Pittsburgh Dispatch* (July 11, 1908).

(32) "When Matty had . . ." From an article by W. W. Aulick in the *New York Times* (June 21, 1908).

(33) "Every independent . . ." Quoted from the *Sporting News* by Harold Seymour in *Baseball* (Oxford University Press, 1960).

(34) "Think of a trust . . ." Al Spalding on the trust system, from *America's National Game* (1911).

(34) "Now for the first time . . ." From A. G. Spalding (1911).

(34) "I'm glad I don't . . ." From Harold Seymour (1960).

(34) "One man yelled . . ." From A. G. Spalding (1911).

(36) "As A. G. saw it, . . ." From Peter Levine (1985).

(36) "I see great things . . ." by Walt Whitman quoted in *An Informal History of Baseball*, by Douglas Wallop, (W. W. Norton & Co. Inc., 1969).

(36) "Baseball is the very symbol . . ." Mark Twain quoted in Peter Levine (1985).

(36) "We owe a great deal . . ." From the *Chicago American* quoted in the *Spalding Official Baseball Guide* (1907).

(36) "I hereby challenge . . ." *Spalding Official Baseball Guide* (1905).

(36) ". . . can prove that one . . ." A. G. Spalding (1911).

(37) "It certainly appeals . . ." From Peter Levine (1985).

Infield Glitter (pages 45–53)

(45) "Lajoie could not go out . . ." Comment by Ty Cobb about Nap Lajoie in a letter to Ernie Lanigan dated 1945 (Hall of Fame).

(45) "He works as noiselessly . . ." Billy Sunday quoted by Red Smith in the *Providence Journal* (February 9, 1959).

(46) ". . . all pitchers and infielders . . ." Nap Lajoie quoted by Stan Baumgartner in *Sporting News*, (August 23, 1950).

(46) "In our day . . ." From Charlie Gehringer's unpublished interview with Rod Roberts, July 26, 1985.

(46) "Few bunts were . . ." John B. Foster, quoted in the *Spalding Official Guide* (1938).

(47) "How he could . . ." Tinker on Evers, *Associated Press* (July 27, 1948).

(47) "We dressed in . . ." Tinker on feud with Evers, *Associated Press*, July 29, 1948.

(47–48) ". . . early in 1907 . . ." Evers on feud, Joe Williams' column, *New York World Telegram* (December 9, 1936).

(48) "Don't get too far . . ." From the *New York World Telegram* (December 3, 1936).

(48) "The final play . . ." Report from the *Pittsburgh Post* quoted in Fleming's *The Unforgettable Season* (1981).

(48) "After Merkle singled . . ." From the *New York Herald* (January 22, 1911).

(49) "These are the saddest . . ." From an undated letter from F. P. Adams (NBL).

(49) "You can have . . ." John McGraw on John Peter Wagner, from *Sporting News* (August 2, 1912).

(50) "It also turned out . . ." From *The Glory of Their Times*, by Lawrence Ritter (Macmillan Publishing Co., Inc., 1966).

(52) "Out of my way . . ." From *Baseball as I Have Known It* by Frederick Lieb (1977).

Brains, Brawn, and Bluster (pages 69–79)

(69) "The very thought . . ." From *Baseball America*, by Donald Honig (Macmillan Publishing Co., Inc., 1985).

(69) "I was born . . ." From an interview with John McGraw by Harry Brundige in *Sporting News* (November 20, 1930).

(69) "I thought I . . ." From *Sporting News* (November 20, 1930).

(69) "Take the bunt. . . ." Wilbert Robinson quoted by Douglas Wallop in *An Informal History of Baseball* (1969).

(71) "That is a contemptible lie. . . ." Quoted from Sweeny in *Sporting News* (August 13, 1906).

(71) "Ladies and Gents! . . ." From *Sporting News* (August 13, 1906).

(71) "I hear you were . . ." From an article by Sam Crane in the *New York Evening Journal (June 10, 1917)*.

(74) "So many batters . . ." From *Spalding Official Baseball Guide* (1906).

(74) "Bresnahan's numerous disputes . . ." *Reach Official Baseball Guide*, (A. J. Reach Co., 1910).

(75) "Of various balls . . ." Christy Mathewson, as quoted in the *New York American* (August 27, 1908).

(75) "It is an exceptionally . . ." Christy Mathewson, *New York American* (August 29, 1908).

(75) "It is not possible . . ." McGinnity quoted by Sam Crane in the *New York Evening Journal* (March 6, 1908).

(76) "Ninety-nine times . . ." Harry Hooper, quoted by Lawrence Ritter in *The Glory of Their Times* (1966).

(76) "You've got to know . . ." John J. McGraw, quoted in an unidentified newspaper clipping (May 7, 1914).

(76) "The reason McGraw . . ." From Lawrence Ritter (1966).

(78) ". . . it was an education . . ." From Lawrence Ritter (1966).

(78) "What a great . . ." From Lawrence Ritter (1966).

(78) "This man McGraw . . ." Charles Ebbets, quoted by Dan Daniel in the *New York World Telegram* (February 26, 1934).

(78) "He was one of . . ." Waite Hoyt, from an unpublished interview with Rod Roberts, October 11–12, 1981.

Philadelphia Stories (pages 80–86)

(80) "The man looked safe . . ." Disagreement between Connie Mack and Umpire McGowan, quoted from an unidentified newspaper clipping.

(80) ". . . a papal bull . . ." From *The Ultimate Baseball Book,* by Wilfrid Sheed (Houghton Mifflin Co., 1979).

(82) "Connie Mack . . ." Rube Bressler, from Lawrence Ritter (1966).

(82) "It wasn't exactly baseball . . ." Connie Mack quoted by John C. Winston in *My 66 Years in the Big Leagues* (1950).

(83) "He was always . . ." Sam Crawford, from Lawrence Ritter (1966).

(83) "He'd jump down . . ." From Lawrence Ritter (1966).

(84) "I'd been watching him . . ." Cy Young, quoted in an unidentified newspaper clipping.

(84) "Mr. Waddell is one of the finest . . ." Drama critic on Rube Waddell, from an undated *Chicago Journal* in an unpublished manuscript by Bill Gottlieb.

(84) ". . . disgusts patrons and players . . ." *Sporting Life* (August 8, 1907).

(85–86) "The claim has been . . ." Connie Mack, quoted in *Sporting Life* (July 3, 1915).

A Peach and an Eagle (pages 87–93)

(87) "He was tough . . ." Donald Honig (1985).

(87) "He didn't slide . . ." Ossie Bluege, from Donald Honig (1985).

(87) ". . . the wonder of baseball . . ." Jimmy McAleer, from Charles Alexander in *Ty Cobb* (Oxford University Press, 1984).

(87) "The greatest player . . ." Comiskey, from Charles Alexander (1984).

(87) "The most sensational . . ." Casey Stengel, from Robert Creamer in *Sports Illustrated* (August, 1985).

(87) "They always talk . . ." Sam Crawford, from Lawrence Ritter (1985).

(87) ". . . not unlike a war. . . ." Ty Cobb, from Charles Alexander (1984).

(87) "Baseball is a red-blooded . . ." Ty Cobb, from Charles Alexander (1984).

(87) "Be good and dutiful . . ." W. H. Cobb quoted in Charles Alexander (1984).

(90) "[He would] aim . . ." From *My Life in Baseball* by Tyrus Raymond Cobb with Al Stump (Doubleday & Co., 1961).

(90) ". . . superbly insolent . . ." From Charles Alexander (1984).

(91) ". . . looked about the size . . ." From Tyrus Raymond Cobb (1961).

(91) "If you put . . ." From Douglas Wallop (1969).

(91) "McGraw is a mucker . . ." From Charles Alexander (1984).

(92) "He treated me . . ." Charlie Gehringer. From an unpublished interview with Rod Roberts, July 26, 1985.

(92) "He put in 100 percent. . . ." From an unpublished interview with Rod Roberts, July 26, 1985.

(92) "He was the strangest . . ." From *Nobody Asked Me, but . . . The World of Jimmy Cannon* by Jimmy Cannon (Holt Rinehart & Winston, 1978).

(92) "He'd take me out . . ." From an article in *Sporting News* by Fred Lieb (December 17, 1958).

The Outsiders (pages 94–99)

(94) "If he had . . ." From *Only The Ball Was White,* by Robert Peterson (Prentice-Hall, 1970).

(96) "If anywhere . . ." From an article in the *National Pastime* by Jerry Malloy (1983).

(96) ". . . in all things . . ." From Lee Allen (1950).

(96) "Charlie, I've been . . ." From Lee Allen (1950).

(96) "I'm not going . . ." From Lee Allen (1950).

(97) "If you play . . ." Andrew Foster, from Robert Peterson (1970).

(97) ". . . the most finished . . ." Frank Chance quoted by John Holway in *Sporting News* (August 8, 1981).

(99) ". . . push it here . . ." Dave Malarcher, from Robert Peterson (1970).

Wets and Wars (pages 100–110)

(100) "I could break . . ." Ed Walsh quoted in *Sporting News* (January 9, 1957).

(100) "When I loaded up . . ." From *Sporting News* (January 9, 1957).

(100) "I think that . . ." Sam Crawford, from Lawrence Ritter (1985).

(101) "We'll get along . . ." From Ring Lardner quoted by Red Smith in the *New York Herald Tribune* (May 31, 1959).

(105) "When I was . . ." William "Rube" Marquard, from Lawrence Ritter (1985).

(106) "An hour and . . ." Rube Bressler, from Lawrence Ritter (1985).

(106) "He had such . . ." Frank Frisch quoted by Ed Rumill in *The Christian Science Monitor* (January 13, 1973).

(106) "Maybe two or three . . ." Hans Lobert, from Lawrence Ritter (1985).

(107) "There can be no . . ." Ban Johnson interview with *New York Evening Sun* from an article in the *National Pastime* by Gary Hailey (1985).

(110) "Exhibitions of baseball . . ." From Gary Hailey, *National Pastime* (1985).

(110) ". . . applied only to business . . ." From Gary Hailey, *National Pastime* (1985).

Scandals (pages 111–116)

(111) "Did you notice . . ." Frank Chance, from *Baseball as I Have Known It*, by Frederick Lieb (Coward, McCann & Geoghegan, 1977).

(112) "He was a little man . . ." From *Eight Men Out*, by Eliot Asinof (Holt, Rinehart & Winston, 1963).

(112) "I don't like . . ." Hugie Fullerton, from Frederick Lieb (1977).

(114) "I believe my boys . . ." From an unidentified newspaper clipping (1919).

The Sultan and the Rajah (pages 117–135)

(117) "Chapman seemed rooted . . ." From an article in *Sporting News* by Joe Vila (August 26, 1920).

(117) "I won over . . ." Carl Mays, from Frederick Lieb (1977).

(117) "Sometimes when I . . ." Burleigh Grimes quoted by Red Smith in the *New York Times* (October 14, 1981).

(119) "I'd tie a can . . ." Stan Coveleski quoted from an unpublished interview with Rod Roberts, August 22, 1981.

(119) "If you can hit . . ." Stan Coveleski, from Rod Roberts (1981).

(128) "I . . . had the ball . . ." In a letter from Edgar Rice dated July 26, 1965 (NBL).

(128) "Sam . . . hurtled the barrier . . ." In a letter from Norman Budesheim to Paul Kerr, president, Baseball Hall of Fame, November 10, 1974.

(130) "Nobody taught me . . ." Pie Traynor quoted by Lee Greene in *Sport Magazine's All Time All-Stars*, Tom Murray, ed. (Atheneum, 1977. Reprinted by New American Library, 1980).

(130) "He could do everything. . . ." From a press release issued by the National Baseball Hall of Fame (July 21, 1969).

(131) ". . . he had none of the raging fire . . ." Stockton quoted by Bob Broeg in *Sporting News* (February 22, 1969).

(131) "I couldn't make any headway . . ." Rogers Hornsby quoted by Frederick Lieb in *Sporting News* (January 19, 1963).

(131) "I learned by standing . . ." From *Sporting News* (January 19, 1963).

(133) "He was a real hard-nosed guy . . ." Billy Herman, from *Baseball for the Love of It* by Anthony J. Connor (Macmillan Publishing Co., Inc., 1982).

(133) "Because he's played . . ." Rogers Hornsby on Branch Rickey in an article with Jack Sher, *Sport Magazine's All Time All-Stars* (1977).

(135) "If you don't . . ." Rogers Hornsby to Judge Fuchs, quoted by Red Smith in *New York Herald Tribune* (1961).

Second Dynasties (pages 155–162)

(155) "I could actually feel . . ." Waite Hoyt on his religious experience, from an unpublished interview with Rod Roberts, October 11, 1981.

(157) "Across the street . . ." From J. G. Taylor Spink, *Sporting News* (1938).

(159) "I liked him on the train . . ." Connie Mack quoted in the *Philadelphia Ledger* (June 7, 1937).

(159) "We made our own. . . ." Robert Moses Grove, from a press release issued by the American League Service Bureau (December 30, 1928).

(159) "Sometimes when the sun . . ." From an unidentified newspaper clipping.

(159) "I had a reason. . . ." Taken from an article in the *Christian Science Monitor*, by Ed Rumill, (n.d.).

(161) "Hello, sweetheart, . . ." From *Baseball: The Fan's Game* by Gordon Cochrane (Funk and Wagnalls, 1939).

(161) "I reported at . . ." Lewis Robert "Hack" Wilson, quoted by Harry Brundige in the *St. Louis Star* (November 7, 1929).

(161) "But John J. [McGraw] . . ." From Harry Brundige, *St. Louis Star* (November 7, 1929).

(162) "You can't fasten it . . ." Taken from an article in the *Chicago Tribune* by Irving Vaughan, (n.d.).

(162) "My sunglasses were nothing . . ." Wilson, quoted by J. Roy Stockton in the *St. Louis Post Dispatch* (January 21, 1932).

Depression and High Spirits (pages 163–175)

(163) "Would have ended up on his ass . . ." From *Babe* by Robert Creamer (Simon & Schuster, Inc., 1984).

(163) "He didn't point. . . ." Billy Herman from *Voices from Cooperstown* by Anthony J. Connor (Macmillan Publishing Co., Inc., 1984).

(165) "Did you really point . . ." Conversation between Ford Frick and Babe Ruth, from Creamer (1984).

(165) "I didn't exactly point . . ." Babe Ruth quoted by Carmichael from Creamer (1984).

(165) "When I was 15 . . ." and "I played baseball . . ." Bill Terry, from an article by Gordon Forbes in *Sport Magazine's All Time All-Stars* (1977).

(165) ". . . before I knew . . ." Stan Coveleski from an unpublished interview with Rod Roberts, August 22, 1981.

(165) "I didn't expect . . ." Edd Roush from an unpublished interview with Rod Roberts, August 22, 1981.

(165) "Bill played the game . . ." From an article by Gordon Forbes, *Sport Magazine's All Time All-Stars* (1977).

(165) "[Bernie] Wefers was brought in . . ." Mel Ott, from an article by Al Stump in *Sport Magazine's All Time All-Stars* (1977).

(166) "The new, dynamite-laden pellet . . ." Garry Schumacher, *New York Evening Journal* (July 7, 1934).

(166) "It is the prevailing belief . . ." John Wray, *St. Louis Post Dispatch* (December 15, 1933).

(166) "But only one of . . ." From *The Unforgettable Season* by G. H. Fleming (1981). (See footnote.)

(170) "I might never . . ." Statement by Frankie Frisch, from *The Dizziest Season* by G. H. Fleming (1984).

(170) "Frisch immediately skied . . ." Jimmy Powers, *New York Daily News* (July 15, 1934).

(170) "Something must be done . . ." Sid Keener, *St. Louis Post Dispatch, St. Louis Star-Times* (July 7, 1934).

(170) "The only way to fool . . ." From an article by Harold Parrott, *Brooklyn Eagle* (July 16, 1934).

(170) "I'd rather pitch . . ." From G. H. Fleming (1984).

(170) "He's a baseball murderer. . . ." From G. H. Fleming (1984).

(170–171) "I just smell . . ." From G. H. Fleming (1984).

(171) "They may not be . . ." From an article by Frank Graham in the *New York Sun* quoted in G. H. Fleming (1984).

(172) "The Mahatma was coatless . . ." From Red Smith, *New York Times*, (n.d.).

(172) "By the time Hubbell's magic . . ." From Paul Gallico, *New York Daily News* (July 11, 1934).

(172) "I'm underpaid, . . ." From the *New York World Telegram* (June 5, 1934).

(175) "I didn't have a thing out . . ." Dizzy Dean quoted by the *New York Times* (October 4, 1934).

(175) "A lot of people said . . ." From *Baseball Between the Lines* by Donald Honig (Coward, McCann & Geoghegan, 1976).

(175) "As a ballplayer . . ." From Red Smith, *New York Herald Tribune* (n.d.).

The Clipper, The Kid, The Hall
(pages 176–191)

(176) "We didn't have . . ." From Joe Falls, *Sporting News* (November 20, 1976).

(176) "I guess I didn't . . ." From Johnette Howard, Knight-Ridder Service (1987).

(176) "endlessly . . ." From *I Don't Care If I Never Get Back* by Art Hill (Simon & Schuster, Inc. 1980).

(176) "Greenberg puts . . ." From *Sporting News* (October 3, 1940).

(177) "And I mean . . ." From Joe Williams, *New York World Telegram* (May 1, 1939).

(177) "On the very first . . ." From the *New York World Telegram* (May 12, 1939)

(180) "The public is with us." From Dan Daniel, *New York World Telegram* (April 16, 1938).

(180) "public sentiment . . ." From the *New York Post* (January 17, 1938).

(180) "I started running . . ." Joe DiMaggio quoted by John Drebinger, *New York Times* (December 12, 1951).

(180) "I got the . . ." Charles "Gabby" Hartnett quoted by Bob Broeg, *Sporting News* (September 5, 1970).

(181) "Just what do . . ." Conversation between by Bill Dickey and Lefty Gomez, from Frank Graham, *New York Journal American* (n.d.).

(181) ". . . there was no time . . ." From Harold Rosenthal in the *New York City Tribune* (December, 1985).

(182) "We had a few . . ." From *Baseball Between the Lines* by Donald Honig.

(182) "You could sit . . ." From *Great Catchers of the Major Leagues* by Jack Zanger (Random House, 1970).

(182) "The throw from . . ." From Dave Kindred, *Louisville Courier Journal & Times* (February 6, 1977).

(182) "He pitched . . ." Recollection by Bill Feller, from Anthony J. Connor (1984).

(184) "The first batter . . ." From an unidentified, undated newspaper clipping (NBL).

(184) "All of us . . ." From Ed Linn, *Sport* (August, 1954).

(187) "I was talking . . ." From Harry Paxton, *Saturday Evening Post* (January 30, 1960).

War and Peace (pages 192–202)

(192) "One night in Cleveland, . . ." From "Joltin' Joe DiMaggio," by Alan Courtney (1943).

(192) "That wouldn't have . . ." From *Day by Day in New York Yankees History* by Mark Gallagher (Leisure Press, 1983).

(192) "I wish you . . ." From Ed Linn in *Sport* (August, 1954).

(192) "I'll tell you . . ." From *The Image of Their Greatness* by Lawrence Ritter and Donald Honig (New York: Crown Pubs., Inc., 1979).

(196) "I honestly feel . . ." Letter from President Roosevelt to Commissioner Landis, January 15, 1942. See *Spartan Seasons* by Richard Goldstein (Macmillan Publishing Co., Inc., 1980).

(199) "Pee Wee Reese was at bat . . ." Warren Spahn, from Joe Reichler, *Associated Press* (September 12, 1963).

(201) "You don't make concessions, . . ." From Joe Reichler (1963).

(201) "He was one of . . ." From *The Man's Own Story*, by Stan Musial with Bob Broeg (Doubleday & Co., 1964).

(201) "I realized that . . ." From Bob Broeg, *Redbird Review* (August 10, 1984).

Opening the Door (pages 203–213)

(203) "When we took off . . ." From *Branch Rickey* by Arthur Mann (Houghton Mifflin Co., 1957).

(203) "There's a couple . . ." Shirley Povich quoted in *Only The Ball Was White* by Robert W. Peterson.

(203) "The very first thing . . ." From *Branch Rickey* by Murray Polner (Atheneum, 1982).

(204) "Colored men are . . ." From Murray Polner (1982).

(204) "The question of . . ." William Judy Johnson from an unpublished interview with Rod Roberts, December 13, 1981.

(206) "The big-league boys . . ." Johnson, from Rod Roberts, December 13, 1981.

(206) "We had good friends . . ." From *Voices from the Great Black Baseball Leagues,* by John Holway (Dodd, Mead & Co., 1975).

(206) "You wrapped your uniform, . . ." From John Holway (1975).

(206–208) "We'd play a semipro team . . ." From John Holway (1975).

(208–209) "I rigged up . . ." From the *New York Times* (June 9, 1982).

(209) "Satchel Paige was . . ." From Buck Leonard with John Holway, *Sporting News* (March 11, 1972).

(209) ". . . the best I . . ." Comment by DiMaggio taken from an article in the *New York Times,* (June 9, 1982).

(209) "There is a catcher . . ." From *Only the Ball Was White,* by Robert W. Peterson.

(210) "I'm for the . . ." From *Branch Rickey* by Murray Polner.

(210) "I had to get . . ." From Murray Polner (1982).

(211) "Jackie raved . . ." From Robert W. Peterson (1970).

(211) ". . . the first time . . ." From an unpublished 1981 interview with Rod Roberts.

(211) ". . . technique, the coordination, . . ." From the Major League Committee's "Report of the Major League Steering Committee NBL," August 27, 1946.

(212) "You can be wrong . . ." From Buck Leonard with John Holway, *Sporting News* (March 11, 1972).

(212) "He'd handle most . . ." From an unidentified, undated newspaper clipping (NBL).

The Outfield Trio (pages 228–240)

(229) "Arm good. . . ." Wid Matthews from *The Man's Own Story* (1964).

(229) "Nobody can be that good." From *The Man's Own Story* (1964).

(229) "I'm tearing it up . . ." Branch Rickey quoted in *The Man's Own Story* (1964).

(229) "Like Eddie said, . . ." Statement by Stan Musial from an unidentified newspaper clipping, on the occasion of his 3,000th hit.

(231) "He looks like . . ." Ted Lyons from an unidentified newspaper clipping, on the occasion of Musial's 3,000th hit.

(231) "As a kid . . ." From Anthony J. Connor (1984).

(233) "I played with him . . ." From the *Ultimate Baseball Book* by Dan Okrent with Harris Lewine (Houghton Mifflin Co., 1979).

(233) "My father kept . . ." From the *New York Journal American* (July 6, 1954).

(233) "Anything that came . . ." From a speech given by Edwin Snider at the Hall of Fame ceremonies, 1980.

(233) "You can go . . ." From an article by Jim Terhune in the *Louisville Times* (August 2, 1982).

(233) "There was a point . . ." From Jim Terhune, *Louisville Times* (August 2, 1982).

(233) "It just seemed like . . ." From Jim Terhune, *Louisville Times* (August 2, 1982).

(233) "He was one of . . ." From Jim Terhune, *Louisville Times* (August 2, 1982).

(233) "I told him right off . . ." From an article by Ed Fitzgerald in *Sport Magazine's All Time All-Stars* (1977).

(234) "Bullshit, . . ." From *How the Weather Was* by Roger Kahn (Harper & Row, Pubs., Inc., 1973).

(235) "I was so scared . . ." From *Willie Mays: My Life In and Out of Baseball,* by Willie Mays with Charles Einstein (E. P. Dutton, 1966).

(235) "The spark was Mays. . . ." From Mays with Einstein (1966).

(235) "My eyes almost popped . . ." From a letter by Eddie Montague to Tim Cohane, sports editor of *Look* magazine, dated November 20, 1954.

(235) ". . . you're going to be . . ." From Mays with Einstein (1966).

(237) "I went out early . . ." From Anthony J. Connor (1984).

(237) "Willie ranks with . . ." From Stan Musial with Bob Broeg (1964).

(237) "When I came into . . ." From Hal Lebowitz, *Cleveland Plain Dealer* (September 14, 1975).

(237) "That space between . . ." Early Wynn quoted by Jerry Izenberg, *Binghamton Press* (December 19, 1971).

A Continental Tilt (pages 254–258)

(255) ". . . with Aaron . . ." From Anthony J. Connor (1984).

(255–256) "I always used to think . . ." From George Plimpton, *Sports Illustrated (April 22, 1974).*

(256) "In that great . . ." From George Plimpton, *Sports Illustrated* (April 22, 1974).

(256) "I almost never . . ." From Gilbert Rogin, *Sports Illustrated* (May 9, 1961).

New Frontiers (pages 274–289)

(274) "All I want . . ." From *The Ultimate Baseball Book* by George V. Higgins (Houghton Mifflin Co., 1979).

(278) ". . . he was the most . . ." From Anthony J. Connor (1984).

(278) "[He played] a kind of . . ." From *Five Seasons* by Roger Angell, (Popular Library, 1977).

(279) "The foot's up . . ." From an undated, unidentified newspaper clipping (NBL).

(281) "When I saw him . . ." From the *New York World Telegram and Sun* (August 28, 1965).

(283) "When the ball is over . . ." From Dave Anderson in an undated column in the *New York Times* (NBL).

(283) "You know you're always . . ." Lou Brock, quoted by Ira Berkow, *New York Times* (July 20, 1982).

(283) "You brace your slide—. . ." Lou Brock, quoted by Ira Berkow, *New York Times* (July 20, 1982).

(285) "Even before Bill . . ." From *Late Innings* by Roger Angell (Simon & Schuster, Inc., 1982).

(285) "Bob Gibson always . . ." From Roger Angell (1982).

(285–286) "He was an intimidating, . . ." From Roger Angell (1982).

New Faces (pages 312–319)

(314) "My brother Pete . . ." Recollection by Jim "Catfish" Hunter from Wells Twombly, *San Francisco Examiner* (October 16, 1972).

The Living Tradition (pages 329–334)

(329) "Whoever wants to know . . ." From *God's Country and Mine* by Jacques Barzun (Little, Brown & Co., 1954).

Alexander, Charles. *Ty Cobb.* London: Oxford University Press, 1984.

Allen, Lee. *100 Years of Baseball.* New York: Bartholomew House, 1950.

Angell, Roger. *The Summer Game.* New York: Viking, 1972.

————. *Five Seasons.* New York: Popular Library, 1977.

————. *Late Innings.* New York: Simon & Schuster, Inc., 1982.

Anson, Adrian Constantine. *A Ball Player's Career.* Chicago: Era Publishing Company, 1900.

Asinof, Eliot. *Eight Men Out.* New York: Holt, Rinehart & Winston, 1963.

Boswell, Thomas. *How Life Imitates the World Series.* New York: Doubleday, 1982.

————. *Why Time Begins on Opening Day.* New York: Doubleday & Co., Inc., 1984.

Brashler, William. *Josh Gibson.* New York: Harper & Row Pubs., Inc., 1978.

Carmichael, John. *My Greatest Day in Baseball.* San Diego: AS Barnes & Co., Inc., 1945.

Chadwick, Henry. *The Art of Pitching and Fielding.* Chicago: A. G. Spalding & Bros, 1886.

————. *The Art of Batting and Base Running.* Chicago: Spalding Library of Athletics and Sports, 1887.

Church, Seymour. *History of Baseball.* S. R. Church, 1902.

Cobb, Tyrus Raymond. *My Life In Baseball.* New York: Doubleday & Co., Inc., 1961.

Connor, Anthony. *Baseball for the Love of It.* New York: Macmillan Publishing Co., Inc., 1982.

————. *Voices from Cooperstown.* New York: Collier Books, 1984.

Creamer, Robert. *Babe.* New York: Simon & Schuster, Inc., 1974.

————. *Stengel.* New York: Simon & Schuster, Inc., 1984

Curran, William. *Mitts.* New York: William Morrow & Co., Inc., 1985.

Durso, Joseph. *Baseball and the American Dream.* St. Louis: The Sporting News Publishing Co., 1986.

Einstein, Charles. *The Baseball Reader.* New York: Lippincott & Crowell, 1980.

Feller, Robert. *Strikeout Story.* San Diego: AS Barnes & Co., Inc., 1947.

Fleming, G. H. *The Unforgettable Season.* New York: Holt, Rinehart & Winston, 1981.

————. *The Dizziest Season.* New York: William Morrow & Co., Inc., 1984.

————. *Murderer's Row.* New York: William Morrow & Co., Inc., 1985.

Frommer, Arthur. *Rickey and Robinson.* New York: Macmillan Publishing Co., Inc., 1982.

Gammons, Peter. *Beyond the Sixth Game.* Boston: Houghton Mifflin Co., 1985.

Goldstein, Richard. *Spartan Seasons.* New York: Macmillan Publishing Co., Inc., 1980.

Hall, Donald. *Fathers Playing Catch with Their Sons.* Berkeley, Calif.: North Point Press, 1985.

Henderson, Robert. *Ball, Bat and Bishop.* New York: Rockport Press, 1947.

Holway, John. *Voices from the Great Black Baseball Leagues.* New York: Dodd, Mead & Co., 1975

Honig, Donald. *Baseball When the Grass Was Green.* New York: Coward, McCann & Geoghegan, 1975.

————. *Baseball Between the Lines.* New York: Coward, McCann & Geoghegan, 1976.

————. *Baseball America.* New York: Macmillan Publishing Co., Inc., 1985

James, Bill. *Historical Abstract of Baseball.* New York: Villard Books, 1986.

Kahn, Roger. *The Boys of Summer.* New York: Harper & Row, Pubs., Inc., 1972.

————. *How the Weather Was.* New York: Harper & Row, Pubs., Inc., 1973.

Levine, Peter. *A. G. Spalding and the Rise of Baseball.* New York: Oxford University Press, 1985.

Lieb, Frederick. *Baseball as I Have Known It.* New York: Coward, McCann & Geoghegan, 1977.

Lowenfish, Lee. *The Imperfect Diamond.* Briarcliff Manor, N.Y.: Stein & Day Publishers, 1980.

McGillicuddy, Cornelius. *My 66 Years in the Big Leagues.* Philadelphia: J. C. Winston, 1950.

Mann, Arthur. *Baseball Confidential.* New York: David McKay Co. Inc., 1951.

————. *Branch Rickey.* Boston: Houghton Mifflin Co., 1957.

Mantle, Mickey, with Herb Gluck. *The Mick.* New York: Doubleday & Co., Inc., 1985.

Mathewson, Christopher. *Pitching in a Pinch.* New York: Grosset & Dunlap Inc., 1912.

Mays, Willie, with Charles Einstein. *Willie Mays: My Life In and Out of Baseball.* New York: E. P. Dutton, 1966.

Morse, Jacob. *Sphere and Ash.* Boston: J. H. Spofford, 1888.

Musial, Stan, with Bob Broeg. *The Man's Own Story.* New York: Doubleday & Co., Inc., 1964.

Okrent, Dan, with Harris Lewine. *The Ultimate Baseball Book.* Boston: Houghton Mifflin Co., 1979.

Parrott, Harold. *The Lords of Baseball.* Westport, Conn.: Praeger Publishers, 1976.

Peterson, Harold. *The Man Who Invented Baseball.* New York: Charles Scribner's Sons, 1969.

Peterson, Robert W. *Only the Ball Was White.* Englewood Cliffs, N.J.: Prentice-Hall Inc., 1970.

Polner, Murray. *Branch Rickey.* New York: Atheneum Publishers, 1982.

Reach Official Baseball Guide(s), edited by Francis Richter. Philadelphia: A. J. Reach Sporting Goods Co.

Reichler, Joseph, ed., *The Baseball Encyclopedia*, 6th ed. New York: Macmillan Publishing Co., Inc., 1985.

Ritter, Lawrence. *The Glory of Their Times.* New York: Macmillan Publishing Co., Inc., 1966.

Robinson, Frank. *My Life in Baseball.* New York: Doubleday & Co., Inc., 1975.

Rogosin, Donn. *Invisible Men.* New York: Atheneum Publishers, 1983.

Rosenthal, Harold. *The 10 Best Years of Baseball.* Chicago: Contemporary Books Inc., 1979.

Rust, Art, Jr. *Get That Nigger off the Field.* New York: Delacorte Press, 1976.

Seymour, Harold. *Baseball: The Early Years.* New York: Oxford University Press, 1960.

Smith, Robert M. *Baseball in America.* New York: Holt, Rinehart & Winston, 1961.

Spalding, Albert Goodwill. *America's National Game.* New York: American Sports Publishing Co., 1911.

Spalding Official Baseball Guide. New York: American Sports Publishing Co., 1890–1941.

Thorne, John. *Armchair Book of Baseball.* New York: Charles Scribner's Sons, 1985.

Tygiel, Jules. *Baseball's Great Experiment: Jackie Robinson and His Legacy.* New York: Oxford University Press, 1983.

Veeck, Bill, with Ed Linn. *Veeck as in Wreck.* New York: The Putnam Publishing Group Inc., 1962.

Voigt, David Quentin. *American Baseball.* Norman, Okla.: University of Oklahoma Press, 1976.

Wallop, Douglas. *An Informal History of Baseball.* New York: W. W. Norton & Co. Inc., 1969.

White, Sol. *History of Colored Base Ball.* Philadelphia: H. Walter Schlicter, 1907.

References to illustrations are in italics

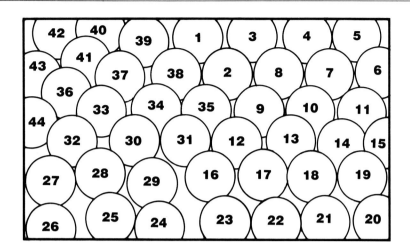

1. Official 1987 World Series ball signed by World Champion Minnesota Twins.
2. Last ball from Don Drysdale's record 58⅔-inning scoreless streak.
3. Official ball used in the Negro National League.
4. Last ball—Game 2 of the 1938 World Series, Yankees vs. Cubs.
5. Ball signed by Jackie Robinson.
6. Early one-piece ball, circa 1860.
7. Ball autographed by the 1924 World Champion Washington Senators.
8. Ball from Ericsson vs. Fleet Wing game, May 25, 1867.
9. Ball from first game of the 1925 World Series—Washington vs. Pittsburgh.
10. Ball hit by Bob Lennon of Nashville AA club, September 6, 1954, for his 64th home run.
11. Babe Ruth's 60th home run ball, September 30, 1927.
12. Ball signed by Clark Griffith and Vice President John Garner at Opening Game of the 1939 season at Washington.
13. Ball hit by Walt Dropo for his 12th consecutive hit, July 15, 1952—Detroit Tigers vs. Washington at Griffith Stadium.
14. Ball from Boston vs. Detroit game in which Babe Ruth was the pitcher.
15. Hank Greenberg's 300th home run ball, September 17, 1946.
16. Ball signed by the 1946 American League Champion Boston Red Sox.
17. Game ball—marked "Seneca, October 25, 1867."
18. Ball from exhibition game in London, England—Chicago White Sox vs. New York Giants.
19. Ball from Warren Spahn's 305th career victory, September 2, 1961.
20. National League Golden Jubilee commemorative ball, February 2, 1926.
21. Game ball from Harvard–Yale baseball contest, June 7, 1884.
22. Ball used in the Negro Leagues autographed by Cool Papa Bell.
23. Ball used in dedicating Candlestick Park, San Francisco, signed by Vice President Richard Nixon and Mayor George Christopher, April 12, 1960.

24. Ball signed by the 1950 World Champion New York Yankees.
25. A homemade baseball used in Canada, circa 1887.
26. Ball signed by the 1940 World Champion Cincinnati Reds.
27. Hank Aaron's 714th home run ball, April 4, 1974.
28. Roger Maris's 61st home run ball, October 1, 1961.
29. Ball with two-piece cover, marked: "M.B.B.C. won from the Continental B.B.C. Nov. 8th 1860, Score 41 to 12."
30. Ball signed by Bob Boone and Al Lopez, after Boone set a record for most games caught in a lifetime with 1,919 on September 16, 1987, thus bettering Al Lopez's old mark.
31. Ball signed by Johnny Vander Meer after no-hitter vs. Boston, June 11, 1938.
32. Ball from Knickerbocker vs. Brooklyn game, July 20, 1858—the first recorded game of baseball where gate money was charged.
33. Ball from the 1869 campaign of the Cincinnati Red Stockings—baseball's first professional team, signed by George Wright and team members.
34. Ball hit by Carl Yastrzemski for the last hit of his career, October 2, 1983.
35. Ball from Dale Long's 8th consecutive home run in 8 games, May 28, 1956.
36. Ball autographed by Honus Wagner.
37. Ball hit by Mel Ott for his 30th home run of the 1938 season, at Forbes Field, Pittsburgh.
38. Gilded game ball, marked: "1866 July 25, Union 45, Chester Norwich 25—9 innings."
39. Ball autographed by the 1952 Hanshin Tigers of the Japanese Professional Baseball League.
40. Ball signed by the 1929 Washington Senators at spring training in Biloxi, Mississippi.
41. Ball signed by the 1929 pennant-winning Chicago Cubs team.
42. American League ball autographed by the 1948 Boston Red Sox.
43. Ball signed by the 1951 World Champion New York Yankees.
44. Ball signed by members of the 1957 St. Louis Cardinals team that played in the Hall of Fame Game, July 22, 1957, vs. Chicago White Sox.